SEXISM IN T

Sexism in the Secondary Curriculum

edited by
Janie Whyld

Harper & Row, Publishers
London

Cambridge
Hagerstown
Philadelphia
New York

San Francisco
Mexico City
Sao Paulo
Sydney

First published 1983

Harper & Row Publishers Ltd
28 Tavistock Street
London WC2E 7PN

British Library Cataloguing in Publication Data

Sexism in the secondary school.
  1. Sexism   2. Education, Secondary
  I. Whyld, Janie
  370.19′349   LB1620

  ISBN 0–06–318251–3

Typeset by Inforum Ltd, Portsmouth
Printed and bound by Butler and Tanner Ltd, Frome and London

CONTENTS

PREFACE

Over the past ten years there has been an increasing amount of research into, and analysis of, the way schooling maintains a male-dominated society, ranging from observation of how young children acquire behaviour appropriate to their sex, to presenting feminist perspectives of advanced academic disciplines. This book aims to draw together and summarize this diverse material so that it is more easily accessible; to show its relevance to the secondary school curriculum, since this is still the highest level of education experienced by most people in this country, and more than anything else forms our concepts of education and knowledge, and is of major importance in determining our career prospects; to offer some new ideas on the way sexism works within the curriculum; and to offer practical advice to teachers on how to counteract sexism in their own classrooms.

The first section of the book deals with the theoretical background to the debate on gender and sex discrimination, and with those aspects of schooling which are relevant to all educationalists regardless of discipline: the way the school is organized and staffed, and relationships between staff and students.

The second section, prefaced by a brief explanation of some concepts common to all the following chapters, contains analyses of the way sexism operates in the major subject areas of the curriculum. The subject-by-subject approach has been chosen for two reasons. First, the analysis of sexism within individual disciplines has been sporadic, uneven and often published only in academic journals which are difficult to obtain. Some areas, such as history, sociology and home economics, have received a lot of attention; others, such as geography and PE, have remained virtually unexamined. Secondly, in order to counteract the tendency in human nature to shift responsibility elsewhere, this approach shows how all areas of school life contribute to the continuance of traditional relationships between the sexes. As the variety of subjects taught in secondary schools is very large, only those subjects most commonly taken by students in the 11–16 age group have been included.

Some subjects which are similar in approach have been grouped together to avoid repetition. Areas of work which are not usually timetabled separately, are included in the chapter dealing with the subject in which they are most commonly taught. While accepting that the structure of the curriculum will need to be examined in order to eliminate sexism, the traditional subject divisions have been adopted because most teachers face the problem of working with such divisions.

The final section of the book suggests action which groups and individuals can take to counteract sexism in education.

Readers who want to concentrate on their own areas of influence are advised to read Section 1, the introduction to Section 2 and their specialist chapter, and Section 3.

CONTRIBUTORS

Pat Browne, born and educated in Scotland, took a diploma in physical education in Dunfermline in 1958. She has taught PE in Australia, New Zealand and South Africa, and now teaches in a special school for ESN(M) children in London. She became involved in the women's movement in 1974, when she came to London, and is now active in the NUT.

Sue Bruley is a feminist historian. She has taught in adult, further and higher education. Her PhD thesis, for the London School of Economics, dealt with the theme 'Women and Communism in Britain'. She is active in the London Feminist History Group, and the Labour Party.

Katherine Clarricoates, who would class herself as a radical feminist, has recently completed her PhD on patriarchal schooling. She has written a number of articles on women and education, and firmly believes that change must come about through the overthrow of the dominant/subordinate relationship of men and women.

Martin Grant is the Research Fellow for the GATE project at the Centre for Science and Maths Education, Chelsea College. He has taught CDT in a boys' secondary modern school, a mixed all-age ESN school, and a large mixed comprehensive school.

Jennifer Hatton was born in 1949 in North Staffordshire where she attended art school in the late 1960s. She became aware of the women's movement while doing a degree in art history at Essex University, and is now Head of Art in a Nottingham comprehensive.

Phil Hingley, born in London in 1950, teaches German and French at Rowlinson School, Sheffield. He is a founder member of the Sheffield NUT Equal Opportunities Group.

Phil Keeley has taught economics and business studies for ten years since leaving Redland College, and is currently teaching at Henbury School, Bristol.

Lene Knudsen, a Dane and living in Copenhagen, is a third-year student specializing in PE and French at Blaagaard Seminarium, a fairly progressive teacher training college. She became involved in the women's movement eight years ago, is active in her union, and tries to fight sexism in the curriculum of her college and in her teaching in schools.

Brekke Larsen, born 43 years ago on a Danish island, was the only girl in a maths and science sixth-form group, so she became an early feminist. After running a geometric observatory in Greenland for a few years, she took a degree in geography, with a thesis on the socioeconomic position of women in Ghana, at Zurich University. She taught geography in Nigeria and Denmark, and now lives in Cambridge with her two daughters, and teaches in a comprehensive school.

Kate Myers trained to teach commercial subjects at Redland College, Bristol. She has taught at Haverstock School, ILEA for 13 years, and has been responsible for equal opportunities in the school since 1980. She is currently seconded to the Schools Council's project on sex differentiation.

Angela Platt, born in Cardiff in 1944, taught in an infant school in Clee-thorpes for eight years, and is now nursery nurse course tutor at Lincoln College of Technology. She researched sex discrimination in the hidden curriculum and in reading schemes for her BEd honours degree in 1981.

Jan Pollock is a socialist feminist. She has taught history and humanities in London comprehensive schools since 1973, and is a member of the Socialist Teachers' Alliance and of Women in the NUT.

Gillian Prout, born in Hartlepool in 1949, worked as a Careers Officer after graduating from Keele University, and is now Head of Careers at a comprehensive school in Essex. She has lived in Cambridge for the past five years, where she has been actively involved in the women's movement and local politics.

Yvette Rocheron has taught various subjects, including French, English and sociology, in France and England, and is presently completing a PhD thesis on sexuality and gender in secondary schools at Warwick University.

Joy Rose, born in Oldham in 1948, trained as a teacher at Bretton Hall,

Yorkshire, then spent a year living rough in South America. She has taught since 1970 in Canada and Sweden, and at present is second in the English department in a large Manchester comprehensive. She has been a member of the *Women and Education Newsletter* collective since 1977.

Judy Samuel took a BSc in biochemistry at UMIST, and a postgraduate certificate in education at Manchester University. She taught for several years in Bolton, before taking up her present post as head of chemistry at a mixed comprehensive school in Sheffield. A member of the Manchester based *Women and Education Newsletter* Group, and of the Sheffield NUT Equal Opportunities group, she was a contributor to *The Missing Half*.

Sarah Sharkey was born in Glasgow, but did her first degree in Sydney, Australia. She has taught mathematics in Australia, Scotland and England, and is currently teaching in ILEA.

Annmarie Turnbull trained as a teacher, and is currently employed as a researcher in a London polytechnic where she is completing a PhD thesis on the history of sexual divisions in schooling. She is an organizer of the London Feminist History Group.

Janie Whyld, born in London in 1946, is a lecturer in general studies at Grimsby College of Technology. She became involved in the women's movement when her daughter was a baby, and has since been active in her union and local politics, run courses on sexism and feminism, and given talks to local women's organizations.

Margaret Winter, born in London in 1949, has taught for ten years, in English and remedial departments, in Liverpool, Great Missenden and Huddersfield. While doing a course on disadvantaged children at Manchester Polytechnic, she became active in the Manchester Women and Education group.

Barbara Wynn has taught home economics in a number of London schools since 1971. She was head of department at Islington Green School until 1983 and is now teaching in Oxfordshire. She has carried out research and has published articles in a number of journals and books on the history of home economics, and on sex-role stereotyping in schools.

SECTION 1

SEXISM IN SCHOOLING

CHAPTER 1

INTRODUCTION

ANGELA PLATT and JANIE WHYLD

Now that Britain has legislation which makes discrimination on the grounds of sex illegal, and, at the time of writing, a woman Prime Minister, many people assume that women have equality of opportunity with men. This is not so. The concept of opportunity implies the existence of choice. Unless we also assume that women *choose* low paid service work, rather than accept it simply because there is nothing else available to them, then an examination of the patterns of women's employment shows that compared with the opportunities open to men, women's choices are still very limited.

We do not believe that paid employment is the only way to a happy and fulfilling life, but most people regard it as a necessary if not entirely sufficient condition for such a life. Education is generally recognized as the element most likely to improve the greatest number of people's chances of getting a good job (and hence money and status). It can be shown that, as well as class and race, sex is a major factor affecting educational success. We contend that the different and unequal achievement of boys and girls in the education system is largely due to the sexism inherent in present patterns of schooling.

Women and work

Despite the Equal Pay Act 1975, the average earnings for women in full-time work have fallen from around 75 per cent of men's in 1976, to 65 per cent of men's in 1982 (*New Earnings Survey* 1976–1982). Between 1911 and 1971, women's share of skilled (higher paid) manual work fell from 24 per cent to 13.5 per cent, and their share of unskilled manual work more than doubled, from 15.5 per cent to 37.2 per cent (see *Table* 3 in Bain and Price, 1972). Half of all women in the productive sector work in only four of the 19 industrial groups: food and drink, clothing and footwear, textiles and electrical engineering. Over half of all female manual workers are employed in catering, cleaning, hairdressing or other personal services, while over half of female non-manual workers are in clerical and related occupations.

Table 1 A survey of jobs obtained by 16-year-old school leavers in 1981 from two divisions of ILEA

Boys	No.	Girls	No.
Electrician	9	Sales assistant	39
Car/bus mechanic	8	Clerk	21
Sales assistant	6	Hairdresser	14
Plasterer	5	Telephonist/receptionist	11
Cabinet maker/carpenter	5	General office work	4
Clerk	5	Typist/junior secretary	4
Plumber	4	Dental nurse	2
Nurseryman/gardener	4	Laboratory technician	2
Fitter/welder	2	Chef	2
Bricklayer	2	Cashier	2
Packer	2	Assembly line worker	2
Messenger	2	Chambermaid	2
Porter	2	Canteen assistant	2
Postal cadet	2	Theatrical dresser	1
Chef	2	Building society cashier	1
Printer	2	Local govt. circuit trainee	1
General office work	2	Keypunch operator	1
Trainee commercial artist	1	Telex messenger	1
Photographic assistant	1	Gem setter	1
Architectural technician	1	Dressmaker	1
British Telecom technical apprentice	1	Stockroom assistant	1
Trainee technician	1	Warehouse assistant	1
Engineering draughtsman	1	Checkout cashier	1
Dental technician	1	Meat packer	1
Solicitor's clerk	1	Packer	1
Library assistant	1	Laundry worker	1
Trainee stockbroker	1		
Trainee manager in timber merchants	1	Total	120
Painter and decorator	1		
Stonemason	1		
Butcher	1		
Engineer	1		
Scaffolder	1		
Saw miller	1		
Waiter	1		
Stockroom assistant	1		
Assembly line worker	1		
Junior army musician	1		
Total	85		

Source: ILEA *Educational Choice at 16*, Research Study Final Report RS 835/82.

Table 1 shows that school leavers in 1981 are replicating this pattern. Despite unemployment, boys are still going into a wider variety of occupations, many of which will include training, whereas one-third of the girls have gone into shopwork, and one-third into office and clerical work, and few of their jobs will offer any training.

Within occupational groups, women work in lower grade and sex-segregated areas. Among electrical and electronic workers, 84 per cent of assembly line workers are female, but only 1.4 per cent of 'linesmen and cable-jointers'. Ninety-nine per cent of all typists, shorthand writers and secretaries are women, but only 14 per cent of office managers. Although women appear to constitute 65.8 per cent of professional and related workers in the areas of education, welfare and health (*New Earnings Survey*, 1979), this statistic masks the fact that most are in nursing and the lower ranks of teaching. Only 17 per cent of GPs, 13.9 per cent of the Institute of Health Service Administrators' members and less than 1 per cent of surgeons and dentists are women. Although 41.1 per cent of women teachers in secondary schools are on scale 1, compared to 22.7 per cent of men, women hold only 871 of the 5198 secondary school headteacher posts.

There are few women in positions of power and prestige. Within the business world, for example, where lower rank jobs are predominantly filled by women, women account for 1 per cent or less of managing directors, bank managers and cost and management accountants. There are only three women high court judges out of 69, and these three are all in the Family Division; and no women judges in the House of Lords. In 1982, the number of women MPs increased from 19 to 21 – still four less than there were in 1945.

Many factors contribute to this pattern: simple prejudice and discrimination; the interruption in some women's careers due to child-bearing and -rearing; women's dual home and work role, which leaves little energy for the extra effort needed to win promotion; poor labour organization in the low-paid service sectors in which many women work. Inherent in some of these factors are assumptions about the roles of men and women. Why do we assume that women are solely responsible for child-rearing and the home, and that a woman's career will be adversely affected by having a family, while a man's will not? As a woman teacher remarked: 'I never ceased to be amazed that women are penalized for having children, but men are promoted because they have a family to support' (NUT, 1980).

Sexism and sex discrimination

It is significant that after more than a decade of a vigorous feminist movement in Britain, 'sexism' is still not a word in most people's vocabulary.
Such is the challenge this concept poses to established culture. Of those who
no longer confuse 'sexist' with 'sexy', few could give a more precise definition than 'discrimination on the basis of sex'. In order to understand the
concerns of this book, it is important to recognize the distinction between
sex discrimination and sexism.

Sex discrimination refers to individual acts or general practices which put
people at a disadvantage because of their sex; men are denied a state pension
until they are five years older than women, married women who pay the full
stamp cannot claim National Insurance benefits for their dependent
husbands and children. Since the Sex Discrimination Act became law in
1975, it has been illegal in Britain to deny anyone access to goods, facilities,
services, premises, education or employment on the grounds of their sex,
although the government exempted from the legislation military employment, immigration laws, tax and social security (the last two directly
affecting most women's financial position). In terms of education, the Act
means that it is unlawful for a school to operate a quota system based on sex,
for example, or only to allow boys to join a cookery class once all the girls
had got places. However, the attitudes of the judiciary (not only with regard
to education) have meant that the Act has been very difficult to enforce. The
judge in the Whitfield case (see Chapter 21, note 1) argued that 'equal
provision' meant 'equivalent', and that to provide cookery for girls was
therefore 'equal' to providing woodwork for boys. This point has never
been clarified in a test case in Britain. Also, the Act refers to discrimination
against an individual, so it has never been possible for a group of parents, for
instance, to show that their girls are being discriminated against by being
given school books which show women in stereotyped and inferior roles,
because this affects all girls (and, it could be argued, boys).

Overt discrimination, such as not allowing girls into technical apprenticeships, or permitting women to compete in non-team sports 'providing
they can prove they're good enough', is becoming less socially acceptable in
a society which admires the concepts of justice and equality. All the same,
many processes which combine to treat people unfairly because of their sex,
go unnoticed because of our sexism, which makes us think such discrimination is justified. Challenging actions as 'discriminatory' involves challenging the sexist attitudes which give rise to them, attitudes which we have

been brought up to believe are natural and normal, and which, in many cases, form the basis of our self-esteem and privilege. This book aims to investigate the attitudes, images and assumptions transmitted in secondary schooling, which lead us to expect certain characteristics or patterns of behaviour from women and men, and hence to discriminate for or against them. Our self-image is also partly determined by sexism. A common argument in support of the status quo is that girls choose nursing, for example, simply because that is what they want to do. We would accept this as an example of free choice, if occasionally more boys than girls chose to be nurses, or sometimes the physics class was predominantly female. But while girls and boys continue to make gender-typed choices, it is obvious that they are affected by what they consider appropriate for their sex.

The eradication of sexism is important for men as well as women. Both sexes suffer emotionally from the constraints of gender expectations. Women also suffer economically and physically. The power structures in our society are weighted in favour of men, and reflect and serve to perpetuate this male-dominated system. It is for this reason that more attention will be given in this book to the situation of girls than to that of boys. For most girls, schooling leads to a position where they have neither the skills nor the attitude of mind to compete equally with boys for jobs, money, and the power that goes with them.

Stereotyping

Our culture is based on deeply embedded views and attitudes about social roles, characteristic traits and psychological and physiological capabilities of groups of people, and these views, which are often unconsciously held, have a profound effect on our expectations of behaviour. In education, we need to be especially aware of attitudes in ourselves and in others, which persistently link certain behavioural characteristics with one sex, to the exclusion of the other. This will affect our self-perceptions as well as our interpretations of others' behaviour.

Generalized assumptions about the capabilities and attributes of men and women have led towards an acceptance of both men and women of supposed limitations in behaviour that are believed to be both real and incontrovertible, resulting in a kind of self-fulfilling prophecy. Once a characteristic is accepted unquestioningly as being 'natural' for a particular sex, this serves as a powerful instrument for discriminatory treatment, and is often used as evidence of the supposed 'natural' difference. The fallacy of this approach has been exposed in several experiments which have shown that the same behaviour is sometimes differently perceived and evaluated, depending on the believed sex of the actor. In one study (Condry and Condry, 1976) the same baby was called a girl for some observers, and a boy for others; in the first case, the baby's crying was described as 'fear', in the second as 'anger'.

Persistent gender linking of behaviour over a period of time often leads to the formation of stereotypes. We all use stereotyping as a convenient method of organizing our thoughts, and most people are aware of the oversimplification involved in gender-linked stereotypes such as 'dumb blonde', 'school marm', 'tart' and 'he-man'. Provided that we do not automatically apply these 'packages of ideas' to individuals without critically examining each case, there is no problem. Unfortunately, where the stereotype is more complex and subtle, it is not recognized, and leads to discrimination, as in the case of Anne Gameau.

In April 1981 the South Australian Sex Discrimination Board acknowledged that Ms Gameau had been discriminated against on the basis of her sex in her application for the position of headteacher at Wanolla School. The Board summarized the evidence of Sue Bettison, a psychologist and expert on sex stereotypes and their possible effects on decision-making, as follows:

> Ms Bettison's evidence was that, looking at cultural stereotypes of sex alone, people who have minimal information about a person other than the sex of the person *assume* other characteristics. If the person is known to be male, then the stereotype characteristics which are assumed are aggression, assertiveness, problem-solving ability, initiative, decisiveness, unemotionality, interest in worldly matters, dominance, ambition, activity – including energy and enthusiasm, physical prowess and strength, leadership, business ability, and administration and ability to deal with crises. Similarly, if all that is known is that a person is female, then the characteristics which are assumed are nurturing, caring, submissiveness, low self-esteem, emotionality, lack of physical and psychological strength, attention to appearance, high verbality, low maths/science ability, low problem solving ability, non-ambition, non-assertiveness and a primary interest in domestic rather than worldly events.

The Board reached the conclusion that the two people in question 'fell quite classically into the error which, on Ms Bettison's evidence, is culturally widespread, of applying stereotypes in the absence of having specific knowledge'. This summary also gives an excellent breakdown of modern gender stereotypes.

Gender

The term 'gender' refers to the behaviour which males and females are expected to show, according to their biological sex. We always decide whether a person is male or female. These concepts are mutually exclusive. There is no place in our culture for people of indeterminate sex. Kessler and McKenna (1978) claim that until we have ascertained whether a person is male or female, we cannot make sense of their behaviour; that 'gender attribution forms the foundation for understanding other components of gender, such as gender role (behaving like a female or a male) and gender identity (feeling like a female or a male)' (p. 2). This conflicts with the usual view that you tell what sex people are from how they look and behave, but would explain why we place such store on making sure that we can tell the sexes apart by encouraging gender differences, for example long hair for girls and short hair for boys.

The commonly accepted definition of gender is that given by Ann Oakley (1972a):

> 'Masculine' and 'feminine' are words which describe not biological realities, but social realities – the 'gender' not the 'sex' of a person. Gender is socially defined and thus varies between different societies. To be feminine in many traditional African societies is to do all the farming and to carry heavier loads than men. To be feminine in our society is to stay at home, look after children, to cry easily and be deferential to men. 'Masculine' and 'feminine' describe cultural complexes of behavioural characteristics and personality attributes assigned on the basis of biological sex and incorporating the values of the society in which and about which they are used.

A more sophisticated conceptualization of gender has been developed by Barrie Thorne (1978) who argues that we cannot properly make sense of gender either by seeing it in terms of individual attributes, or defining it in terms of roles. We have to see gender as part of a system of relationships.

There are relatively few well-established psychological differences between the sexes, but many similarities; and there are no characteristics which always apply to one sex but never to the other. Differences are always relative – more men than women show aggression – yet these are often presented in a mutually exclusive way. Even with 'concrete' characteristics which can be measured, such as height and weight, there are far greater differences between the extremes of one sex, than between the male average and the female average. Seeing gender in terms of attributes ignores how change takes place. Once 'masculine' and 'feminine' characteristics have been grouped together to form a stereotype, there is a tendency for the 'atypical' characteristics to be discouraged, and the 'typical' to be accentuated, so the norms move further apart. Girls who show a special aptitude for ball games are unlikely to be actively encouraged, and boys will be actively discouraged from 'feminine' pursuits such as ballet, and so the merging of male and female genders will be socially prohibited.

Building on the concept of gender as sex-assigned characteristics, most people define gender in terms of the parts, or roles, which men and women play in society, and examine gender acquisition in terms of how and why we are prepared for our future roles. But the use of role theory to explain gender is also unsatisfactory. Clearly, being male or female is not a role in the same specific sense in which 'nurse' or 'neighbour' is a role. The 'male' role cuts across all other roles which men perform. Role theorists have had to coin a variety of different terms, such as 'basic role' and 'unfocused role' to explain a concept which does not fit the usual notion of roles.

Thorne's approach sees gender not just in terms of belonging to the person who is being described, but as being affected by the presence, actions and perceptions of the observer. A man who defends his ideas positively may be described as 'assertive', whereas the same behaviour in a woman would be considered 'aggressive'. The response to the behaviour of others may differ, depending on what the observer believes the sex of the performer to be. In a study similar to that of Condry and Condry (1976), Lloyd (1980) presented four six-month-old babies to eight mothers. The babies were dressed for half the presentations in a pink frilly dress and called 'Jane' and for the other half in a blue jumpsuit and called 'John'. When the babies appeared to be boys, the first toy usually presented was a hammer-shaped rattle, while a soft pink doll was usually chosen for the 'girls'. 'Boys' were verbally encouraged to vigorous action, while the 'girls' were praised for their cleverness and attractiveness. Waving arms and legs was encouraged in the 'boys' by bouncing them up and down further, but the 'girls' were calmed down. (The experimenters were unable to detect any statistically reliable evidence of difference in the amount of movement in their 'actor' babies.)

Infants soon learn what behaviour brings them rewards of affection, and so will soon establish a 'masculine' or 'feminine' mode of behaviour. As soon as they learn to distinguish gender in others, they will also learn that some behaviour will produce different results with men and women. Gender becomes more important in some situations, like courtship, than in others, and tends to be more important at the beginning and ending of any social interaction when power relationships are being established and confirmed.

Seeing gender as a facet of any interaction means that we cannot discount the effect of our own gender upon the person(s) with whom we are relating, simply because we may choose to act in a 'non-sexist' way, by being aware of, and choosing not to respond to, their gender. A part of being actively anti-sexist, as opposed to passively non-sexist, means challenging the expectations that others will have of us because of gender.

Sex differences – real or supposed?

Explanations for differences in the behaviour of males and females are usually based either on the idea that such differences are innately linked to biology, or are socially and culturally learned – the nature/nurture debate.

Biological factors

Because of their biological productive function, women have traditionally been limited in their role in society, although the degree of limitation has varied with the type of economic organization and level of technical development. Although biologically stronger in terms of endurance, able to withstand pain developed in bearing children, and with a longer life-span, women have come to be regarded as the 'weaker' sex. In developing these particular strengths, women were confined to the home by the burdens of maternity. Frequent pregnancies were usual, and nursing and child-rearing took up most of their adult life. The division of labour which evolved as a result of this biological difference in capacity became more clearly demarcated when industry moved out of the home into factories after the industrial revolution.

As a result of the occupational division between the sexes, where men faced danger in hunting for and providing food, and 'protecting' women in times of threat, attitudes have evolved which imply that a woman's strength is really a weakness which impairs her ability to function in any role unrelated to her traditional nurturing one. Despite this, many women nowadays do not choose to follow this pattern. Men who may be more suited by their particular interests and capabilities, to performing a 'nurturing' role, are still regarded as odd in choosing a role more akin to that of the 'second-class citizen'. Our society has given high status to the acquisition of wealth, professional expertise and ambition at the expense of the 'caring' occupations, largely peopled by women.

The difference between male and female amounts to one pair of chromosomes in 23 contained in human cells; the female has an XX pair, the male an XY pair. In the absence of the Y chromosome, the foetus develops into a female. That, in theory, is where the difference ends, and a great number of similarities begin.

When we examine research for further evidence of any additional factors in genetic make-up to account for behavioural differences between men and women, we are further confounded by differences in interpretation, which are made to support innate, environmental views. For example, Oakley (1972b), studying gifted children in America, found a close correlation between the I.Q. of the boys on a particular test and their later achievement as adults. Two-thirds of the girls with a high I.Q. of 170 or above became housewives or office workers, occupations which did not reflect their true potential and capabilities. It was found that the I.Q. of the girls studied had actually fallen in adolescence and adulthood.

An 'innate' interpretation of these findings could be that highly intelligent American girls later naturally average out and retain an intelligence test score related to their traditional 'biological destiny'. Environmentalists, on the other hand, would suggest that it is the lack of intellectual demands in the occupational roles of these women, along with socialization pressures at puberty, which contribute to an accompanying decrease in mental agility.

In the absence of any studies which have taken boys in large numbers and reared them as girls and vice versa, no research finding can fully and conclusively eliminate other interpretations put upon it. Men and women secrete both male and female sex hormones; a difference in amount alters the balance and manifests itself in physical differences which at opposite ends of a continuum represent the male and female.

Beach (1948) claimed that the secretion by both men and women of progesterone, a female sex hormone, and androgen, a male sex hormone, had a profound effect upon the emotions. Because progesterone, when administered in large doses, acts as a sedative, and androgen sometimes produces unruliness and aggressive behaviour, research such as that by Hamburg (1967) has been interpreted to suggest influence of these hormones on brain function. But 'aggression' is not a clearly defined term. In studies of young babies, it has been associated with high activity levels, frequency of cries, 'greediness' at the nipple, etc. In nursery-aged children, 'assertiveness' and physically hurting others are both interpreted as aggression. In adults, aggressiveness has been observed in contexts of physical pursuits, crimes, the desire for dominance and the exploratory urge.

Aggression in educational terms has, apparently arbitrarily, been taken to include wide areas of behaviour such as untidiness, carelessness, truancy, rebelliousness, failure to do homework or the drive needed for success. The corresponding 'lack of aggressiveness' of schoolgirls is interpreted as covering behaviour ranging from reticence, less physical activity, submissiveness, shyness and avoidance of responsibility.

Certain educationalists have said that these 'natural' differences should be accepted, and not tampered with (Dale, 1975). Yet, because too much 'aggression' by boys can disrupt the classroom, it needs to be contained within 'healthy' acceptable limits, and action *is* taken to curb this. The 'lack of aggression' often displayed by girls, because it is not disruptive, is not considered a problem, and is therefore ignored, even though it may serve to limit their capacity for active learning (see Chapter 3).

Between the ages of two and five years, with the development of language and cognitive skills, as well as personality characteristics, behaviour differentiated by sex becomes measurable. A number of studies have described boys as more active, aggressive and disruptive, and personal preferences for 'boys' toys' have been observed. Studies of parent–child interaction have, however, shown that parents channel their children's toy interests from a very early age, which may later affect the child's choice of toys.

Differential treatment by teachers

Exploring differences in teacher behaviour at nursery school, Serbin et al. (1973) found that teachers responded to boys' disruptive behaviour with loud reprimands. The teachers gave equal attention to girls and boys, but to girls only at close range, while boys received attention even at a distance. They largely ignored disruptive behaviour from girls, thus decreasing the probability of its recurrence. In boys, disruptiveness was constantly reacted to, thus reinforcing that behaviour pattern. In the same study, the teachers were found to give more information to boys in the form of longer direction, and more conversation.

This type of attention given to boys may at least partly account for later differences in performance between boys and girls, particularly in mathematical skills. Differences in performance at reading and mathematics may also partly be accounted for in terms of the amount of reading and maths taught to boys and girls. Results of observations show that girls receive one-tenth more instruction and contact from teachers than boys in reading, and boys receive one-tenth more contact in mathematics (Leinhardt et al., 1979). These results confirm that teachers behave differently towards male and female pupils and that this behaviour varies according to the subject being taught.

The most significant finding from all the research so far mentioned seems to be that there are very few, or possibly no, innate behavioural differences between men and women; those that emerge are almost certainly learned. As long as there is any doubt about *how much* is learned socially, there is always the possibility that 'innateness' will be used as a convenient argument for not tampering with what is 'natural', and thus allow educational provision to remain inadequate.

Social factors

It is within the family, in whatever form the family takes, that we absorb most of our ideas about gender. The long-term continuity of the parent–child bond does much to shape the course of our early lives. Research shows that parents' and adults' behaviour towards babies is very much influenced by the sex of the baby. In exploring attitudes of 'parents of the future', 100 psychology students were found to consider certain play and toy activities as more appropriate to one sex than to the other (Fagot, 1973). Mothers and fathers have been observed to have touched male infants more than females and to have paid more overall attention to the former. With girl babies, parents were more concerned to elicit smiles and sounds.

Much of the research conducted before the 1960s which purported to have found behavioural differences between newly born girls and boys has since been questioned and not replicated in repeat studies; follow-up research has shown that differences in behaviour between girls and boys increase with age. This strengthens the view that the social environment has an increasing influence on gender-linked behaviour (Bell et al., 1971). A further aspect of this social learning has been suggested by Thorne (1978), where children can be seen to utilize gender in complex ways as a means of imposing their will upon others, in a form of social control.

Girls between the ages of two and three years have been shown to explore their environment and manipulate objects less than boys, with more sitting still, imitating, attending, persisting longer with tedious tasks and being generally non-disruptive. However, experiments with nursery and infant groups have shown that where the female teacher displays active participation in playing with constructional toys, girls will gradually imitate and take an active part where previously no interest was shown. Lack of active participation and a limitation presented by infant and nursery staff models may therefore be seen as an important factor in social learning for girls.

Cultural variations

Assumptions about appropriate gender behaviour can be challenged if we look at societies and cultures outside Europe, although some of the early research in anthropological studies needs to be examined with some caution. In the ancient civilizations of Egypt and Sparta, for example, women held power in terms of property rights; men provided dowries for women, adopted the name and nationality of their wives who alone had the right to divorce; children took their mother's name, inheritance and social position and girls were valued more highly than boys.

In the matriarchal society, women stabilized their power and secured for themselves greater freedom by providing food for the dependent sex. Occupations of women lay outside the home; men took care of the home and family. It is particularly notable that in this setting, men apparently developed what in Western society today are regarded as typical feminine characteristics – use of placatory techniques in achieving goals and a tendency to greater personal adornment and modesty. The outside occupations of the women, along with their greater freedom of movement and activity, resulted in taller, stronger women; the inferior strength of men was considered 'natural', and they are reported to have displayed tendencies towards depression, a condition symptomatic of the long-term performance of repetitive, unchallenging tasks (Vaering, 1946). It is tempting to make a comparison here with Western society today. In 1966 Gavron drew attention to the common problem of depression among housebound mothers with pre-school children. Research by Brown and Harris (1978) revealed that 19 per cent of women in this situation are depressed, psychiatric cases, and in poorer areas the proportion is as high as 31 per cent.

In her observations of three American Indian cultures, Mead (1950) found that in one tribe both men and women displayed Western stereotyped feminine characteristics; in another, both sexes displayed 'masculine aggression', while in the third, a variety of behaviour undifferentiated by sex was observed. Whatever value we now attach to these early studies, they do serve to suggest, if nothing else, that sex-linked behaviour is largely determined by cultural factors.

More recently, in a cross-cultural study of sex differences in attitude and attainment in different subjects studied in education, Keeves (1973) found wide variations between cultures, displaying a whole range of human behaviour possibilities. Each culture manifested expectations related to gender-typed behaviour in certain subjects, which led to self-fulfilling prophecies in motivation, attitude and examination performance. Where mathematics was interpreted as a 'masculine' subject, girls obtained poorer results. In comparing 'O' Level mathematics examination papers, where boys consistently obtained higher scores, a factor not generally taken into account was found to be exposure to previous mathematics-related experiences elsewhere in the curriculum, such as technical drawing and physics. In an investigation of one year's candidates taking 'O' Level mathematics with the Cambridge Examination Board, Sharma and Meighan (1980) found that boys and girls with equal technical drawing experiences performed equally well in the mathematics papers on most questions, as did girls and boys from physics groups.

Sex differences in educational achievement

A comparison of boys' and girls' educational achievement from primary level through to higher education shows two major features; first, girls start school doing rather better than boys, and gradually fall behind during secondary school; and secondly, the qualifications obtained by girls prepare them much less well than boys to earn a living (*Tables* 2–4). Throughout primary school, girls tend to be better readers than boys, and some research (Douglas et al., 1968) has shown that at the age of 11, girls are slightly ahead of boys in tests of reading, arithmetic and verbal and non-verbal intelligence. Certainly, in the days of the 11 +, many authorities used to calibrate the results to bring the boys up to the level of girls, otherwise the grammar schools would have had a disproportionate number of girl pupils.

Statistics are not available to chart boys' and girls' success across the whole curriculum in the first years of secondary school, but the experience of Stamford County Secondary Modern, Ashton-under-Lyme (*Times Educational Supplement*, 18 July 1980; see also Chapter 21, p. 300) illustrates what happens in maths. All the first-year pupils are tested a few weeks after arrival, and average scores of boys and girls at this stage are roughly equal. By the end of the first year, the average test score of the boys is significantly higher, and during the second and third years the gap between the average marks of the boys and girls tends to increase considerably. Consequently, by the fourth year, boys outnumber girls by four or five to one in the two top sets. The same trend is seen in science (Kelly, 1981). At both 'O' Level and CSE in 1978, the pass rate for girls was marginally better than it was for boys, although boys were entered for a slightly larger number of subjects

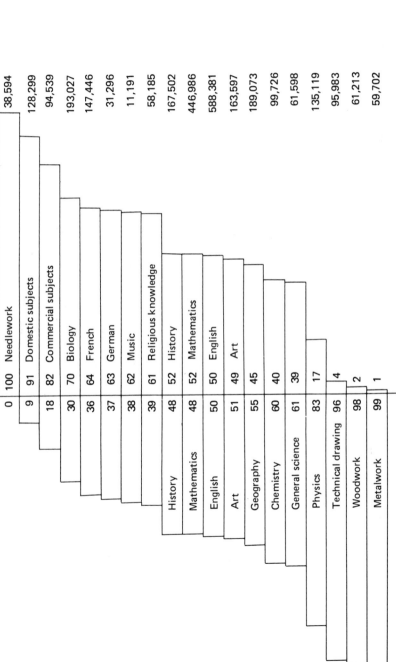

	BOYS (%)	(%) GIRLS		Total Entries
	0	100	Needlework	38,594
	9	91	Domestic subjects	128,299
	18	82	Commercial subjects	94,539
	30	70	Biology	193,027
	36	64	French	147,446
	37	63	German	31,296
	38	62	Music	11,191
	39	61	Religious knowledge	58,185
History	48	52	History	167,502
Mathematics	48	52	Mathematics	446,986
English	50	50	English	588,381
Art	51	49	Art	163,597
Geography	55	45		189,073
Chemistry	60	40		99,726
General science	61	39		61,598
Physics	83	17		135,119
Technical drawing	96	4		95,983
Woodwork	98	2		61,213
Metalwork	99	1		59,702

Source: The GATE Project, Chelsea College.

Table 3 The percentage distribution of boys and girls in GCE 'O' Level entries (Summer 1980)

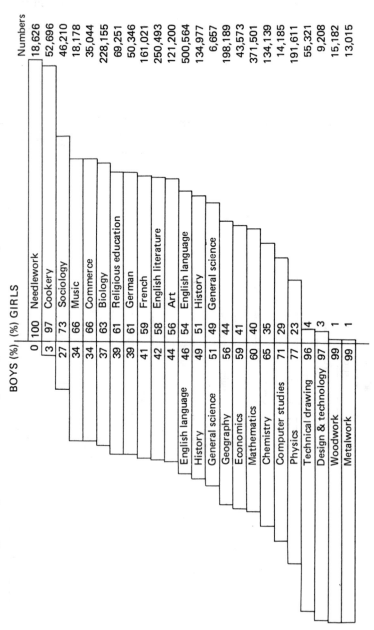

BOYS (%)	Subject	(%) GIRLS	Numbers
0	Needlework	100	18,626
3	Cookery	97	52,696
27	Sociology	73	46,210
34	Music	66	18,178
34	Commerce	66	35,044
37	Biology	63	228,155
39	Religious education	61	69,251
39	German	61	50,346
41	French	59	161,021
42	English literature	58	250,493
44	Art	56	121,200
46	English language	54	500,564
49	History	51	134,977
51	General science	49	6,657
56	Geography	44	198,189
59	Economics	41	43,573
60	Mathematics	40	371,501
65	Chemistry	35	134,139
71	Computer studies	29	14,185
77	Physics	23	191,611
96	Technical drawing	4	55,321
97	Design & technology	3	9,208
99	Woodwork	1	15,182
99	Metalwork	1	13,015

Source: The GATE Project, Chelsea College.

Table 4 The percentage distribution of boys and girls in GCE 'A' Level entries (1980)

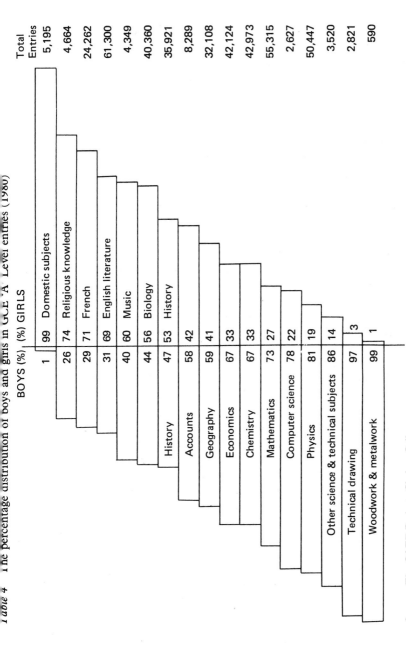

	BOYS (%)	(%) GIRLS		Total Entries
Domestic subjects	1	99		5,195
Religious knowledge	26	74		4,664
French	29	71		24,262
English literature	31	69		61,300
Music	40	60		4,349
Biology	44	56		40,360
History	47	53		35,921
Accounts	58	42		8,289
Geography	59	41		32,108
Economics	67	33		42,124
Chemistry	67	33		42,973
Mathematics	73	27		55,315
Computer science	78	22		2,627
Physics	81	19		50,447
Other science & technical subjects	86	14		3,520
Technical drawing	97	3		2,821
Woodwork & metalwork	99	1		590

Source: The GATE Project, Chelsea College.

than girls. This could indicate that teachers perceive boys as being more
intelligent than girls (Stanworth 1981; *see also* Chapter 3), or that teachers
are prepared to risk more public money on entering boys for examinations,
because they consider boys have a greater need for career qualifications.

At 'A' Level, for academic subjects only 43 per cent of entries were for
girls, despite the fact that girls had passed more academic subjects than boys
at 'O' Level. This trend of girls being under-represented in higher education becomes more marked at higher levels: only 38 per cent of under-
graduates in 1978–1979 were women (compared to 31 per cent when women
were first admitted to university in the 1920s) and 30 per cent of post-
graduates. Men still outnumber women in higher education, particularly in
medicine, engineering, science, administration and business studies, and
architecture and other professional subjects.

The most important comparison to be made is between the type of
courses girls and boys follow at school. Woodwork, metalwork and technical drawing are much more valuable for securing employment than domestic subjects; and biology without the accompaniment of physics or
chemistry is not regarded as adequate qualification for science-based training. *Table* 3 shows that although 63 per cent of biology passes were gained
by girls at 'O' Level in 1980, they gained only 40 per cent of maths passes,
and 25 per cent of physics passes. In 1977 only 2.7 per cent of passes in 'O'
Level technical drawing were by girls, and more girls (33 063) passed 'O'
Level cookery than passed chemistry (31 621). Even for the bright girl,
education is still linked to the home-centred nurturant role.

At a less academic level, the DES Rosla Report *Four Years On* (1979)
notes: 'It was disturbing to find far fewer girls than boys on some science
courses in the fourth and fifth years and, in one girls' school, no physical
science at all. Similarly, work experience schemes involved more boys than
girls while child development courses strongly demonstrated the reverse.
Among the link courses offered to pupils in the fourth and fifth years, the
boys largely selected technically based studies while the girls were mostly
found taking commercial subjects and courses such as hairdressing.'

Traditional vocational education qualifies girls only for a very restricted
range of jobs and occupations which, because they are traditional for
women, are low paid and low status. Although there are almost as many
women as men going into further education, the majority of women are on
non-advanced full-time courses, in secretarial studies, catering, nursing
and hairdressing. On average, the girls will stay on their courses for a
shorter time than boys and will attend a full-time course, hence they are

unpaid. In contrast a boy with an apprenticeship would expect to get paid not only for the work experience but for his day spent at college. Only 8 per cent of girl school leavers go into apprenticeships, compared to 37 per cent of boys (*DE Gazette*, December 1980). Of the 150 000 apprentices in the manufacturing industry, only 5000 are girls which represents only about 0.25 per cent of female employees in manufacturing ('Learning the job', *DE Gazette*, September 1980). Although women can expect to make up 40 per cent of the labour force over the next few years ('Labour force outlook to 1986', *DE Gazette*, April 1981), girls are leaving school without the qualifications necessary to secure training for a career, nor, in many cases, the expectation that they should do this. In doing this, they are conforming to the stereotype of femininity.

In a study by Broverman et al. (1970), mental health clinicians, both male and female, were asked to describe a mature, healthy, socially competent man, woman and adult. The clinicians rated the 'healthy male' the same as the 'healthy adult', but the 'healthy female' was perceived as significantly less well adjusted by adult standards: less objective, less adventuresome, less aggressive and competitive, more submissive and dependent. If women display more acceptable 'adult' traits of social competence, then they are perceived as less feminine. It is little wonder that girls, at the age of 14, when the pressures to be feminine are greater than ever before, do not press to take 'boys' ' subjects which will bring them disapproval from their friends, parents and teachers, even though they may be aware that they are disqualifying themselves from a wide range of 'male' occupations.[1]

Society as a whole suffers because girls' potential is wasted. Teachers, who are in a position to influence, are doing an even greater disservice to girls by not taking more positive steps to help them escape their gender expectation of incompetence and dependence.

Changes in the philosophy of education

The history of girls' education and its implications have been well documented and analysed (Marks, 1976; Wolpe, 1977; Byrne, 1978; Deem, 1978; Love, 1980). We therefore present only the briefest summary here, concentrating on government reports because these reflect official ideology. At the introduction of compulsory education in 1870, the basic element of the curriculum for girls in elementary schools was domestic economy, which included cookery, laundrywork and sewing. Education for the working classes has always been vocationally linked. The introduction to the

1904 School Code states: 'The purpose of the Public Elementary Schools is to form and strengthen the character and to develop the intelligence of the children entrusted to it . . . assisting both girls and boys, according to their different needs, to fit themselves practically as well as intellectually, for the work of life . . . to implant in the children habits of industry, self control and . . . perseverance.' The 'work of life' for women was seen as domestic service, and being housewives and mothers. The 'needs' of children were differentiated according to sex only. The predominant concern was to produce a docile and sufficiently skilled work force to serve the needs of industry and the state.

By 1923, with the Board of Education report on curricular differences, educational philosophy had become more progressive, recommending child-centred work for boys and girls. In 1943, the Norwood Report also advocated individual treatment: 'The purpose of education (is) to help each individual to realise the full powers of his personality – body, mind and spirit' (p. viii). However, the Committee's thought is as sexist as its language – individuality only applies to boys – for later in the report the justification for including domestic subjects in the curriculum is 'that knowledge of such subjects is a necessary equipment for *all* girls as potential makers of homes' (p. 127, our italics). Domestic skills were no longer seen as marketable, but as a preparation for marriage, a belief that was reiterated in the Crowther Report, 1959: 'With the less able girl, however, we think schools can and should make adjustments to the fact that marriage now looms much larger and nearer in the pupils' eyes than ever before' (para. 51). This does not affect boys: 'There can be no doubt that at this stage boys' thoughts turn more often to a career, and only secondly to marriage and the family' (ibid.).

As the number of women in the work force increased during the 1960s, later reports could not ignore the fact that girls would expect to get jobs, but they still considered that women should be confined predominantly to the wife/mother role, with work as an optional extra. In 1963, the Newsom Report *Half Our Future*, on 13- to 16-year-olds 'of average or less than average ability', stated: 'For all girls too, there is a group of interests relating to what many, perhaps most of them, would regard as their most important vocational concern – marriage. . . . many girls are ready to respond to the wider aspects of homemaking and family life and the care and upbringing of children' (para. 113). This reflects the Committee leader's earlier feelings about the suitability of a career for women, ambitious women being 'normally deficient in the quality of womanliness and the particular physical and mental attributes of their sex' (Newsom, 1948, p. 109). The Plowden Report, in 1966, was the first to advocate the concept of positive discrimination, calling for a redistribution of resources 'to improve the educational chances of the least well placed' (para. 146), but saw these children exclusively in class terms, as the offspring of manual workers, and made no mention of girls as a distinct group with problems of their own.

The education of middle-class girls followed a different pattern. In the 19th and early 20th century, middle-class girls were usually privately educated, thus avoiding the 'domestic' routine of elementary schools. Two names associated with the development of education for girls are Miss Buss and Miss Beale. They had two conflicting philosophies. Dorothea Beale, who became headmistress of Cheltenham Ladies College in 1858, worked on the principle of equivalence and separate needs. She believed that girls' education should be worthy of comparison with boys' education, but different. This formed the pattern for most girls' public schools. Frances Buss, who had to work herself while she was a student, was more concerned to produce a style of education to fit girls for a life of independence. She founded the North London Collegiate School and the Camden Girls' School, which established the style of the girls' public day school. Her students were encouraged to enter public examinations in open competition with boys, and the rigorous academic curriculum made no concessions to femininity. This tradition was reflected in the Regulations for Secondary Schools (1904) which laid down that both boys and girls should receive not less than seven and a half hours a week of science and mathematics, of which at least three hours must be devoted to science.

The provision of education for girls on an equivalent level with boys was strongly resisted by the medical profession, amongst others, who warned of nervous troubles and harm to the reproductive organs as a result of receiving education during menstruation, thus impairing a woman's ability to breastfeed her young. These fears were only expressed about upper-class women; the possibility of ill effects on working-class girls from continuous work as servants and factory hands was ignored.

Justifications for the different patterns of girls' and boys' education were based on the simple sexist notion that men and women had different aptitudes and intellectual capacities. In papers written by a group of headmistresses, girls were said to 'lack reasoning power, were unable to give a lucid direction, an accurate description or a clear and logical direction' (Burstall and Douglas, 1911). The belief that girls find maths and science too hard, because they are not innately disposed towards such subjects, is still fairly common today, indicating how entrenched ideas can become, and how hard it is to remove them.

In 1922 the Hadow Report confronted the problem of appropriate curriculum content for boys and girls. The academic experts, Cyril Burt and R.L. Thorndike, were called upon to establish the differences between the sexes in terms of educability and intellectual capacity. They concluded that:

> There are important physical differences (between boys and girls), there are also important differences in temperament and emotion; there are, too, fairly broad differences due to training and tradition. But in the higher intellectual levels, at any rate before adolescence is completed, inherent sex differences seem undoubtedly small. (Burt, 1917)

Unfortunately, the observations made by the teachers at the time of the Hadow Report carried more weight than the conclusions of Burt, which noted the strain on girls imposed by the secondary curriculum. However, mainstream philosophy seems to have gradually accepted that girls are capable of achieving academic excellence without physical collapse. The question is, though, of what constitutes excellence, and this is generally seen as what is established as a suitable education for boys. The Crowther Report commented of more able girls that 'there is not much scope in school hours for giving them any education which is specifically related to their special needs as women' (para. 51), and in 1963 the Robbins Report on higher education recommended that more girls be encouraged to read applied science. Although he was thinking in quite different terms, Newsom had a point when he complained that 'equality of educational opportunity became synonymous with imitation' (Newsom, 1948, p. 69), for there has been no attempt to take what is best from the tradition of girls' education and offer it to boys. Excellence is male defined.[2]

Since the Sex Discrimination Act 1975 came into force, government directives on education have all paid some attention to the 'problem' of girls. The Green Paper of 1977 says: 'Positive steps may be necessary to encourage girls to broaden and modernise their aspirations' (para. 2:17), although it does not give any indication of what these steps should be, nor should it be assumed that 'positive steps' refer to any form of 'positive discrimination' whereby resources or opportunities are offered to one group at the expense of another. The Green Paper is conceived largely in liberal individualistic terms, with emphasis placed on career opportunities being dependent on 'girls' choices', with no mention of the pressures of the hidden curriculum. Although the paper does suggest that both sexes should learn how to cope with domestic tasks and with parenthood, it supports the principle of equivalence, that 'Equal opportunity does not necessarily mean identical classroom provision for boys and girls' (para. 1:20). The Sex Discrimination Act is ambivalent on this point, although the Equal Opportunities Commission (EOC) firmly maintains that 'equal' should, in the context of provision, be taken to mean 'the same'.

The EOC has recently become much more forceful in arguing for positive action to favour women and girls, including, for example, with reference to retraining, single-sex training courses for non-traditional employment, the reservation of a quota of places for women on mixed-sex courses, and the provision of childcare facilities (EOC, 1981a). However, the EOC bemoans the fact that the MSC consultative document *A New Training Initiative* 'was not seen as an opportunity to propose a programme of positive action for girls and women' (ibid.). Not surprisingly, the EOC stands out as a lone voice among government agencies, and its stance should not be taken as typical of government educational policy.

It is on the international scene that the outlook seems the most promising. In 1979, at the Standing Conference of the European Ministers of Education, at The Hague, the ministers reached the conclusion that 'formal' equality has not led to actual equality of opportunity for girls, and asked each country to commit itself to 'a new overall policy designed to ensure that in all areas of life equality between the sexes becomes a reality'. This would include initial and in-service teacher education, positive discrimination, the development of new teaching programmes, and effective monitoring.[3] They also declared that 'Education systems should . . . prepare *all* pupils for the sharing of domestic and parental responsibilities, and equip girls as well as boys to earn an independent living, to cope with the technical elements of practical life and to participate in democratic decision-making and public life.'

The acceptance that both men and women should expect to share work within and outside the home is of vital importance. Girls' expectations are limited by seeing marriage as the most important part of their future life. Consequently, they attach less importance to career prospects, which ultimately leads to financial dependence on men. It is equally important that boys do not see their future only in terms of employment outside the home, since this cuts them off from parenting and childcare, and as long as men do not take an active role in childcare, women will continue to be restricted.

Unfortunately, attitudes conceived at international and even national level take a long time to seep through to the classroom. Rosemary Stones

(1980) relates an incident at her child's primary school, where a class of nine-year-olds, asked to write an essay on what they would like to be when they grew up, were helped along by their teacher suggesting that 'you boys might like to think about being mechanics or engineers, and you girls might like to think about becoming nurses' (Stones, 1980). This took place a few days before the publication of the Finniston Report which states: 'There is no reason why women should not become engineers'. In these circumstances, it would be useful to remember, and to remind others, that there is an international mandate for action. The UN 1979 Convention requires that member states 'shall take all appropriate measures – to modify the social and cultural patterns of conduct of men and women, with a view to achieving the elimination of prejudices, and of customary and all other practices which are based on the idea of the inferiority or the superiority of either of the sexes or on stereotyped roles for men and women'.

Early feminist analyses of education concentrated on the history of girls' education, and the way the organization of the school and the content of the curriculum prepared girls and boys for their expected work roles in future life (Marks, 1976; Sharpe, 1976; Wolpe, 1977; Byrne, 1978; Deem, 1978). Such analyses also focused on the way young children acquired gender identity through play and role models (Belotti, 1975) and particularly reading schemes (Lobban, 1976). Recently, work has focused more on the interaction between boys and girls, and the dominance of boys over girls, both in acquiring space, such as in playgrounds, and verbally; and on teachers paying more attention to boys (Clarricoates, 1978; Spender, 1980a, 1980c, 1981, 1982a; Stanworth 1981). From this, two major problems can be identified. Males command more attention, and are seen, by both men and women, to be more worthy of it; and secondly, our culture, knowledge and traditions have been selected and designed by males for the interest and encouragement of males. It is these problems which we will try to explore in this book – how does what is taught in secondary schools contribute to making men more successful than women? How does it give them real power (by providing boys with saleable skills which are able to command a higher price in the labour market than those appropriate for girls, and encouraging the development of physical strength) and how does it create the impression that men are more worthy than women, so that we would prefer to employ them in almost any situation where responsibility, authority and initiative are called for, and so that we choose to listen to what they have to say, rather than to women?

We shall try to show how the subject matter of the secondary curriculum reinforces the impression given by the social system, and by men and boys themselves, that they are superior; and to suggest ways in which teachers can challenge and change this. Awareness is the first step to our liberation.

Notes

1   Many girls, however, are not aware of career implications. 'These girls (in the EITB scheme), not knowing the educational requirements for technician training, thought they had received career advice too late at schools, as they had already made some decisions about subject options' (EITB, 1979).

2   I am indebted to Jill Lavigueur's *Co-education and the Tradition of Separate Needs* (Spender and Sarah, 1980, appendix) for most of the ideas in this paragraph.

3   See Chapter 21, p. 308 for use of the EEC directive 76/207/EEC.

CHAPTER 2

SCHOOL LIFE –

ORGANIZATION AND CONTROL

JANIE WHYLD

Socialization is a very subtle process which induces us to view our behaviour as natural, and stops us from seeing any alternative to it. It is usually extremely difficult to identify how we are being sexist. Even feminists who have spent years developing their awareness of sexism are occasionally filled with remorse because their behaviour has unwittingly been influenced by gender prejudice.[1] The processes of control involved in naming and in sexual harassment are only now being fully uncovered. But there are some aspects of school life which show overt sex discrimination. Many schools still adopt different standards for boys and girls, for example with regard to dress and access to subjects, segregate the sexes unnecessarily and, despite the Sex Discrimination Act, allocate scarce resources to one group on the basis of their sex. To eradicate such discrimination does not require any greatly heightened consciousness, or careful and continual modification of behaviour, but only sufficient commitment to overcome organizational problems and bureaucratic obstacles.

I will not examine all the arguments for and against topics such as timetabling, since these are well covered in many standard works on education. I shall concentrate on those aspects of school life, unrelated to particular subjects, which reinforce gender differences and keep men in a position of privilege and power over women.

Emphasizing the difference

According to child psychologists, children can distinguish between male and female by the time they are one year old, and know their own gender by the age of 18 months (Belotti, 1975, p. 51). In school, children learn that their sex is their most important distinguishing feature. (At the same time, though, secondary schools require students to repress their emergent sexuality.)

Teachers divide classes into smaller groups for a variety of purposes, ranging from the organizational, where there is a clear need for boys and girls to be separate, such as visits to the school nurse; through the practical – 'Boys put the clay back in the bin, and girls wipe down the tables'; to the educational, such as quizzes. Whatever the purpose, the most common basis on which to divide a class is sex. In many cases, division is quite unnecessary.

The 'girls first' approach for getting pupils to leave a classroom in an orderly fashion does nothing to help create the sense of self-discipline necessary for this to be carried out without teacher control, but merely reinforces the 'polite to ladies' and 'frail female' attitudes and is often time-consuming. Where it is considered necessary or desirable to rank a class in order, or divide a class into smaller groups, more thought could be given to the bases for division, linking them to the purpose. If the teacher wants a random mix for a quiz, then a complicated basis for division, such as birth signs, could be appropriate. A teacher might make the division on different lines each time, and check how quickly pupils respond – those with a 't' in their name, those born on odd dates, anyone who had toast for breakfast. Occasionally, more serious or meaningful factors may be appropriate, such as professed belief (atheist or religious, punk or reggae) or whether the pupil lives in private or rented accommodation. If the idea of emphasizing social class shocks you, why does the emphasis on gender not produce the same response? The effect of constantly dividing a group by sex is to rank our biological sex above any other aspect of our personality, to play down real similarities between girls and boys, and to distance the sexes from one another.

Tasks around the school are usually shared out on the basis of expected aptitudes. Typical sexual division of labour involves boys moving the furniture, even in the first year, when girls are frequently bigger than the boys and as strong, while girls get the tea ready for staff at break, and do the washing up afterwards. When visitors come to the school, the home economics classes, usually all girls, are often expected to make and serve refreshments, and the most presentable pupils, with the most civil manners, again usually girls, are used to show visitors around (hostess training!). On speech day, the headboy may make the speech and the headgirl present the flowers. Girls are used to clean out and tidy up stock cupboards, because they can be trusted out of the teacher's sight. Experiments to get boys to share in 'girls' ' tasks, such as washing up, have sometimes resulted in massive breakages as boys rebel against doing 'women's work'.

Registration

Most schools register boys and girls separately. This practice often leads to further segregation in lining up, filing into assembly, dismissing the class, giving out reports, and allocating resources, such as books and desks. Since boys come first they are seen to be more important, and girls at the end of the list are the ones who suffer when resources are scarce. Sara Delamont found that in two schools she observed, the use of the class list to allocate places in craft laboratories led to girls being given inferior facilities (Delamont, 1982).

The DES requires that form 7 on the back of registers gives details of boys and girls in separate lists. This information is needed for the creation of statistics which help provide the rationale for the need for positive action on sex discrimination. However, it is possible to desex class lists, as at Haverstock School, ILEA, where class lists, printed internally, are in simple alphabetical order. Possible opposition from school secretaries because of the extra work must be balanced against the advantage to pupils. In any case, pupils in computer studies could be given this simple practical task to carry out on the school computer.

Space

Some schools still have segregated playgrounds although most are mixed now, with an area set aside for ball games. This will usually be dominated by boys, while girls congregate around the edges, or in secluded corners. Wolpe (1977) described an experiment in having mixed 'noisy' and 'quiet' playgrounds, which had to be stopped after three weeks, because of boys rushing from one playground to another through the school building. So the quiet playground was given back to the girls only, who then saw it as boring because nothing ever happened.

By secondary school, and the onset of puberty, girls have usually succumbed to the role of spectators, watching the boys. This conversation with third-year girls shows how they feel that the boys' control of play space is approved of by the teachers.

- At break and dinner, the boys play football and that, but if we try joining in, they won't let us on the pitch.
- It's not theirs.
- They think we're not good enough.
- Yeah, they think we shouldn't be there, so we just hang around the concourse.

– In this school, the playgrounds are for boys, and we're stuck on the concourse, and then if we run around there's always a teacher trying to stop us, but we can't go on the playgrounds.
– We get chucked out of school, but we can't go outside 'cos there's nowhere to play outside.
– And if the boys are mucking about on the concourse, the teachers just walk past, sort of ignoring it, and just tell them to stop it. Girls would get separated and sent off.

(Pimlico School, 1982)

The problem of girls hanging around the edge of a boys' activity area does not seem to occur where the school building is open to pupils during breaks. Then only those pupils who want to will take a walk or play sport, and the rest can take their break, relaxing with friends in the warmth in the same way chosen by most teachers. Where facilities such as pool and table tennis are available for pupil use, these are frequently monopolized by the boys, with the implicit condonement of staff. In order to challenge boys' dominance of leisure facilities, schools might initiate 'girls only' sessions for a limited period so that girls can practise using unfamiliar equipment, and improve their performance so that they do not feel so uncomfortable playing under the critical and sometimes hostile gaze of boys. The experience of the National Association of Youth Clubs[2] has proved both the need and value of 'girls only' sessions.

The architecture of schools frequently separates boys and girls. Although schools are rarely built with separate entrances nowadays, it is common to find toilets placed on either side of the entrance, instead of next to each other, thus leading to a segregated use of the entrance, and of cloakroom facilities and lockers which may be placed nearby. An interesting exercise in social interaction which could be undertaken by pupils on a general or social studies course, or by staff trying to initiate action on sex discrimination, would be to chart who controls what space in the school (Thorne, 1978; see also Chapter 12, p. 185).

Uniform

Elementary school dress was standardized at the beginning of this century to protect deprived children from ridicule and embarrassment. However, it followed the tradition set by boys' public school uniform, which had been developed to be distinctive. Girls' school uniform had to be ultra-respectable, as Delamont (1980) explains. At the turn of the century, wearing a gymslip which was free fitting and did not need stays, was a liberating and daring experience, but drew the criticism that girls who went to school were in danger of becoming 'mannish' (being educated in male subjects and not wearing approved feminine dress). To counteract this criticism, the strictest standard of 'ladylike' dress, including hats and gloves, was insisted on in public. This standard of public presentability has continued, but whereas boys' ordinary clothing has not changed much during this century, girls' uniform, which was once 'avant garde', is now more restrictive than ordinary dress.

Uniform identifies the wearer as belonging to a particular institution. It is supposed to give the wearer a sense of pride and an *esprit de corps*, useful for competitive sport, interschool quizzes, speech days and concerts. It also makes it easier for neighbours, shopkeepers and bus conductors to identify vandals, and can provoke gang warfare between rival schools. However, being distinctive is rarely the main reason given by teachers for the desirability of school uniform. Many schools now adopt a system of 'standard dress', without distinctive badges, blazers, hats or ties, but generally this is still thought of as uniform: 'We have school dress, a very wide choice, but because some things are prohibited, some pupils regard it as school uniform' (Humberside teacher, 1982).[3]

Apart from the debatable issue of cost (school trousers, shirts and skirts may cost less than high fashion clothes, but more than oddments from the market), the interpretation of what is suitable clothing for school is clearly based on the work ethic: 'A dress code has developed for the male members of the Sixth Form; they wear what they consider to be suitable for business occasions' (11–18 urban secondary school). 'Basically we aim at explaining that school is a place for work, and that one should dress in a "workmanlike" manner' (semi-rural 11–16 secondary school). As most 'workmen' wear denims, the work envisaged here is clearly office work.

Collar, tie and jacket for boys, and skirt and blouse (or twin-set!) for girls imitate the conventional dress of the middle aged and middle class, a group which few pupils will identify with, and against which most will rebel. Safety is often given as a reason for not allowing jewellery, long hair (for boys) and high heels (for girls), yet it is never used to justify girls wearing trousers. Underlying these overtly sensible justifications of uniform is the knowledge that a homogeneous group is easier to control. Studies of institutions have shown how uniform is used to strip individuals of their external identity (Goffman, 1961). 'Wearing distinctive clothing indicates that students belong to certain groups, and we wish to discourage that'

(Humberside Teacher, 1982). The only group to which the pupil is allowed to belong is the school, where values are not created by the pupils.

Because pupils wear uniform, and staff do not, uniform becomes a badge of inferiority. Although many schools relax their standards of uniform for sixth-formers, 16-year-olds are often required to dress in the same way as 11-year-olds. Uniform is used to deny pupils the expression of their emergent sexual identity, which girls in particular are socially encouraged to demonstrate through dress:

> Parents want standards of dress laid down for their children to follow . . .
> Parents of teenage girls particularly are horrified at what they might be going
> to school in. . . . (Humberside teacher, 1982)

One Lincolnshire comprehensive, otherwise progressive in that it allows girls to wear trousers, specifies in its uniform list that girls' blouses should not be see-through!

Although some schools claim that they are 'anxious to keep abreast with changing fashions' (13–18 urban secondary school), others banned girls from wearing ties when it became 'trendy' for girls to wear them (in 1981). Ironically, although school uniform may curb the excesses of female dress, such as tight skirts and high heels, it forces many girls to be more traditionally feminine, by wearing a skirt, with all its attendant 'modesty behaviour', than they would choose to be outside school. There is also the problem that insistence on skirts poses for girls of Asian origin.

Standards of uniform for boys seem equally concerned with enforcing a conventional form of masculinity, by banning long hair, jewellery and earrings, often allowed for girls, and at the same time avoiding any show of male force:

> (Following a press report that the county council was going to abolish school
> uniform) I had two or three lads (turn up) with denim jackets and studs all
> over them, which I found unacceptable . . . and which quite a lot of the girls
> found very menacing. (Humberside teacher, 1982)

Some schools seem to have reached a successful compromise where the school retains some control over the standard of dress, but the pupils are allowed some choice:

> Girls moving into the sixth form choose their own uniform prior to joining the
> Sixth, to overcome the difficulties of fashion-conscious competition. (11–18
> urban secondary school)

> Grey or blue, black optional for fifth formers. Variations introduced every
> year by changing fashions, or by a committee at school. (Last year, 1975,

wider trousers, longer skirts, platform shoes, etc.) Unenforceable by anyone, but because of 'variations' is approved by majority opinions, and the minority is willing to be cajoled. (11–16 urban secondary school)
(Other schools in the county were banning platform shoes at this time.)

The experience of the school quoted above, of Kingswood School, Northamptonshire, of free schools and of further education colleges, where there is no uniform or standard dress, seems to prove that wearing clothes which express personality does not hinder academic performance or pupils' relationship with staff.[4] I have lads with studded jackets in almost every class I teach. To me, they are just clothes; for them, it is their 'uniform'. The 'menace' disappears with familiarity.

The standard dress of most schools enforces the division between boys and girls, and denies them the expression of their individuality, which could draw them closer together. Some girls wear studded leather jackets, too!

Control of pupils

Corporal punishment

Boys and girls are disciplined in different ways, and for different offences (see Chapter 3, and Davies, 1977). Corporal punishment is generally reserved for boys, sometimes only the younger boys:

Corporal punishment is regarded as suitable for some minor offences for smaller boys, usually under 13. It is used where a parent might smack a child. (11–18 secondary school)

More often it is only given for serious offences – bullying, stealing, vandalism – and for insolence to teachers, and smoking. Almost all schools see it as the most extreme form of punishment:

Verbal rebuke is used in the majority of cases of minor misdemeanour though in the infrequent cases of bullying, lying, cheating or stealing, corporal punishment is used as a last resort. (9–13 middle school)

It may be that because corporal punishment is so often reserved for boys, it is seen as the only real or 'manly' form of punishment. Equality, or lack of gender-linked distinction, can be achieved by applying the same standards of required behaviour to boys and girls. I support the following statement: 'The school does not believe that violence can be eradicated by officially sanctioned violence' (13–18 secondary school). Violence is a form of control sanctioned in male-dominated society. It would be profitable to draw on women's experience of controlling relationships verbally, and by the withdrawal of affection.

Reynolds' work (1976), comparing differences in delinquency rates between similar schools, indicates that less insistence on rules is associated with greater academic success and less delinquency. Those schools which caned boys most often also provoked the greatest amount of disruption. However, there is a temptation to infer that since, compared with boys, girls are rarely physically punished, they have less to rebel against, and are therefore less troublesome.

Naming

Teachers' language inevitably reflects their own conditioning and bias which they unconsciously pass on to their pupils. The old habit of calling boys by their surnames still persists in many schools, and is often used in a meaningless way to distinguish boys and girls in prize and honours lists. Similarly, in staff lists, male teachers are called by their initials and surname, whereas female teachers are given a courtesy title. In a coeducational school, this reinforces the view that boys and male staff share a common experience unknown to girls, and that boys deserve to be treated more brusquely than girls. Senior male staff sometimes continue this tradition by calling junior male staff by their surnames. An interesting variation on this is the teacher who proudly declares that he treats all his pupils the same way by calling them 'chaps', even the girls!

On the other hand, the worst insult you can give a boy is to call him a girl – gender is a powerful mechanism of control! Both male and female teachers are known to control boys' 'unsuitable' behaviour by calling them girls. Valerie Hey (1982) cites an example of a black woman teacher who disciplined a noisy boy who was displaying 'gay' mannerisms, by saying that the sooner he turned into a girl the better. And at my own college, a course tutor, telling his group they were the worst he had ever had, ended with 'You're just like a gang of big soft girls!'

Counselling and discipline

Girls may be better served than boys by counselling, since it is assumed that girls are more emotional and need to discuss their problems more. However, dwelling on the emotional is generally regarded as a sign of weak character, so unless there is an obvious problem, boys will be encouraged to 'keep their chin up'. The use of a same-sex member of staff for discipline and counselling reinforces the idea that difference of sex is an insuperable barrier to both understanding and control.

Girls appear to be more willing to ask for help over personal matters. They may also learn how to exploit their situation in the same way as they use/abuse their sexuality to get out of being disciplined by staff – perhaps because of lack of attention and help in class (see Chapter 3) and perhaps because they are brought up to recognize and value showing emotion.

When boys are caught swearing or fighting in school, they are likely to be dealt with differently from girls. A group of boys scuffling in the corridor would probably be sharply reprimanded and moved on, or told to sort out their argument out of school. Girls scuffling would provoke much more concern about the cause of the fight, since such behaviour, considered 'unnatural' in girls, would be interpreted as having a serious emotional cause. Similarly, a girl heard swearing would not simply be told off, but reminded of correct lady-like behaviour (Pimlico School, 1982).

It is generally accepted that boys are 'told off' more in class, and are dealt with more harshly by the agencies of social control such as the police and educational welfare officers. Jenny Shaw[5] has shown that girls are absent from school rather more than boys, but are less likely to be labelled 'truant', or stopped by the police. The milder label of 'non-attender' is more likely to be applied to a girl, and consequently, less action will follow. There is the expectation that girls should adopt domestic responsibilities in the home, and should not be penalized for doing so during school time.

Not surprisingly, boys are often resentful because, as they see it, girls talk and misbehave as much as they do, but the boys are reprimanded more severely and more often. More attention needs to be given to what teachers and pupils consider to be acceptable behaviour. 'Subversive' behaviour is usually taken to mean aggressive, 'male' activity, and the sullen, bored, withdrawn behaviour of girls is overlooked because it is not immediately disruptive. When normally quiet girls become noisy, they may be controlled more quickly, in an attempt to stop disruption spreading, if attempts to deal with those (boys) who are the real cause of the trouble have met with failure.

Sexual harassment

Physical sexual harassment includes groping, pinching and men rubbing themselves against women. In school, this occurs when a group of boys squash a girl into the corner, or grab at her in the corridor. If she fights back, she risks being told off by staff who have not witnessed (or refused to notice) the assault. Bea Campbell elicited the following from some 11–12-year-old girls in a south London mixed comprehensive school:

> It's as if the boys rule us and there's nothing you can do about it. They get girls in corridors and say 'How big are your tits?' and start feeling them up. It makes you feel sort of terrible about your body.

Carol Jones (1982) also identifies non-physical forms of sexual harassment in schools. Visual forms include large penises drawn in books, on posters, on desks and on the blackboard, graffiti abusing women staff and pupils, violent images in many of the books and videos used in schools, and boys showing off their 'macho' physique in public, by practising karate punches against a wall. Verbal harassment includes comments on women's bodies, their sexuality – 'slag, bitch, cunt, begging for it' – as well as jeering, wolf whistles and threats. Male teachers also subject girls to sexual comments and 'appraising' looks and leers. Angela McRobbie (1980) describes the blatant forms of humiliation to which women can be exposed:

> One teacher's authority is undermined by her being labelled a 'cunt'. Boredom is alleviated by the mimed masturbation of a giant penis and by replacing the teacher's official language with a litany of sexual 'obscenities'. The lads demonstrate their disgust for and fear of menstruation by substituting 'jam rag' at every opportunity.

A woman teacher has authority because of her status as a teacher, but lacks it because she is a woman. Just as Dale Spender notes that 'if a woman can be classified as promiscuous, then her ideas can be classified as unreliable and not worthy of serious consideration' (Spender, 1982b), male pupils and staff who wish to attack the female teachers' authority will do so by humiliating her as a woman. Valerie Hey (1982) argues that the female teacher is afraid to identify with girl pupils and the sexual harassment to which (she may be aware) they are exposed, because by doing so she loses her authority as a teacher (which should make her invulnerable to such attacks). If she admits that she is intimidated by male pupils, she will not be seen as an able teacher, will jeopardize chances of promotion and other jobs, and may feel that she is showing up all women as having special problems because of their sex. The problem, of course, lies with the men who practise sexual harassment and our culture which condones it and not with the women who are the unfortunate recipients of such attacks.

Many male teachers maintain their authority over pupils by a 'hard-line' rule of fear, and are often competitive about their ability to establish firm discipline. They also patronize women staff with offers of help, often when there is no problem. This 'tough male' approach, with which some adolescent boys identify strongly, only makes matters worse for staff who want to establish attitudes of self-discipline, since they are then labelled 'soft'.

Timetabling

Although more than three-quarters of secondary schools in England are coeducational, almost all these schools separate boys and girls for some lessons. Sometimes this may only be for PE, but two out of eleven Hudders-field comprehensive schools studied in 1980 separated boys and girls for careers lessons, so that they could specialize in boys' and girls' careers (Benett and Carter, 1981). The Sex Discrimination Act 1975 makes it illegal for a school to restrict any subject which it offers to pupils on the basis of their sex, so although the Huddersfield schools were probably not in contravention of the terms of the Act, because all pupils were receiving careers education, they were certainly contravening its spirit. East Sussex County Council recently found that seven out of 39 secondary schools were still offering craft subjects on traditional lines (the schools were told they must change their timetables), and a survey of school brochures in London found that only 18 out of 107 mixed schools said that they offered the full range of practical crafts to boys and girls.[6]

Until the early 1980s, the response of all education authorities to the Sex Discrimination Act had been extremely cool. A Nottinghamshire teacher observed that for most changes in educational policy, the LEA asked headteachers to state what they were doing to comply with new regulations, but that this seemed not to have happened for the Sex Discrimination Act.[7] Schools tend to feel that they have fulfilled their commitment to the Act if they formally offer all craft subjects to first-year girls and boys. They do not question why boys and girls resort to traditional choices, since this rein-forces their own feelings about sex differences. It is extremely important how the offer of a subject is made. In 1973, Lynn Davies found that the head of one Birmingham upper school said that there was 'absolutely free choice of subjects', yet the craft and typing teachers along the corridor said that their subjects were not available to both sexes. The situation has not changed appreciably: 'Girls in the scheme have told the Nottingham researchers about the difficulties they had in taking practical subjects at school. In some cases this was due to absence of equipment and facilities but in others because the school discouraged them' (EITB, 1979).

Conversations I have had with girls who left Humberside schools in the summer of 1981 have shown they believed girls were not allowed to do woodwork, metalwork or technical drawing. Sometimes they had been told this outright by a member of staff, frequently their form teacher, and although they knew that this was supposed to be illegal, they had not known how to persist without the support of their parents. Tradition, parental pressure, media and peer-group influence, as well as the attitude of some teachers, all influence pupils to opt for traditional subjects. It takes courage and determination to be the only member of your sex in a group, and if you have to fight to get into the group, it is no surprise that so few pupils take 'non-traditional' subjects. In recognition of this problem, Somerset County Council issued an official instruction to all headteachers that there was to be no allocation to craft subjects along traditional sex lines, and that it was not sufficient to tell parents that they could request their children take a cross-sex subject.[8]

Single-sex groups

In most schools boys and girls still do crafts separately in practice, if not by design. Some, but not all, of these schools suffer from lack of facilities, because until the late sixties, schools were built to provide craft facilities for only half their pupils. This can be overcome by having twice as many pupils use the facilities for half the time, thus developing a rotating craft circus. Formal objections to this are that there is insufficient time with any one group to give meaningful grounding in the subject. In practice, objections are more likely to be based on tradition and teacher attitudes. The home economics teacher who has only ever taught groups of girls cannot imagine how to motivate or control rough boys, and the outdoor studies teacher will argue against the practicalities of mixed camping, and will say that girls cannot keep up with boys on long walks. The difficulties envisaged can be traced to the teachers' stereotyped expectations of pupils' reactions. Where all crafts are taught to both sexes but in single-sex groups, there is a tendency to confine girls' metalwork to jewellery[9] and boys' needlework to heavy textiles.

Timetabling single-sex groups can create organizational problems for a school, but these should be accepted as worthwhile if it is believed that pupils will benefit. There is much debate still as to whether pupils learn better in single-sex groups (see Chapter 21), and this should be the main area of concern when deciding to adopt single-sex teaching, and not which areas of study are appropriate for each sex. It has been shown that girls benefit from single-sex teaching in maths (see Chapter 7) and possibly science, and boys may benefit from single-sex oral work in languages. Ideally, boys and girls should have some opportunity for single-sex discussion in sex education and assertiveness training.

Curriculum choice

It is vital that careers counselling starts before subject choices are made, usually at the end of the third year, so that pupils are aware of the vocational implications of dropping subjects. Biology alone is insufficient for entry into careers requiring a science education, yet for most girls it is their only science subject. When pupils choose crafts in the second year, careers guidance is seldom given, and pupils often do not realize that they cannot take up subjects again in the third or fourth year once they have dropped them. Wherever choices are offered, pupils should be fully aware that dropping a subject in one year may exclude them from taking a related subject later on; for example, technical drawing may only be available to those who have studied metalwork in the third year. The DES *Education Survey 21* found that 27 per cent of schools operated a pre-emptive system of the kind in which the qualifying subject was not available to one sex. EOC advice to parents (EOC, 1982a) on choosing subjects suggests a choice of subjects which develops a pupil's potential, and does not limit a pupil to a specific career. The EOC warns against choosing subjects such as childcare or car maintenance, which may appear relevant but which are not essential for a chosen career, at the expense of dropping subjects which give access to a wide range of careers.

The grouping of fourth-year options often channels pupils towards traditional choices. Few schools have the resources of time and staff to offer pupils a totally free choice. Option systems have been devised to ensure a balance between academic and non-academic elements of the curriculum, so that girls end up taking arts and domestic science, and boys science and technology; or to provide a package of skills fitting the non-academic pupil for his/her future role (Crowther, 1959; Newsom, 1963), so that girls take English, typing, domestic science and childcare; or to allow early specialization in the arts and sciences. The rationale for alternative subject groupings might include the ideas that an all-round practical education should include home economics, childcare, and home and car maintenance; that all technologists should study a social science; and that home economics should be linked to science. This leads to the question of what is considered to be essential knowledge. Science is considered so important at Billericay School, Essex, that all pupils are expected to take one 'hard' science up to examination level. All pupils also take a two-week keyboard course suitable for commercial or computer work.

The 1976 'Great Debate' argued that there should be a very limited core to the curriculum, which was related to the 'basic educational right of the country'. Many now argue that basic education should be the sole concern of secondary education, and that optional leisure and vocational interests should be the province of further education. We need to ask why some subjects such as maths are considered important enough for all pupils to study, while others such as science are optional. If subjects are considered important enough to be taught at school, then surely they should be taught to all pupils? This would deny any element of individual choice, except in areas which develop the same skills, so there could be a limited choice of sports, arts and music. However, those who argue for individual choice imply that it has the virtue of freedom, whereas the results of the option system prove that 'choices' are bound by social expectation. If in one year 90 per cent of the candidates taking childcare were academic boys, then we could accept that the choice was free!

Preferential treatment

When resources are insufficient to meet demands, the basis on which they are shared out reflects the relative power and prestige of the recipient groups. In Western society, the people most likely to acquire wealth and its attendant power will be male, white, from a non-manual background and will live near to an industrial area. A similar situation applies in schooling. Byrne (1976) has shown that a less able girl, living in the country for her middle years of school, will be quadruply disadvantaged. In schools, prestige and often resources go to male areas of interest, and men teachers are promoted more quickly than women.

Resources

Schools that were built as single-sex institutions did not generally include facilities for subjects associated with the opposite sex, hence girls' schools seldom had science facilities, and in those areas of the country where single-sex education is common, it is still the case that girls' schools will be comparatively poorly equipped for science, probably with no on-site facilities for technology. In mixed schools where facilities for science are limited, it is common for boys to be timetabled into science laboratories for chemistry and physics, while girls use converted classrooms for biology (Byrne, 1975). Where there is a limited number of places on a sex-typed course such as metalwork, it is common for the sex concerned to be given preference. Proportionately more money is spent equipping 'boys' ' subjects like metalwork and car maintenance than on 'girls' ' subjects like childcare or home economics. It could be said that technical subjects are expensive to equip, and that resources are allocated where they are needed, but pupils, mostly girls, following CSE office skills courses do not generally have access to word processors (see Chapter 16, p. 238). Money goes to examination groups, and because girls are not encouraged to achieve at CSE Level, they are allocated less of the available resources.

Since 1981, schools have been encouraged to buy items such as micro-computers, and there is some concern that where these are based in the maths department, they are reserved for the best pupils in maths, namely the boys. Baroness Lockwood, chairperson of the EOC, in a speech on vocational courses for women (3 March 1982) said: 'Information filtering through is already indicating that girls are losing out in some schools on the opportunities being provided. Where computers have become school-based there has been such enthusiasm that pupil usage numbers have had to be restricted and boys have been given preference.' Certainly publicity in the local press advertising Lincolnshire's new venture of a travelling 'new technology' classroom indicated that it was intended for boys by showing only boys in the photograph. Paul McGee, the Croydon HM Inspector for computers, suggests that computers be kept out of the maths department, if girls are to have a chance to use them. (*TES*, 20 Aug. 82)

In the use of school funds for extracurricular activities, it can be seen too that girls get much less than their fair share. Funds are frequently spent on financing sport, involving more boys than girls. Consideration should be given to funding some equivalent activities of interest to girls.[10]

Staffing

At the end of the 19th century, women made up 75 per cent of the teaching force in elementary schools and held 56 per cent of the headships. In 1978 women made up 59 per cent of the full-time teaching force, but had declined to 38 per cent of headships. In 1976 women teachers in middle and second-ary schools made up 43 per cent of the full-time teaching force, but less than 1 per cent held headships, compared with 3.4 per cent of the men; 71 per cent of men, but only 57 per cent of women had succeeded in achieving scale posts. Among reasons suggested for women's inferior position in the educa-tion hierarchy are that employers see women as a 'bad risk' and are reluctant to promote them, and that they assume that married women follow their husband's work, often leaving a job with promotional prospects, or not applying for a job in another area. The NUT survey *Promotion and the*

Woman Teacher (1980) effectively refutes the claim that women do not apply for promotion. Over half the women surveyed had applied for promotion in the last five years. On the other hand, Byrne (1980b) argues that 'one of the continuing hidden barriers of inherited and separate sex roles (is) women's own conditioning to accept a secondary place in the queue for opportunities where these are limited through lack of resources'.

As girls' schools disappeared, during the move to coeducational schooling, so did the number of headships reserved for women, who then had to compete with men, but on unequal terms. Where men were deemed capable of controlling girls, women were not considered suitable for controlling boys. Many female heads of coeducational schools are in that position largely by virtue of the fact that they were already head of a girls' school before it admitted boys. Also, headship requires experience of timetabling and very few women acquire this. A woman's traditional nurturing role is seen to fit her for pastoral care, not for planning or staff management. A woman teacher, quoted in the NUT survey, complained: 'Two posts were advertised, one for the pastoral care of girls, and one for curriculum development post. . . . I was only asked about pastoral care'. The posts of head of department, on the promotional ladder to the posts of deputy head and headteacher, are largely held by men. Many schools operate a system where there is a head, a deputy head (or two, if it is a split-site school) and a senior mistress, which indicates that the deputy headships are intended for men. As Valerie Hey (1982) remarks, the job description of a senior mistress should read responsibility not for welfare, but for flowers, Tampax, visitors and note-signing.[11]

Table 1 Full-time teachers in maintained nursery, primary and secondary schools

	Men	Women
Heads	17 789	11 131
Assistant heads	163 821	250 287

Source: DES, *Statistics of Education*, vol. 4, 1979. Reproduced with permission of the Controller or H.M.S.O.

Table 1 shows that far fewer women than men can expect to progress from the position of assistant head to head, and since this table includes nursery and primary schools, where a larger proportion of women hold headships, the position in secondary schools is far more extreme than indicated here. The sexual division of labour in society is replicated among the non-academic staff of a school. Male porters and caretakers are responsible for the buildings; women service, as secretaries, cleaners and dinner ladies. Yet again the microcosm of the school reflects wider society. Women staff are generally paid less than men, and occupy fewer positions of authority. This model is clear for all pupils to see.

Notes

1 Maggie White, talking at the 'Curriculum for Girls' evening organized by the PTA at Norwood School, London, related how she ruined an exercise designed to see which sex children would see a leader as being, by herself referring to the leader as 'he'.

2 Information can be found regularly in the *Working with Girls Newsletter*, available from the NAYC Girls Project.

3 Quotations in the sections on uniform and on corporal punishment come either from the Humberside Report on School Rules, Uniform and Discipline, agenda item no. 12 of the Humberside Schools Sub-Committee 22 April 1976 (where indicated with type of school) or from a meeting of teachers' representatives with Humberside Education Authority, 9 February 1982, about the abolition of school uniform.

4 Humberside, along with some other Labour-controlled authorities, have now made the wearing of school uniform non-compulsory, i.e. children may not be refused entry to school because they are not wearing certain items of distinctive or specified clothing. Schools are still allowed to request that a uniform be worn, but not to enforce this. It will be interesting to observe how long it takes before uniform ceases to be an 'issue'.

5 Jenny Shaw contributed the sections 8:10, 8:11 and 8:12 of the Open University Course E353 Block 5, unit 13 Family, State and Compulsory Education.

6 Quoted in *Women and Education Newsletter* no. 23, summer 1982.

7 The EOC *Comments on the DES Report — 'Local Authority Arrangements for the School Curriculum'* (1979), noted this apparent lack of concern, shown by the fact that at that time, only 14.5 per cent of LEAs had any form of monitoring.

8 In a letter dated 22 May 1981, to heads of all schools and colleges, the chief education officer of Somerset County Council, Mr Barry Taylor, suggested 'that in order to avoid any possibility of misunderstanding all parents should be asked to specify their choice before allocations are made. Obviously, it is understood that it can never be possible to guarantee any parent his or her choice of subject where subjects are over-subscribed However, in such cases the allocations should not be made on the basis of the sex of the pupil.'

9 In a London comprehensive, it was decided to teach boys and girls separately for metalwork, so that the girls could develop confidence in an area of work which was unfamiliar to them. The programme was very successful while the teacher who initiated the scheme was at the school, but when this non-sexist teacher left, the new 'traditional' metalwork teacher reduced the girls-only metalwork syllabus to making jewellery, and 'nice, small pieces'. Single-sex teaching should be reviewed regularly to assess direction and performance.

10 Ideas for girls' activities are set out in the *Brighton Girls Project Report* (1980), available from NAYC Girls Project.

11 Marian Carter, now head of De Brus School, Skelton, told how she became aware of sex discrimination when she realized that her main function as senior mistress in a mixed comprehensive school was to dispense cups of tea to visitors and to deal with what the male headteacher referred to as 'girls' sanitary problems' (EOC, 1982b).

Acknowledgement

I would like to thank Jane Rylands-Bolton for all her help and suggestions with this chapter, and for contributing to the section on discipline.

CHAPTER 3

CLASSROOM INTERACTION

KATHERINE CLARRICOATES

In this chapter I want to concentrate on how classroom life forms and reinforces gender divisions in schools. I shall look at the interaction between teachers and pupils, and between the pupils themselves, and show how such interaction is suffused with notions of gender. If we can identify those forms of interaction which directly and indirectly perpetuate beliefs in 'appropriate' gender behaviour, it helps us to avoid such action.

Teachers' strategies for dealing with pupils' demands

In order to explore how and why gender is used to organize the classroom, we need to look beyond the 'chalk and talk' and the generalities of social organization in school. Many people assume that relationships in education are concrete and clearly demarcated – teachers provide knowledge and at the same time maintain control in their classrooms, and pupils absorb this knowledge and provide evidence of their learning in public examinations. Many people also realize that there is nothing simplistic in this 'conveyor belt' idea of education (Hargreaves, 1967; Sharp and Green, 1975). Human beings are very complex, and much that goes on within classrooms is taken for granted, since it is seen as commonplace and not dramatic.

Let us start with what could be seen as a fairly innocuous example of everyday life in a primary classroom,* to illustrate what goes on between teachers and pupils. Most readers will recognize this, if not as teachers, then almost certainly from when they themselves were at school.

A second-year infants' class is in the middle of a 'word construction' lesson. One of the children, Jonathan, is having difficulty with the construction of a particular word. The teacher, Miss Nicholson, takes him aside and produces a large word card set. Holding a card up to him, this is the context of the conversation that ensues.

---

* *Editor's note.* Although this exchange takes place in a primary school, I have experienced the same type of exchange, with the same latent function of disruption, in a college of technology.

Miss N.:	Now can you tell me what the word is? Look at the picture and it will help you . . .
Jonathan:	(looking carefully at the card, suddenly says) Do you like my jumper, Miss? (jerking the waist of his jumper towards her).
Miss N.:	(with infinite patience) Yes, it's very nice, but can you try and tell me what this word is?
Jonathan:	My Mum knitted it for me, but there's a hole in it (jutting his elbow into her face).
Miss N.:	(removing his elbow from her face) Perhaps your Mummy will mend it for you when you get home. Now, about this word.

Jonathan, however, has got the bit between his teeth, so to speak.

Jonathan:	Did your Mum knit your jumper for you, Miss?
Miss N.:	No. I bought it at a shop. (But neither is she to be put off). Try the first letter, Jonathan. Come on b . . .
Jonathan:	At what shop? (refusing to let go).
Miss N.:	(with a slight edge to her voice, which should tell him that he has gone too far) Marks and Spencers. Now that's enough. Where I got this jumper is not going to tell you what this word is. What is it?
Jonathan:	(either ignoring the warning or not having recognized it) Can't your Mum knit?
Miss N.:	(now with slightly raised voice) Enough, Jonathan. The word.

Jonathan gives a deep sigh. Miss N. remains impassive.

Jonathan:	One of my teeth 'cem' out and I'm going to put it under the pillow and then I'll get 5p . . . Look!

And with that he reveals his gums and teeth, and the inevitable gap.

It takes a further seven minutes for Miss Nicholson to 'extract' the word from Jonathan. Meanwhile, during the exchange, the teacher has somehow managed to keep an eye on what is going on around her:

– Matthew, kindly get down off that desk . . . if you fall you will hurt yourself . . .

– No, Gillian! You're not to play 'snap' with the word cards.

– Michael Andrews, the class abacus is for counting with, and not bashing your classmates with it over the head . . . put it down.

Now, the exchange between Jonathan and the teacher has had different meanings for both of them. For Jonathan it was an exercise to manoeuvre himself out of a situation, and he attempted to play on the 'maternal instincts' of the teacher. What he does not know is that Miss Nicholson has been the teacher of that class for ten years and is adroit at countering the tactics of children like himself. However, this exchange is symptomatic of the 'problem' that teachers have to cope with in their classes. Such an example also reveals that pupils are not merely passive objects, but do exert influence on the teacher.

Certain types of behaviour exhibited by pupils present 'management problems', and a prime example of the pressures teachers face is disruption from boys. It is a well-researched fact that boys do tend to be more disruptive than girls (Spender and Sarah, 1980; Stanworth, 1981). In many of the discussions I had with teachers, they informed me:

– The boys are more difficult to settle down.
– It's a bit harder to keep the boys' attention.
– The lads can really play you up if they're in that frame of mind.

Sarah et al. (1980), in a discussion of 'management problems', noted that gender was an important category when defining such problems. It would seem that the classroom behaviour of girls and boys makes different demands upon the teacher, and has a particular bearing on classroom practices. Some teachers were 'forced' into situations where they would have to stop the lesson, or could not even start it.

– Until the boys quieten down, we're not going to start.
– Alright, I'm waiting for some of the boys to sit down and then we'll begin.
– When Michael stops playing the fool, I'll tell you what we're going to do.

A great deal of research in classrooms, spanning two decades, shows that boys are at the centre of teachers' strategies to maintain control. Meyer and Thompson, as early as 1963, found that in each of the three classes they studied, boys received significantly more disapproval or blame than the girls did. In a much larger study of the same year, Spaulding (1963) produced a similar result, using categories such as violation of rules, personal qualities of child, thoughtlessness, task mechanics, lack of knowledge or skill, lack of attention, poor housekeeping. Boys exceeded girls considerably in the violation of rules. Both in praise and in punishment, it is generally agreed that boys do get more attention in class than girls (Brophy and Goode, 1970; Martin, 1972; Frazier and Sadker, 1973). British studies of classroom life would tend to support such findings (Deem, 1980; Spender and Sarah, 1980; Delamont, 1980), but not all studies agree.[1]

Faced with a greater demand from boys for attention, and difficulty in controlling their behaviour, teachers adapt to the situation by using particular strategies. Many segregate their pupils on the basis of gender to simplify administration in class (see Chapter 2). Some teachers also have particular notions of the 'ability' and 'skills' of girls and boys. This perpetuates an inevitable dualism. Certain activities, subject matter and project topics are presumed to be appropriate for girls, and others for boys. So lesson content is directed to specific groups:

- You boys will like this topic, it's right up your street . . .
- I know that this subject mainly appeals to the girls, but you boys have had sessions on the Vikings . . .
- Right! The boys can choose the topic today, and please make it different from the usual boys' projects such as war.

Choosing a topic specifically with boys in mind is a teacher strategy to deal with the greater demands from boys, who seek the most attention and who present teachers with greater difficulties in coping with their behaviour (Clarricoates, 1978; Spender and Sarah, 1980). Teachers hope to maintain classroom control by making the lesson appeal directly to the boys; the girls may not agree or be entirely content with the situation but will 'tag along'.

This also has a particular influence on pupils in that it reinforces the already held belief that girls and boys have different 'natural' abilities in specific subjects, thereby leading towards 'feminine' and 'masculine' skills. In a collection of papers, Alison Kelly (1981) pointed out that such an attitude, no matter how tenuous, may well influence girls in their choice of subjects, in particular to avoid science.

Teachers have perceptions that there is a greater difficulty in teaching boys. Elizabeth Sarah (1980) states:

> I found I spent a lot of my time focussing attention on the boys who were misbehaving and practically ignored all the girls who were getting on with their work. (p. 160)

Similar statements have been echoed in numerous studies, whether observational or accounts of teachers' views (Davies and Meighan, 1975; Clarricoates, 1978; Spender and Sarah, 1980):

> The boys take a long time to settle down to their work . . .
> They are so easily distracted . . .
> I find myself putting a lot of energy into keeping the boys occupied.

Such statements were made by teachers during my research in four schools in the north of England. In the study by Davies and Meighan (1975) the boys were seen as: '. . . restless, independent, noisy and careless' (p. 175).

Girls, on the other hand, were seen to be the most 'sensible' pupils:

> You can rely on the girls to get on with their work and not to act up in class.
> I can leave the girls on their own, but I wouldn't trust the boys . . . I'd keep
> them with me . . .
> It's such a relief to know you can depend on the girls . . . they make life so
> much easier in class . . .

(Clarricoates, 1978)

Manipulated by the necessity to maintain control and provide instruction, teachers appear to be drawn into the stereotyped attitudes towards gender-orientated subjects and activities. Eileen Byrne (1978) reports that in primary and middle schools:

> A predominantly female staff looks for ways of interesting boys in mechanical
> toys, activities, projects, because these are rightly thought to hold their
> attention . . . (p. 91)

It is very common for topics to be chosen and taught with a view to evoking the interest of the boys, whilst the girls are expected to tag along. Anne Lee (1980) reports:

> It seems that teachers work harder on trying to provide examples and experiences that will hold the boys' attention. (p. 125)

Marion Scott (1980) supports this supposition by inferring that because of boys' rigidity and unwillingness in class they can: '. . . determine the nature of the lessons to an unfair extent' (p. 105). This clearly indicates that a teacher does not have to be sexist to produce a gender-divided class. The social dynamics of gender, in fact, are worked out in every classroom, every day, not just by teachers but by every pupil in his or her own peculiar way. Treating girls and boys in an equal way may be made difficult for the teacher, or even impossible, by the pupils themselves. It is to be remembered that previous to their schooling, children have already learned certain notions about appropriate gender behaviour, and these notions will affect their conduct in the classroom.

Scott's point (1980) that boys' 'rigidity and unwillingness' in class can 'determine the nature of the lessons' (p. 105) is particularly salient to the following extract from my own fieldwork.

In a class in a suburban school, a project on the planets has been going on when a boy called Justin suddenly exclaims: 'I don't like this . . . it's for girls'. The teacher, Miss Peters, is not to be put off: 'Nonsense, Justin, you should enjoy this just as much as the girls . . .'. She moves in quickly to quell any slight disturbance, and proceeds with the lesson.

Miss P.: Who can tell me what is the importance of the moon?

But neither is Justin to be put off: 'I think it's cissy.'

One or two other students join in: 'No, it's not.'

Miss P.: (carries on) Who can tell me what is the difference between the sun and the moon?

Justin: (intent on sabotage) The sun comes out at night.

Jenny: (another student) No, it doesn't.

Kevin: It keeps you warm.

Miss P.: What does?

Kevin: The moon.

Lisa: Silly, that's the sun.

Miss P.: That's right.

Justin: (who is now in his element) But Miss, the sun's shining now and it's cold. Look, I think it's snowing.

Miss P.: (still trying to relay information) We've discussed the seasons and why it's cold.

Kevin: I still say it's the moon.

Miss P.: What is?

Kevin: That keeps you warm, 'cos look outside. It's cold . . . Justin says so.

Lisa: The moon only comes out at night . . . and it's got something to do with the sea.

Justin: Next she'll be telling us it dives in.

Jenny: You're just being daft.

Miss P.: (thinking it has gone far enough, brings the class to order, and raising her voice slightly, states) I'll tell you once more, it is the sun that shines during the day; it gives the earth light and warmth. The moon comes out at night and it controls the sea tides. And Justin Bateson, remind me when there's another trip to the moon to put you on it.

It is this sort of discourse that the teachers regard as evidence of boys' lack of concentration. It also shows how some pupils attempt to subvert what is going on in class, and incite others to join in.

Even when teachers do not segregate the class along male and female lines, some pupils, particularly boys, take the initiative themselves. In a music lesson, the teacher asks: 'Michael, will you move next to Lisa and make more room?'

Michael does not move, but glares at Lisa. The teacher tells him again: 'Michael, go and sit next to Lisa'.

Michael: I'm not sitting next to her.
Teacher: (surprised) Why?
Michael: She's a girl
Teacher: That's very observant of you. Now, move.

Michael does so, but not before he has managed to hold the class up for at least seven minutes.

What is to be noted from this boy's refusal to sit next to Lisa is his implicit idea that girls are inferior. This is not an exaggerated statement. Such an imputation is apparent in many aspects of Western culture in the form of advertising, stock jokes, crude innuendoes in our language,[2] and the inferior status of 'women's work' with regard to pay, conditions and prestige. It is of paramount importance that teachers assess their interaction with pupils, as they may unconsciously be perpetuating such a superior/ inferior relationship among pupils, particularly by perceiving girls and boys as 'different' and unequal groups.

'Hard work or talent?' Achievement related to girls and boys

Just as teachers accept the generalizations about differences between the behaviour of girls and boys, such differences are believed to exist in ability. First, let us take what is fact. Teachers and researchers generally agree that girls, on average, are ahead of boys at 11 years of age both in physical maturity and scholastic competence (Douglas, 1964; Sharpe, 1976; Clarricoates, 1978; Hannon, 1981). Douglas (1964) reported that girls were more successful than boys at primary level in most subjects, particularly in reading, writing, English and spelling. In my own research, the majority of the teachers supported such a distinction by reporting to me:

> . . . the girls have always been my brightest pupils.
> There's simply more girls at the top of the class than boys.
> The girls tend to do better at most of the subjects.

Greater interaction with the boys was justified on the basis that they needed more attention in order to 'catch up' with the girls in their scholastic work:

> You have to encourage the boys more as they soon drop back in their work . . .
> The boys lose their concentration more easily . . .
> I have to cajole the boys that bit more as they tend to lag behind in their work.

So, more time was spent listening to, talking to and helping the boys, not only because they needed more control, but because they needed 'drawing out' (Spender, 1981). Another major reason put forward is that teachers give the boys more attention simply because they find them 'more creative', and therefore 'brighter'. Davies and Meighan (1975), for example, state that girls' 'ability' was perceived as being: '. . . more conscientious, precise, organised, and better at written work', whereas boys were perceived as: '. . . more logical, more enthusiastic, quicker to grasp new concepts and better on the oral side' (p. 175).

Ricks and Pyke (1973) surveyed the attitudes of 30 Canadian teachers of both sexes, the majority of whom thought that male pupils were more interesting and critical. In general, research in this field suggests that male pupils are more likely to be perceived as having 'creative ability' whilst the girls are noted for their 'conformist' and 'sensible' behaviour.

Robert Spaulding (1963) found that teachers accorded to boys' work and efforts in the class more approval than they accorded to the girls' work. Glennys Lobban (1978), in her synthesis of research on the 'hidden curriculum', which may throw more light on the matter, noted that most of the research on teachers (of both sexes) shows that they interpret behaviour according to stereotypes and that it is the male pupils who are destined for the 'real career'.

Societal myths of stereotypes pertaining to 'femininity' and 'masculinity' do influence teachers' beliefs about what girls and boys are like. Such behaviour as 'adventurous', 'boisterous', and 'disruptive' in boys was seen as being linked to their supposed 'high creativity' and 'imagination'. And yet there is no evidence to suggest that high activity is connected with intelligence (Broverman et al., 1968). In their study of four schools, Broverman et al. recorded the observation that girls' real ability was attributed to conformity to institutional expectations and that the academic achievement of girls in schools is explained in terms of the 'feminine' stereotype. A statement in Delamont's (1976) study of an upper middle-class girls' school sums it up that there can be few boys of whom it could be said, as it was of one girl in her study: 'She only answers when she's sure she's right' (p. 70).

It seems quite clear that the interpretation of the socially constructed term 'creativity' relies upon the personal, subjective beliefs of the teachers. In an Australian study, Terry Evans (1978) focused on the relationship between what he termed 'sex role'[3] socialization and creativity within the context of schooling. He found that teachers are more inclined 'to give encouragement to the males whom they see as most creative, rather than females'. He goes on to conclude that such 'sex differentiated patterns of teacher–pupil interactions, implies that teachers may not be teaching as fairly as they might' (p. 153).

If teacher–pupil interaction is to the overall advantage of boys and they are also perceived as the 'creative' pupils, what should we expect the social learnings of girls and boys to be as they go through both primary and secondary schooling? Research has consistently itemized the fact that girls reveal a higher degree of anxiety about both the teacher and other pupils (Davie et al., 1972; Galton and Simon, 1980). This is usually interpreted as 'wanting to please the teacher' and as a sure sign of 'conformity'. However, the self-esteem of pupils is being looked into, and some of the results are very disquieting. Girls' self-concept of mental ability has been found to be significantly lower than that of boys with the 'same intelligence' (Spaulding, 1963; Stanworth, 1981). Jennifer Shaw's statement (1980) that mixed schools are ultimately boys' schools may be borne out by the fact that 'they are dominated by boys' interests' (p. 73).

Research material on the schooling of adolescent girls is rapidly growing and revealing some contradictions. The study by Davies and Meighan (1975) gave examples of perceptions of life in school by girls who were aware of the differential treatment they themselves received from the teaching staff. The authors state that the girls complained of the boys '. . . receiving more attention and friendliness . . .' (p. 174).

E. M. Chandler (1980) attempted to assess the extent to which girls generally felt they were valued by the school they were attending or had just left. The question was asked: 'Do you think that at school you were approved of, disapproved of, or just accepted?', and some of the following answers were given:

> I don't think they really noticed . . . They noticed if I didn't do my essays and when I was successful in sport . . . They didn't see me.
> I don't know. Good ones go unnoticed . . .
> A successful person is someone who doesn't get in the teacher's way. (p. 74)

It is hardly surprising that girls have a greater level of anxiety about the effect they have on teachers if they go through their school life unnoticed. One of the girls in Chandler's study felt she had been approved of in that: 'No-one has disapproved' (p. 74). Angela McRobbie's sensitive work (1978) on adolescent girls' youth culture indicates how girls combat what they see as the oppressive features of school, and to gain the attention that otherwise is given to boys, they

. . . assert their 'femaleness' to introduce into the classroom their sexuality and their physical maturity in such a way as to force the teachers to take notice. (p. 104)

The view that girls are conformist or only interested in 'boring and insular' life-styles of romance, pop stars and make-up, however, is being questioned. Lynn Davies, for example, has found that teachers' perception of what is important to girls, namely 'immediate youth values', could be misplaced. Davies found that the girls were much more concerned about examination achievement which may help them to get good jobs (Davies and Meighan, 1975).

> The question is whether this imperfect insight into what is important to girls means that other interpretations of girls' personality characteristics are also inaccurate, affecting their entire attitude to and relationship with them at school. (p. 175)

Certainly the view typifying girls as 'conformist' needs reviewing. Madeleine Arnot (1980) suggests that the 'setting up and transmission of gender stereotypes as a form of social control does not necessarily imply that individuals become what the stereotype demands'.

The situation becomes more complex when we turn to the analysis of the subculture of black girls in a particular school. Mary Fuller (in Deem, 1980), in a study of West Indian schoolgirls in a London comprehensive, describes how they rejected the 'conformist' routine:

> As a strategy for present and future survival the girls had adopted a programme of 'going it alone' in which those aspects of schooling to do with acquiring qualifications had an important part. No more tolerant of the 'irrelevant' aspects of schooling (e.g., the daily routines) than their male black peers, the girls were in some ways a good deal more effectively independent of adult authority than any other group of pupils (male or female) in the school. (p. 64)

A similar study of Asian schoolgirls by Sue Sharpe (1976) echoes Fuller's findings. Sharpe indicates that despite the ambivalence of the girls' response to education, they place more emphasis on the importance of qualifications and of education itself (p. 252).

It is obvious, due to the classroom studies of adolescent girls (Davies, 1973; Fuller, 1980; Llewellyn, 1980), that traditional and uncontradictory views of teenage schoolgirls need to be revalued. Much of what we usually term 'feminine behaviour' has been reinterpreted as the resistance to lessons and teachers. Mandy Llewellyn (1980) has pointed out that this resistance takes the form of day-dreaming, filing and painting nails, writing initials on desks and books, or 'skiving off' school. An essential part of this resistance can be seen in girls' clothes and hairstyles – an important aspect of 'feminine' youth culture – which is often at odds with the school's idea of 'suitable' dress or uniform (see Chapter 2). This oppositional style is expressed similarly within the 'masculine' youth culture of boys, but there all similarity ends. The collective challenge of the 'lads' to the teachers' authority is quite different to the individualized and personalized challenge of the girls (Llewellyn, 1980). The working-class 'masculine' culture of the lads in school is shown not only through anti-social and anti-academic values and behaviour, but also in anti-women and sexist terms (Willis, 1977). Smoking, drinking alcohol (particularly on the last day of term) and boasting about sexual experiences are the main ways of resisting the school and excluding 'outsiders', namely ethnic minorities and, above all, females. Whatever else the 'lads' may or may not be, 'at least they are not girls' (Shaw, 1980, p. 71).

The limitations of girls' resistance – escaping from what they see as the meaningless authority and activity of school life – can be related to the fact that they have to negotiate and/or avoid the 'slag' and 'drag' categorization, which is essentially male-defined. Discovery of a girl's sexual experience leads inevitably to moral censure even amongst her own peer group. There is a hypocritical belief amongst males, and in society in general, that females are only to be sexually attractive, and not sexually active. Equally, girls are ambivalent about the 'drag' category (having a steady boyfriend), as many see themselves as being too young for a serious and permanent relationship, which the 'drag' category implies (Robins and Cohen, 1978).

Such double standards and notions of female inferiority are found in many levels of interaction, notably amongst the peer group. Gender 'appropriate' behaviour is learned from birth. This is made more complex by the intersecting dimensions of class, race and age. Young children even within primary schools are already putting their 'world' into an order which is essentially based on gender identity and status, related to their class position and/or ethnic group in society.

During conversations with all-female, all-male and mixed groups, I was able to discover how the various groups expressed themselves in relation to gender. I noted particularly that working-class boys hinted at the lack of scholastic success as part of their peer group status. It seemed to represent more of an 'achievement' than a disability. Girls, on the other hand, valued academic success. Obviously it is not as simple as this. Some boys were actually quite good at their work and were keen to do well, while some of the girls found study tedious and difficult. But it seems that some of the girls and boys were already preparing themselves to be part of the anti-school culture which exists in a concrete form in secondary schools, as outlined by Willis (1977) and Llewellyn (1980). It is significant that, among the peer group, values and status hierarchies associated with gender are being formed quite apart and distinct from the teacher(s) in the classroom, although teachers may unwittingly be assisting in the formation of these 'feminine' and 'masculine' subcultures.

Implications of the gender preference of teachers for pupils

Just as teacher expectations seem often to be sex-specific, so their preferences would seem to be gender based. It has been indicated in previous research that teachers actually prefer those children with graded and 'acceptable' gender-typed behaviour (Feschbach, 1969; Levitin and Chananie, 1972). Davies reports that 72 per cent of the teachers (both male and female), in response to a questionnaire, said they would prefer to teach boys, giving a variety of reasons including ease of relationship, career prospects and such attributes that are seen to be connected with boys' 'dynamic personality' (Davies and Meighan, 1975, p. 175). Stanworth's research (1981) also pointed to the fact that teachers, on the whole, have a greater regard and interest for their male pupils. Such a preference is linked to boys' greater involvement in the class and to their future careers.

Preference for teaching girls has been documented by researchers like David Hartley (1977) and Mary Fuller (1978). However, Fuller implies that this preference only exists for girls in primary schools and that the situation is reversed in the secondary school. Phil Clift and Barry Sexton also conclude that primary schoolteachers prefer girls (A. Kelly, 1981a). It would seem we must take a closer look at those attributes and characteristics that are at the basis of teachers' gender preference.

Levitin and Chananie's work (1972) highlights the dichotomy of the teachers' *professional* values about how children ought to behave, and their *personal* values about how each sex ought to behave. As they suggest, it is not difficult to ascertain that noisy, active and aggressive girls would be least liked, as they violate *both* sets of values, whereas boys with similar behaviour only violate one set of values. David Hartley (1977) noted that although some of the teachers did not like the boys as 'pupils', nevertheless they liked them as 'boys' (p. 203). It would seem there is a significant sex-and-behaviour interaction effect between teachers and pupils.

But what influences such preferences? In my own research, 'preferences' varied among the four schools I studied. In the working-class dockland school, the pupils were viewed as 'material' which frequently came below the par of the derived ideals of what teachers hoped to achieve. The persistence of the *belief* that girls and boys behaved in exactly the opposite mode and the acceptance of the school in a 'poor area' affected ongoing social interaction. The teachers perceived the boys as 'rough and ready', and saw their unwillingness to accept authority as part of the 'boys will be boys' syndrome. The girls were expected to be orderly and good at getting on with their work. By attributing behaviour to gender and seeing 'mis-behaviour' as an attribute lodged within the male (naturally or learned), teachers transfer a toleration message to the boys that their noise and disruption is acceptable, by virtue of insisting that the girls accede to their expectations of the 'feminine' stereotype. These expectations actually rein-force the tendency of boys to express that behaviour further.

In the middle-class school of Applegate, scholastic achievement and behaviour 'becoming of white collar workers' children' were expected from all the pupils (despite the fact that a minority came from working-class backgrounds). The boy who achieved well and was successful in sports was given high status, since his behaviour reflected the value structure of the whole school. However, in no way did a girl receive similar status when participating in all that was required of her. Disruptive behaviour from the boys was seen as an expression of high spirits but girls were expected to acquiesce to the middle-class notion of 'femininity' with all its contra-dictions, encompassing what Delamont (1978) termed as the 'double conformity trap'.

During the interviews with male teachers in my study of four schools, many of them agreed that they did tend to reprimand girls more leniently than they did the boys:

> I would clearly be much more severe with the boys in my class when it comes to punishment. I think this is partly to do with the fact that trouble tends to come more from the boys than the girls, therefore I tend to overlook the odd misdemeanour from girls.
>
> You have to remember that girls are not as physically strong as boys so I tend not to treat the girls as I would the boys.
>
> The girls respond more to verbal reprimands than boys do.

During observations in class, teachers were seen to indulge in such prac-tices. They were clearly inculcating ideas about traditional stereotypes, by having a different discipline procedure for girls and boys. This tended to increase the antagonism, often held by the boys for the girls, when subjected to what they saw as discriminating policy to the advantage of the girls. I am not suggesting the 'equal right' of girls to be physically punished, but that girls and boys be treated the same – with respect and consideration.

Such differentiation in treatment, with its implications of gender preference, has alarming consequences, and gives rise to some disturbing manifestations.

Wolpe (1977) gives clear examples of how male teachers encourage girls by praising their 'femininity' or suggesting that they use it, not only to gain attention, but in 'achieving particular ends'. One specific illustration of Wolpe's epitomizes this form of interaction:

> Text books of a particular lesson had to be collected from another male, young, equally 'mod' teacher. Mr B. selected one of the prettiest girls in the class (and also one of the cleverest) for this chore and advised her to 'go to Mr A., and charm him, use a lovely voice, say thank you sir, and smile at him when you ask him for the books'.

Whilst unaware, at the time, of the implications of this form of interaction, Wolpe later realized that:

> . . . he was coaching the girls and telling them that being pretty, and being nice, and being charming, were all essential ingredients to achieving particular ends. (p. 36)

However, there is another side to this coin, which distinctly points to the sex-and-behaviour interaction previously indicated. Lynn Davies (1973) reported that girls felt they were often discriminated against by female teachers. They made accusations of being 'bitched at' and 'shouted at' while the boys were 'pandered to' and their demands met with a more positive response. In a later paper, Davies (1979) argues that 'any probing into girls' disaffection with school' should take into account the way that girls' behaviour and resistance to school is categorized by both male and female teachers. Boys' physical confrontation is often seen easier to deal with in that it can 'be seen to start and stop' (p. 69). I have lost count of the times I have heard secondary school teachers tell me that they are having trouble with the girls in their class; and it is to Davies I turn to for an explanation:

> The initial greater conformity amongst girls at school can be related to the overall absence of alternative typescript for women in society; and also to the fact that the conforming girl fits neatly into the good pupil script at school. The difficulty school has in dealing with disruptive female pupils indicates the lack of appropriate deviant typescripts for them. Boys are expected to be

naughty. But for girls the punishment structure is not there; and the teachers have to fall back on the wider 'social immorality' typescript. (p. 69)

It is not difficult to see from these various examples of fieldwork and research that teachers relate differently to pupils because of their gender. Obviously, such practices inform pupils that the divisions based on gender are an inevitable part of their everyday lives.

Summary

It would appear that despite the fact that girls and boys may attend the same school, they are clearly being prepared for different social worlds. Girls' ability, though equal to that of boys, is scanned for a different meaning, so that their achievement is seen as 'conformist' and merely 'wanting to please'. The different expectations that teachers have of boys and girls may in some part explain the persistent failure of state schooling to radically improve the chances in the lives of women in general It is understandable that teachers respond more to boys who are 'difficult' and need coaxing with their work. Sarah (1980) states that she herself often 'responded with praise or encouragement' to her male pupils. Such responses are viable when one wishes to reduce negative, disruptive behaviour and reinforce positive, cooperative behaviour. However, it is increasingly evident that boys are able to dictate classroom life to their own advantage. Lesson content and subject matter are invariably chosen with boys in mind, with a reliance on the 'gender appropriateness' of particular skills and activities. Recent research has documented this critical issue of skills, learning and behaviour which are considered 'appropriate' to either female or male, and the thorough research of people like Alison Kelly (1976, 1981) and Gaby Weiner (1980) has strongly contested the theory of gender in relation to performance in science and mathematics, and found it wanting. But attitudes that certain skills are a 'natural concomitant' of being either male or female remain entrenched, especially when one group is able to amass a great deal of power and prestige through the existence of such a dichotomy.

It would be naive and simplistic to place the blame of gender divisions squarely on teachers' shoulders, as pupils themselves are 'ordering their own world' on the basis of gender and do, in fact, exert some influence on their teachers.

In the television documentary on 'Education and Equality' in December 1981, which dealt specifically with gender, Dale Spender noted that even when teachers were aware of such discrimination and set about correcting it, they found it impossible to do so. The physical arrangements of the classroom and the behaviour of the pupils exert an influence on teachers making it impossible for them to divide their attention equally between male and female pupils.

By identifying patterns of behaviour which reinforce gender divisions within schools we can at least attempt to interrupt such patterns in order to bring about change. The road to change will mean not only monitoring behaviour as teachers but as people. Our teaching methods must acknowledge that categories of gender exist, and must attempt to counteract them. This will include challenging our own perceptions, and those of pupils and their parents. It is essential that collective discussions among teachers, pupils and parents take place in an informal setting either through lines of communication specifically set up to challenge the situation or through those lines which already exist, such as the PTA, Board of Governors and/or open nights. Once we begin to question or displace the prevailing norms defining what it is to be female or male, we will ultimately challenge the dominant–subordinate relationship of men over women, and develop equal relationships.

Notes

1   See Maurice Galton's work on the ORACLE studies (Galton and Simon, 1980).

2   The classic work of Dale Spender *Man-made Language* (1980c), deals with this aspect in a thorough and unique analysis.

3   The term 'sex role' is now seen as a rather questionable concept; see Thorne (1978) and Chapter 1.

SECTION 2

THE SUBJECT CURRICULUM

CHAPTER 4

SUBJECT IMAGE, EXAMINATIONS AND TEACHING MATERIALS

JANIE WHYLD

Although individual subjects differ considerably in the way they are sexist, for example the invisibility of women in history, or the 'male is normal, female is deviant' approach of biology and psychology, there are many aspects of sexism which are common to most subjects.

Image

A survey carried out by Weinreich-Haste (1981) confirms that pupils think that to a greater or lesser degree certain subjects such as cookery, typing and French are 'feminine' while woodwork, physics, maths and chemistry are 'masculine'. Weinreich-Haste and others have also shown that pupils have quite complex ideas about the nature of various subjects, the skills they require and the attitudes they engender. Woodwork and physics are both considered masculine, but the masculinity of woodwork stems from it needing some physical strength, and being training for an appropriate career and for the role of 'man about the house', whereas the masculine qualities associated with science include objectivity, rationality and a lack of concern with feelings or appearance (the 'absent-minded professor' stereotype). The images of individual subjects, where relevant, will be explained in more detail in the specialist chapters. Here I am concerned not with what the image is, but with how it is created and perpetuated. No one point is sufficient to explain the build-up of a gender-typed image, but the following factors all contribute.

The sex of the teacher

Statistics showing the distribution by sex of teachers in various subjects are not collected, but if it is assumed that most teachers are teaching the first subject of their degree, then *Table* 1 shows that male physics teachers outnumber female ones by four to one; that there are twice as many men as women teaching maths, geography and history (almost); and that women predominate only in the areas of English and modern languages. The NUT survey (NUT, 1980, table 19) found that among 1316 women teachers who replied, only one specialized in woodwork/metalwork, and six in engineering science, compared to 293 who taught art, music and craft.

Teachers present role models for children, just as much as do parents, workers in industry and commerce, who may be known to the child, and characters in books and on television. There are few children who, at the age of 11 or 12, will have met a scientist or linguist in person, except at school, so a woman physical science teacher may help to dispel the myth that the female mind is not capable of dealing with the abstract complexities of science. One or two teachers of the non-traditional sex will not be sufficient to change an image, only to modify its application. Although many English teachers are men, English is still seen as more of a girls' subject (Weinreich-Haste, 1981), and the men who teach it may be regarded as cissy, particularly by working-class boys, since more importance is attached to the physical aspects of gender in working-class culture (muscles for men, babies for women).

Future career

At the end of the third year, pupils' attitudes to schooling tend to be very instrumental, and subjects are chosen on the basis of what will be suitable for getting a job, or for continuing education. This is particularly true of boys who intend to leave school at 16. Consequently, the gender appropriateness of subjects is determined by the relevance they are generally believed to have to work as currently performed by men and women.

Educational tradition

As has been shown in Chapter 1, until recently governmental philosophy of education has been to educate less able girls primarily for a life of domesticity, and to train middle and low ability boys in technical skills. Although current educational philosophy has changed direction (e.g. EOC, 1981b), and efforts are being made to involve more girls in design and technology, old habits die hard. Boys may be encouraged to take cookery as a preparation for a career in catering, but cookery and needlework are still taught to girls in a manner which has as its aim to prepare them for a life of meticulous and careful housekeeping, rather than seeing these subjects as saleable or survival skills. For the academic girl, the emphasis on languages, the arts and humanities, leading to the top 'feminine' career of multilingual

Table 1 Full-time teachers in maintained secondary schools by named subject as first subject of degree

Subject	Men	Women
Maths	5445	2668
Physics	3960	769
Chemistry	5022	1176
Biology	3446	2919
Geography	4802	2372
English	6003	6953
History	6201	3530
Modern languages	6159	6658

Source: DES, *Statistics of Education*, 1979, vol. 4, table 9. Reproduced with permission of the Controller of HMSO.

personal assistant to the managing director, is reminiscent of the finishing school preparing the cultured companion.

Schoolchildren do not have long memories. Their own experience of tradition will be limited to less than ten years: what they as first-formers observed of the behaviour of sixth-formers, and have learnt from older brothers and sisters. If the school building is old, the layout and equipment, or lack of it, may be constant reminders of earlier gender expectations. But by far the most powerful source of traditional expectation will be parents and teachers.

People or things

From early childhood, girls are encouraged to nurse and care for dolls and people (Belotti, 1975, p. 57). Not unnaturally, in adolescence they tend to choose subjects which they see as people-orientated. Biology is the 'female' science, partly because it is necessary for nursing, but largely because it is seen as the study of the human body. Psychology and the social sciences also appeal to girls because they are seen as being 'about people', whereas in practice the concepts they involve are often quite abstract. Boys, on the other hand, who have never been dissuaded from spending their time looking at how things work, rather than paying attention to the needs of people around them, show more interest in abstract subjects, such as maths, or those which emphasize the mechanical, such as physics and technology.

The media

Although some modern plays, television programmes, films and books are beginning to show men and women in non-traditional roles, the majority of doctors, skilled manual workers, managers and experts in all fields of science and technology are still shown as men. Women are largely relegated to the home, or shown in service roles such as secretary or nurse, and are rarely given the opportunity of offering expertise even in 'neutral' areas of knowledge such as history and geography.

Other pupils

Probably the most potent factor determining the image of subjects in any one pupil's mind is how many other pupils take them. ('It takes courage and determination to perhaps be the only girl in, for example, a technical drawing class' (EOC, 1981a). This would account for the proportionally larger number of boys studying languages and girls studying science in single-sex schools, but begs the question of how an image becomes established. I do not know of any research charting the increasing participation of pupils in a non-traditional subject, but personally I know of several instances where once a few boys or girls have ventured into a non-traditional area, a lot more have followed the next year.

Examinations

Teachers who attempt to provide an alternative non-sexist curriculum have to face the problem that pupils expect to be prepared for public examinations, which are generally conservative and hence sexist in their approach.

Exam questions

Exam questions are often sexist in both wording and content. Maths exams, for example, may often test ability to apply theoretical concepts, with sport-based problems. The recent APU test[1] asked children to find the batting average of a famous cricketer. I remember lots of questions about football scores and the size of cricket pitches, but none about netball or hockey. Since most girls are excluded by their school from taking cricket, it is unlikely that they would know what a batting average is. Exam questions may also demand certain attitudes from the pupil. Imagine the reaction of a boy taking home economics, faced with this question: 'Your brother and his friend are arriving for breakfast after walking all night on a sponsored walk.

Press a pair of trousers neatly for him to change into. Cook and serve a substantial breakfast for them.'[2]

Syllabus

For the final two years of compulsory schooling, most of what is taught is defined by a small group of academics who devise the syllabus and set the exam papers. Most of these academics are men, since it is men who are promoted by other men to positions of power within the academic hierarchy. As Dale Spender (1982a, b) argues, men control knowledge. They decide what is of value and relevant on the basis of their own (male) experience. With regard to women's ideas, says Spender, 'If they like them, they use them; if they don't they lose them'. Whether women's experience is appropriated or discarded, it becomes invisible.

The control of the curriculum by examination boards is not always a disadvantage; some are more progressive than many teachers and textbooks, for example AEB Sociology (see Chapter 12). Also, it is probably easier for feminist teachers to influence the curriculum by being examiners than by any other single method, and it is often not difficult to secure the position of chief (or only) examiner for an exam board, since these positions are notoriously badly paid. However, by and large, exam syllabuses reflect a male view of life. The set book lists for literature exams are dominated by books written by men about men; language and secretarial exams expect pupils to know that a married woman should be addressed by her husband's surname and Christian name, and history is more about kings than about conditions of life, more about warmongers than about women.

Assessment techniques

Harding's analysis of sex differences in science examinations (Harding, 1981) shows that the only part of any examination in which girls were more successful than boys was the 'conventional' (essay type) biology paper. Boys tended to achieve higher marks in multiple choice questions. Similarly, Murphy (1982) found that in a wide range of 'O' and 'A' Level examinations, male candidates performed better on objective tests than they did on other types of assessment. The exception was mathematics, where girls performed better on the objective tests than they did on other parts of the paper which required numerical computation. Possible explanations for this male advantage in objective tests is that other methods of assessment usually place greater emphasis on written language skills, which tend to be more highly developed in girls, and give more opportunity for girls to display neat handwriting, which is likely to bias examiners in their favour.

Murphy concludes that the best way of minimizing bias could be to include a variety of assessment techniques. Harding notes that structured questions appeared to show the least bias.

Teaching materials

Almost all teachers use a considerable amount of commercially produced educational materials – books, posters, films, filmstrips, tape–slide sets. Most are sexist in some way, and although it is quite impracticable to think of ridding the classroom of all sexist material, an awareness of the way sexism operates in written and audio-visual material should enable teachers to avoid the worst examples. Alternatively teachers should be able to use them as consciousness-raising devices with their pupils, and to introduce into the classroom material which will help to redress the balance. The checklist at the end of the chapter gives specific guidance on how to identify sexism in teaching materials. The following pages give a more general description of the ways in which a sexist impression is developed.

Gender stereotypes

Stereotypes are essentially clichés. Ready-made phrases, as George Orwell said in his essay *Politics and the English Language*, are the prefabricated strips of words and mixed metaphors that come crowding in when you do not want to take the trouble to think through what you are saying. They emphasize a few characteristics which are supposed to belong to the 'normal' subject. But this 'norm' has always been an ideal – white, middle class, male-defined and male-dominated. In fact, only 17.6 per cent of families with children, or 5 per cent of all households, fit the 'cereal-packet' image of working husband, economically inactive wife and two children (from *General Household Survey*, 1978 and 1979). And in the days when *Janet and John* was first published (1949), the family with a car, a privately owned detached house and only two children, reflecting the values of patriarchal consumerist culture, was far from the reality of life in post-war Britain.

Gender stereotyping concentrates on the characteristics which are supposed to go hand in hand with biological sex, and on the roles which men and women are supposed to perform.[3] Hence, men are shown in a great variety of work roles, while adult women are limited to the roles of wife and mother. Analysis of the Caldecott prize-winning picture books in the USA revealed that the only adult women depicted, apart from wives and mothers, were a fairy, a fairy godmother and an underwater maiden (Weitzman et al., 1976). Not one woman in the sample held a job.

The invisible woman

The most subtle way in which the inferior position of women is 'taught' in educational materials is by simply ignoring them and their contribution to life. Analysis of the Caldecott winners (Weitzman et al., 1976) found 11 pictures of males to every one picture of a female. Women are severely under-represented in most areas of school study (Frazier and Sadker, 1973; Maccia et al., 1975; Lobban, 1976; Nightingale, 1977), even in subjects such as literature, where there is a shortage of published material by women and about girls and women. 'Masculine' pursuits and qualities are frequently valued more highly than 'feminine' interests.

In history textbooks, it is not uncommon to find more space devoted to detailing the weaponry used in a particular war, than to a description of the injuries sustained and the effect the war had on the soldiers and their families. In a section entitled 'Mining today' (Harben, 1978 in Macdonald, P. *Mines and Mining*) we are told, 'Mining still runs in families and often sons follow their fathers in learning the skills of the miners'. No mention is made of the present-day legislation which debars women from working at the coal face, nor of women miners in other countries such as Bolivia and the USA. Where women's contribution is mentioned, it is frequently trivialized. In *The Ancient Chinese* (Lai Po Kan, 1980) the usurpation of political power by the dowager Empress Wu of the Tung is reduced to: 'The next emperor Kao-tsung, was rather lazy, and allowed one of his wives, Wu Chao, to deal with government affairs'. Collections of essays about famous people usually give a lot more space to men than to women. *Famous Names in Medicine* (Stevens, 1978) lists 15 men and only one woman (Florence Nightingale). The book could well have included women like Marie Curie, Elizabeth Garrett Anderson, Elizabeth Blackwell and Dorothy Hodgkis. Also, the 'famous names' approach means that women's contribution over the centuries to herbal medicine and midwifery is not covered.

Language

Another area which contributes to the problem of the invisibility of women is language, particularly the generic use of 'man' and 'he' to denote, at some points, people of both sexes, and at others only males. Geography, history and social studies materials in particular use 'man' to mean people, e.g. the ascent of man, prehistoric man, *Man, A Course Of Study*. American pupils were tested to discover the visual images they had when confronted with (1) 'man', 'mankind', 'man' and 'he'; (2) 'people' and 'humans'; and (3) 'men and women'. The group asked to depict 'man' and 'mankind' produced images of males for every activity except childcare (Harrison, 1975). When I see 'Man, the potter' supported by a picture of a man making pots, I do not feel that this refers to women, even when I know women were probably the first potters. It is customary in the English language to write in the singular, and to use the masculine pronoun with common gender words, e.g. doctor, leader, child . . . he . . . The only case when 'she' is used is when the group being described is assumed to be all female, e.g. the infant teacher, nurse, housekeeper. In either case, the effect is to limit the reference to one sex.

Apart from the problems caused by generic terms, other linguistic conventions also carry certain sexist assumptions. The use of the courtesy title for women, but not for men, as in 'Pierre and Madame Curie' implies that women need especially delicate treatment. The gratuitous use of the term 'lady' in 'cleaning lady', instead of 'cleaner' or 'cleaning woman', implies that to be a woman is to be of indecently low status. Quite common phrases like 'George Smith and his wife Mary' include the idea that the woman is owned by the man, as does more explicit phrasing such as 'Pioneers moved west, taking their wives and children with them', which also suggests that only men were pioneers, and completely devalues the part played by women.[4] Many texts refer to women in a denigrating or patronizing way, e.g. 'gossip', 'shrew', 'scatter-brained female', 'fair sex', and it is not unknown for educational materials to portray women as sex objects.

Illustrations

Often books which are quite non-sexist in the sense that they cover 'neutral' areas like science or geography, and do not refer to people at all, can be sexist in their choice of illustration. First, men are likely to figure far more often and more prominently in illustrations than women. Secondly, where illustrations are used sparsely, they often tend to present the most common examples of their subject matter, hence pictures of workers will usually all be of men. Drawings of men and women together show men as bigger than women, and husbands as older than their wives. And women in the house always wear aprons! (Nilsen, 1975). Line drawings of hands are male in technical books, and female in domestic science or needlework books. Also important are background images, such as the all-female group of typists in an office scene, nurses in the hospital, girls in a domestic science class or shoppers in the high street.

Visual imagery can be more subtle than words, and can therefore be used to express our perception of normality without making an explicit point which might be obtrusive. Posters[5] and photographs can be bought singly or 'home made', so it is relatively easy for a committed teacher to introduce positive and challenging images into the classroom, without inviting too much discussion which may prove distracting to the lesson if done frequently.

It is unfair to criticize authors of books written in the past for following the linguistic usage of their times. However, teachers need to be aware of the way sexism operates in materials, so that they can redress the balance by offering carefully chosen passages or images which give less restricted presentations of women and men, or at least give verbal explanations for women's under-representation. Since the publication of the EPC guidelines (1981) we should voice criticism loudly to publishers of new material which continues in the sexist tradition.

Guidelines for recognizing sexism in educational materials

Character stereotyping

- Are males associated with knowledge, technical ability, confidence, where females are not?
- Are females associated with emotion, sensitivity and instincts while males are not?
- Does the text polarize 'masculine' and 'feminine' characteristics? For example, 'She was technically gifted, but feminine'. 'He was a good sportsman, but gentle.'
- Are girls instructed by, led by, or rescued by boys?
- Are girls ever shown engaged in outdoor, active games?
- Are boys ever shown playing indoors, quietly on their own, or learning from a woman? (Lobban found that boys were often shown watching and learning from men in adult occupations.)
- Are husbands shown as older than their wives?
- Is marriage held up as the main goal in every woman's life?
- Are phobias, e.g. of spiders, or the dark, always associated with girls/women, and trivialized? Are strength and daring always associated with men/boys, and glamourized?

- Are women always shown as concerned with their appearance? Are women's appearance and clothing emphasized, as opposed to their achievements, or referred to in inappropriate situations? e.g. 'Who would have thought this trim, petite young woman would have discovered radium?' (of Marie Curie).
- Are statements by fiction characters like 'Boys make the best architects' and 'Girls are silly' allowed to go unchallenged?
- In a situation where a male and a female face a problem together, is the female shown as looking to the male for leadership and support?
- Are women shown as squeamish, weepy, passive, frivolous, inept, nagging, and easily defeated by simple problems, and men as brutish, violent, crude, harsh and insensitive?
- Is it assumed that women work for pin money, and are not interested in career advancement?

Role stereotyping

- Are men shown coping competently with domestic work and childcare?
- Is it assumed that women should take responsibility for looking after the family instead of, or as well as, their jobs? This attitude is very common in home economics textbooks.
- Are men and women shown as working in a variety of jobs and careers, or are jobs shown as restricted to one sex?
- Are women shown in positions of authority, in managerial positions, in charge of men?
- Are all men shown as self-employed or in paid employment?
- Is it assumed that sex role divisions were the same in the past, and are the same now in other cultures, as traditional sex role divisions?

Content selection

- Is equal attention paid to the work of women as to the work of men?
- Is 'progress' measured in terms of power stations and railways, instead of, for instance, the development of contraception, and how long it takes to prepare a meal or do the laundry?
- In books dealing with the history of science and technology, is any explanation given for why there is almost no mention of women? (They were traditionally and sometimes legally excluded from technical and scientific training.)
- Is equal, or at least 'fair', representation given to women in texts concerned with famous lives, events and important achievements?

- Do stories about the 18th and 19th century concentrate on the upper middle classes, where sex roles were exaggerated, instead of the working class, where women took on a much wider range of responsibilities?
- In anthologies, are male and female contributors equally represented?
- In quoting literature or documents that make heavy use of the generic forms 'man' and 'he', is it indicated that the terms are used to include men and women?
- Is the material presented in such a way that boys will feel superior to girls?

Language

The following is a list of sexist terms with suggestions for non-sexist alternatives:

Man, mankind	People, human beings, the human species, men and women, individuals, humankind
Men of science	Scientists and discoverers
Man and his world	History of peoples
Man and the environment	People and the environment, human influences on the environment
When men first discovered fire	When fire was first discovered
If one man takes four hours to	If it takes four hours to
The working man	The worker, labour, work force
The man in the street	Ordinary people
Manned by	Worked, staffed, run by
Founding fathers	Ancestors, forebears
Man-made	Artificial, synthetic, manufactured
Workmanlike	Competent
Manhood	Adulthood
Right-hand man	Chief assistant
Man-sized	Enormous, huge
Businessman	Business executive, industrialist
Salesman	Salesperson, representative, assistant
Fireman	Firefighter
Policeman	Police officer
The woman doctor	The doctor . . . she . . .
The child . . . he	Children . . . they . . .
The farmer and his wife	A farming couple
Managers and their wives	Managers and their partners, spouses
Young lady	Young woman

Recommended reading

Sexism in Children's Books (Writers and Readers Publishing Collective, 1976) – a collection of essays which includes Glenys Lobban's analysis of British reading schemes.

Words and Women by Casey Miller and Kate Swift (Penguin, 1976).

Man-made Language by Dale Spender (Routledge and Kegan Paul, 1980).

Sex-stereotyping in School and Children's Books (Educational Publishers Council, 1981).

Notes

1 The National Foundation for Educational Research carried out tests for the government's Assessment Performance Unit on the mathematical ability of 11-year-olds, reported in *Times Educational Supplement*, 1 February 1980.

2 From a CSE Housecraft paper, quoted in the *Gender Trap, Vol. 1* by C. Adams and R. Laurietkis (Virago, 1976).

3 See section on 'Gender' in Chapter 1 for a critique of these concepts.

4 An ironic example of the prevalence of this devaluation appeared in the ILEA magazine *Contact*, introducing an article on differences in achievement between boys and girls. A husband and wife team was described as follows: 'In the preparation of these articles Dr Mortimer has been assisted by his wife, Jo, an educational researcher'.

5 Feminist and Left bookshops carry a variety of non-sexist posters suitable for educational use, and the EOC has recently published a set for classroom use. Poster-Film Collective, BCM-FPC, London WC1N 3XX, has 13 posters on women and history.

CHAPTER 5

ENGLISH

JOY ROSE

English is a subject which is popular with girls and one in which they often succeed (see Chapter 1). How then can English teachers be accused of failing to provide for the needs of their female pupils? Apart from the disservice of channelling girls into arts subjects which offer such limited career prospects in our increasingly technological society[1], it is sadly the English lesson which can actually damage a girl's self-esteem and aspirations.

The problem was first brought to my attention when my fourth-year girls complained that all the texts we studied were boys' books. It was not feminist consciousness that prompted this comment, but a recognition that their interests were being disregarded. An analysis of CSE set texts led me to the same conclusion: books written by men, about boys and men. The scarcity of female characters in the novels read in school implied that they were less worthy of attention. Where women did appear, narrow, traditional images were portrayed. In an attempt to compile a list of books which appealed to girls, I surveyed the books which they chose to read themselves. I found that while the novels they chose were mainly written by women and featured girls as central figures, the conventional stereotypes remained unchallenged.

A closer look at other aspects of the English curriculum reveals more subtle forms of sexism. Essays and writing assignments too often indulge male interests. In discussion lessons, boys are allowed to dominate, while the passivity valued in females encourages girls to submit quietly to lessons not aimed at them. Even in the language used in the classroom teachers unwittingly transmit messages about the expected future role of girls, thus limiting their aspirations. Finally, the structure of the English department itself, with predominantly female teachers but (usually) a male head of department,[2] conveys implicitly the message that despite women's aptitude for English, their status within the subject is lower. The social expectations for each sex are communicated in every English lesson, widening the gap between girls and boys, perpetuating the myth of female inferiority, and teaching girls that career or intellectual fulfilment is not for them.

Literature

Early readers

Before our pupils reach secondary school they have been exposed to a process of conditioning in which their expected future roles are defined according to sex, irrespective of levels of perceived ability. Early readers present male and female worlds as quite separate and without overlap. Male characters appear more frequently in leading roles, are more active and more adventurous. They are shown with constructive toys, planning, inventing, thinking about careers and giving instructions – usually to girls. Female characters are portrayed in domestic situations with domestic-related toys or dolls, often watching boys indulging in much more interesting activities. Early readers offer models of desirable feminine behaviour and personality for girls to emulate. They are presented as pretty, smiling, passive, and hesitant when faced with the prospect of action. No wonder they always keep their clothes clean! Activity and adventure having been proscribed, perhaps girls' rapid progress in reading is a direct result of being condemned to vicarious experience through fiction. It is not surprising that by the time they reach adolescence, believing this pattern of behaviour to be natural, girls attempt to conform to the image and role which society has set for them.

Fiction popular with adolescent girls

The fiction generally popular with adolescent girls communicates several damaging ideas: to be womanly is to be traditionally feminine and involves submerging your interests and capabilities; glamour and beauty are important female attributes; energy and enterprise are acceptable in young girls but must be repressed at the onset of womanhood; women who are different from the stereotype are abnormal, lonely and open to ridicule; women, especially mothers, cannot be taken seriously as responsible people.

To a teenage girl the future must look very bleak. Marriage and motherhood are what society offers, and despite attempts by the media to persuade them that the roles of wife and mother are fulfilling, the evidence of life around them is unlikely to be convincing. Because it is necessary to endow the future monotony of domestic servitude with an aura of romance, there are numerous stories about romantic love which are fervently read by teenage girls and women. Notably they always end, rather than begin, with marriage. Pick up any of the ten new titles published by Mills and Boon[3] each month and observe the image of the ideal woman: unambitious, beautiful, dutiful and compliant. In *Wild and Wonderful*, for example, Bruce, the unrequited lover, informs Glenna that she looks "more like a woman now . . .". The difference dawned on him slowly. "You look vulnerable now. Always before you seemed so confident and self-assured, capable of tackling anything . . . you look lost and a little afraid . . ." ' Finally, the real message is explicitly conveyed when Bruce takes 'Glenna's hand extending it to Jeff. "I believe she belongs to you," he said calmly as if he were returning lost property.' Glenna's worth is not measured in terms of integrity, personal achievement or career. Is it surprising that so many of the girls we teach lack motivation to succeed academically and have low job aspirations?

Perhaps this explains the popularity of the escapist fantasy novels written by Noel Streatfield. In her books, heroines are preoccupied with looking decorative, and achieving recognition in the glamorous world of entertainment seems to be their only escape from dreary, conventional, domestic life. Alternatively, horse stories describe a socially acceptable active life, and satisfy the caring instinct fostered in young girls.

Another genre of fiction popular with adolescent girls, is domestically based. The recurrent theme is the quelling of creative energetic instincts in a prominent character, a 'tomboy' who is eventually reconciled to her domestic, traditionally feminine role. *What Katy Did* by Susan Coolidge and *Little Women* by Louisa M. Alcott are didactic. Katy aspires to be 'beautiful and beloved and amiable as an angel' while the four 'little women' are urged by their father to 'do their duty faithfully, fight their bosom enemies bravely, and conquer themselves so beautifully'. These books continue to appeal despite being so dated, because girls can easily identify with heroines undergoing a painful inner struggle against impulses which are difficult to control but which are deemed by society to be undesirable.

Some novels popular with teenage girls do include female characters who have not repressed their lively and independent selves. Unfortunately, these characters are often ridiculed and occasionally severely punished. In *Skinhead* by Richard Allen the reward for conformity is to be acknowledged as a desirable sex object, and the penalty for independence is rape. The message reinforces the one generally conveyed by the media – that a woman who is not 'feminine', and does not subordinate herself, puts herself outside the boundaries of respect and makes herself vulnerable to attack.

Where such female characters are not violently repressed they are presented as deviant compared with 'real' girls. In *Pippi Longstocking* by Astrid Lindgren, which offers younger readers a positive and determined female central figure, it is quite plain that society expects girls to identify, not with Pippi, but with the girls who make up Pippi's admiring but shocked audience. The penalty of Pippi's independence is the loneliness of being exceptional. Enid Blyton withholds approval of her tomboy characters, and hints that they will grow out of their boyishness. Both George and Henry of *The Famous Five* series are expected to conform eventually to the cosy image of motherhood, despite the author's ambivalence towards that role. The children are openly contemptuous of adult women, who are not regarded as positive decision-makers, and are unable to cope in a crisis. 'There's no grown up here tonight except Mrs Johnson' says Henry, who turns to a schoolboy for help.

CSE set texts

In the past ten years, CSE boards have shown imagination in choosing set literature texts which are topical and address current problems. Books giving a more honest picture of the working classes, condemning the glorification of war or confronting racism, have become popular in schools. The ALSEB syllabus includes many pioneering works of contemporary fiction, but written predominantly by men, about boys and men. Apart from the initial obstacle of arousing a girl's interest in a book apparently not intended for her, the English teacher finds that the pattern of undeviating sex roles is being reinforced with each novel studied.

Lord of the Flies is supposed to be an examination of human nature, set apart from the social constraints of everyday life. Golding obviously interprets 'human' as meaning male, there being a total absence of female characters in the story. In *The Loneliness of the Long-distance Runner* girls and women exist only in minor roles, in relation to the anti-hero, a Borstal boy. The lone woman in *Shane* bakes apple pies, models new hats and watches anxiously as her men defend their land. Women passively await the return of their men in *All Quiet on the Western Front*. In *Kes* Mrs Casper, neglectful and ineffectual as a parent, appears to be responsible for Billy's aberrant behaviour, while the absconding father is romanticized and apparently blameless. The anti-hero in *Billy Liar* is surrounded by doting young women aspiring to be his wife. A male teacher in *To Sir with Love* actually instructs his female pupils in ladylike behaviour; modesty, deportment, charm and attractive appearance are the criteria for winning his esteem. Such female characters do not offer role models for young girls who aspire to be anything more than decorative and supportive of their male partner, once they have ensnared him.

These novels are familiar and widely used as CSE set texts, along with numerous others which are equally well respected in literary terms, but nevertheless damaging to a girl's self-image and subtly undermining her hopes of a career. CSE boards are quite willing to adopt books recommended by teachers as set examination texts, and it is up to us to suggest novels which raise new issues and challenge reactionary stereotypes.

Recommended literature for secondary schools

Literature in secondary schools can be valuable in countering the distorted reality presented in early reading schemes and popular adolescent fiction. Many of our pupils live in high-rise flats, with an exhausted mum who juggles housework, job and parenting. It cannot be healthy for such children always to be asked to identify with nice nuclear families with smiling mums, who live in 'respectable' semi-detached suburbs.

What should we look for in the books we choose for schools?

1. A more honest depiction of society as it is, including women who work outside the home, women as the chief wage-earner in the household, women in positions of authority with well-paid, prestigious occupations and in non-traditional jobs, and men in domestic roles, or sharing domestic responsibility.
2. Female central figures with whom girls can identify, even if they conform to a stereotype. Girls, as central or background figures, who show initiative, daring and leadership are essential as positive role models, although ideally they should retain the feminine virtues of caring and gentleness.
3. Recognition of the value of qualities other than resourcefulness and courage, including sensitive and compassionate male and female characters, and supportive, sharing friendships between girls.
4. Topics of interest to girls which are traditionally regarded as 'women's issues' – marriage, pregnancy, abortion, parenthood, feminism.
5. Books about girls who cope with being different from the stereotype.
6. Books written by women.

One book will not combine all of these points, but it is possible to find novels which satisfy some of these requirements, as the following selection illustrates. It is time that novels read in schools acknowledged that one in five households has a woman as breadwinner; that there are 825 000 one-parent families in the UK (1978);[4] that there are mothers who work night shifts and fathers who fill domestic roles.

In *The Night Daddy* by Maria Gripe (Chatto and Windus) Julia's single-parent mother works at night while a young man babysits. *Jenny and the Sheep Thieves* by Griselda Gifford (Puffin) describes Jenny, a nine-year-old in handed-down dresses, who regrets that her mum cannot afford to buy jeans. She leaves her mother's London flat to convalesce with grandparents in the country. 'Grandpa did much of the cooking because his cough prevented his going out to help Grandma with the sheep.' In Mildred Taylor's *Roll of Thunder, Hear My Cry* (Puffin), Cassie's mother combines teaching with running the farm while father works away on the rail-road. Mother and grandmother shoulder rifles to tackle alone the attacks from white Southerners upon this black farming family. Valerie Avery's *London Morning* (Pergamon) is an autobiographical account of life with the author's mother in south London, her father having been killed in the war.

How many of our pupils don't live in a family unit at all? *The Great Gilly Hopkins* by Katherine Paterson (Gollancz) is the painful story of an 11-year-old girl, toughened by a life in care, coping with a new foster mother who compares unfavourably with the glamorous mother-figure of her fantasies. *Knock and Wait* by Gwen Grant (Heinemann) describes an 11-year-old at a residential school coping with homesickness and fighting against being institutionalized. *Edith Jackson* by Rosa Guy (Gollancz) describes life in foster homes, separated from sisters and brothers, and the pain and guilt arising from being subjected to state care.

Do the books on our classroom shelves offer girls central figures with whom they can identify? We are more likely to find girls appearing as sisters, mothers and wives of the central character. When token females exist they usually conform to a stereotype. Yet there is a wealth of exciting literature offering role models with which girls can identify without loss of self-esteem. In *The Turbulent Term of Tyke Tiler* by Gene Kemp (Puffin), Tyke, whose mum is a night nurse, emerges as an adventurous and irrepressible heroine, combining courage with loyalty and compassion. *Harriet the Spy* by Louise Fitzhugh (Fontana Lions) is the tale of an enterprising 11-year-old who, disguised as a spy, snoops and records all she observes in the neighbourhood. *The Farthest Away Mountain* by Lynne Reid-Banks (Knight) presents Dakin, a brave and resourceful girl who breaks the spell over the mountain. Rosemary Sutcliffe's *The Chief's Daughter* (Piccolo) recounts how Nellan defies the tribe and frees an Irish captive intended for sacrifice. In *The Lightkeepers* by Elizabeth Renier (Hamish Hamilton) Helen, whose father, the lightkeeper, has been kidnapped, realizes that shipwrecks are being caused deliberately for their loot. As in the true story, she lights the beam and averts disaster. *True Grit* by Charles Portis (Peacock) tells of Mattie's determination to avenge her father's murder. *Song for a Dark Queen* by Rosemary Sutcliffe (Pelham) retells the famous story of Boadicea.

Despite the impression created by comics, magazines and romances, girls' lives do not revolve entirely around boys. Are warm, supportive relationships between girls and women presented positively in school books? *The Friends* by Rosa Guy (Puffin) is an excellent account of everyday life without adventures other than those experienced by most teenage girls, this one a West Indian immigrant to New York. *The Loneliness of Mia* by Gunnel Beckman (Bodley Head) recounts a lonely adolescent's close relationship with her grandmother, once a suffragette, after the separation of her parents. *Go Well, Stay Well* by Toeckey Jones (Bodley Head) describes the friendship between two 16-year-olds – Candy, white, and Becky, black – in South Africa despite apartheid.

Of equal importance in fiction is the recognition of qualities other than strength and daring. Sensitivity and tenderness are not exclusive to girls. In *The Midnight Fox* by Betsy Byars (Puffin) we have a hero who is afraid of cows and disturbed that the black fox should be shot for stealing chickens. Ivan Southall's *Josh* (Puffin) tells of a boy who writes poetry and weeps on seeing a rabbit beaten to death. *Alan and Naomi* by Myron Levoy (Bodley Head) deals with sex stereotyping as it affects boys. Alan wants to be accepted as one of the boys, but also struggles to free himself from the limitations of appearing to be tough and manly.

It is quite likely that some of the girls we teach will have slipped through the net of social conditioning and envy the relative freedom experienced by their male peers. Through literature we can increase their awareness of social injustice, and reveal that this can be changed. Cress in *That Crazy April* by Lila Perle (Fontana) discovers that it is not easy having a campaigning feminist mum and suffers difficulty and embarrassment explaining things to her less liberated friends. For older readers Robert Leeson's *It's My Life* (Fontana) presents love, sex and fear of pregnancy through adolescent eyes. Jan's mother, questioning the domestic role, abandons their home. Ironically Jan is expected to assume responsibility for the domestic chores and sacrifice her education. Gradually, but painfully, she is awakened to the cause of her mother's dissatisfactions. Lots of issues – shared housework, the role and image of girls, equal opportunities at school – are raised in these novels and can be used to promote awareness of alternative behaviour, or as a stimulus for classroom discussion.

If only a few books find a place in the syllabus, a more honest view of society will be presented. Heads of department may need to be persuaded to order new books (perhaps on grounds other than their non-sexist content). If it is impossible to buy a full set, you might read aloud to the class. Despite their façade of sophistication, secondary school pupils do enjoy a relaxing lesson being read to, regarding it as an escape from real work; but it is also an exercise in developing their ability to listen and concentrate. Excerpts from novels, autobiographies, newspaper articles and periodicals can be used to supplement inadequate stock cupboards, to stimulate debate, or as a starting point for related work. It is possible in this way to present examples of positive female images, raise feminist issues or simply motivate female interest. It is not necessary to focus attention on the feminist content every time; resource materials can simply replace the usual passages used to test comprehension or punctuation.

'O' and 'A' Level set texts

At 'O' and 'A' Level the same pattern continues. Set texts reinforce society's message that the feminine point of view is divergent and present the masculine experience and perspective as the complete human experience. Women's contribution to literature is not recognized by examination boards despite current interest in women's writing. Virago, The Women's Press, Sheba Feminist Publishers and Onlywomen Press publish mainly books written by women, describing the experience of women, or commenting on society's effects on female aspirations and achievements.

Elaine Showalter, in *A Literature of Their Own* (Virago), analyses the lives and works of 213 prominent literary women born in England after 1800, of whom at least 21 are sufficiently well known to be indisputably worthy of study in schools and colleges. *The Penguin Book of Women Poets* (ed. by Carol Cosman) includes selections from the work of 198 women poets. Louise Bernikow's *The World Split Open* (The Women's Press) is an anthology of women poets, 44 American and 29 English. Scholars are beginning to accept that women's experience is important, and often significantly different from the male experience.

The 'great' women novelists, Jane Austen, the Brontës, George Eliot, Virginia Woolf, are occasionally set for 'A' Level, but how do the exam boards justify excluding such writers as Elizabeth Barrett Browning, Christina Rossetti, Sylvia Plath, Anne Bradstreet, Amy Lowell, Marianne Moore, Denise Levertov, Anne Sexton, Adrienne Rich, Stevie Smith, Elizabeth Jennings, Katherine Mansfield, Edna O'Brien, Doris Lessing or

Rosamond Lehmann? In 1977 the London University Exam Board set one book written by a woman for study at 'A' Level, as opposed to 26 written by men. In the same year, the AEB set 15 texts by men and none by women. It is possible in a two-year 'A' Level course to supplement the study of set texts with a wider, more balanced course. Recommended reading lists could be issued in which women writers are fairly represented, or at very least the work of women writers can be chosen as practice for the paper requiring pupils to analyse 'unseen' passages.

Teachers can use the set texts as starting points for analysing the life-style of the female characters, and the effect of their gender upon their aspirations and achievements. Many authors offer opportunities for teachers to question the credibility of their depictions of women. Would a woman writer have portrayed them in the same way? Can female pupils accept the Lawrentian towering matriarch living vicariously through her son, or the idolizing, self-abasing young Miriam vying for Paul Morel's attention in *Sons and Lovers*? How credible is Ursula's convenient failing of examinations and settling for the role of contented housewife in *The Rainbow*? Questioning D.H. Lawrence's image of women, whose fulfilment lies only in fecundity, can lead to the study of other images of women.

Lynne Reid Banks' *The L-Shaped Room* and Margaret Drabble's *The Millstone* portray women who retain their independence and self-respect, while determining to face unmarried the joys and sorrows of childbirth. Jane Austen's Fanny Price offers a spirited image of woman in *Mansfield Park*. George Eliot in *Mill on the Floss* shows how the passionate energy of her heroine is crippled by her family. Virginia Woolf presents a portrait of the artist as a young woman, describing the obstacles facing a woman writer and insisting upon the need for economic independence, in *A Room of One's Own*.

It is possible to incorporate such women writers in the new, alternative 'A' Level English Literature course offered by the AEB, which combines the conventional unseen passages and set texts for examinations with course work. Teachers select their own six texts, though these must be submitted to the Board for approval, and set their own essays for assessment. This allows much more freedom in the choice of books for study, encourages a wider range of reading and allows a different type of assignment to be set.

Writing assignments

'This passage was written by a woman' (NUJMB 'O' Level English language, 1978) – a rare event indeed, and possibly unique to find a passage about a girl, describing her childhood adulation for another girl; the assumption is evidently that most passages are not written by women. Male bias is evident in the choice of writers of, and subjects for, comprehension passages, as well as in the choice of authors of set texts. It would not be surprising if pupils concluded that writing is not an occupation available to women, or that women's writing lacks merit. Elaine Showalter (1982) makes it clear that this is a false assumption, and in *A Literature of Their Own* she explains why women writers have drifted into obscurity. The absence of females in English language teaching materials, including grammar and punctuation exercises, leads pupils to the conclusion that women are insignificant. Too often we indulge male interest in the topics chosen for essay writing, or we expect girls to identify with male characters. Women's issues and the female experience are consistently ignored; yet we persist in asking girls to write, while simultaneously conveying negative messages about their worth and ability. Is it surprising that girls are often said to produce perfunctory writing, neat and accurate, but uninspired?

Motivation

Since the 1960s the idea that children require motivation if they are to express themselves vividly and imaginatively, has become widespread. They need to be emotionally as well as intellectually involved in their writing. If we set essays about action and adventure we must include the learned female interests, by widening the perspective to take in relationships and feelings. Instead of 'Journey through space' why not get a class to write about 'Life in space', emphasizing food, household gadgets, clothing, games, making contact with space beings, etc? Teachers could set stories involving action and excitement in everyday life: a chip pan fire, a night nurse on an emergency ward. It is possible that girls assume that all firefighters, divers, pilots are men so the teacher should avoid the word 'space man', and use the pronoun 'she', e.g. 'When the space traveller climbs into her rocket she . . .'. It may be necessary to draw attention to females as central figures. Before writing about a diver, the class could compile a list of characteristics which she requires to perform the dangerous task of retrieving the very fragile remains of lost treasure from the sea bed.

For older pupils essay topics could include issues which girls regard as relevant to their lives, but it is important not to label them as 'women's issues', to avoid alienating the boys. These may well be experiences which will occur in the lives of both boys and girls; for example, baby battering is a

topic about which there is immense concern amongst adolescent girls and boys, and about which they feel stirred to write. I have found that using a facsimile of a medical report on a battered baby as a starting point prompts concerned discussion, followed up by written work such as:
- a social worker's case-study of the mother, commenting on her education, background, life and home conditions, stating what action is to be taken.
- a story in which a young parent is driven to harming a child.
- an account of the causes and prevention of child abuse.
- a newspaper report on such an incident.

Taking Liberties[5] and *Women's Rights*[6] are useful teaching packs with information sheets, facts and figures, to stimulate discursive writing, or to counter myths about marriage, divorce, adoption, abortion, cruelty to children, equal pay, inequalities at work and taxation. Letter-writing is an essential skill, and teaching it can be an opportunity to present ideas raised by these packs. Pupils can write to newspapers or magazines, complain to the local tax office, or inform the EOC of cases of discrimination. The salutation in such letters can be Dear Madam/Sir, and this is an occasion to raise the issue of Ms as opposed to Mrs or Miss, especially when writing to a stranger whose title we do not know.

Sexist imbalance is evident in the essay questions set in CSE and 'O' Level GCE literature examinations, but within the constraints of the syllabus, it is possible to shift the emphasis somewhat. When studying *The Merchant of Venice* the question 'How far does Portia conform to the stereotyped image of a female?' demands the same literary analysis of a pupil as does a conventional character study. When the set text is *The Pearl*, the answer to 'Describe Juana's way of life' will differ more in focus than in content from 'Describe the way of life of Kino and his family', as does 'How does *Hobson's Choice* illustrate that women can be cleverer than men?' Some texts allow more searching questions: 'How far is Tess's tragedy the consequence of dual standards for men and women?' (*Tess of the D'Urbervilles*) or 'Give an account of the ways in which Henchard causes suffering to all the women closely involved with him' (*The Mayor of Casterbridge*).

Provoking awareness

When we ask children to write, our aim extends beyond the development of writing skills, for a process of intellectual development occurs during the writing. Writing can be an opportunity to organize our perception of experience: the articulation of a thought or a feeling often makes us see more clearly. Thus the writing assignments set in the classroom can be invaluable if they draw pupils' attention to the artificiality of gender-related personality traits and social roles. Through writing we can expose the socialization process. Possible assignments could be:

– Compile lists of toys and clothing that might be chosen for a baby, one list for each sex. Indicate which are common to both sexes and which are specific to one sex. Deduce what kind of future is being planned by these early choices.

– Read *Project Baby X*[7] and discuss. Write an account of how we learn our sex roles.

– Read aloud a non-sexist fairy tale.[8] Analyse sex roles in traditional fairy tales. Rewrite a traditional tale in a non-sexist way, or reverse the roles, or write a fairy tale with a heroine who does not conform to a stereotype.

– A study of the media's role in socialization could include redesigning the usually sexist cartoons, reversing the roles, or rewriting captions; rewriting dialogue for romantic stories featured in comic strips;[9] writing more realistic stories about love and relationships; designing advertisements aimed at women with interests apart from their home and appearance; designing advertisements in which the women selling the product are in positions of authority, or expert in areas other than the household.

Writing assignments, while allowing pupils to practice linguistic skills, can also be used to promote awareness of alternative career opportunities. Myths about 'men's work' and 'women's work' can be challenged, and pupils' attention can be drawn to the limited career prospects and poor financial rewards of occupations traditionally regarded as women's work. When the stated aim of 88 per cent of girl school leavers is to 'get as good jobs or careers as possible' (Schools Council, 1968), then it is particularly important that they are made aware of the wide range of career opportunities available outside the traditional areas. This can be combined with a programme intended to develop a variety of skills.

– Vocabulary exercises: (1) pupils compile a list of jobs and choose appropriate adjectives to describe each job from a list supplied, e.g. repetitive, demanding, varied, skilful, etc. (2) The US Department of Labour revised 3500 occupational titles which were considered to be discriminatory because they excluded women and suggested women's entry into such jobs was inappropriate. Pupils can compile their own lists and make their own revisions, e.g. dustbin man – refuse collector, cleaning ladies – cleaning staff (see p. 75).

– Exposition: (1) give an account of qualities and qualifications required to be a nurse, draughtsman/woman, taxi-driver, police officer, sales assistant, nursery teacher, social worker, milk deliverer. (2) Write a formal job description for a company's official manual.

- Persuasive writing: (1) write an advertisement for the local paper to fill a vacancy for one of the above jobs. Use a persuasive style, omitting or rephrasing less desirable aspects of the job.
- Letter-writing practice: (1) write an application for a job not traditionally done by a person of your sex. (2) Write a reference for someone applying for a non-traditional job explaining why she/he is suitable. (3) Write a letter of acceptance to the applicant saying why she/he is chosen for the job.
- Imaginative writing: (1) write accounts of a day at work in two jobs, one traditional and one non-traditional.

It is not only girls who are faced with limiting social stereotypes. The male stereotype is equally damaging to boys. Excerpts from literature can be used to present alternative modes of behaviour, showing men who are gentle, compassionate and sensitive. Poetry can be used to reveal that men and women experience the same anxiety, fear and despair, that the tough male image is only a façade and conceals a range of emotion too often thought of as exclusively feminine.

Discussion arising from such reading can be aimed at analysing how and why we express or repress our feelings and whether this is beneficial to the individual. Boys may be reluctant to talk about their own feelings, regarding them as weaknesses, but they are often more willing to express such emotions when asked to write briefly and imaginatively of an occasion when they have been sad, lonely, unhappy, angry, deeply moved, afraid, elated, or proud of an achievement. It helps to insist that such writing is brief and that the cause of the experience remains shadowy, so that the writer can concentrate on the mood, its effect and its expression. Free poetry is a form which pupils find more conducive to conveying emotion, than narrative.

Even grammar exercises can be purged of sexism, by eliminating 'brides' veils' and 'housewifes' aprons' from apostrophe exercises, for example, and replacing them with equal numbers of women and men participating in as wide a range of activities as occurs in reality. Girls *do* climb trees. Women *do* explore, pioneer and sail around the world. Men *do* cook, clean the home and care for the children. Doctors are often female, and nurses male. It is a distortion of reality to show women exclusively involved with domestic tasks, or in service occupations.

Working in groups

Traditional classroom organization is not conducive to high attainment by diffident pupils, or by those who have learned that quiet passivity is required to maintain an image acceptable to their peers. While teachers concentrate on the more demanding members of the class, compliant pupils can be swamped or neglected (see Chapter 3). Working on an assignment in a small group can encourage cooperation and remove the feeling of failure that may be caused in a competitive atmosphere. Self-initiated tasks, and research guided by worksheets, can promote active participation in learning. Group work allows the teacher to give up the formal, authoritative position in front of the class, and to work in turn with each group. A project for group work could be to investigate the life of a famous or successful woman, or to discover the unrecognized contribution of women to science. Such a programme might include the following:

- Finding information about the achievements of such a woman.
- Finding information about her domestic and personal life.
- Discovering difficulties and obstacles she encountered.
- Compiling a list of questions to ask her in an interview.
- Preparing a radio programme in which she is a guest, for taping.
- Writing a newspaper article about her first achievement.
- Writing a daily diary.
- Writing a letter to her, or from her to someone she worked with.
- Writing a short story based on fact, but using imagination to enliven it, about any times in her life when she experienced joy or despair.
- Writing a poem at a moment of sadness or despair in her life.
- Finding a poem about some related topic, to copy out and analyse.
- Writing her epitaph and obituary.
- Holding a 'balloon debate' involving all the figures the class has researched.
- Preparing a brief report to present to the class.

Oral work

The stereotyped image of a female is of an excessively talkative and gossipy person. When she is angry she is 'hysterical'. If she asserts her opinions she is 'strident'. A more positive image would be of an 'eloquent', 'passionate', 'forceful' and 'articulate' woman. In reality neither of these extremes apply to most women. Research has shown that boys are the talkers (see Chapter 3); that they exert more control over conversation, and interrupt more often than girl pupils. Women do not talk as much as men in mixed company and girls do not talk as much as boys in mixed classrooms (Spender, 1982a). Boys volunteer answers, hazard guesses, or command the attention of the teacher by noisy disruptive behaviour.

Both sexes regard talking in class, particularly in the form of questioning or challenging, as masculine behaviour (Parker, 1973), so participation in debates and discussions forces girls into an 'unfeminine' role. The idea prevails that the desirable female is quiet, passive and a good listener. Furthermore the image of a successful woman as partnerless and childless may cause anxiety to girls who succeed at school. Some girls avoid success by withdrawing from competition and reducing their academic performance, preferring popularity with their peers (Horner, 1974). It is not surprising then that girls usually submit quietly to using materials intended for boys, withdrawing into inattention rather than disruptive behaviour. The structured formal setting of most classes promotes and rewards the passive behaviour which makes classroom control easier. Thus the acquiescent girl is encouraged in her reluctance to participate.

Questions and answers

How can inhibited girls be persuaded to participate more fully in classroom interaction? A patient teacher in a supportive atmosphere is the most important factor. Equipping pupils with jotting paper and giving them time to write down ideas, offers them the reassurance of answering with the aid of notes. Open-ended questions, requiring opinion and imagination rather than a correct answer, avoid exposing pupils to failure and ridicule. In this situation the teacher can select pupils to respond, instead of relying on volunteers. An approach to poetry which I have found successful is to ask all pupils to choose a line or lines which they found interesting, enjoyable or unusual, and to say what they liked about their choice, or what thoughts it prompted. Gradually they realize there is no wrong answer.

Discussions and debates

Class discussions pose another problem (see Chapter 21, p. 311, where the difficulties of such lessons are discussed). Diffident or anxious pupils need a chance to express their thoughts without a large audience. Initially pupils can work in pairs, which are easier to control, and give each a chance to talk. I have found that paired talk is successful, given a short period of time and a clear subject such as:

- giving instructions or directions;
- explaining a principle or rule learned in another lesson;
- sharing ideas as a preliminary to creative writing, by talking about loneliness, being bullied, memories of childhood, accepting a dare, discrimination experienced, failure, fear, hardship, being new, how you would react to a nuclear warning.

From here progress can be made to small group discussions which demand more tolerance, and encourage appreciation of a wider range of viewpoints. Some suggestions for group work are:

- exchange opinions about a topical or political event;
- discuss the benefits and dangers of television, drugs, euthanasia, nuclear power.

Talking in groups is often more constructive if pupils are given a goal, which may be to come to a conclusion, make a decision, present a summary of opinions or a consensus. To give purpose to the discussion, notes can be taken and written up for assessment. Discursive essays are inevitably less dogmatic and more interesting when pupils are informed with a variety of opinions. Alternatively, individuals can report to the class, armed with notes to which others have contributed, as well as a sense of solidarity.

Natural social groups are more encouraging at first to less confident pupils, but it is possible gradually to steer a class into different groupings to facilitate a wider interchange of ideas. (Chapter 21 looks at how groups function and at ways of reorganizing them.) Some pupils will never progress comfortably to public speaking, but life rarely demands such skills. More important are the skills required in the small group, the increase in fluency and the confidence which develops in that situation.

Materials to stimulate discussion

If girls are to be encouraged to participate in oral work, then teachers must suggest topics relevant to the female experience, or of which they have some fundamental knowledge. Older girls will talk, and feel that they can do so with authority, about responsible parenthood, combining motherhood and paid occupations, or causes and prevention of cruelty to children. *Taking Liberties* is packed with easily absorbed information and suggestions for discussion on issues directly relevant to women's lives. *The Experience of Parenthood* (Longman Imprint) includes a newspaper article by Rick Sanders about his decision to care for the baby at home while his wife continued her career as a journalist, John and Elizabeth Newsom's survey of male participation in childcare, Margaret Mead's account of Samoan childhood, and an excerpt from *Silas Marner*.

If the syllabus demands the study of war, why not include a study of the domestic front? Excellent source material is available in *Bombers and Mash* by Raynes Minns (Virago), on rationing, women involved in war work, evacuation, etc. *While They Fought* (Longman Imprint) includes material on Gladys Aylward, Sybil Hepburn – a woman setting up Resistance cells in occupied France, an interview with a female teacher in Belgium, and a transcript of *Woman's Hour* answering the question 'What did you do in the war, mummy?'

Determination is needed to root out non-sexist resources but this can be rewarding, especially because such materials will be fresh and so much more inspiring. Group work should not be used as a way of distributing sex-appropriate topics. Nor should such topics be introduced as being particularly relevant to either sex. It can be emphasized that many of the class will be faced with parenthood, for example, and that during the war, all men were not at the front all of the time. Boys and girls have acquired different interests through their experience of the socialization process. Our intention should be to narrow, and not widen the gap.

Language

A close examination of the language used in school books will reveal many sexist assumptions. Often, by our careless choice of words, we allocate limiting social roles to both women and men; we demean women, we imply that they are dependent on male initiative or are possessions, and we ignore the contribution women have made to science, history and the arts.

However successful women are in their own right, the language used by the media tends to emphasize their irrelevant traditional domestic role. Both male and female public figures should be referred to in the same way; but reports on Wimbledon persist in speaking of Bjorn Borg and Mrs King. Billie Jean King's status as a tennis player is more important in this context than her role as someone's wife. A female shopper in a supermarket is a customer, not necessarily a housewife, and assumptions about her role as a wife or mother are irrelevant.

Unwittingly, language allots women a particular place in the world. Too many occupational terms end in 'man' or 'woman' and suggest that entry into such jobs would be inappropriate for the opposite sex. By using terms like 'housekeeper', 'office cleaner', 'business executive' or 'camera operator', we do not by implication limit these jobs to one sex. Many jobs are not explicitly designated to one sex, but are popularly thought of as being performed by only one sex; so there has arisen the practice of labelling those who contravene the norm, for example 'women doctors', 'male nurses', 'lady lawyer', 'female pilot' and 'woman engineer'. If occasions arise when it is necessary to distinguish between male and female, a subsequent pronoun will clarify. 'The judge made her remarks to the court' is preferable to 'lady judge' with its implication that it is exceptional for a woman to occupy this position.

Vanishing women

By using a vocabulary which appears to refer only to men, school textbooks effectively present a world without women (see Chapter 4). When we refer to 'the best man for the job' we may actually mean 'the best candidate', and as alternative expressions are more accurate, we should use them. Equally the use of the masculine pronoun instead of a generic singular pronoun signifying both he and she, has the implicit effect of excluding women from implied participation in a variety of human activities. This can be avoided by using 'one', 'you', 'he or she', or recasting into the plural. Thus 'When a motorist buys a car he must insure it', becomes 'When motorists buy cars they . . .'.

Too many girls lack self-esteem and have low aspirations. Many of the patronizing and offensive stereotypes in our language contribute to that poor self-image. Do we want girls to identify with 'the little woman', 'scatterbrained female', 'gossip', 'shrew', 'dumb blonde', 'henpecking wife', 'nag', 'scold', 'interfering mother-in-law', 'accident-prone woman-driver'? Yet what alternative do we offer? To differ from the stereotype is to be abnormal and scorned: 'tomboy', 'unladylike', 'Women's Libber', 'career woman', 'frustrated spinster', 'blue-stocking'.

As English teachers we must ensure that our own language is at least neutral and does not reinforce stereotypes. We can redress the balance by adding riders to textbooks, or by supplementing exercises with examples that include females in untraditional roles. We can actually draw attention to the distortion of truth in the way we use language. One useful exercise is the study of pejorative vocabulary as applied to men and women. This can form the basis of a wider study of emotive language, particularly of the persuasive style of the press. Some exercises could include:

– List common expressions applied to women. Indicate what status is implied and what assumptions are reflected. Try to find parallel expressions applied to men. For example,

Female expressions	Status	Assumptions	Negative/ positive	Male equivalent
Spinster	low	unattractive, lonely	negative	bachelor?
Old maid	low	ugly, unwanted	negative	nil
Housewife	medium	no career, dependent		nil
Career woman				
Office girl				
Little old lady				
Weaker sex				
Tomboy				
Bird				
Tart				
Little woman				

Female adjectives
Shrill
Hysterical
Nagging
Coy
Feminine

- Find alternative words or phrases which are more positive: for example, spinster – single, independent woman; little old lady – elderly woman, senior female; tomboy – lively, energetic girl.
- For lower ability pupils teachers can provide the two lists, but jumble the positive alternatives, and ask pupils to pair off appropriate phrases.

Maura Healy, in *Your Language – Three* (Macmillan Education), a non-racist, non-sexist language course for secondary schools, draws attention in a lively way to the bias in language in Unit 18, 'Girl talk, boy talk'. She offers some suggestions for follow-up work. One useful idea is to tape a class discussion for the class to analyse (as Dale Spender has done), assessing the amount of time each sex speaks, and the number of interruptions made by each sex.

Conclusion

If we are genuinely interested in fostering the development of all our pupils, then we must attempt to minimize the impact of society's stereotyped view of what girls ought to be and do. We must begin by examining our own expectations of sex differences in achievement and conduct, and then reassess our teaching methods.

As English teachers, we are faced with a dilemma, for a part of our work is to inspire a love of literature in which girls are too often portrayed in limiting roles. However, there are also advantages, for in English we are not wholly restricted by the demands of imparting a body of knowledge. Materials are available, assignments can be set, and classroom practice may be adapted, to develop an awareness of alternative roles and behaviour, for both girls and boys.

The views expressed in this chapter are not necessarily those either of the school where the author works, or of its department of English.

Resources

Thinking, talking and writing

Language and Thought by J.B. Carroll (Prentice Hall, 1964).

Language and Woman's Place by R. Lakoff (Harper and Row, 1975).

Talk – A Practical Guide to Oral Work in the Secondary School by D. Self (Ward Lock, 1976).

The Development of Writing Abilities (11–18) by J. Britton et al., Schools Council Research Studies (Macmillan, 1975).

Why Write? by N. Martin et al. (Schools Council/London University Institute of Education, English Department, 1973).

Classroom material

Bombers and Mash: The Domestic Front 1939–45 by R. Minns (Virago, 1980).

For Better, For Worse: Marriage and the Family by J. Gillott, Connexions Series (Penguin, 1971).

The Gender Trap (3 vols.) by C. Adams and R. Laurikietis (Virago, 1976).

His and Hers by J. Groombridge (Penguin, 1971).

Different Therefore Equal by Peggy Seeger (Blackthorn Records, BR1061).

Children's books and women's writing

A Literature of Their Own: British Women Novelists from Brontë to Lessing by E. Showalter (Virago, 1977).

Catching Them Young 1: Sex, Race and Class in Children's Fiction by B. Dixon (Pluto Press, 1977).

Children's Book Bulletin. Available from 4 Aldebert Terrace, London SW8.

Racism and Sexism in Children's Books by J. Stinton (Writers and Readers Publishing Cooperative, 1979).

Reading for Young Women: Annotated Bibliography of Fiction and Non-fiction by V. Carpenter and K. Stirling (Sisterwrite, 190 Upper Street, London N1).

'Urgent voices: gender and English teaching', *The English Magazine*, no. 9.

Now Read On. Recommended Fiction for Young People by Bob Dixon. (Pluto Press, 1982).

Gender Workshop, ILEA English Centre (available from Schools Council). (See Appendix C.)

EOC list of non-sexist books, available free from the EOC.

Sex Differences and Reading: An Annotated Bibliography by E.M. Sheridan (International Reading Association, 1976).

Silences by J. Olsen (Virago, 1980).

Spare Rib List of Non-sexist Children's Books by R. Stones and A. Mann. Available from 27 Clerkenwell Close, London, E1R CAT.

Teaching packs

Taking Liberties: An Introduction to Equal Rights by J. Coussins (Virago, 1978).

Women's Rights by M. Lowe (Rights for Women Unit, NCCL, 1980).

Women in Society. Available from the Labour Party, Smith Square, London SW1 (free).

Notes

1   There are more places available in maths and science courses in further and higher education than there are in arts courses. Often girls do not realize that even the traditional areas of employment for women, such as nursing, hairdressing or catering, demand these qualifications.

   Over 60 per cent of girls going to university study arts subjects and around 35 per cent of arts graduates have no job to go to when they graduate; 95 per cent of electrical engineers find permanent jobs (EOC, 1982a).

2   *Promotion and the Woman Teacher*, an NUT research project published jointly with the EOC, offers an interesting analysis of the position of women in the career structure of schools. See also Chapter 2, pp. 42–44.

3   Mills and Boon recently launched a £1 million mass advertising campaign and are spending £530 000 on TV advertising, unprecedented in publishing. They produce ten new titles each month, each 157 pages long and all romances (*The Observer*, 8 February 1981).

4   National Council for One-Parent Families.

5   *Taking Liberties: An Introduction to Equal Rights* by J. Coussins (Virago, 1978).

6   *Women's Rights* by M. Lowe (Rights for Women Unit, NCCL, 1980).

7   *Project Baby X* by L. Gold (see p. 196)

8   *Myths and Legends for Young Feminists . . . and for Old Feminists — The Original Version* by Beryl Whyatt (90 Plane Ave., Wigan, Lancs WN5 9PT – 35p plus p + p); *The Prince and the Swineherd*, *Red Riding Hood* and *Snow White* (Fairy Story Collective, 53 Sandown Lane, Liverpool LI5 4NU – 30p each plus postage).

9   *Shocking Pink* is an alternative comic/magazine available from Shocking Pink, 4 Essex Road, London W3. Price 20p plus a large s.a.e.

CHAPTER 6

MODERN LANGUAGES

PHIL HINGLEY

The image of modern languages

There is no immediately obvious reason why modern languages should have become a girls' subject, but the figures that are available, such as those from the DES (*Table* 1), paint a quite unambiguous picture. If we consider French and compare the 'being offered' column with the 'taking' column (in other words, the percentage of pupils to whom the subject was made available by the school and the percentage who went on to study it in the fourth and fifth years), we see that in mixed schools, 3 per cent more girls then boys are offered French,[1] whereas in single-sex schools the difference is 17 per cent. In single-sex schools this latter difference is reflected exactly in the take-up. In mixed schools, however, the 3 per cent difference becomes a 15 per cent difference by the time the pupils have made their choice. What happens in between is the mystery. In the case of German, there seems little mystery – it is simply an amazingly unpopular subject.

Table 1 Pupils being offered and taking particular subjects (modern languages) (1973)

| | Being offered | | Taking | |
| | Single sex | Mixed | Single sex | Mixed |
	Per cent of totals of pupils		Per cent of totals of pupils	
French				
Boys	75	87	28	24
Girls	92	90	45	39
German				
Boys	33	36	7	4
Girls	44	38	8	8

Source: DES, *Education Survey No. 21* (HMSO, 1975). Reproduced by permission of the Controller of HMSO.

These figures show the position in 1973. One might imagine that greater awareness of the situation, combined with the official rubber-stamp on sexual equality provided by the Sex Discrimination Act, would have had some discernable impact over a period of five years. But a DES survey in 1979 found that of the pupils in the sample schools taking French in the fourth year, 68 per cent were girls and 32 per cent boys. It must have been uncomfortable for the educational establishment to recognize that mixed schools were dividing, rather than integrating.

We need, then, to look at the specific factors that turn a reasonably equally offered subject into a very unequally studied one. The clues must lie, at least in part, in the attitudes, both spoken and implied, and the encouragement, both given and withheld, that come into play when the time comes to make crucial choices.

Helen Weinreich-Haste's study (1981) of the image of science (see Chapter 4) provides some interesting, if oblique, insights. The combined view of her sample of university students and female and male school pupils was that French was the third most feminine subject after cookery and typing. Since the pupil sample was drawn from single-sex comprehensives where subjects are generally less firmly linked to gender (DES, 1975), her findings probably understate the extent to which images and hence attitudes are already fixed in the school population.

A study conducted by Sabin Parsonage (1979, unpublished) certainly seems to confirm this view. She sampled the attitudes of both third- and fourth-year pupils (those about to make an option choice and those who had completed a year of the examination course in German). The third-year boys seemed to have few misgivings about possible problems. The girls were, by contrast, expecting the subject to be 'difficult but stimulating'. Having faced the actual difficulties, the fourth-year girls attributed any loss of interest on their part directly to the difficulty of the subject, whereas the boys also listed as significant factors boredom and other subjects being more important. This was no great surprise since they had already listed craft and history as being of greater value before they had even started German. They had also received little encouragement (and some discouragement) from family and peers to study German. The girls had been positively encouraged from the same sources and had given the subject a higher importance rating. The overall impression is that the boys seem predisposed or preconditioned to cast the subject aside as soon as it becomes irksome and to depress its status further, by describing it as boring. The girls seem more inclined to retain a positive attitude despite difficulties. Could it be a question of them expressing a 'for better or for worse' feeling about their narrower range of opportunities?

A great deal has been written and said about why girls either cannot or do not take up sciences (see Chapters 7 and 9), but if we look at the most recently available figures (*Table 2*), the discrepancy between the percentage of boys taking physics to exam level and that of girls is massive. The same discrepancy in chemistry is still very serious, but if the genders were reversed, it would match that found in modern languages and French.

Table 2 Percentage by sex of candidates entered for individual subjects and groups of subjects (GCE and CSE examinations) (Summer 1979)

	Girls (%)	Boys (%)
Physics	21	79
Chemistry	37	63
Biology	66	34
Physics		
Chemistry	45	55
Biology		
Chemistry		
Physics	28	72
French	61	39
All modern languages	61	39

Source: DES, *Statistics of Education*, vol. 2 (1979). Reproduced by permission of the Controller of HMSO.

It might be tempting to assume that the imbalance in modern languages is caused by girls avoiding physics and chemistry and that the effort put into restoring the balance in science will solve both problems at once. This is not just simplistic but also dangerous, because it works on the same premises as an argument that says that, if we take the figures for all the sciences in *Table 2*, we have nothing to worry about, while at the same time ignoring the individual figures for physics and chemistry.

Attitudes and influences work much more subtly and insidiously. Could there be some feedback to both boys and girls of career expectations? A study of Scottish school leavers (A. Kelly, in Kelly, 1981) showed that boys seemed to overestimate the importance of science in career terms, and girls to underestimate it. We might infer from this that taking a science suggests to the pupils a particular level of seriousness about their career, and that boys will often study sciences for the wrong reasons. Carrying over this inference to modern languages, it may be that girls are choosing them in the knowledge that their direct applications are very limited, and those they are normally told about are traditionally female, e.g. air hostess, bilingual secretary and courier. Are girls obeying unspoken rules that they should step out of the way of boys in the jobs game? Or are they limiting their choices themselves, anticipating the disappointment of having them limited later on by others?

Careers advice to all pupils could be a great deal wider and emphasize a greater range of practical applications for modern languages, such as selling abroad, diplomacy, long-distance road haulage, hotel management, journalism, foreign language broadcasting, etc. Syllabuses could be adapted to include practical elements to fit such career possibilities. Models for such syllabuses already exist in colleges of further and higher education.

Are girls unwilling to compete within school? In mixed schools, options are usually open to both sexes. In practice, of course, some of them are pre-empted semi-deliberately. For example, fabric craft can be offered to boys as a fourth-year option although the craft circus has excluded them from the subject since the first year. In some schools, a second foreign language is timetabled in opposition to games, with predictable results. In most cases, however, the only barrier to a girl or boy stepping out of a traditional pattern is her or his own confidence to deal with the added burden of the expectation, either overt or implicit, that she or he will fail in some way. For a girl who finds the prospect of working in the male atmosphere of a craft workshop or a physics laboratory daunting, the alternative (the language laboratory or a mainly female option group) may appear as a haven of relative peace. Behind it all, no doubt, is the myth that languages, along with English literature, is a subject that belongs on the 'soft' margins of education and is best dealt with by the 'less logical girl's mind'. Languages are neat and clean and reward neat, accurate, written work; through primary school, girls have been praised more than boys for neat work and are considered to be more verbally adept at the start of secondary school. If the latter is the case, teachers could emphasize variety of expression and intonation, the value of gestures and facial expressions in communication and at the same time reduce the overwhelming value placed on painstaking written accuracy and other exam-orientated tasks. This may go some way to involve both boys and girls more equally in classwork. It certainly is a help to the less able of either sex.

'Ou est Madame Marsaud maintenant?' Sexism within the subject

When new course materials were developed in the 1960s, teachers welcomed them because of the greater authenticity of the language and the immediate appeal of the back-up material – reading books, flashcards, film strips, etc. However, virtually all the courses in this 'new wave' settled upon the lowest common denominator of European life as their vehicle – the nuclear family. They depict a stereotyped norm where father makes all the decisions, goes out to work and waits for his meals to be prepared by the wife with the occasional assistance of the daughter. The son is indulgently allowed to be noisy, greedy and disobedient; the daughters are usually quiet, helpful, punctual, deputy mothers, but in a tight spot they have to be busily frightened while the (otherwise irresponsible) male child takes charge of the situation. The most widely used course of this type was written by Moore and Antrobus and published by Longmans. The first two years of the course revolve around the Marsaud family and a not unreasonable answer to the question 'Where is Madame Marsaud?' might be 'She is under house arrest'. The one advantage of the Longmans course is that it is rather dull and lifeless and therefore less likely to have any impact on the pupils.

The same cannot be said of the Schools Council German course *Vörwarts* (E.J. Arnold) which is very attractive and lively. It relies heavily on realistic dialogue which, with the help of a variety of visual clues, is intended to be repeated by the pupils and assimilated into their active vocabulary. But the dialogues include such phrases as *'bitte nicht unterbrechen, meine Liebe'* (please don't interrupt, dear), said by Herr Schaudi to his wife when she was presumptuous enough to ask a question while he was reading a letter out loud. Frau Schaudi's meek reply is *'Verzeihung Heinrich'* (sorry, Heinrich). Later in the course, the pupils are supposed to repeat *'ich habe Angst'* (I am frightened) while they are watching Lieselotte saying this to Hans during a thunderstorm. I know that teachers, aiming for further authenticity, often split the class into boys and girls for such dialogues. By doing this, they not only strengthen the link between the helpless character and the girls in the class, but they also force them to imitate her whimpering tone of voice. The boys, of course, are protected from saying 'soppy' words, thus avoiding any fear of protest from them. Alternative ways of dealing with dialogue material of this kind are discussed later.

What has happened since the boom period of the 1960s and early 1970s? Have subsequent courses shown any improvement in the images they project? The answer is that any improvement is patchy. Two popular courses *Eclair* (ILEA, Mary Glasgow) and *Chouette* (ILEA, E.J. Arnold) certainly show girls more actively involved in adventures, accidents, etc. and more women driving cars without having accidents, but the norm of the nuclear family still prevails. What is more disturbing is to find offensive visual material amongst these more positive images. *Eclair* includes a flashcard for the word '*la jupe*' (skirt). It shows a woman in front of a mirror, trying on a skirt that is so short that it exposes stocking tops, suspenders and frilly underwear. One can only wonder who it is supposed to appeal to, let alone educate.

The *Tricolore* course (E.J. Arnold) has at last moved away from the tedious family group and includes very varied images of people, taking part in activities, some of which are refreshingly non-traditional. But again, when there is a temptation to be humorous, the 'well it's only a joke' mentality comes bouncing back and gives us (all in the cause of motivation) the good old sexist stereotype. On page 34 of *Tricolore 1* is an exercise which asks pupils to select four captions for the same number of cartoons. The correct solution for one of the cartoons which shows two people playing is '*Elles jouent au football*' (they [feminine plural] are playing football). In the very same book, on page 74, there is a cartoon story intended as a stimulus for oral and/or written work which includes a scene in a restaurant. A woman diner in the background is given unnaturally large and uplifted breasts, on which her male companion seems to be fixing his gaze.[2] Throughout the book, there are more caricatures of women with their bodies distorted in the same seaside postcard manner. The publisher's answer to criticism of these images is to describe them as unconscious idiosyncracies of style and therefore harmless. Surely the more unconscious they are, the more reason there is for concern!

There is, however, some very good material available. *Formidable* by Anne Topping (Edward Arnold) is a slim booklet of short illustrated stories, all of which include more than the usual quota of girls who are a definite departure from the old goody-goody type. Perhaps the best of all the stories is where Thérèse prevents her brother from falling while rock-climbing. When she appears later, having climbed the overhang where he had lost his footing, she gives him a thumbs-up sign and he says: '*Merci Thérèse, tu es formidable*' (Thanks Thérèse, you're great). The most appealing feature of the story is that it is told without the slightest hint of the self-consciousness that is sometimes evident when traditional roles are reversed.

Deutsch Aktiv by Neuner et al. (Langenscheidt) is intended for use by adults, but it could well be used in schools. It treats people throughout as individuals and not in terms of their relationship with another person. It also includes a number of photographs and drawings of female doctors, girls in engineering workshops, etc. However, I find it almost unbelievable that as recently as 1978 a book for German beginners was produced – *Multiple Choice German* by R.T. Thorpe (Blackie) – in which every single picture of a woman is stereotyped and the book even includes one of a young woman in a short skirt being ogled by two small boys and is intended to elicit the correct answer: '*Die ist aber schön*' (she's pretty). 'Our course books are filled with stories and pictures which make us angry with their driving, working, speaking, male characters and their meal-preparing, house-cleaning and deferring women' (Chris Green, private communication). This is the reaction of a colleague in Sheffield to some of the material she has to work with. It is a reaction which has made her develop a variety of positive strategies and these she describes in detail herself later in this chapter.

Why cannot teachers simply put aside the offending courses and refuse to use them? The major reason is economic. In the past, teachers were given textbooks and, if they had any imagination, they developed supplementary material around them. Now, courses come in large expensive packages, consisting of tapes, filmstrips, magazines, teacher's books, pupils' books, and so on. To keep up with the routine replacement of lost or damaged items is the most one can normally manage. Probationary teachers also find the support of a pre-planned course, complete with standardized tests, invaluable. Realistically, there is only one thing left to do and that is to intervene, and there are different ways in which this can be done.

Selective rejection

Sometimes, you may feel that a whole passage is unacceptable and that you simply have to give up all hope of challenging it successfully. The passage that the teacher refers to here is a piece of comprehension from the German *Vörwarts* course. It is one that is also rejected by many other teachers.

> It is called '*Elke spielt Hausfrau*' (Elke plays housewife) and is a gripping story of how a girl, extremely proud of herself, cleans a house in preparation for her parents' homecoming. Usually, because I need to fall back on the textbook, I will simply point out any sexist remarks or statements in a story and ask the students if they would be happy to be talked of in such a way. I will not allow a class to work on this piece at all, because I can't find anything positive in it. (Chris Green)

When a tape or a filmstrip (or both simultaneously) demands a particularly offensive phrase to be repeated such as that of Herr Schaudi to his wife (see above), I will stop the tape and say that I do not want the class to repeat it and will give my reasons. With the Schaudi example, I will then expand on the boorishness and meanness of Herr Schaudi, by giving instances of the way in which he treats Frau Schaudi in later episodes.

Adaptation – the oblique attack

I was also faced with a sexist comprehension passage which had been irritating me for some years and was supposed to be used with a mixed-ability second-year class. In the passage, a woman is asking her husband for a new leather jacket for Christmas. He first deliberately ignores her and continues pointedly to smoke his pipe and read his book, then offers her a pullover on the grounds that her old jacket is not sufficiently disreputable. She, in despair, begins to weep. The passage ends: "And Herr Mehle? What does he do? Of course! He buys a leather jacket for his wife!" (my translation – original punctuation). The implication, of course, is that the wife has employed unfair female tactics on the poor husband, so I produced a new set of questions in English.

1. How do you know that Herr Mehle is deliberately ignoring his wife?
2. Why is he doing this?
3. Would it be better for Frau Mehle if she did not have to rely on him for her clothes?
4. Is it surprising that Frau Mehle begins to cry?

The pupils, though puzzled at first, answered the questions, on the whole, thoughtfully, trying at the same time to work out why I had asked them. This was quite clear from the discussion that followed. The girls all disapproved strongly of the husband's behaviour and offered some interesting corrective policies. The pro-husband group of boys, having lost the support of the text, may not have changed their views, but they looked beleaguered.

The head-on approach

For this approach you need to have planned your strategy carefully enough to have the confidence to carry it out.' Chris Green describes how she dealt with a much more extensive piece of work: ' "Die Modeschau" (*Vörwarts*) chooses to teach description of people and their clothes with a story of a fashion show. From our point of view this is one of the worst possible subjects. Often I simply omit stories that are sexist. In this case, I asked the students to use it as an exercise in finding stereotyped characters. They were surprised, but discussed it in groups and found that the women were only interested in one thing – clothes, and the older male was interested in two things; (1) ogling the young (tall, slim, blond, green-eyed) model in a miniskirt (1974), and (2) avoiding having to buy anything for his wife.

'The boys, mainly, sniggered at the sexual implications, but the girls objected to the idea that the woman had to ask her husband for money. I was pleased, and hope that they will meet other concerned teachers and, in the end, decide that the financial dependence is intolerable. I threatened a beauty contest for the boys for the next week and rather surprised myself by going through with it. When the boys were told that they would have to try to win because we were going to have a vote, they acted quite well, with only the occasional hip-swaggering and baring of the knees. While the vote was being counted, I asked them how they felt and received the reply: "Scared that no-one will vote for me." Only four of the eight got votes and I'm sure they understand not only more German, but more about the ethics of beauty contests than they did before. I can't say that they arrived at their conclusions without any nudging on my part, but they are nudged in other directions from so many sources that I feel glad to have been able to counteract at least some of their prejudices.'

Making your own materials

This is very expensive in terms of both time and energy but, in the preparation of this chapter, other ideas have occurred to me which can reduce that load. Photographs can be used as a source of materials, either directly or indirectly. Enlarged, they can supplement the usual tourist board poster and can, since they are the teacher's own choice, include positive images of either sex. Once they are on the wall as a display, they can also double as a teaching aid. Features of smaller prints can be traced out and used as line drawings for worksheets. To replace an unacceptable flashcard, take an appropriate slide, project it onto card, follow the outlines of the section required, and colour it in. In this way teachers have some control over the images their classes see and can make them as personal as they like.

The greater impact of the personal image was proved to me when I drew a cartoon on the blackboard for a first-year group to illustrate the verb '*fahren*' in German, which has a sound change in the third person singular. I knew that the class had been discussing friction with their science teacher in terms of the brakes on her motorbike, so I drew her riding her bike, with me on the back thinking the appropriate German sentence: 'She's going fast' ('*Sie fahrt schnell'*). The class asked me to redraw the cartoon two or three times during that year and remember it even now, 13 months later. It remains a very positive image for them and I hope to produce more of its kind.

Feminist magazines from France and Germany could provide a further source, not just of images and ideas, but also of non-sexist language for use in the classroom. The most easily available German magazines include *Emma* and *Courage*. *Le Nouveau F* from France is rather glossy and may not be regarded as feminist, but as a working women's magazine it is sufficiently different from the normal textbook.

The classroom – interaction

In modern languages, shyness is a particular problem for pupils. Uttering foreign sounds in front of others can be very intimidating. Boys have a different way of coping with this than do girls. Boys are simultaneously defensive and aggressive. They are very ready to laugh at anyone who makes an obvious error. Also they have a great tendency to dress up their own mistakes to look deliberate, often using the ploy of the exaggerated English accent. It is often a girl who overcomes her reserve and, out of obvious exasperation with this silly tactic, gives the right answer. If she does so, she risks muttered disapproval from the boys.

In the first case, any laughter at mistakes has to be stopped as soon as it happens and disapproval very clearly expressed and then reinforced periodically. I now anticipate such laughter, and make a rule against it before I start work with a class at the beginning of a school year.

In the second case, I have found it counterproductive to challenge the boys in front of the rest of the class because first, some kind of collective ego seems to make them join forces, and secondly, they have probably had more than their fair share of attention already. I usually take them aside after the lesson in question and tell them that I would rather they did not cover up their nervousness in that way. I find that particular approach quite effective, because it tends to defuse and deflate, rather than antagonize.

Role playing, because of the possibilities of role switching (not necessarily reversal, because it implies recognition of the original position), can be a very useful exercise. If in the textbook it is the girl who has the accidents and is looked after by the boy, then change it round until the text has been sufficiently distanced, but not for so long as to allow the girls to assume a nursing role. Role playing also gives the opportunity of rearranging the classroom and, in doing so, of breaking down some of the established territories which themselves become defined by gender (see also Chapter 9).

Games and quizzes in modern languages tempt teachers to divide the class into boys' and girls' teams, no doubt partly in the hope that the boys will copy the girls and take the lesson more seriously because they see it as a way of achieving their main aim – to win. I have always found the good effects short-lived and the long-term effects divisive and negative. I now always refuse any requests by a class to divide the class by sex, and explain that I find the aggressiveness unpleasant. I never quite know whether the pupils understand, but I do find that after I have given the explanation, the boys seem relaxed in their mixed teams. I wonder at those times if I have, successfully, let them off a hook and they feel they don't have to perform to each other or to me. I hope so.

Beyond our control

Grammar is usually sexist and male orientated. For example, why is it that in French a group of females from two to an infinite number can only be called '*elles*' until a male turns up and they have to be referred to as '*ils*'? Why are German articles and personal pronouns always listed *er*, *sie*, *es* and *der*, *die*, *das* (masculine, feminine, neuter)? There is little that you can do about this, apart from to point out the unfairness and illogicality of the first case, and occasionally to alter quite purposely the order of things in the second case, explaining why you are doing it. Certainly no examples of this kind of structural sexism in language should be allowed to pass without comment.

Examinations

For years, teachers have been fuming inwardly when they find themselves having to prepare their candidates to answer questions like these for the oral examination: '*Was hat die Hausfrau vor und nach dem Essen zu tun?*' (What has a housewife to do before and after a meal?); '*Was fragt eine deutsche Mutter ihre Familie nach dem Essen?*' (What does a German mother ask her family after a meal?); or the incredible: '*Sollte eine Mutter arbeiten gehen?*' (Should a mother go out to work?).

All three questions are taken from the JMB Syllabus B oral syllabus. The first two are still current and the last one was on the syllabus until 1981. The dilemma is clear. Do teachers prepare an answer which challenges the question and risk losing the candidates marks for impertinence or flippancy? Do you go for an expansive answer which weighs up all the arguments and risk overloading the candidate with complexities? Or do you bite your tongue and accept the values of the question? I have tried all three and now offer all the possibilities, explaining my own feelings about the questions, allow the candidates to make their choice, and simply offer my help individually, according to their decision.

Examinations as a whole, much like the teaching materials we use, are extremely traditional and conservative in the image of life they project (CILT, 1980). The Southern Universities Joint Board, for example, actually managed to produce a whole examination which totally excluded females! Teachers who have the opportunity to set their own examination, by opting for mode 3 CSE, can make the material as non-stereotyped as they like, but it is the regionally set papers which have the most influence, not only in the exam room itself but on the whole scheme of work that leads up to the examination. But when such a highly respected body as the Centre for Information on Language Teaching and Research, having conducted an exhaustive study of examinations at 16+, makes a statement as forthright as the one that follows, you begin to feel that there is reason to hope for a change:

> Such overwhelming evidence suggests that examiners are the crudest of male chauvinist pigs. They would surely reject such a statement, but their choice of examination material certainly suggests their latent prejudices. It is time a healthier and truer view of society were given.

> (CILT, 1980)

Notes

1   The survey, published in 1975, was carried out in 1973, so schools would not have been in contravention of the Sex Discrimination Act 1975 by offering different subjects on the basis of sex. The 3 per cent difference may be due to strict banding or a grouping of subjects such that some boys were not offered the option of a modern language.
2   The publisher, E. J. Arnold, refused permission for the actual illustrations to be reproduced in this chapter.

Acknowledgements

The views expressed in this chapter are not necessarily those of either the school where I work or its faculty of modern languages.

I wish to thank the following people for their help: Judy Samuel, Chris Green, Kim Clark, Dominique Borel, Sabin Parsonage and Peter Eustace.

CHAPTER 7

MATHEMATICS AND SCIENCE – INTRODUCTION

JUDY SAMUEL

Introduction

Chapters 7, 8 and 9 of this book deal with the areas of maths and science. This chapter begins with a section of statistics describing the underachievement of girls in maths, chemistry and physics. It continues with reviews of biological, socialization and political theories that attempt to account for this underachievement. The final part examines some aspects of school organization. In contrast to this, Chapters 8 and 9 examine classroom practice in maths and science respectively. The emphasis in these chapters is on examples of good practice and suggestions for action that can be effected by individual teachers.

What is the problem?

It is usual practice in secondary schools for science subjects to be part of the options system[1] in the fourth and fifth years; most commonly pupils are advised to choose at least one science subject. This may be a single science, e.g. physics, chemistry, biology, human biology, rural science, etc.; alternatively, it may be some kind of general or integrated science, e.g. Schools Council Integrated Science Project (SCISP – a 'double' 'O' Level course), or one of the general science courses which abound at CSE level. In order to simplify the discussion in this chapter, only the separate subject sciences (physics, chemistry or biology) are considered.

The classic data on the uptake of science option choices (DES, 1975) are shown in *Table* 1. The information is now somewhat dated, since in 1973, when the survey was carried out, there were fewer mixed schools and fewer comprehensive schools than there are now. However, the figures in a more recent survey, *Aspects of Secondary Education in England* (DES, 1979), show very little difference: in most categories there has been an increase of approximately 2 per cent in the numbers of girls and boys taking a particular subject. *Table* 2 shows similar data from a recent local survey (Sheffield

NUT Equal Opportunities Group, 1982); in Sheffield all secondary school pupils are in mixed 11–18 comprehensive schools.

It is clear from *Tables* 1 and 2 that physics and chemistry are 'boys' subjects', while biology is a 'girls' subject'. *Table 2* shows higher percentages of pupils in each category than *Table 1*, but similar ratios of girls to boys, except in physics where there is an improved ratio.[2]

Table 1   The percentage of girls and boys being offered, choosing and taking science subjects in the fourth and fifth years

		Being offered (% of fourth- and fifth-year students)	Choosing (% of column 1)	Taking (% of fourth- and fifth-year students)
Physics	Girls	71	17	12
	Boys	90	52	47
Chemistry	Girls	76	22	17
	Boys	79	35	27
Biology	Girls	95	52	49
	Boys	88	31	28

Source: DES, *Education Survey No. 21* (HMSO, 1975). Reproduced by permission of the Controller of HMSO.

Table 2   The percentage of girls and boys taking science subjects in Sheffield

		Taking* (% of fourth-year students)
Physics	Girls	30
	Boys	61
Chemistry	Girls	34
	Boys	45
Biology	Girls	61
	Boys	38

Source: Sheffield NUT Equal Opportunities Group (1982).

*All three subjects are available in all schools, although this is not the same as saying that these subjects are offered to all pupils. A few schools operate banding systems, according to ability, which make it impossible for some pupils to choose these subjects.

Mathematics is almost always compulsory for all pupils until the end of the fifth year so, unlike science, girls' success in maths cannot be measured in terms of option choices, and a different comparison must be used. The 1978 examination results indicate that the difference between the sexes is small at CSE level (DES, 1978). Although more boys (15.6 per cent of candidates) than girls (12.3 per cent) gained a grade 1 pass in mathematics, girls had a marginally higher success rate (i.e. grades 1–5) over all. The discrepancies occur at 'O' Level, with more boys than girls being entered for the examination, and substantially fewer girls gaining A, B or C grades. More recent statistics (ILEA, 1980) show that only 44.2 per cent of 'O' Level maths entrants in London were girls, of whom 47.1 per cent gained a grade A–C pass. On the other hand, 55.8 per cent of the entry were boys, with 55.3 per cent gaining grade C or higher.

The polarization by sex in uptake or success in maths and science subjects is similar to the position of the subjects on a scale of femininity, as observed by Ormerod (1981). Physics is seen as the most masculine subject, then chemistry and maths which are slightly masculine, and finally biology, which is the feminine science, sometimes described as the 'soft' science.

Given that this is the situation by the age of 16, what happens as girls and boys progress through the education system? *Table* 3(a) shows that this scale of masculinity continues to operate beyond 16: for example, approximately twice as many boys as girls enter for 'O' Level chemistry, but by PhD level there are almost 10 male chemists for every female chemist. However, *Table* 3(a) (bottom line) indicates that women are under-represented in further and higher education as a whole, and *Table* 3(b) shows that, in general, women are no more under-represented at the higher levels of science than at 'O' Level.[3] One exception to this general pattern is evident in the transition from 'A' Level to first degree in maths and physics (*Table* 3(a)). At 'A' Level many physics students are also studying maths, and vice versa, but whereas the relative representation of women in maths improves at first degree level, it worsens in physics. This suggests that female students of maths and physics at 'A' Level tend to choose maths in preference to physics as a degree subject, while their male peers tend to choose physics rather than maths. This is in agreement with the position of these subjects on the scale of masculinity discussed above, and is also reflected in the composition of the teaching force; it is common to find that there are several women teaching maths in a particular department, while it is much less usual to find women physics teachers in mixed schools.

Thus it is evident that whatever factors operate to cause women to drop out of physics and chemistry, they do so before CSE and 'O' Level, that is, in the pre-school years, during primary school and the first three years of secondary school, before option choices are made. Generally speaking, what happens in the fourth and fifth years, during these option courses, may influence the grades achieved, but will not affect the numbers entering for 'O' Level and CSE exams. Similarly with maths, the decline in girls' performance begins before the fourth year, and continues through the next two years, leading to the under-representation of girls in 'O' Level exam entries in maths.

Is it inevitable that there should be this under-representation of women in maths and the physical sciences? In an international study,[4] Alison Kelly showed that boys consistently did better than girls in a standard science test in all the industrial countries studied, but the girls in some countries (notably Japan and Hungary) did better than the boys in almost all other countries. Kelly also showed that in some countries (particularly, but not exclusively, in Eastern Europe), women form a large proportion of the science students. Even so, within each country, girls achieved lower standards than boys in physics, chemistry and maths, and, in every country studied, the relative underachievement was worst in physics, and the situation was reversed for biology.

This, then, is the problem: girls and women underachieve, and are under-represented, in physics, maths and chemistry; in biology they retain, throughout the education system, the relative over-representation that is evident at CSE and 'O' Level.

Biological theories

Clearly there are physiological differences between girls and boys, but are there also innate (i.e. genetic in origin) differences of an intellectual or emotional nature? There are real difficulties in measuring these innate characteristics; as Margaret Sutherland (1982) explains, 'As soon as children are of any age at all they have been subjected to social influences'. She goes on to point out that in attempting to measure differences in the abilities and interests of children, we 'may be assessing what they have learned as well as their innate capacities'.

The most popular versions of the biological approach to explaining the underachievement of girls in science, hinge on the idea that girls have superior verbal ability to boys, and boys have superior visuospatial ability to girls.[5] (Visuospatial ability involves the perception and manipulation of

(a) The number of males for every female studying science subjects at various levels of the educational system

Subject	Attempt CSE	Attempt 'O' Level	Attempt 'A' Level	Advanced FE courses	Universities[2]		
					Obtain first degree	Do post-graduate research	Obtain PhD
Biology[1]	0.4	0.6	1.1	2.0	1.3	2.6	3.8
Mathematics[1]	1.0	1.5	3.8	3.8	2.6	8.0	9.7
Chemistry	2.1	2.1	2.4	6.7	4.7	7.0	9.7
Physics	7.5	3.8	4.9	13.1	7.2	9.6	17.1
All subjects	1.1[3]	1.0	1.4	3.1	2.0	4.1	6.3

(b) The representation of females in science compared to their representation in the educational system as a whole at various levels[4]

Biology[1]	0.4	0.6	0.8	0.6	0.7	0.6	0.6
Mathematics[1]	0.9	1.5	2.8	1.2	1.3	2.0	1.5
Chemistry	1.9	2.0	1.8	2.2	2.4	1.7	1.5
Physics	6.8	3.7	3.5	4.2	3.7	2.4	2.7

Source: A. Kelly (1981), derived from DES, *Statistics of Education*, vol. 2 (1976) and vols. 3 and 6 (1975).

[1] At 'A' Level, mathematics includes all mathematical subjects; at university level, biology includes all biological subjects, but excludes medical and paramedical students.

[2] The university figures refer to all British universities.

[3] The figure for 'all subjects' shows more boys than girls attempting CSEs. This is because there are more boys than girls in the population; it does not indicate that girls are under-achieving at this level.

[4] The figures in (b) are: 'number of males for every female studying subject' divided by 'number of males for every female studying all subjects at that level'.

spatial relationships, for example identifying which of a series of shapes is a rotation of a sample shape.) However, while it is true that the average scores achieved by boys on tests of this kind are slightly higher than those achieved by girls, there is also a large degree of overlap in the scores of the two sexes, with the majority of individuals falling within the same range of scores, regardless of sex (Oakley, 1972b). Further, in some countries (e.g. the Soviet Union), a high proportion of women are successful in the physical sciences, despite these sex-based differences.

Scores on tests aiming to measure spatial ability do not simply differentiate according to sex; different researchers report significantly different results; younger people (pre-puberty) do not show such marked sex differentiation in scores as older ones do; physical science pupils perform significantly better than arts, social science or biological science pupils, and cross-cultural studies fail to show sex differentiation of spatial ability scores in some countries. Recent work (Kelly et al., 1981; Sutherland, 1982) shows that girls' scores on tests of visuospatial ability improve significantly if they receive appropriate teaching for these skills; this suggests that their lower scores may be the result of socialization rather than being genetically determined. And, is it not anyway a function of education to compensate, as far as possible, for any handicap an individual may have, whatever the origin?

In contrast to physics, where ideas concerning visuospatial ability have been invoked in an attempt to account for sex-based differences in performance, the development of visuospatial ability has traditionally been regarded as central to the learning of mathematics.[6] Yet sex differences in mathematics performance are not as great as in physics, and, moreover, no specific biological model of other aspects of mathematical ability has been proposed.

Thus it seems that for maths and the physical sciences, the biological theories of the origin of girls' underachievement are, at best, unhelpful; the issue becomes that of enabling girls to use to maximum advantage the abilities they do have and of developing the skills they are lacking.

Socialization theories

This is the other side of the nature/nurture debate: the biological theories for the underachievement of women in science suggest that females and males are born with innate differences; the socialization theories involve the idea that women's underachievement is a consequence of the interaction of individuals with their immediate social environment – peers, parents, teachers, books and the media. From birth onwards, children experience the world in a different way, depending on whether they are girls or boys. As Alison Kelly (1980) puts it, this is important in that 'girls are brought up in our society in a way which restricts their capabilities and narrows their horizons, and that science (in particular) has a masculine image and is therefore unattractive to girls'.

Pre-school and primary school experiences

Even at an early age girls and boys behave differently, and consequently induce different reactions in the adults around them, though whether this is cause or effect is unclear (Oakley, 1972b). By four or five years of age, boys tend to show a pattern of non-compliant, demanding, attention-seeking behaviour, and therefore get punished (both at home and at school) more often than girls; however, this does confer the advantage of more frequently gaining the undivided attention of parents or teachers.

At a similar age, boys are (generally) encouraged to become tough and independent, whereas girls are encouraged to become, and rewarded for being, gentle and caring, interested in people rather than 'things'. This same training is also being learnt from books: girls helping mum in the home, boys outside, active, doing, being the leader (see Chapter 4 for a discussion of children's readers). It has been suggested that girls who learn to be more self-reliant at this early age will find it easier to develop more positive attitudes to the physical sciences later on (Maccoby, 1972).

By the time that girls are in primary school, they already have attitudes towards satisfaction and success in school work that will stay with many of them throughout their academic career. Girls are more interested in people than are boys, and are more anxious to please: thus they learn to aim for the approval of the teacher (for example by being quiet and well behaved) in preference to completing the set task (which may involve being assertive and demanding in order to get assistance) (Oakley, 1972b). There is also considerable evidence that girls and women do, in general, attribute reasons for success and failure in an opposite way from boys and men. Females attribute success to luck or extra effort, and failure to lack of ability. Males, on the other hand, see their success as a consequence of ability, and failure as bad luck or lack of effort. Though often unconsciously, teachers hold these same stereotyped views as the children they teach, and may indeed expect their pupils to react in these ways (Blackstone and Weinreich-Haste, 1980).

The GIST project[7] found that when 11-year-olds were asked to compare their attainment with that of their peers, 13 per cent of the girls and 19 per cent of the boys described themselves as better overall at school work than their peers, even though at this age girls are usually doing better at school than boys. They found, too, that boys were more likely than girls to give their own ability as the reason for their success in maths, which agrees with work done in the USA which showed that, when confronted by the same low mark in a maths test, girls saw it as a sign of inadequacy, but boys simply saw the need for more work. From this follows the idea that girls learn 'helplessness' to avoid repetition of situations in which they have already failed.

When girls enter secondary school they already have very different methods of working, interests and attitudes from boys. There has been a great deal of anecdotal evidence of this, which has been substantiated by the results of the GIST initial survey (Kelly et al., 1981). This shows that although girls and boys have a similar knowledge of science at age 11, they have differing experiences of relevant practical activities, and that there are large differences in their scientific interests. By far the biggest difference in experience is in 'tinkering' activities; for example, boys were more likely than girls to have experience of using saws or screwdrivers, of helping to maintain a cycle or a car, and of playing with electrical or constructional toys. And because girls have less experience of using or maintaining machines, they are less confident about their ability to control or understand the 'machines' they encounter in science and craft lessons.

One of the preliminary conclusions from the GIST project, based on the results of visuospatial tests and the findings concerning the scientific activities in which the pupils have engaged, is that the development of visuospatial skills may be directly related to concrete experiences. Girls have often missed these experiences, either because they were never offered the opportunity (girls are only rarely invited to help maintain a car), or because their earlier socialization led them not to choose, for example, constructional toys. Girls' lack of involvement in these and similar activities 'may well be the major explanation for their poorer performance (on tests of visuospatial ability)' (Kelly et al., 1981).

The dilemma of being an adolescent girl

Girls mature ahead of boys, and for many girls making option choices in the middle of the third year coincides with the middle of adolescence, the period of becoming aware of, and then established in, their femininity. This is the very time at which girls are most likely to conform to gender norms, and are most concerned to be seen as entirely separate and different from boys. It is, therefore, the most difficult possible time for girls to choose subjects with a strong masculine image, especially when this is combined with self-doubt about their own ability. This is also the stage at which many girls become aware of their own sexuality. Elinor Kelly (1981) describes how it is still unacceptable for the majority of girls to ignore the traditional sexual and marital codes. They have to try to prove their sexual attractiveness without making 'mistakes', while their male peers enjoy the time-honoured privilege of the double standard: licence to gain sexual experience, while, at the same time, decrying the girls who partner them. This is the context in which girls get drawn into a feminine adolescent subculture which, because of its very nature, encourages sex-typed behaviour. Making option choices (see later in this chapter) at this period ensures that many girls effectively narrow their horizons, and reject the opportunity to break the mould of marriage, children and work inside the home (or poorly paid work outside the home), choosing to return to the same narrow range of school subjects as were available to their mothers, 20 or 30 years previously.

Some girls, having made very traditional, and limiting, choices at 13+, will have regrets later, when they emerge from adolescence to become second-class workers in 'time-filler' jobs. In the meantime, however, the subculture of adolescent girls is not only important, but working in opposition to school. One aspect of this is described in detail by Angela McRobbie (McRobbie and MacCabe, 1981) who documents the attitudes presented by *Jackie* magazine (which has a weekly circulation of about 600 000, aimed at 11- to 14-year-old girls). From her study, McRobbie observes that 'beautification is, then, the ideal hobby for a girl'; girls are encouraged to conform, to spend a great deal of time on make-up, experimenting with hair styles, manicuring their nails and ironing their clothes. Beauty, McRobbie concludes, becomes more important as education to these girls than the education which they receive in school; first, they learn to regard marriage as the most important career, and then, in order to make this possible, they learn the techniques of beautification to attract a suitable partner. And some schools reinforce these same ideas in an attempt to arouse the interest of low-achieving girls; options in making cosmetics and projects on hair care not only create ghetto areas of girls' science, but are also 'bad' science, encouraging recipe following without developing any understanding.

The image of science

Ask almost anyone to think about the word 'scientist', and then to describe the image they have, and it is likely that they will describe 'a man, wearing a white coat, working on his own in a laboratory, a cold and entirely rational being'. This view has now been investigated in many studies[8] and seems to be almost universally held in our society. Is the description true? Certainly not in the literal sense: some scientists are women, some don't work in a laboratory, and many are less rational, objective, cold or logical than the public image of a scientist indicates. This image is a simplified view, and there is a serious difference between it and the reality of science for many scientists: it ignores the human, and the social and cooperative, aspects of their work. So the image of a scientist is of someone who is abnormal; the reality is someone less strange, but still, in general, someone male. Here lies the problem for girls: they are more likely than boys to be bothered by the abnormal image (Smithers and Collings, 1981), and anyway as science stands at present, it is very largely a masculine activity.

Physics and chemistry are viewed as difficult subjects by both boys and girls, but girls are more likely to be adversely affected by this. The GIST project found that girls are more likely than boys to see science as 'difficult, only for brainy people, something they don't expect to be good at themselves'. Even at 11, girls are pessimistic about their ability in science, they lack confidence and need encouragement, a view endorsed by HM Inspectors in their survey of schools where girls did particularly well in science (DES, 1980). Boys, at 11, are far more likely than girls to think that girls who do science are 'a bit peculiar', and not very good at it (according to the GIST survey results), and it is likely that this attitude may well be transmitted to girls in the first three years of secondary school. On the positive side, girls are more likely than boys to be favourably impressed by some understanding of the social effects of science, and this too has important implications for the way that science is presented in the early years of secondary school.

This image of maths and the physical sciences as 'hard, complex, based on thinking rather than feeling, concerned with things not people' (Weinreich-Haste, 1981) and divorced from the social context, is in stark contrast to the image of biology, which shows concern with living things, and is more personal and alive. For adolescent girls the image of maths and the physical sciences fails to fit with the qualities that they are learning as appropriate for womanhood, whereas the image of biology fits better with their view of their future selves, and so the choice of biology involves fewer incongruities.

Science as a political activity

An alternative view of the image of science is offered by Esther Saraga and Dorothy Griffiths (1981). They argue that there is more involved in the masculine image of science than the numerical domination of male scientists, and the stereotyped (male) personalities of successful scientists. In their view, socialization theories do not go far enough, 'because they do not attempt to explain *why* socialisation follows particular patterns' (Saraga and Griffiths, 1981).

They urge that the history and practice of science need to be considered, as well as the development of girls in relation to science, if girls' underachievement in the physical sciences is to be explained. They describe how science has specific functions in society, namely to promote both technological innovations (leading to improved products and increased profits) and military developments. Thus science develops in the service of the dominant interests in any society, and the status of the different science subjects varies according to their economic and military usefulness.

Saraga and Griffiths conclude that the 'problem' of girls in science is a direct consequence of the political nature of science. In the short term, improvements can be made by countering (or better still, changing) girls' early socialization. However, as the position of girls and women in science is a reflection of their position in society as a whole, it can only be fundamentally changed through political changes.

School organization

Mixed or single-sex sets?

There has been much discussion of whether girls do better at maths and science in mixed or single-sex schools; indeed the DES itself has effectively contributed to both sides of the debate (DES, 1975, 1979). When HM Inspectors considered the issue of girls and science in their survey of secondary education (DES, 1979), they found that only for physics in grammar schools was it true that more girls chose the subject in single-sex than in mixed schools. There was no significant difference between numbers of girls choosing each science subject in mixed or single-sex comprehensive schools. Despite this statistical evidence, there are increasing numbers of teachers who feel that girls do not receive a fair share of their attention in mixed classes,[9] and there are currently several experiments (either running or being set up) to investigate the performance of girls who are placed in all-girls sets for maths and/or science in mixed schools.

This has been tried with maths classes at Stamford High School in Tameside since autumn 1978, with very encouraging results.[10] During the period of the initial experiment, the performance of girls in an all-girls maths set was compared with that of both boys and girls in an equivalent mixed set, taught by the same teacher. At the beginning of the first year there was no difference in the maths test marks of these three categories of pupils; but by the middle of the second year, while the girls in the all-girls set were still scoring nearly as highly as the boys, the scores of the girls in the mixed set had dropped behind those of the boys by an average of more than 20 per cent. This school now has a policy of single-sex sets in maths in the lower school, and hopes to extend it through the school. It was commented that in the mixed sets boys continually monopolized the teachers' time in many ways, and the girls received much more individual attention in the all-girls set.

A similar experiment is being tried in a Sheffield school, where all the girls who have opted for computer studies in the fourth year have been put into the same set (not, unfortunately, all girls but girl-dominated). This is because it was found that in boy-dominated sets (five times as many boys as girls choose computer studies in this school), girls had very little access to the machines; the boys clamoured very assertively for machine time, and the girls repeatedly relinquished their places in the queue. As Mary Harrison (1982) writes, 'I observed in a secondary school and was quite horrified to see that when computers were used, girls sat back and refused to have a go, fearing to lose face by making mistakes, while the boys gleefully monopolised the game.' Computer studies has already become a more masculine subject than physics in terms of option choices (Sheffield NUT Equal Opportunities Group, 1982), and any organizational strategy which may lead to a rapid improvement in the reaction of girls to computers is to be encouraged.

Making option choices

Physics, chemistry and biology (and frequently a course in general or integrated science, as well as other science subjects are usually included in an options system in the fourth and fifth years, as evidenced by the comments of HM Inspectors (DES, 1980) and the results of a local survey in Sheffield (Sheffield NUT Equal Opportunities Group, 1982). In most schools in Sheffield, pupils are advised to choose at least one science subject; in most, but not all, of these schools it is possible for a pupil to choose all three subjects of physics, chemistry and biology if she/he wishes. The DES report that nationally the most common exception to this pattern is in the small number of schools where a science subject forms part of the compulsory element of the curriculum, along with English and maths.

Investigating pupils' reasons for their science choices, Alison Kelly (1981, ch. 9) found that the most important reason concerned their perceived relevance of science to their future lives. Girls saw science as being less useful than did boys, and seriously underestimated the need for science and maths qualifications, whereas boys overestimated the usefulness of science subjects. One implication of this is that boys often cling to high-flying career plans although their current achievement may make such plans seem ludicrously unrealistic, whereas girls downgrade their plans in response to every minor setback. Even where boys did not have a specific scientific career in mind, they were still more likely to choose science subjects than the equivalent group of girls. A parallel situation exists in maths; the Cockcroft Report (1982) comments, 'Mathematics often acts as a "filter", whose absence as a qualification can exclude girls from many fields of employment, training and further education.'

Twice as many boys (10 per cent) as girls study three science subjects (DES, 1980). The figures average out at nearly one and a half (1.45) science subjects per boy, compared with just over one (1.15) science subject per girl in the fourth and fifth years. As the science most frequently chosen by girls – biology – is the one that by itself is of least use as a scientific qualification, it becomes clear that the one step of making option choices effectively closes many careers to girls, and simultaneously confirms their position in a traditional female role.

All of this underlines the need for a very positive programme of guidance in the third year, before option choices are made. It is essential not only to inform pupils of the science qualifications needed for particular careers and of the careers which will be closed to them if certain science subjects are dropped, but also to provide clear information about careers and jobs which do not traditionally employ large numbers of women.[11] This is where the pupils are least likely to have gathered information from parents, the media or from knowing women already working in such jobs.

Encouraging signs are beginning to emerge of official concern to eliminate sex bias from the information and advice offered in preparation for making option choices. HM Inspectors (DES, 1980) recommend that LEA policy should place greater emphasis on this area, and some LEAs have responded, notably ILEA, Manchester and Somerset.[12] This does not, of course, mean that more thorough, and less biased, advice and preparation for making option choices will automatically follow in all schools, but it is certainly a welcome initiative. A different approach is being tried in Tameside,[13] where the LEA has appointed two teachers with the particular brief to 'encourage interest and enthusiasm for the sciences among girls'. Each of these teachers has half a teaching timetable, and the rest of their time is available for developing work with science departments in the borough.

One aspect of the problem which will remain, despite such an 'official' improvement, is the views and attitudes of some of the teachers who provide advice and discuss possible option choices with individual pupils. The Sheffield survey (Sheffield NUT Equal Opportunities Group, 1982) found that a high proportion of such interviewing is done by senior members of staff (deputy heads, senior teachers, careers masters [sic]), rather than by form teachers or subject teachers. Although one would hope that such senior staff would have the most up-to-date information and clearly thought-out policies of non-discrimination, it is all too frequently the experience of more junior teachers that these are the very people who hold the most strongly prejudiced views and are most resistant to accepting changes in women's role in society.

A simple expedient used in some schools, which reduces the likelihood of a pupil receiving biased advice, is that options interviews are conducted by pairs of staff interviewing together, and it might be desirable that at least one of these interviewers should be of the same sex as the interviewee.

An illustration of the effect that unconscious bias can have (in this case, for or against science) is provided by HM Inspectors (DES, 1981), and is reproduced in *Table* 4. This shows the average number of science subjects chosen by pupils in a mixed school where the guidance was provided within a house system, against the background specialism of the housemaster (sic).

Employment barriers are broken down at times when there is a labour shortage; in the current climate of unemployment, women are being pushed back into traditional areas of work, and these problems are further exacerbated by the introduction of micro-electronic technology. Thus it becomes crucial to encourage girls to appreciate the implications of options choices if they are to have the appropriate qualifications when seeking employment.

Compulsory physical science – one way to stop girls from dropping out?
One way to overcome the problem of girls opting out of physics and chemistry is to make the study of some physical science compulsory up to the age of 16 (although this would not, of course, solve the problem of

Table 4 Average number of science subjects chosen by each pupil in a school where guidance is provided within a house system

Specialism of housemaster (sic)	Engineering	Theology	Maths	Commerce	Maths
Average number of science subjects per pupil in that house	1.92	1.08	1.64	1.41	1.62

Source: DES (1980). Reproduced by permission of the Controller of HMSO.

underachievement; girls also underachieve in (compulsory) maths). Alison Kelly (1980) and HM Inspectors (DES, 1980) describe schools where some physical science is compulsory up to the age of 16, and comment on the reactions of girls who have followed such courses. They found no particularly marked resentment at the compulsion involved, possibly because the schools offered interesting and relevant schemes of work, including applications of physical science. Many girls remarked that they were glad, in retrospect, not to have had the opportunity to drop the physical sciences, although they would have done so given the chance. (In other schools, girls who have dropped physical science have later regretted doing so, and have often found great difficulty in returning to the subject.) This is clearly an area worthy of further consideration; as yet few schools have tried this approach, and little has been written about the experiences of the teachers involved, or of the girls (particularly the lower achievers) following compulsory physical science courses in the fourth and fifth years.

It is important not to become over-optimistic about the advantages of compulsory physical science; it is worth remembering that in (compulsory) maths, girls drop out of the top sets and achieve poorer examination results than boys. Thus, beyond those aspects of school organization described here, it is to practices in the classroom that we must look if we are to raise the achievements of girls in maths and the physical sciences.

Notes

1 See section on 'Timetabling' in Chapter 2.

2 Without earlier Sheffield figures (or indeed national figures for 1982) for comparison, it is not possible to make any deductions as to the significance of the high percentage of girls in

Sheffield studying physics; it may simply be a consequence of the small number of schools in the sample (20 schools).

3   For a fuller discussion of the numbers of women at various levels in science and technology, see Ferry (1982).

4   For a fuller discussion of this study see A. Kelly (1981), Chapter 2.

5   For a fuller discussion of biological theories see Gray (1981), and Saraga and Griffiths (1981).

6   See Chapter 8 for further discussion of this issue.

7   The GIST project is described in Chapter 21.

8   For further discussion of this, see Weinreich-Haste (1981).

9   See, for example, Spender (1982a) and Stanworth (1981).

10 See Schools Council Programme 14, *Reducing Sex Differentiation in Schools*, Newsletter 1, September 1981.

11 Examples of useful materials for this include the film *What's a Girl Like You?* (distributed by the Central Film Library), the booklet produced by the EOC, '*Getting it Right Matters*', and the tape–slide sequence created by Margaret Hotine for the ASE, *Why Science?*

12 See Schools Council Programme 14, *Reducing Sex Differentiation in Schools*, Newsletter 2, April, 1982, and EOC (1982) *Research Bulletin No. 6.*

13 Further information about the Tameside Scheme can be obtained from Ms Janet Dawe, Tameside Girls and Science Initiative, Education Resources Centre, Waterloo Road, Stalybridge, Cheshire.

CHAPTER 8

MATHEMATICS

SARAH SHARKEY

Mathematics is generally regarded as one of the most important subjects in the secondary school curriculum. It is a compulsory subject in England for virtually all pupils aged 11–16 years, and occupies a comparatively large share of their timetabled time. Nevertheless adolescent girls do not seem to see achievement in mathematics as being important for them – an impression which may be created by socialization and culture, and not always contradicted in our secondary schools.

One of the ways this impression is reinforced is by the continual and frequent lip service paid to the popular myth that girls are not good at mathematics. The results of public examinations (see Chapters 1 and 7) give statistical evidence of girls' under-representation in the higher levels of mathematics (and show that they are increasingly more likely than boys to be entered for CSE rather than 'O' Level). However, one must not be misled into the belief that boys have more ability in the subject. The similarities between the sexes are just as important as the differences; and the idea that all pupils seem to find mathematics a somewhat difficult subject, is probably a more accurate assessment of the real situation. This is borne out by the Education, Science and Arts Committee Report (1981) which expressed concern that in mathematics, unlike other subjects, there had been scarcely any increase in the proportion of 'O' Level passes over the past ten years. In spite of the evidence that all pupils seem to find it difficult, the supposition that boys are good at the subject and girls are not, continues to permeate much of mathematics teaching and colours the attitudes and expectations of parents, teachers and society in general.

One example of this is the commonly held belief that both spatial awareness, and an interest in activities which might enhance its development, are lacking in girls. The unquestioning acceptance of this belief has serious implications for girls' education, as was shown by Walden and Walkerdine (1982) in a recent British study. The researchers found that when children at a nursery school were allowed to choose whether or not they would engage in a construction activity using Lego bricks, 'as many girls as boys chose to do the task' (p. 19). This however had not been inticipated by many of the staff. Indeed, 'you won't get the girls to do this', was a typical comment (p. 18). Not only did the girls engage in the activity but no difference was found in the types of structures built by either sex. This study serves to highlight the way in which the fixed, firm but erroneous ideas teachers have about girls and their socially defined interests, influence the classroom experiences they provide.

It is likely that secondary school teachers are no more free from such prejudice than their primary and nursery school counterparts. Mathematics teachers frequently teach higher-level mathematics and three-dimensional topics in particular, already entrenched in the belief that girls cannot, or will not, go very far in either field. It is hardly surprising that such teachers simply experience results which bear out their own self-fulfilling prophecies and which have negative consequences on the self-image and motivation of girls in the subject. This whole attitude towards three-dimensional work needs to be examined further. It is rooted in early childhood, with teachers and other adults being convinced that boys and girls almost exclusively engage in different play and activities which result in facilitating (in the case of boys), or hindering (in the case of girls), their spatial development. This play experience is somehow linked to their later success (or otherwise) in mathematics, in spite of the fact that in primary school, when opportunities for play are greatest, performance differences between the sexes are negligible. The links between early play activities and later success in mathematics are very tenuous. Reservations about both the definition and measurement of spatial ability have been dealt with in Chapter 7. It is important here to realize that even if one accepts that boys are more successful in particular spatial tasks, 'the relationship of these tasks to overall mathematical ability is not well understood' (St John-Brooks, 1981, p. 411).

Is mathematics sex neutral?

Mathematics is frequently claimed to be an impersonal, totally rational and heavily authoritarian subject, and it is precisely this last aspect which allows and encourages the power structures within it. While it is probably true that many people suffer from its authoritarian image, girls in particular are the victims of the power structure. When speaking of girls being good at mathematics, it is frequently remarked that they are only good at computa-

tion or rule following. In this context a number of questions need to be raised.
- Why is computation such a poor skill at which to excel?
- Surely employers are seeking just such skills in their employees?
- Why is it that within mathematics, and no other subject, the areas in which boys are traditionally thought to be proficient are regarded as being important, whereas the topics at which girls succeed (e.g. modern algebra, computation) are made to seem hardly worth while?
- Is it just by chance that language is used, first, to maintain the power structures within the subject, and secondly, to negate girls' success at the very instance of its being mentioned?

It could be that men and boys see mathematics as a male province and the message is deliberately conveyed so that things stay that way.

> Since males stereotype mathematics as a male domain, they undoubtedly communicate this belief in many subtle and not so subtle ways.
>
> (Fox et al., 1980, p. 87)

Even if this is somewhat overstated, the view of mathematics as male, is perpetuated in the recent wave of textbooks, particularly those designed for the 'maths applicable' and 'maths for everyday life' trends. At least the traditional mathematics textbook with its football league tables and boys on paper rounds, was confined in its male orientation. Adding a new dimension to such limitations, it is a serious retrograde step that negative female images are now finding their way into mathematics books. Examples of this are to be found in a series of six books by Chester et al. (1980, 1981) which contain, in book 1 alone, some 31 images depicting men only, four showing females only (of which one is advertising Spain and another singing), and four scenes including both males and females, but in a ratio favouring males. In the quiz show on page 11, the token female is also the token black and of course she is not winning. Other examples are found in Burkhardt's book (1981) in which photographs depict extremely negative images of women and girls, who are shown wallpapering across the door of a room (p. 43), as prizes to be won by competing males (p. 67), as onlookers while the boys cheer *Match of the Day* (p. 146), as items to be scaled down from fat to thin (p. 154), etc. Image is infinitely more powerful than text.

It is hardly surprising that girls who are continually exposed to such material become more and more alienated from mathematics as they progress through secondary school. Should it be the case, however, that any of them have failed to internalize the message that mathematics is male, the public examination papers which they take at the end of their fifth year will rectify the situation. Questions outlined in terms of girls or women only are virtually impossible to find, while almost every paper contains questions which support boys in claiming mathematics as their subject:

15. Four boys each in turn toss a coin. What is the probability that the fourth boy will toss 'heads'?

29. In a group of twenty-seven men, eighteen smoke, sixteen drink beer, and . . .

49. A man is x years old now and his son is y years old now . . .

   (Paper 1, London 'O' Level syllabus B, January 1981)

6. Last year a man and his family took their holiday abroad . . .

14. Each member of a class of thirty supports one and only one of three football teams . . .

   (Paper 2, London 'O' Level syllabus B, January 1981)

17. Each quarter a consumer uses a total of x units of electricity at night and y units of electricity during the day. He uses at most . . .

   (Paper 3, AEB 'O' Level 105/3 June 1980)

The situation is no better at CSE level:

A8.   Two boys have x pence each, three other boys have y pence each and a further four boys have z pence each . . .

A22.   A man had to deliver 21 parcels to a firm . . .

A28.   A boy completes a journey of thirty-five kilometers in two stages . . .

B44(b). The graph in Fig. 9 illustrates a journey which was made by a man during a period . . .

   (Paper 2, LREB, 740000/A2, June 1981)

B14.   A boy recorded the temperatures in . . .

C15.   An applicant for a job in which a high level of colour sense was required was given ten colour cards each of a slightly different shade of green. He was told . . .

   (Statistics LREB, 924809, June 1981)

Since many of the skills and situations of interest in mathematics are defined as male, it is no great shock to find that girls tend to attribute their success in mathematics to luck rather than ability or expertise (Foxman, 1981). Mention has already been made of the way in which language is used to undermine girls' achievements in the subject. Articles concerned with girls' progress are frequently headed: 'Why do girls fail at mathematics?' One seldom sees: 'Why are boys poor at computation?' or 'Why cannot boys simply follow the rules?'

It is also true that the language in which research is reported can exaggerate boys' success in mathematics and diminish girls' achievement by comparison. A recent report from Sheffield Polytechnic states

> In the problem paper, the boys performed better on questions about area and the girls did better on problems involving simple money operations. (p. 108)

The 'simple' money problems under discussion were concerned with the rate of exchange, council house rents and an error in a supermarket bill; surely 'relevant' would have been a more appropriate adjective. In the light of such insensitive use of language, it is not so surprising that girls find it difficult to make explicit the real basis for their success or failure in mathematics. It is, however, absolutely essential to discount the luck theory, since if girls perceive their progress to be one of luck, they are not likely to use it as a basis for future planning or allied subject choice.

Positive practices

A review of the literature would seem to indicate that girls' performance in mathematics is closely linked to broader social attitudes which are particularly influential during adolescence. It is important, therefore, to undermine as much as possible the masculine image which mathematics seems to have acquired (Ormerod, 1975) and which probably adversely affects girls' achievement in the subject. Possibly one of the best ways of neutralizing this is to provide positive female-role models both within the subject itself, and in the teaching environment.

Models within the subject

Writers, publishers, examination boards and teachers must review written and oral material to ensure that positive female roles become established practice. One such example which I have used is a workcard[1] in which Bob's aunt who is a mathematician and 70 years old, writes to Bob outlining four ways in which she is prepared to leave him some of her money. Bob's task is to reply to her letter choosing one of the schemes and giving reasons for his choice. This task is useful, because the female role mentioned is both positive (she is a mathematician) and powerful (she has money to leave), but the setting is one of social correspondence and not merely an impersonal computation. Other examples are to be found in the work of Perl (1978) which portrays the history of women in mathematics, with related classroom activities. There is a chapter on Hypatia's life and work which outlines ideas on conic sections, an area of mathematics in which Hypatia was interested.

The impersonal and masculine images of the subject will also be counter-acted by having the mathematics arise out of female interests and situations. One such possibility is Kitty[2] who never fails to arouse the interest of the lower-school pupils, particularly the girls. The difference in this approach to early probability work is simply one of centering it around a personal dilemma, rather than rolling a die or tossing a coin. The task itself still leaves ample room for class discussion on ideas such as randomness, expected results and extensions of the original problem. In general, if one cannot devise situations which appeal to both sexes, then it is better to choose problems which are based on work in which the pupils have little prior experience. For example, in introducing three-dimensional work, I have found it useful to begin with tetrahedra and other pyramids, rather than the traditional cuboid and cube. Pyramids seem to me to be more neutral territory which helps to set up an atmosphere of cooperation and novelty.

Classroom interaction

By far the most important area for positive intervention is within the classroom. Many teachers (and others) believe that boys occupy the major-ity of teacher time, attention and interest, and that this cannot be allowed to continue (Spender, 1982a). One of the remedies mentioned in Chapter 7 is the move towards single-sex sets, and this may be particularly helpful in schools in which the number of boys is far greater than that of girls. In my own experience, I have found that if the room is arranged so that the pupils are expected to sit in groups of twos or threes, then these groups will be single-sex ones. Teacher attention can then be more readily and overtly monopolized by one or two unruly (frequently male) groups. Alternatively, if enough tables are pushed together in the centre of the room so that 12–15 pupils can sit around three sides, such positions will tend to be occupied by both boys and girls. This helps alter the power structures and interactions which take place within the classroom itself.

Learning mathematics requires much individual attention, and on the question of teacher–pupil interaction I have found it best to circulate among the pupils, rather than stay behind a desk or in front of the blackboard. If the pupils can be set to work on a definite task while the teacher moves around the room, there is more likelihood of a fairer distribution of time and attention. A teacher who remains in one place for most of the lesson may well be adding to the already impersonal image of the subject, and fre-quently places the onus on the pupil to publicly seek help or quietly admit defeat. This latter path is the all too familiar route taken by many females in learning mathematics (Spender and Sarah, 1980, pp. 5–11).

Departmental strategies

Apart from individual teachers, mathematics departments as a whole can do much to counter some of the issues which have previously been mentioned. They could, for example, establish close links with the careers service to ensure that girls are constantly being made aware of the importance of mathematics both as a filter and as a basic requirement of even such traditionally female careers as nursing and teaching.

Whatever form of assessment is used in a school, effort should be made to diagnose the areas, if any, in which girls appear to be disadvantaged. Wood (1977) has suggested that disadvantage occurs in two areas: those involving quantification and those concerned with spatial visualization. If, after scrutiny, individual departments find that such is indeed the case, then as Wood concludes:

> if we can see where to concentrate effort and training on fractions, proportion and, more generally comparison factors – some improvement ought to be possible. (p. 21)

Heads of department might be particularly vigilant to ensure that female participation in the department does not go unnoticed, and to encourage female teachers to apply for promotion posts. This might help to redress the imbalance which exists in many secondary schools with more men than women teaching mathematics[3] and occupying the positions of seniority. Some of the literature on girls' diminishing achievement in mathematics should be made the subject of several departmental meetings. The traditional content-based syllabus, with its authoritarian and rule-bound approach, may well be worthy of review.

Some of the alternative teaching styles (e.g. individualized, investigative) which are currently being used in schools throughout the country, offer a genuine choice to mathematics departments[4] and should undoubtedly be the subject of many departmental meetings. It is my own belief that individualized learning, in which pupils are not directly in public competition, provides a more humane, cooperative and sensible environment for learning mathematics. This has already proved particularly successful with girls.[5] Whether individualized or otherwise, an investigative approach to the teaching and learning of the subject challenges many of its existing authoritarian aspects. While there may be good practices and procedures to be encouraged in investigations and open-ended work, there is certainly no one correct and final solution, and no single method by which the situation can be probed. This is very different from most people's experience of the mathematics classroom and of the way in which the subject can be learned.

Beyond the department

The school itself should encourage departmental initiatives in this vital subject in which girls are seen to underachieve. For instance, (1) time should be allocated to teachers to enable them to devise and run any necessary compensatory courses; (2) teachers must be released more easily to attend conferences on the issue; and (3) outside speakers could be invited to address the department, the pupils or both.

One of the more recent and most promising developments in mathematics teaching is the setting up of the Girls and Mathematics Association (GAMMA)[6] which seeks, among other things, to provide a national network of current research on the subject, and which will undoubtedly prove a valuable source of information and ideas for many mathematics teachers.

The search for factors to account for the diminishing progress of girls in mathematics is one which requires commitment, monitoring and reappraisal by mathematics teachers. Support and resources are required from both the school and local education authority. It is hardly surprising that given the complexity of the problem, few easy solutions can be identified. Nonetheless, school-based initiatives must be recommended as one of the most positive means of altering the situation which leaves many girls unprepared to share in the benefits of the post-school employment market.

Computer studies

It is probably true that in most schools computer studies has found its way into the curriculum through the mathematics department. In view of the carry-over effect of the mathematics image, together with the apparent alienation of girls and women from technology in general, one can hardly describe this situation as commendable. Many LEAs have been quick to realize the adverse effects. Mr Paul McGee, Croydon's HM Inspector for computers, considers it a priority to have more girls involved in computer studies and to this end he has made a call for computing to be kept out of mathematics departments.[7] ILEA also seems to be moving towards creating a separate computer studies department in all schools. This alone, however, will not solve the problem. There is a need to adopt some or all of the following practices which have been initiated in various schools to different degrees:

1. A school policy which insists on equal numbers of boys and girls in the computer option groups.
2. No boys allowed into the school computer club unless accompanied by a female enthusiast.
3. Teachers to be kept abreast of the work on the position of women in technology, currently being undertaken in Greater London and Avon, under the auspices of the Schools Council.
4. Women who work with computers (e.g. members of the Women and Computing Group[8]) to be invited to address pupils in the school. This might encourage girls to think in terms of a career in computing.
5. A syllabus to be devised in the subject, which will be taught to all pupils in the lower school, thus ensuring that every pupil becomes accustomed to a micro-computer.

It could be argued that the micro-computer will eventually become demystified, with most departments using it as a learning aid across subject boundaries. Such progress takes time, and meanwhile pupils are being confronted with a wave of textbooks which reflect the masculine image of the computer and its technical, rather than human, interest. There is an urgent need for a directive from LEAs encouraging schools to refuse to buy such books before it is too late. Unless this happens, girls will continue to be presented with alienating material on the grounds that the money has been spent and the books have already been bought.

Every effort must be made to include girls in the field of technology so that they acquire a realistic awareness of the computer's potential and can take an active part in determining the direction and meaning of society's 'progress'.

Notes

1 This activity comes from a Smile workcard (number 1425). Smile is an individualized learning scheme in the Inner London Education Authority, and information can be obtained from The Smile Centre, Middle Row School, Kensal Road, London W10.
2 Kitty first appeared in a mathematics magazine for lower secondary school pupils, produced by The Smile Centre. Kitty appears in various guises of logical, probability, calculator Kitty, etc. Most of these are now workcard activities as a result of their popularity with the pupils.
3 ILEA carried out a secondary school staffing survey in 1977. The results, for mathematics, were as follows:

Mathematics teachers* in ILEA

	Male	Female
Full-time	789	413
Part-time	42	75

*Defined as teachers who spend more than 60 per cent of their time teaching mathematics

Although there were no figures available for the distribution of senior positions within the sex groupings, recent research has shown that fewer women than men apply for senior posts in secondary schools (ILEA *Female and Male Teaching Staff in the ILEA: Equal Opportunity Research Study* 833/82).

4   Most local examination boards offer provision for mode 3 CSE examinations so that teachers can (and currently do) write examination papers in keeping with their teaching styles. The Associated Examining Board also offers a mode 2 'O' Level in which all 'O' Level pupils take the first two papers written by the Board's examiners. The third can (with negotiation) be written by groups of teachers in the style of their choice. Smile teachers have negotiated such an 'O' Level and it includes some marks being awarded for course work.

5   Tony Gomme, head of mathematics at Christchurch Girls' School, Chatham, has commented (in a letter to GIST, 7 March 1980) that as a result of using an individualized system (KMP) 'girls now enjoy their Maths whereas before the vast majority just "switched off" in Maths lessons'.

6   The Secretary of GAMMA is Susan Wright at the Department of Teaching Studies, Polytechnic of North London, Prince of Wales Road, London NW5 3LB. GAMMA endeavours to link all groups working in the field of girls and mathematics. They have run one-day conferences and are currently looking at teacher training, producing resource packs, nursery education, etc.

7   An article on p. 4 of the *Times Educational Supplement* of 20th August 1982 describes the initiatives being undertaken in Croydon, under the direction of Mr Paul McGee.

8   The London branch of the Women and Computing Group can be contacted c/o A Woman's Place, 48 William IV Street, London WC2. They are interested in demystifying technology and assessing it from a woman's point of view. They produce a newsletter, run conferences, etc. and are willing to talk to girls in schools.

CHAPTER 9

SCIENCE

JUDY SAMUEL

Introduction

It is reassuring to know that, according to the GIST survey (Kelly et al., 1981), girls and boys have a similar *knowledge* of science at age 11; at least girls do not start off at a disadvantage in this respect when beginning secondary school science. However, given the underachievement of girls by sixteen plus, the corollary to this is the inescapable fact that somewhere between the beginning of the first year and making option choices in the middle of the third year, lies the 'heart' of the problem. And however much we point to factors beyond our immediate control (such as those discussed in Chapter 7), at least part of the responsibility for girls' underachievement in the physical sciences lies with science teachers, and it is up to us to do something to improve the situation.

Clearly the crucial period is the first three years of science in the secondary school, and in this chapter I consider science teaching, learning and courses in years 1, 2 and 3. I also discuss some aspects of upper school work in physics and chemistry, as these influence both what is taught and how it is taught lower down the school, particularly in the third year.

Applications of science

When asked to comment on their science courses, girls frequently mention that the work becomes more interesting when the relevance and applications of the work are clearly indicated[1]. Discussion of applications in a science course is clearly desirable for boys as well as girls; however, it is girls who are particularly concerned when such aspects are missing. This relevance is obvious when the science concerned is human biology, but it is usually obscured to a greater or lesser extent in almost all other science subjects. It is not that every minute of the lesson should relate to everyday life, but that within each topic or section the relevance should be clear. The work should be *based* on practical applications and everyday situations, rather than these being added at the end, as if as an afterthought.

Many science teachers agree that these are sound principles for the construction of a first- and second-year course, but find such aims quite impossible to achieve when teaching exam courses in chemistry and physics (CSE, 16+ and 'O' Level). Many of the exam syllabuses at this level are overloaded with conceptual and factual knowledge, with little mention of, and therefore little time for, applications to, and relevance for, everyday life. The result is that the crucial third-year course is where the two quite different philosophies meet. The third-year course becomes a compromise: a rapid increase in pace, some applied physics or chemistry and some conceptual or more difficult work as a taster for the fourth- and fifth-year courses. It is a situation in which (until the mode 1 examination syllabuses become more relevant) the teacher cannot win: third-year work which is too much like first- and second-year work means that pupils don't find out what fourth- and fifth-year work will be like, and anyway there will be too much left to cover in these two-year courses; third-year work which is too much like fourth- and fifth-year exam courses mean that few pupils will want to opt for the subject with girls (who have less confidence in their own ability than boys) being most affected.

There are beginning to be some signs of change. The revised JMB 'O' Level chemistry syllabus (first examined in 1981) has replaced small sections of the most conceptually difficult (and most mathematical) work, with a small amount of applied chemistry, concerning pollution and fertilizers.[2] One useful consequence of such syllabus development is that textbooks are beginning to appear which, whatever their other faults, pay more attention than is usual to applications of chemistry.[3]

Changes in 'O' Level syllabuses are likely to be followed by changes in CSE mode 1 syllabuses, and together these improvements will reduce, to a small extent, the compromise involved in designing a third-year course. (At least this is true for chemistry; I know of no parallel developments in physics.) Meanwhile, many schools, and groups of schools, operate excellent CSE mode 3 courses which include physical sciences, and which stress both the relevance and the application of scientific principles. (However, there are no data available to show whether such courses lead to greater uptake by girls, as the girls themselves predict.)

Another development is the introduction of science and society studies, and although, so far, these courses are aimed at sixth-formers,[4] some of the ideas and materials in them could be adapted by teachers for use with younger groups. Some of the philosophy of science and society studies is discussed by Solomon (1980).

To return to the science lab, what do we do to make the application of science more apparent to girls? It seems to me that there are two distinct approaches here: one is to include more applications, and (in many cases) to alter the order of teaching so that the application comes first instead of last; the other is to change the applications which are used.

A good example of the first approach (in this case with a CSE group) is described in detail by HM Inspectors (DES, 1980, p. 32). The question, arising from previous work, was 'Why is sulphur removed from fuels?' Answers to the question were used as a reason for burning sulphur; the effects of the product (sulphur dioxide) on everyday materials were tested by the class, and the results used to lead into a discussion on air pollution. This is clearly an example of good practice, with theory and applications so intimately linked. A further possibility here is to mention the effects of science on society at an earlier stage than is usual in traditional courses. For example, practical work on burning fuels is part of our third-year course and I have found that third-year pupils (both girls and boys) have a good general knowledge of, and interest in, the effects on people and the environment of pollution by carbon, carbon monoxide and lead, arising from the burning of hydrocarbon fuels.

An example of the second approach (using applications which are more familiar to girls) concerns the separation of mixtures of liquids. It is common practice to use oil/water or petrol/water as examples of liquids which do not mix. An alternative is to start by showing pupils a bottle of French dressing (oil and vinegar salad dressing), asking them to describe its appearance, and then to suggest why the oil and vinegar always separate into two layers. This leads easily into the usual work on using a separating funnel to separate two immiscible liquids.

A third, and more long-term approach, would be to extend the background experiences of girls, so that some of the traditional examples (especially in physics) are less alien to them. The GIST survey results (Kelly et al., 1981), discussed in Chapter 7, show that girls indulge less frequently in tinkering activities than do boys, yet these are the very experiences that would enable girls to better appreciate the use of such examples as pliers as a lever or a wheelbrace as a simple machine. Kelly et al. suggest that technical skills 'playschemes' in schools might be one way in which girls could compensate for their lack of mechanical expertise. This idea is being tried in a few schools: instead of more conventional science clubs, girls are being offered the opportunity to 'play' with toys such as Fischer Technik and Meccano.

Role models

It has frequently been suggested that the lack of suitable female role models is a factor which discourages girls from opting for physics and chemistry, and it is certainly true that girls notice the absence of women teachers in these subjects. Despite the obvious attractions of suggesting that more female teachers would help to improve the proportion of girls opting for physical sciences, HM Inspectors (DES, 1980) found no evidence of any correlation between the number of women teachers in a department and the number of girls opting for that particular subject. Indeed, this is not entirely surprising, for a woman teacher (of whatever subject) is unlikely to act as a positive role model for low-achieving girls.

A woman working in science or technology, at a level which the girl might herself achieve, would be far more use as a role model. For many of the areas of work that girls traditionally consider, such as nursing, hairdressing or secretarial work, such role models are already well known to the girls, and provide both an example and a source of information. In discussing option choices and possible jobs with different third-year forms over a period of years, I have heard comments from girls such as, 'My Mum will get me a job where she works, doing the same as she does' and 'I'd like to be a nurse, my auntie's a nurse', many times. But most of these girls don't know any women working in the fields of science or technology, so there is no opportunity of informally passing on information about such jobs. This is where schools need to take positive action to fill the gap, as all schools in the GIST projects are doing at present with the VISTA programme.[5]

The VISTA programme brings women working in science and technology into schools; whenever possible these are women with qualifications such as 'O' Level or CSE rather than at degree level (although in practice this has proved rather difficult). The women talk to one class at a time, as part of the normal science lessons in the first, second or third year. The aim of each visit is twofold. One aim is to illustrate an application of science; for example, when a class was learning to use thermometers, they had a visit from a gas engineer, who spoke about the different ways of measuring temperature she uses in her work, including a demonstration of heat-sensitive crayons. The second aim, of providing a role model, comes not only in the physical presence of the woman engineer, but also when the discussion after the 'talk' involves asking the woman about other aspects of her life, such as the attitudes of male colleagues and of family members. On a small scale, many of us could arrange something similar for our own classes, using our own contacts, or contacts made through school–industry links. The next step would then be to extend the scheme to involve other members of the department/faculty.

Written materials

Textbooks for physics and chemistry, particularly those aimed at the 11–16 age range, have become much more attractively presented in the last few years, with more drawings, more photographs, more colour. Many of these books have illustrations on every page. Although only a small proportion of the drawings and photographs show people, it adds up to a significant number of illustrations of people, mainly male people, in each book.

A careful and detailed study of the gender of people in illustrations in some current physics books has been carried out by Geoffrey Walford (1980). His survey shows that in the *Exploring Physics* series by Tom Duncan there is an overall bias in the illustrations of about four to one in favour of male characters. There are even fewer females in most of the other books examined in the survey. Analysis of the lavishly and colourfully illustrated chemistry book we use with third-, fourth- and fifth-year pupils (Groves and Mansfield, 1981) gave an almost identical ratio of four illustrations showing men for every one showing a woman. Walford further comments that many of the illustrations featuring women show 'women pushing prams, a woman floating on the Dead Sea, girls blowing bubbles, women cooking, women as radiographers, nurses or patients, women used as sex symbols, women looking amazed or frightened, or simply women doing "silly" things'.

One small way to redress the balance in illustrations is now offered by the Equal Opportunities Commission, who are publishing a series of posters of women scientists. These posters (which are available free from the EOC) give information about both the woman's scientific achievements and more general aspects of her life. They are suitable for use with secondary pupils from the first year upwards. A colleague had the idea of producing a collage to accompany the posters, showing contemporary women in scientific occupations, but found extreme difficulty in finding suitable pictures. Women's magazines yielded little beyond nurses, and the glossy publications of the major chemical companies usually produced only a token woman; the sole reliable source of photographs was university prospectuses!

While there is little we can do in the short term to improve the image of girls and women in science textbooks, we can influence the many written materials produced within the school. Workcards and worksheets (especially for use with first, second and third years), sheets of homework questions and internal examination papers can all be cleared of sex bias by taking action within the science faculty or department. In unbiased materials, males and females will be equally represented in illustrations, not only numerically, but also in terms of the activities in which they are engaged. Questions about pupils carrying out experiments will refer equally to girls and boys, the applications of science used as examples will be equally familiar to both sexes, and care will be taken to avoid excessive use of technical or militaristic examples in physics.

Sex bias appears in a quite different way in examinations, according to the work of Jan Harding (1981). She shows that there is a small, but significant, difference in the performance of girls and boys on different types of science examination questions. In Nuffield 'O' Level examinations, boys perform better than girls on multiple choice questions, both sexes perform equally well on structured questions, and girls score better than boys on essay-type questions. If this pattern applies generally to science exams at sixteen plus[6] then the implications are considerable, particularly at CSE level, where essay questions are not normally used, and for the development of new examinations in physics and chemistry for a common system of examining at sixteen plus. It is encouraging that this point is noted in the report on draft national criteria in chemistry (Southern Examining Group, 1982).

In the laboratory

Confidence and organization

Teachers have noted that girls often lack confidence in tackling practical work when they begin formal science courses in the first year, and girls themselves often feel that they start at a disadvantage.[7] This is particularly evident when dealing with hot or unfamiliar apparatus, or with electrical equipment. For example, girls rather than boys need to be reassured that the collar on a Bunsen burner is not hot and can be safely touched to alter the flame, or that when heating a liquid in a test tube, the metal holder will not burn their fingers. The teacher has an important role here, in encouraging and involving girls who are rather hesitant: I have found that girls respond well when I show them the best/safest way to use apparatus, and then offer encouragement while they carry out the task themselves. I have observed similar situations when acids are first introduced: boys are generally much less concerned than girls with the safety aspects of the subject, and it seems likely that girls are deterred from tackling experimental work by the strongly worded warnings that are, of necessity, delivered to the boys.

This lack of confidence is manifested in a slightly different way, particularly in physics, in schools where there is a change in the third year to a more formal, teacher-centred method of presentation. This approach frequently includes the teacher giving experimental instructions verbally (while pupils listen, or hastily note them down), and girls often lack the confidence to proceed from this basis. One method of tackling this is to put the experimental directions onto worksheets, so that girls can refer back to them as often as they find necessary. A male physics teacher found that making this change in presentation helped to improve the attitude of third-year girls to physics, and led to an increase in the number of girls choosing physics as an option subject.

It is also important to consider the order in which topics are taught in the third year: for example, simple current electricity should not be covered just before the making of option choices. Girls see this as a particularly masculine part of physics, a view which is reinforced in the laboratory by the clearly evident skill with which many boys set up circuits, while the girls find themselves struggling with a new and unfamiliar topic[8] – a situation which acts to discourage them from opting for physics. It is interesting to note here that chemistry does not seem to include any such clearly defined masculine areas; in discussion with other chemistry teachers it emerged that the topics which pupils described as 'boys' chemistry' varied from teacher to teacher depending, apparently, on the way the topic was approached. However, 'experiments that didn't work' were tolerated less readily by girls than by boys, particularly when it was an experiment done by the pupils themselves that had failed, rather than a demonstration experiment. I suspect that this is again a matter of self-confidence in the laboratory.

Outside the classroom, girls often need extra opportunities to go over the work covered, so that they gain confidence in their ability to cope with it. It is important that physics and chemistry teachers make it clear that girls (and boys) are welcome to come and discuss their work. The teacher must be prepared to make such offers of support reliable – by indicating availability at specific times, or by postponing other work. It is my experience that when I have offered such assistance to fourth- and fifth-year pupils, girls have made much greater use of the opportunity than boys, a finding which is endorsed by HM Inspectors (DES, 1981).

The invisibility of girls compared with boys in mixed classrooms has been thoroughly documented (see, for example, Sharpe, 1976; Stanworth, 1981; Whyte, 1981; Spender, 1982a; see also Chapter 3 in this book). Boys make more claims on the teacher's time than do girls, and teachers spend a disproportionate amount of time with the boys in a mixed group. I find this is often because boys shout out far more than girls, and are less prepared to wait their turn for help. My immediate reaction is always to deal with those pupils causing the disturbance. This is particularly evident with a fourth-year CSE group I teach, where girls outnumber boys by two to one, yet at the end of a lesson it frequently seems to me that I have spent at least half my time helping boys. Some teachers have tried taping their lessons, and have found the same result as Spender (1980a, 1982a): even where the teacher is a feminist, and thinks that she is allocating more than half her time to girls, she is still, in fact, allocating more than half her time to boys!

In attempting to counter this situation, I find that the most difficult part is establishing a relationship with the boys where they do not continually demand attention; only when this has been done is it possible for me to attempt to divide my attention fairly. It also helps to have a good proportion of the girls sitting in the centre of the room. I have a third-year group that I teach in two different labs in the course of each week; as a consequence of which pupils were first through the door at the beginning of the year, girls and boys sit in different places in the two labs, which differ in layout. The girls almost always take a more active part in the lesson in the lab where they sit near the centre of the room. A colleague noticed that whenever she asked a fourth-year class to bring their stools to the front, the boys were sitting in the centre, and the girls behind them. She used the simple expedient of instructing the girls and boys to swop places, and then discussed the reasons for this with the group. The arrangement with the girls at the centre has been maintained ever since, with the girls contributing more to the lesson than they did previously.

Additionally, the behaviour of the boys needs to be under control so that they do not interrupt by calling out or doing silly things such as falling off their stools (which third-year girls do far less than their male peers). In physics and chemistry, particularly, it takes only a little of this kind of behaviour to discourage the girls, and tempt them into easing themselves out of the lesson.

Questions and overt sexism

It is much more difficult to involve girls than boys in answering questions: often a girl will readily offer an answer only if the question is direct rather than open-ended, and she is confident that she has the correct answer. In contrast to this, boys (especially younger boys) are often over-eager to answer – they stand up, and shout, 'Miss, Miss!', so that it is very difficult to ignore them. Occasionally younger girls do this too, but much more rarely than boys, and it is usually the same one girl in a class. Thus the issue of question technique is crucial. I try never to accept answers when only boys are volunteering to answer the question, but always try to reword, or to break the question into smaller parts, or to offer hints. Such hints are often particularly successful with high-achieving girls, who know the answer but do not have the confidence to offer it.

To illustrate what I mean, the following example arose recently with third-year groups. The question was, 'What name is given to the process of making small molecules, like ethene or petrol, from the large molecules obtained from crude oil?' No girls offered an answer, so I continued, 'Hint, it's got eight letters, beginning with "c",' and, on a second occasion, with a different group, 'Hint, it's what you do when you want to use an egg'. (The answer is cracking.) The point here is that there were girls in the groups who, like many of the boys, knew the answer when the question was first asked, so it would have been patronizing (and unnecessary) to simplify the question; the hints provided confirmation to the girls that their answers were correct and, as a consequence, they participated in the lesson. In other circumstances, different techniques (such as dividing the question into simpler parts which can be tackled separately) are more appropriate for building confidence and maintaining the involvement of the girls.

Boys in a science class often undermine the confidence of the girls in very direct ways, as the following examples show: boys grabbing the best apparatus, boys commenting unfavourably on the girls' work, boys laughing, groaning and making derogatory remarks when a girl makes a mistake in answering a question. This kind of harassment is particularly difficult to control; as a colleague remarks (Kath Thorpe, private communication), 'I always put the boys down with a quick verbal comment, but would be much happier if it didn't happen'.

While trying to eliminate the subtleties of indirect discrimination, we must also counter the more overt sexism that is still too often found in science faculties. Delamont (1980) recounts several such incidents, including one of a chemistry lesson in a comprehensive school where the teacher asked the class what was special about Pyrex beakers and commented, 'The girls will know more about this'. HM Inspectors comment (DES, 1981) that teachers are often unaware of possible impressions (of stereotypes) created by casual remarks, and give examples to illustrate the point, including the following from a dissection lesson, 'Now which of the boys will do the cutting? – Girls let me know if you feel sick'. And, from my own experience, a physics teacher who mentioned to colleagues that he expected only boys to be interested in a new fourth-year course in control technology, gave options talks on the subject to third-year pupils and found, when the option choices were made, that his expectation was fulfilled. Nastier (because it is more personal), but even more common, are sexist remarks addressed to individual girls by male teachers (and female teachers who are unaware of the issues). Again, an actual example: to a high-achieving fourth-year girl, who wanted to be an engineer, 'What do you want to do that for? (laughs), you'd get all sorts of comments from the men you worked with!' If male teachers in a science faculty are making remarks such as this, then the other staff have a responsibility to challenge them on behalf of the girls, who are in no position to do so.

Conclusion

The factors contributing to the underachievement of girls in physics and chemistry are complex and inter-related. In this chapter, I have outlined some of the ways in which an individual teacher or science department/ faculty could tackle the issue; other approaches, which may involve policy changes in the school as a whole, were described in Chapter 7. Some individual teachers and departments have developed their own strategies, and these are described from time to time in *Education in Science*, the internal journal of the Association for Science Education. The GIST project is currently using, and evaluating, a variety of intervention strategies in schools in Manchester, and intends to publish details of the most successful schemes when the project is completed.[9]

Notes

1 See, for example, DES (1980), pp. 20–21.

2 The JMB also offers an alternative 'A' Level chemistry syllabus (syllabus A), which embodies the philosophy that chemistry is an activity not only done by chemists, but that it affects everyone, whether or not they are a scientist. The core part of this syllabus begins with a section on 'The social and economic implications of chemical technology', and the course also includes two applied chemistry options, where pupils apply their 'A' Level chemistry to areas of science where chemical principles are used. Examples of such options are 'The chemistry of living systems' and 'Metallurgy'.

3 See, for example, *Chemistry About Us* by A. H. Johnstone, T. I. Morrison and N. Reid (Heinemann Educational, 1981) as an 'O' Level chemistry book; *Chemistry in Context* by G. Hill and J. Holman (Nelson, 1980) as an 'A' Level book; and *New Chemistry Teaching Materials* by N. Reid (1978) (Scottish Council for Educational Technology, Downanhill, 74 Victoria Crescent Road, Glasgow) as background materials for 'O' Level/CSE.

4   At present only one such syllabus is in operation, the ASE 'Science in society' course. A second syllabus, 'Science in a social context' (SISCON) is undergoing trials and will be published in sections, beginning in January 1983.

5   For details of how this 'Visiting Women Scientists' scheme operates see Smail et al. (1982).

6   Sadly this work has not, to my knowledge, been repeated with other 'O' Level examinations, nor with 16+ or CSE examinations.

7   See, for example, DES (1980) and Samuel (1981).

8   The GIST project team (in conjunction with some teachers in Manchester) intends to consider more closely the teaching of electricity, with a view to developing a sample teaching scheme which is more appropriate to the needs of girls.

9   Readers who would like to pursue further the issues raised in this chapter are particularly recommended to read: DES (1980) *Girls and Science*. HMI Series, *Matters for Discussion No. 13*. London, HMSO; Kelly Alison (ed.) (1981) *The Missing Half, Girls and Science Education*. Manchester University Press; and Harding Jan (1983) *Switched Off: the Science Education of Girls*. Longmans Resources Unit.

Acknowledgements

I would like to thank Margaret Bell for typing Chapters 7 and 9, and the following people for reading and commenting on earlier drafts of these chapters: Phil Hingley, Alison Kelly, Jill Norris, Sarah Sharkey, Kath Thorpe and members of the science faculty at Rowlinson School, Sheffield.

CHAPTER 10

HISTORY

ANNMARIE TURNBULL, JAN POLLOCK AND SUE BRULEY

School history teaching

History has always been a popular subject with girls, but in spite of its image as a feminine, literary and people-orientated subject, the context of school history is overwhelmingly male centred, which is not surprising as most of it is, and always has been, written by men. The 'famous men' approach is still used in many schools. This perspective assumes a relentless line of human advance. It is both anglocentric and androcentric – the success story of the wealthy white male. History is neatly structured into a series of discrete 'historical events' which are explained primarily as the actions of powerful men. The tasks assigned to pupils are passive: dictated notes and straight comprehension. Too often pupils are expected to absorb 'facts' uncritically from secondary tests, and with no discussion of competing interpretations of historical evidence.

This presentation of history as an impartial body of data concerning biographies of the famous and the story of the relentless march of progress, has rarely made it a contentious subject in the curriculum. But the sun has set on the empire, and the schoolteachers' vision of the past is at last being re-examined.

In the 1960s the development of a more child-centred approach began to emerge throughout the curriculum. It is now considered that subject matter must be of relevance to pupils, and so we have seen the growth of social and economic history, focused generally on 'the ordinary people'. Teaching methods and tasks set have also undergone change in some schools. For example, pupils are asked to write of themselves as a 19th-century factory worker. Empathy is tested as well as memory; many pupils are asked to examine short primary source extracts.

World history courses have also been developed by examining bodies. These developments mark progress in school history. The choice for 'O' Level and CSE exams now usually lies between British social and economic history, or world history. As the latter is political history, the question of how British and world history connect or indeed how social and political aspects relate, is left untouched. For example, the work of women in factories is often presented without consideration of its economic background or the place of working-class women within the power structure. World history syllabuses and textbooks contain little or no references to women, and exam questions continue to ask for isolated paragraphs on this or that personality or event rather than seeking the background causes or results. All this leaves the study of women in history isolated from ruling-class men or anything that happened in other countries.

The record of school history teaching has left a stultifying legacy. The sexist content and approach to the subject can be neatly illustrated by a quote from a 1952 government pamphlet on history teaching, which informs us that girls have an interest 'in costume and in household matters'. Boys, on the other hand, 'are fascinated by cause and effect' (Ministry of Education, 1952). Although this was written over 30 years ago the history that is taught in schools today is still male-dominated and continues to perpetuate outdated stereotypes. The school plays a crucial role in building a young person's identity. At present girls go through 11 years of state education, during which they come into contact with scarcely any historical material concerning women, except token gestures to such women as Florence Nightingale or Elizabeth I. One could be forgiven for thinking that women's history was the history of saints and queens!

This lack of material focused specifically on women contributes among girls to a lack of self-esteem, from which boys are much less likely to suffer. Thus, the absence of 'women's history' in schools can be related to the feeling among many girls that they are inferior to boys. There is another reason why sexual bias in history is an important issue. If consideration of women's lives (i.e. the ordinary experience of women, not just 'great women') is neglected, then history itself is impoverished, because it reflects the historical experience of only one half of humanity. It is, therefore, partial and inadequate.

There is already a substantial and ever-growing body of work on women's lives in the past (see section on 'Resources', p. 161), but we still await its incorporation into general school history texts and teaching. This is as much a result of women's unequal status in society today, as in the past. Academic bodies such as the Historical Association have yet to acknowledge that a problem exists in school history teaching. From May 1969 to June 1979 *Teaching History* made no mention of women's history. In October 1979 it published a book review that declared 'Most books written about the history of women are either biased or boring' (p. 40). Not one article gave positive encouragement to teachers to fundamentally reappraise what they are teaching from the point of view of its sexism. There has always been a tradition of sexual bias in both history as a discipline and in history teaching. This is not something that each generation of history teachers consciously takes up; rather it is unconsciously passed on through the profession. The history that is taught in universities and polytechnics is often biased, and this in turn reflects and consolidates the sexism found in the wider society.

Although there is no agreed body of historical knowledge that all children should know, there is an implicit assumption in much of history that it is fundamentally concerned with the process of change, and that as women have had little importance in initiating change their inclusion as subjects of study is irrelevant. Such is the belief of one critic of women's history. Commenting upon history's concern with change, the influential American historian J.H. Hexter says: 'We know who is mainly behind those trends and developments and movements . . . For better or for worse it was men' (quoted in Lewis, 1981, p. 55).

If men have occupied the stage of history it is only because of a myopic approach to the subject. If we emphasize change and 'great men and movements' in a vacuum, we risk sacrificing an understanding of society as a whole, and particularly the underlying relationships between men and women. What is noticeable about the oppression of women over the centuries is how its essential features have endured, not how much it has changed. Having said that, we must be careful not to go too far in the opposite direction and overdo the role of women as helpless victims. There were 'great women' in history and significant movements of women. Both the oppression of women and the resistance to it must be integrated into our history courses.

Much is made in history teaching of stimulating children's curiosity and of developing their understanding of themselves and others. The connections between history as a subject and the formation of social attitudes can be seen by the fact that history is increasingly being called upon to help reinforce among youths the 'right' ideas about values, standards and responsibilities. We can use this trend to our advantage. By illustrating and examining the origins and historical development of sexual divisions, the teacher can provide an ideal milieu for an explanation of the current situation. The sexism of the past should, we believe, be presented to pupils in an open and critical manner, like every other aspect of human injustice. Efforts should be made so that boys do not 'switch off' when a topic involving women is being studied. The emphasis should be on the relationship between women and men, not 'women's history' and 'men's history' as separate categories.

History teaching could be educating children to understand the reasons why a non-sexist society is desirable. The gender stereotypes of man as hunter/warrior/worker, and woman as wife/mother/homemaker are oppressive. Girls, in particular, need to be shown that they cannot achieve their full human potential under such a system.

So far this section has been rather gloomy, pointing to faults and criticisms of present school history teaching. But the British education system presents less of a centralized monolith than that of some other countries. The child-centred and more progressive approaches in our schools have opened up opportunities for tackling sexism in history teaching. It is important, and possible, to provide young women with some information about women throughout history, about their struggles and triumphs as well as their grim conditions. It is also possible to provide both girls and boys with information which can help them to counter current stereotypes.

Towards an anti-sexist school history

In this section we discuss the restraints and possibilities facing the teacher who is persuaded that an anti-sexist history is an ideal worth aiming for.

The Restraints

'Hey, *Dad*, when was history?'
'It IS any time at all – in fact you are making a tiny part of history right now!'
'But I'm not famous, like *Richard the Lion Heart* fighting in the crusades.'
'That's true enough, but although normally you only hear about the famous people in the past, ordinary people *like us* have been making history all the while. In fact if you look carefully you will see history all around you.'
The boy was surprised by *his father's* answer, but history is all around just waiting to be noticed. Even people's surnames often tell part of the story about the work, home or characteristics of their *forefathers*.
(Pitcher and Harris, 1978, p. 6 – our emphasis)

These opening lines of a 'progressive' history textbook illustrate the androcentric tone of so much school history. Both the language and the content show the child that history is made by and for males.

The language which historians use to convey historical data into easily assimilated textbook form is not neutral. It plays a crucial role in the interpretation of history which the child learns. Most historians are men and the language they use (usually unconsciously) is male centred. Sexist language in history texts operates in a number of ways. First, simply by omitting women. Most vexing here is the use of 'men' or 'man' (see Chapter 4). To those who think this is carping consider the accuracy of the following:

> Cooking began thousands of years earlier, possibly when men found some animal roasted by forest fire. Later men learned to roast whole animals on a spit, turning the carcass from time to time to cook it evenly. When they could grow wheat, they ground the ears into flour with stones and baked rough bread.
>
> (Quoted in Adams, 1981, p. 24)

It is little help to change 'man' or 'men' to 'people' if the text still assumes that only the male of the species did anything significant. This only succeeds in keeping women invisible, or at best tagging them on as secondary. When they do appear women are too often portrayed as 'the wife of . . .', implying they are not important in their own right. R.J. Unstead's *Tudors and Stuarts* (1974) is a typical example, 'A merchant and his family . . .', 'A citizen's wife' (p. 33), and 'Everyone enjoyed himself on Mayday' (p. 42). In some instances this can completely distort the historical experience described. To read about 'Ancient Egyptians and their wives' entirely falsifies a situation where the marriage ceremony involved a man's promise to obey a wife, and inheritance in the earliest times was matrilineal.

Turning to content, one of the most striking aspects of history textbooks is their stereotyped image of women as full-time wives and mothers. For any period in human history you can find a text which states, in one way or another, that 'a woman's place was in the home'. L.F. Hobley's *Knowing British History 1900—1939* (1976) tells us that,

> At the beginning of the twentieth century the British family consisted of a father, who went out to work and earned the money, mother who looked after the home and their children. (pp. 30–31)

Hobley has oversimplified the facts and, as a result, distorted them. At no time in British history until the post-1945 economic boom have men, on the whole, earned enough to be the sole breadwinner of the average family. In 1900 only middle- and upper-class women and the wives of highly skilled craftsmen could stay at home and be economically inactive. The wives of the majority, i.e. semi- and unskilled men, took in washing and sewing and looked after lodgers. Many women also worked outside the home – in textiles, the sweated trades and many other occupations. Single working-class women were in an even worse position. Many were forced into domestic service.

In the interests of clarity, there is a tendency to exaggerate the division of labour between the sexes. As a result, the role of women as wage-earners has been almost entirely overlooked. An extension of this is the fact that when more advanced work is done on the history of the labour movement, pupils rarely learn anything about women and trade unionism, except perhaps for the match girls' strike of 1888.

There are many other aspects of 'school' history from which women's history is simply excluded. For example, descriptions of the mediaeval period devote a lot of space to the monastries and monastic life. The majority, however, fail to give more than a passing reference to nunneries. Education is another vastly neglected topic. *Ancient Egypt* by R.J. Sheppard (1960) contains information about the training of boys as scribes, but no mention is made of the education of girls, so the reader does not know whether or not girls in ancient Egypt learned to write. Then there are the number of school history books on wars, battles and armies which have an exclusively masculine orientation: DuGarde Peach's *William The Conqueror* does not mention women at all, nor do M. Gibson's *Knights and the Crusades* (1975) and B. Oakshott's *Dark Age Warrior* (1974). These books have an exceptionally narrow focus. This type of history may present an exciting story but it also glorifies war. Should we encourage schoolchildren to study wars and battles in isolation, without situating them in the social and economic context? Why are women in a period of war ignored?

Another feature of textbooks is the assumption that the nuclear family of mother, father and children is a stable institution, universal throughout human history. The family is not a natural, unchanging institution, based on human nature. It has a story of its own, which is very complicated and not yet fully known. The idea that women are inevitably destined for motherhood and men for fatherhood, renders invisible all those, including lesbians and gay men, who are not part of conventional families. Few books mention, for example, the persecution of lesbians and gay men by the Nazis. The full complexity of the history of sexuality may be difficult to convey to pupils, but some indication could be given, with examples, of the changing character of the family and of the many different family types which have existed in human history. At the moment, the way in which families are portrayed is unnecessarily simplistic and ahistorical. More importantly for us, it overemphasizes the role of woman as 'wife and mother' and conveys the idea that throughout human history women's primary identity has been that of wife and mother, as if this were her 'natural' and only function in life.

As we might expect, the illustrations in history textbooks, on the whole, reflect the narrative that they accompany. Thus, many of the sexist themes which we have examined receive amplification in the illustrative material. A more extreme version of this tendency is when women are not so much marginal characters, but written out of history altogether. It is not unusual for an illustration to include a couple engaged in some joint activity but for the caption to refer only to the man. Yet again, the reader gets the message that women are too insignificant to mention. However, quoting isolated examples of poor illustrative material does not adequately convey the cumulative effect of the hundreds of textbooks that rarely provide images of women amongst their visual representations of men making history.

Textbooks reflect the content of the examinations. There are so many different boards and syllabuses that it is difficult to generalize about this. One can say, however, that most GCE boards are fairly conservative, and are unwilling to step beyond the traditional bounds of male-dominated history. Many examination syllabuses (and therefore questions) carry the sexual bias which we have already examined, 'The attitudes of men in Britain to the problems of the empire . . .', etc. GCE 'O' and 'A' Level modern British history may contain a question on 'the emancipation of women' or, as it is sometimes put, 'the changed status of women'. London University 'A' Level British history 1815–1939 (syllabus B) sometimes (roughly once every three years) asks a question like this, 'What had been achieved by 1929 and what still remained to be achieved, towards the political and social emancipation of women?' (June 1975). This, and similar questions, have the advantage of not limiting themselves to suffrage, but asking candidates to bring in the wider factors. We should not, however, overestimate the 'women's history' component of this examination. This subject is one topic out of 40. Many teachers using this syllabus do not touch it at all.

If we look at non-British history papers, women are rarely mentioned in the questions. London University's 'A' Level paper on 'Europe of the dictators 1919–1941' covers the Russian Revolution, Stalin's Russia, Germany during the Weimar Republic and the Nazi era, the Italy of Mussolini, etc. Questions could have been set on many aspects of 'Women and the dictators', for example (a) What did the Russian Revolution achieve for women? (b) Were women better off under Stalin in the 1930s than they had been before 1929? (c) What did fascism in Germany mean for women? But, there has never been a question specifically on women, because they are not mentioned in the syllabus. Questions on such topics as artists, intellectuals and culture in Hitler's Germany have been set. Why are artists and intellectuals considered by the examiners to be more important than women?

The majority of pupils take the CSE exam. It provides for greater opportunity, through teacher control, of varying methods of examination: course work, orals, etc. Schools have been able to develop their own courses through mode 2 or mode 3. The more usual mode 1 exam treats world history as entirely separate from British social and economic history. Thus, while there is often a question on women in British society, or on the suffragettes, women do not exist in world political developments. Current proposals for the 16+ exam show no marked difference from the traditional approach, and as teacher control here will be replaced by 'mere consultation', the opportunity to develop an anti-sexist curriculum will be more limited.

The possibilities

Whilst not wishing to underestimate the problems that texts and examination syllabuses present to teachers, we do believe that much can be done in the classroom. From the first to third year teaching offers plentiful opportunity for developing an anti-sexist school history curriculum.

It may seem easier to accept classwork on wars and weapons because this seems popular with boys, while perhaps giving the girls a project on costume. But pupils may thus learn more about what present-day society expects of them, than of history and the lessons it can provide to help us understand and change society. Women's history is a part of a wider struggle to reclaim the experience of all oppressed sections of society. Jane Lewis (1981, p. 55) reflects on the recent emergence of women as a focus of historical enquiry:

> The fact that women's contribution to society had been ignored in the past made it easier to deny women's contribution in the present: it also helped to perpetuate woman's poor self image. Keenly aware of this, writers of the new women's history were fired with the dual purpose of 'restoring women to history and history to women' (Kelly-Gadol, 1976, p. 809). *Hidden from History* and *Becoming Visible* are two of the titles that reflect this preoccupation with discovering women's past (Rowbotham, 1973; Bridenthal and Koonz, 1977).

Six approaches

Anti-sexist history teaching cannot be developed unless pupils are given access to information about the role of women. The fact that no woman's name appears in a list of 'The immortals of history' may not strike anyone as strange unless they have been able to explore a little of women in history first. We cannot run before we can walk, nor can we hope to teach in the near future a history where the past concerns and actions of all the human race are covered adequately. But there are some positive steps that we can take to integrate aspects of women's history into existing courses. Below we outline six approaches for putting women back into the history curriculum. Each has advantages and disadvantages, but we think that they provide a useful framework by which teachers can measure their own awareness and responses to the challenge of history.[1]

Remedial

A heightened awareness of women's absence from courses may lead a teacher to plug in any information about women that is relevant and to hand. This should not appear as an artificial appendage, but should be integrated into the structure of the enquiry. For example, an analysis of the role of women in the Paris Commune of 1871 adds to a fuller understanding of the Commune as a whole.

Great women

Whilst it is important to portray a positive image of women, it is difficult to replace previously unquestioned facts about famous men with information on famous women. In a male-dominated world few women have reached the exalted heights of fame. Those who have may appear as freaks, unrepresentative of ordinary women. It is progress to include women like Boudicea in the syllabus; such women provide images which girls can at least begin to identify with, but this does not necessarily challenge assumptions and rarely allows a consideration of the dynamic between the sexes in history.

If there is to be an emphasis on heroines and notables, it might be as well to try to extend the range beyond the more commonly presented monarchs, philanthropists and novelists.

Oppression

Constant references to women's subordinate position in history may over-emphasize the image of women as victims, but this question will have to be tackled, because the constant presentation of positive images raises the question, 'Well, if women were so great why aren't we equal now?' Whilst it is important to present the restraints on most women's lives, it is nevertheless still possible to show them in most cases responding to those restraints with some degree of opposition or at least awareness.

Women in . . .

Turning to events already established as important and looking for women's contribution to them provides both riches and pitfalls. The contributions of women to art, science and politics, for example, are important to note but this genre is unlikely to establish new criteria for evaluating woman's historical achievement. Moreover, by singling out women we segregate them, distort their roles and the degree of their involvement.

Social history

This is probably the most common means of including women's experiences in history teaching. The development of social history from the 1960s has provided rich sources, and its apparent relevance has made it particularly acceptable to many teachers. Further, it allows teachers to widen their methods of teaching and use, for example, oral history and fictional work. The problem here is that the rich evidence on women's domestic lives will lead them to be once again segregated, this time in discussions of homes and families.

Political movements

Women's political activity can be presented simplistically, with reference to their involvement in suffrage and feminist movements alone. Whilst important, these should not be presented as comprising the totality of their political activity. Women have been involved in social movements including Chartism, temperance, bread riots and rent strikes, and in right-wing and left-wing movements.

Each teacher will use the strategy or combination of strategies with which she/he feels most comfortable. The exam syllabuses and textbooks may look impenetrable, but are never completely so. Much can be done, by our sensitive use of language, to make women, hitherto invisible, magically materialize on the pages of a text or worksheet. Even the youngest pupils are capable of discussing who decided 'man' should be the generic term, and why the simple question 'Who did the sewing?' asked of a class embroiled in the actions of the men depicted in the Bayeux Tapestry, shifts the emphasis and lifts women out of their seclusion. More difficult to deal with are the absent women: those areas and issues, like the oft-taught 'Voyages of discovery', that we know did not feature any females. Again, questioning the absence with a class is preferable to ignoring it.

In dealing with the past it is not always possible to apply the anti-sexist standards we would expect of modern writing. While modern writers all too often judge women's achievements by standards different from men's, e.g. 'for a woman, Ms G. has made a remarkable success of . . .', the total elimination of such wording when referred to historical achievements may be misleading. Florence Nightingale or Boudicea's achievements *were* remarkable given the contemporary restraints placed upon women and should be acknowledged as such.

From an American publisher came, ten years ago, a suggestion that might be usefully applied to history texts, and their use by teachers:

> If, after careful consideration, an editor finds it desirable to use selections that contain sexist attitudes, these attitudes should be discussed in accompanying descriptive material or discussion questions. Otherwise the text will convey to the reader the impression that sexism is socially acceptable, rather than a form of prejudice or a lack of sensitivity.[2]

Of course, we do want writers and publishers to change their sexist language and alter the text, but teachers and pupils live in a society where the media continues to promote sexist imagery and assumptions. So it becomes essential to teach a critical reading of both words and pictures. Carol Adams (1981, p. 24) has pointed the way forward:

> If women's history is seen only as a special study or is presented as just another version of events, passed on by the teacher, and as 'biased' in its way as the rest, then it has little to do with sound history teaching. Rather, we must continually encourage pupils to be critical and raise their awareness of the invisibility of women in the material they study.

Boys can sit through a whole series of lessons on women, noting down facts, and yet the teaching does not actually change their consciousness. It is still the teacher pouring out one form of 'propaganda' instead of another. This is why the learner must have an active role. Girls who have had the chance to develop their ideas can challenge the stereotypes of other pupils far more effectively than the teacher. For this reason history teachers cannot ignore the general ethos and organization of the school and what happens in other subject areas. Teachers cannot exist in a vacuum and, wherever possible, the history teacher must tackle sexism on a whole-school basis. Equal opportunity working parties and women's groups have been set up in secondary schools. The question has to be taken up in the teaching unions too. The NUT, for example, has pledged itself to positive action on women and the curriculum (see Chapter 21).

Within history specifically, the work set for pupils needs to follow the progressive/discovery model. Group work, where pupils can discuss together, is important and the sorts of task set need constant reviewing. Some boys will raise protests at being asked to put themselves in a woman's shoes. Here again the best approach is to ask the girls what it is like to constantly be asked to pretend that you are a man. This again depends on the class having a few confident and articulate girls, who can batter their way through the boys' objections.

The use of oral history is especially important for women's history as there is much less written about women than there is about men in the recent past. It can be a useful means of obtaining information about women since 1900. Questionnaires can be used, and older pupils could use cassette recorders, so that more accurate and detailed information can be obtained, and dialects recorded.

Examples from three schools illustrate the enormous potential of oral history. One class was asked to find out what life was like for their grandmothers when they were the same age as themselves. The respondents were asked about 'everyday topics like clothes, work, food, shopping, school, travel and entertainments'. The pupils wrote down the answers, and also collected so many different items of clothing and other objects that a class 'museum' was set up. In another school the teacher wanted to introduce the idea that 'Women have always worked'. The class was asked to find out what work their grandmothers did in the 1939–1945 war. There was some initial resistance from the boys, but this was soon overcome, and the class produced an enormous amount of information which they gathered into a highly informative book. In addition, the children learnt that women can do such jobs as engineering or mucky manual labour, which are often regarded as 'man's work'. In a third school, one result of the dialogue between the young women from the school and their mothers who had come to Britain from the Caribbean in the late 1940s and 1950s, was the production of a play examining their experiences – *Motherland*.[3]

What can teachers do about examination courses that emphasize economic, political or even military history? Just as a teacher can alert pupils to aspects of social history within the restraints of a syllabus covering, for example, 'Europe and the modern world 1870 to the present', so the same can be done with women's history. Mentioning women, however peripherally, is better than ignoring them altogether. Alternatives are beginning to appear. The London and Cambridge examination boards offer 'O' Levels with syllabuses covering women's rights in the 19th and 20th centuries. The recently introduced London Alternative 'O' Level exam is divided into a compulsory section and an option. One of the eight options is 'Women in Society in Britain since 1850'. The first part is on 'historical method and sources' and can roughly be described as the philosophy of history. The option on women has a very interesting syllabus, which includes topics such as women in education, literature, employment and entertainment and other aspects of the subject such as birth control. It stretches up to the present day and deals with the modern working woman and mother and with equal pay. History teachers in single-sex girls' schools may like to offer this course in addition to the traditional 'O' and 'A' Level history courses.

Mode 3 CSE examinations, which allow a particular school or consortium of schools to write their own syllabus, can tread beyond the scope of the traditional history exams, providing that they obtain the approval of the exam board. This could, in theory, allow considerable scope for a 'women's history' component. Loughton College of Further Education in Essex runs an Associated Examination Board mode 3 'O' Level history course (roughly 1850–1950) which takes the question of women's history seriously. Here are three of the questions which have recently been set on women:

1. What disadvantages did the working woman suffer in the 50 years before 1914 (a) In domestic service? (b) As manual workers in the manufacturing sector?
2. Briefly outline the main problems of women during the lifetime of any one of the following, discussing the contribution that she made to the lives of women: Caroline Norton, Elizabeth Garrett Anderson, Emmeline Pankhurst, Sylvia Pankhurst.
3. Why did the feminist (women's) movement grow up in the nineteenth century and with what issues were its campaigns concerned?

Other questions in the Loughton papers refer to 'she/he' or 'his/her', so that the dominant use of the male gender is avoided.

Thus history no longer appears as the lives of 'great men' and 'little women', but of society as a whole – both women and men. The Loughton mode 3 also includes a project (30 per cent of the total mark) and here again work on various topics in the history of women is strongly encouraged and there is a bank of resources (chiefly sets of articles) to facilitate this. Some CSE examinations are run along similar lines to the mode 3 'O' Level. It is theoretically possible, therefore, to introduce a considerable amount of material on women's history into these courses, both in formal classwork and in project work.

Resources

Again and again, teachers will be faced with areas, topics, patches, periods, eras, etc. where they will know little or nothing about women's lives. Ensuring some kind of equitable treatment looks, and unfortunately often may be, a gargantuan task. Below are some of the resources that teachers might seek.

Museums and galleries

The education departments of museums and galleries offer background information, materials and talks to school groups. Some have collections specifically relevant to women in history, and staff who are aware of women's absence from traditional history and who may be willing to give talks focusing on some aspect of women's lives in the past. It is well worth exploring the possibilities at your local museums and galleries.

Meetings and libraries

The isolation of teachers seriously hampers the production of good teaching materials. Organizing a group of like-minded teachers would be a useful way of sharing the work involved, and would be facilitated by approaching sympathetic LEA advisors and teachers' centres. For example, in East London a group of women teachers formed the Newham Teachers Women's History Group to solve problems of isolation and limited resources. They have close links with their local museum's extension services department, hold regular workshop sessions, and monthly open meetings with visiting speakers. They have produced teaching materials called 'What did you do in the war, mummy?', which are available for loan to primary and secondary schools.

If you live near a local feminist history group this could be a valuable way to increase your own knowledge of sexual divisions in history. Groups already exist in London, Birmingham, Liverpool, Manchester and Sheffield.

The two most comprehensive library collections on women's history are based at the Fawcett Library, City of London Polytechnic, Calcutta House, Old Castle Street, London E1 and at the EOC in Manchester. If you cannot visit them, both will be able to provide you with references for the topic that interests you.

Films, posters and books

Films

Coalmining Women (United States and Britain) 30 mins.
Donna (Women in the Italian Resistance) 64 mins.
Long Shadows of the Plantations (black women in the United States) 30
   mins.
My Survival as an Aboriginal 50 mins.
Some American Feminists (United States, 1960s) 55 mins.
Women of the Rhondda (Women in Welsh mining communities in the 1920s
   and 1930s) 20 mins.
Union Maids (textile workers in Chicago) 45 mins.
Swiss Graffiti (animated feminist history of Switzerland) 7 mins.
Rosie the Rivetter (women's work during World War Two, United States).
Contact: COW Films (Cinema of Women), 27 Clerkenwell Close, London
EC1, for details.

Posters

A two-part poster series on women and history is available from the Poster
Film Collective, BCM–PFC, London WC1N 3XX. Part I comprises 13
posters on topics which include feudalism, the age of science and reason, the
industrial revolution, the beginning of the modern state, women in the
1930s, women and fascism, women as a reserve army of labour, the welfare
state, and consumer society. Part II looks at aspects of the above in relation
to the present day.

Books and articles

We cannot provide a full bibliography here, but list below some of the most
useful and easily available material which is for use up to the sixth form.
There is still a dearth of accessible material other than that on European and
North American women in the 19th and 20th centuries.

Teaching methods

Sally Purkiss (1977) 'Oral history in the primary school', *History Workshop
   Journal*, no. 3.
Jane Lewis (1981) 'Women lost and found, the impact of feminism on
   history', in Dale Spender (ed.) *Men's Studies Modified* (Oxford, Pergamon Press).

Teachers' books

Margaret Barrow (1981) *Women 1870–1928: A Select Guide to Printed and Archival Sources in the UK* (London, Mansell).

Barbara Kanner (ed.) (1979) *The Women of England from Anglo-Saxon Times to the Present. Interpretive Bibliographical Essays* (Connecticut, USA, Archon Books).

Anna Davin (1979) *Women's History. WRRC Booklist No. 10*. An extensive reading list, restricted to European and American Studies, available free with s.a.e. from WRRC, 190 Upper St., London N1.

Gloria T. Hull, Patricia Bell Scott and Barbara Smith (eds) (1982) *All the Women Are White, All the Blacks Are Men, But Some of Us Are Brave, Black Women's Studies* (New York, The Feminist Press).

Sheila Rowbotham (1973) *Hidden From History* (London, Pluto Press).

Sheila Rowbotham (1972) *Women, Resistance and Revolution* (Harmondsworth, Penguin).

Jill Liddington, *Hurrah for Life in the Factory!* (A teaching pack of cassettes, photos and teaching notes on Lancashire mill women based on oral history, produced by Cotton Industry Records Project, Manchester Studies, Manchester Polytechnic, available on loan from Manchester Polytechnic library).

Eileen Power (1975) *Medieval Women* (Cambridge University Press).

Source material for use by pupils

Carol Adams (1982) *Ordinary Lives — A Hundred Years Ago* (London, Virago).

Votes for Women, folder of material available from the Museum of London.

Julia O'Faolain and Laura Martines (eds) (1973) *Not in God's Image* (London, Fontana).

Pupils' books

A. Turnbull, A. Davin and P. de Wolfe (1982) *Women with a Past: A Brief Account of some Aspects of Women's History* (Schools Council).

Lee Davidoff and Ruth Hawthorn (1976) *A Day in the Life of a Victorian Domestic Servant* (London, Allen and Unwin).

S. Raven and A. Wier (1981) *Women in History* (London, Weidenfeld and Nicolson). Short biographies of women from different countries.

A. Davin (1972) 'Women in history', in M. Wandor (ed.) *The Body Politic* (London, Stage I).

Notes

1   Glenda Riley first outlined these methods, with reference to North American courses, in 'Integrating women's history into existing course structures', *The History Teacher*, August 1979.

2   Sexism in Textbooks Committee of Women at Scott, Foresman and Company (1972) *Guidelines for Improving the Image of Women in Textbooks*.

3   Sally Purkiss, in 'Oral history in the primary school', *History Workshop Journal*, no. 3, spring 1977, describes the project on 'grandmother's childhood'. In 1979 Doreen Weston, a mature student at Avery Hill College, devised the project on women's work in the Second World War. *Spare Rib* no. 123, October 1982, and no. 124, November 1982, contain articles on *Motherland*.

CHAPTER 11

GEOGRAPHY

BREKKE LARSEN

Maps and chaps: invisible women in school geography

At first encounter, school geography appears to be neither a male nor a female subject. The subject's status in the pupils' minds (Hutt, 1979, p. 26) is only slightly weighted in favour of it being a boys' subject (*Fig.* 1). In most mixed schools there are both male and female geography teachers, not least to comply with fieldwork regulations. The teaching groups, even after option choices, are not noticeably imbalanced. The teaching materials are not obviously sexist. Therefore little work has been done to date on the sex differences in the geography curriculum.

On closer study it appears a bit like the myth of talkative women (Spender, 1980c, 1982a). We are in fact dealing with a subject in which women are largely invisible, and in which sex differences could be on the increase due to the changing style of teaching. Geography is chosen by fewer girls than boys, girls get relatively fewer top grades and more fail the subject altogether (*Table* 1). Although there are both women and men teaching the

Fig. 1 Geography as a subject for boys or girls or both

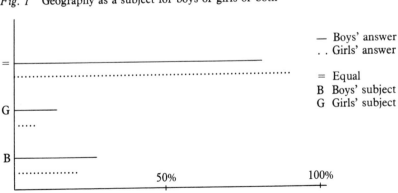

Source: Hutt (1979)

subject, there were, in 1980, only 2417 specialist graduate women compared with 4829 men (DES, 1980, vol. 4). The leaders within the subject are, not untypically, mostly men. Only 1 in 15 geography department heads in Cambridgeshire is a woman. The textbook writers, the college of education lecturers and, not least importantly, the chief examination officers, are men. Guess the sex of the Geographical Association lecturer who spoke of Swindon football club or of the examination officer who wrote the Cambridge 16+ paper (summer 1978) where the weather map question asked the pupils to forecast the weather for a cricket match. Who knows how wind speed and direction, humidity and cloud cover affect that game?

The subject has become dominated by the male view and perception of the world. The subjectivity of perceptions has led to a prevalence of male preoccupations and criteria of relevance. Is shopping a leisure activity or a chore? What is it to work? What is development? Men and women may not answer these questions in the same way. The male bias is highlighted by book titles where the word 'man' appears. It is as if in a subject that tries to generalize and discuss norms, the norm has become male; this is particularly worrying in the light of the subject's movement towards a more personal view of geography and away from impersonal global views.

Combined with this development is another movement towards a less

Table 1   Numbers and results of pupils (boys and girls) taking CSE and 'O' Level geography (1975–1980)

| | | CSE | | |
	Entries	**Grade 1** (%)	**Grades 1–5** (%)	**Increase** (1975–1980)
Boys	103 938	14.38	91.59	30.6
Girls	89 135	12.73	91.71	30.0

| | | 'O' Level | | | |
	Entries	**Grade A** (%)	**Grades A–C** (%)	**Unclassified** (%)	**Increase** (1976–1980)
Boys	110 045	9.86	57.32	14.37	13.2
Girls	88 144	9.05	53.26	17.20	8.3

Source: DES, *Statistics of Education* (1980). Reproduced by permission of the Controller of HMSO.

balanced subject away from the guided geography lesson which girls like and towards testing methods where girls score less well. Geography is running the risk of becoming yet another male subject.

The clearest representative of the world of women is shown in Peterson et al. (1978) (*Fig. 2*) where the different ways women and men perceive their world are depicted. I suggest that as geographers we should aim at a square, or put equal value on all levels of the triangles.

Geography as a school subject

It is difficult to show the connection between the maleness of school geography and its choice of materials, and the uptake and success rate of girls at external examination level. There are too many other variables at the time of choosing options. What can be shown is that girls are disadvantaged

Fig. 2   Differing ways in which women and men perceive their world

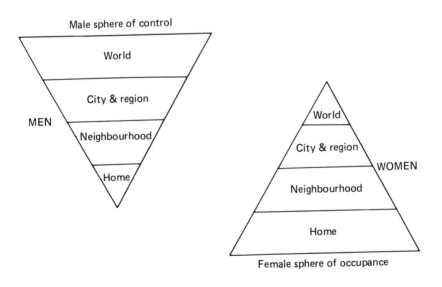

by gender differences in learning style, in the type of classroom practices on which geography relies, and in the type of geography being taught. The development of the school discipline at present is away from the type of geography where girls would do better both in examination syllabuses and lower school courses. A main area of difference is that of mapwork, which makes up a very large part of any geography syllabus. Girls like it less than boys do (Long, 1970; Bartlett, 1979) and do less well at it (Peterson, 1971; Broadman and Towner, 1979).

In classes where teacher interactions with the pupils are frequent the girls' poor self-image and lack of confidence allow them as little as 25 per cent of the teacher's time (see Chapter 3). The interaction pattern of discussion and problem solving, such a dominant feature of modern geography, is a further area where girls are less confident (Carey, 1958).

Physical geography includes several areas of disadvantage to girls. Long (1953) showed that fear is a common reaction of girls to pictures of physical landscapes. Girls have smaller home territories (Saegert and Hart, 1978), they are not encouraged to roam and explore their home environment, especially the so-called 'wildscapes'. Fewer girls than boys know the local river from fishing there, and in my own area, few girls in the first-year intake have cycled as far as our only 1:10 gradient hill five miles away, whereas the boys have often cycled there. Physical geography also includes the problems of fieldwork. Interestingly, the Australian survey of teaching style preferences (Bartlett, 1979) shows fieldwork at the top of the list for both boys and girls. In Britain, fieldwork for the urban girl probably involves not having the correct clothes, so she may get wet, her shoes may not give support, her trousers may be too tight and make walking uphill and climbing over fences difficult. It spoils the day. Getting dirty and looking bulky is something she is not normally encouraged to do and like. When these restrictions are combined with the fear of unknown and empty spaces (possibly linked with rape fears and with being brought up not to speak to strange men), then it is not surprising that fewer girls than boys choose to go on fieldwork excursions and often enjoy it less, and get less out of it in terms of geographical learning.

Modern geography is scientific in its methods and relies heavily on numeracy, a disadvantage to the girls. Geography in the past relied more on neatness, hard work and a good memory. Now it is a question of finding solutions to problems using a multitude of resources: graphs, maps, interviews, knowledge of the home environment. Could this be partly why girls are doing less well? As the subject has become more scientific it has moved away from the traditional testing methods of the essay, to objective tests. Murphy (1982) showed a greater descrepancy in the AEB 'O' Level geography results of girls and boys after objective testing had become part of the examination style.

In the last decade a new style of enquiry method has been filtering into schools in a more personalized, more human perception-based geography. This new style of geography could be an improvement, from a feminist point of view. We have, as geographers, started to look at the various value systems imbedded in our geographies; imperialist, racist, marxist, eurocentric, etc., but so far little attention has been paid to the female perception of the world; this can be remedied. Reading a book like *Women's Worth* by Leghorn and Parker (1981), would show that the value system of women and their sense of place are very different from those of men. It points out that the woman's world is smaller, poorer and far less concerned with measurable quantities. Women are less likely to see cost and speed as prime considerations when, for example, choosing a location. Human well-being is a major concern, and development is not seen in terms of steelworks, etc. Therefore it is important that positive moves are made to make the school subject less male dominated – to make more women speak and give more prominence to women's values and concerns.

Mapreading

Whichever style of geography the pupils study, the spatial component through mapwork remains. In a way this is the trademark of the subject. It is therefore disturbing that girls as a rule are less competent map users, and find maps less interesting. In most external exams one-eighth of the marks come from a compulsory Ordnance Survey map question. As much as 40 per cent of the total marks may derive from mapwork in some form or other (atlas work, remembering places to be named on a blank map and the general visual memory for the spatial relationship between places).

Mapreading is a very complex skill. Apart from the mathematical skills in measuring and calculating distance, counting in contour intervals, etc, it is mostly a spatial visualization competence. Psychologists have got much mileage out of debating whether such skills are innate and sex linked or learned differentially depending on gender, or whether there is no difference at all between the sexes. For geographers the main areas of concern can be seen in two studies (Peterson, 1971; Broadman and Towner, 1979) which attempt to establish in which areas of mapreading the differences occur.

Broadman and Towner's study involved fifth-year CSE and 'O' Level pupils in tests based on standard examination questions from an Ordnance Survey map with an aerial photograph of part of the same area. The test involved four sets of tasks: (a) imagining relief from contours; (b) relating photo and map; (c) relating a cross-section with the map; (d) route description. The girls did less well than the boys on virtually all tasks and at all ability levels. They scored particularly badly on direction, relating photo to map (orienting) and on route description. The test left out those map-reading skills which are mainly dependent on memory, for example map symbols, and those dependent on mathematical skills, for example using scale and grid references. The girls stated they did not like mapwork and that they did not use maps outside school as much as boys did.

The Swedish study examined pupils from 7–15 through the compulsory school years. It was concerned with general map skills such as knowing where places were on a map, projections, townplan use, position, etc. In most tasks the boys again did better. Sonia Peterson's explanation of these differences involved the experiences with which the pupils start their mapreading course, their outside interests and the TV programmes they watched, as well as society's expectations of them. The study further showed improvement of map competences with age and teaching.

In the psychology debate, Sherman (1978) states convincingly that there is no conclusive proof of innate spatial ability differences. She points out that the standard test of spatial ability, the 'frame and rod test', is a test carried out in a dark room, often by a male tester and involving the girl being assertive, insisting that the rod is not yet straight; hardly conditions where a girl would perform best! She also points to the connection between spatial ability and the general life-style of boys involving more movement, and to the later maturation of spatial competence in girls. She finally states that spatial ability in girls frequently is not developed to its full potential.

The relevance of these studies to geography teachers is manifold. At the very least it is reassuring that map competence is subject to training, but more than that, it seems it is subject to outside factors such as the area pupils use around their home, and how far they may go on their own; and how often they use maps in other situations. The most concrete area where we as teachers may be able to improve the girls' performance is by considering carefully when we introduce mapwork, the extent to which we repeat using it and the scale and size of maps we use. What must also be considered is that the girls must not be put in a failure position. A task should not be considered taught when in a mixed group a reasonable number of pupils have grasped it, that is all the boys and a few of the girls. If teachers are aware that girls are more likely to have problems in understanding an area of work, they should pay more attention to them. Girls are quite capable of learning mapwork but may need extra encouragement and time.

Since spatial competence is transferable from one area of life to others, the importance of mapreading to girls has wider implications. Unlike maths and science where spatial skills are also important, geography does not have the label against it 'girls are no good at geography'. So the girls might learn spatial competence for other areas of life, through learning mapwork which may be transferable.

Geographical teaching resources

Geography is not a subject where one takes a textbook and starts on page 1 working on to page 253 by the end of the year. A multitude of different resources will be used, ranging from newspaper articles, video-taped TV programmes, interviews and surveys, e.g. of classmates, Sunday colour magazine articles, leaflets from travel agents, aid organizations and town planning departments, and statistical materials from the HMSO. Text-books, as such, may only form a small part of these resources and many pupils will in their lower school years not use any textbooks but rely on worksheets produced by their teacher or the school geography department.

My knowledge of what goes on in schools other than my own is mostly obtained from printed textbooks. I made a small survey of some current textbooks for the captive audience in geography – 11–14-year-olds and the 14–16 exam groups. Books suited to the types of aspects of geography most commonly studied had the following main topics:

– Mapreading
– British Isles (home region, industry, farming, power, settlement)
– Developing world contrasted with a developed region, e.g. Europe (farming, population issues, industrialization, urbanization, health and migration)
– Landforms and weather study.

These revealed some recurring biases that could be classified as sexist or sex biased. I feel most of these errors stem from unawareness and ignorance rather than from any serious intent to keep women down.

I have already pointed to the prevalence of titles which include the word 'man', not least stemming from the educational initiative of the Geography

Department of the London Institute of Education with their 'man environment' approach to geography. 'Man' was a generic term but research has shown that it is losing that place fast so that 'man' now means 'male' and 'he' does not mean 'she' (see Chapter 4). (Sorry colleagues!)

Geography relies heavily on the pictorial aspect of learning and the absence of pictures of women is a serious shortcoming of most books. When present they are often ornamental rather than active. Women are mostly shown in stereotyped roles as pretty receptionists, dressed up for the photographer, for example doing farm work in party dress, or pushing prams. *A Sense of Place* (1980) has as many as six photos of women and prams!, but few of women in other roles. This does not support the teacher's attempt to encourage the girls to take a more involved role in the world around them, to see that motherhood only lasts a few years and that it is important to want to do more than marry and have children. The pictures do not help to highlight the relevance of the topic to the lives of women. *Maps and Mapping* (p. 2) shows five different groups of people using maps, all men. As that book is written by a woman let it be clearly stated that awareness of sex bias is not itself related to sex! Even in areas where women traditionally are active in the economy, e.g. market gardening, bush fallow, Third World farming and the textile industry, textbook pictures are often of men.

The assumption that social life in the Third World is similar to that in Europe leads to errors. That this ignorance can have expensive consequences was seen in the World Health Organization in Upper Volta where an attempt to increase subsistence crop production failed for the simple reason that the project addressed itself to the men. *Oxford Geography Project 3*, in its chapter on Third World farming, has no picture and no hint of the very substantial part played by women in agriculture there. In its dealings with cash versus subsistence crops, it does not mention the way increased cash crop production in the hands of men has led to the women having to walk further to the food fields, that the women have to do more of the food farm work than before, as men are too busy, and that the women and their children as a rule get little benefit from the cash that mainly goes on consumer goods, transistor radios and cycles, if not cigarettes for the men.

The male workplace of the steelworks, the coal mine and the car plant seems ever present along with the various types of power production plant. I asked some teenage girls to look through a few of the books I am looking at here; it seemed that if the initial chapters were on those male topics, they classified the books as books for boys. I remember the afternoon when I did yet again shopping as part of the GYSL (Geography for the Young School Leaver, Schools Council Project) unit on 'Cities' and the boys were restless and less responsive than normal; one boy finally said: 'this is for girls' and started telling me how he hated shopping. Girls switch off more quietly and are not conditioned to expect the lessons to be of relevance to their lives (see Chapter 3). At least we could include the locational factor 'the steelworker spouse' in the treatment of side industries in, for example, Scunthorpe in *Eastern England, 1976* (p. 17). The mention of decline of these male industries is today part of most geography lessons. However, we do not help prepare the pupils for the problem of ego loss men face in families, e.g. in the North-East where the woman is the main breadwinner. We should give more attention to the importance of the female workforce also from that point of view.

What happened to the married woman's property act? In the sample studies we read of the farmer – Mr Bloggs and his family – it has disappeared. Coming from a rural background I am not so sure this represents Mrs Bloggs' contribution fully. I am still looking for a sample study of a farm, where that team effort is made clear. Is it not part of our study to show in some way how domestic life differs between farm and suburban terrace? Statistics are partly to blame, as female spouses are not counted in the employment figures.

In settlement geography, we study planning for leisure – leisure as defined by men. Amanda, in response to a question about the provision for leisure, which contained a photograph of a cramped Victorian inner-city terrace, said that she did not know what clubs and other activities were inside the houses, while Peter spoke naturally of the lack of outdoor play-space. Girls must learn that leisure space means male leisure space if they are to succeed. Would you give marks for mentioning the High Street as a leisure space? For many girls Saturday shopping is a main leisure activity; although men would not define it as such.

Population geography presents problems of its own. Family planning is a topic still not touched on in some schools. One is easily left with the impression that it is women who are to blame for the population growth. The impression that family planning is only a female concern is given by pictures of women queueing and a women's sterilization team, in *Sense of Place 3*. In other ways population pyramids offer a good discussion basis for the differences in life pattern between men and women and between women here and in the developing countries.

A very gentle but nonetheless harmful type of sex bias is found in the way books introduce and develop a topic. A great number of authors start with large-scale studies and generalized views of the topic. Bearing in mind that our teenage girls have a small-scale conceptual world, the teaching materials we give them must start at a scale which they can manage to visualize, and then move on. I am not suggesting here that we should not teach the girls to have a bigger world, but so many topics, like *Patterns in Geography I* (N. Farleigh Rice, Longman, 1975, p. 42) start by drawing a large map of the South-West peninsula and then proceed to fill in relevant information in relation to, for example, dairy farming. Why not start with the milk on the doorstep and move on from there?

Simulation games have shown themselves to be a very effective way of teaching inter-relationships of geographical factors as well as promoting decision-making abilities. Sadly many of the games are presented with roles with names on but usually the only female roles are mums and housewives. This last example in a way highlights the risks carried within the new, more humanized geography compared to its traditional dehumanized predecessor. Fifty-one per cent of the population is female and what women do is *not* unimportant and is not restricted to domestic roles only. It is no better to show passive women than to show invisible women. It is not enough to present women in stereotyped roles only.

Several of the relief aid organizations provide leaflets on the position of women and the *New Internationalist* considers the position of women as one of their criteria by which to assess Third World countries' degree of development. The demand for visible women in textbooks must not be allowed to result in a separate chapter. Colin Ward's book *The Child in the City* has one chapter out of 20 called 'The girl in the background'. Bearing the 51 per cent figure in mind, something is wrong. What we need is women integrated and not seen as a separate issue.

Reducing sex bias

There are three areas in school geography where a gender imbalance shows up; women are invisible, the point of view is male and the scale of study is too global. All these could easily be balanced up with a minimum of extra work. The most important step towards getting the correct gender balance is a general educational rather than a specific geographical one. Make the lesson equally geared to boys and girls, and make sure that 50 per cent of the involvement in the lesson comes from the girls. A student teacher once took my class. Initially the girls put up their hands to answer questions; when they realized they would not be asked, they stopped participating. It is, by the way, more work to teach 30 active pupils than just 15. The girls may not all like to have demands made on them if they are not used to it, but one thing I am sure of, they will not say 'that teacher only cares about the boys', a comment I have often heard from teenage girls. Remember to praise girls for the content of their work, and not just for presentation; tell them when the content is weak, since only then will they know what we expect from them.

When considering women in the content of the lessons I am not in favour of lessons of the type 'women in . . .' etc. I want to integrate a female view into all lessons, and not see women as a separate issue. To suggest a few ways where this can be done, a 30-second comment within the usual lesson will often suffice:

- In Southern Italy there are many one-parent families due to male migration to the North European industrial areas.
- Swedish and North American women work underground in mines but may not do these best-paid jobs in Britain.
- West African farmers are not men; subsistence farming and the retailing of food products is in the hands of women.
- A well-planned town, from the homeworking spouse's point of view, has day-time social space.
- A city environment has dark, lonely roads at night. Consider lack of rape fears, public transport facilities late at night and street lighting provision as some of the criteria for a good environment.
- In towns where a traditional heavy (male) industry dominates, labour-intensive industries have followed to be near the female workforce.
- Use fashion trade to show the extent of the town centre.
- The micro-electronics industry in South-East Asia owes its existence not least to the women there; their hands are smaller than ours and they expect less diversity in life!
- The 'Oilies' in Peterhead bring change to the lives of teenage girls, who will be a scarce 'commodity' and will perhaps move far away if they marry.
- What constitutes an area of high unemployment is determined largely by *male* unemployment. In Washington New Town, there is relatively low unemployment among women.
- If you devise a simulation exercise, make some of the important roles, such as chief planning officer, female.

There is a growing list of geography studies on women at the more academic level. The Women in Geography group at the Geography Department of Reading University monitors this and also keeps in contact with the Association of American Geographers, a similar but much older group. There is now a long bibliography on women in geography. Six units for use at lower university and sixth-form level with a gender-balanced slant have been developed, e.g. an analysis into women's dependence on childcare and public transport as a limiting factor in their job searches. This will also help raise teachers' awareness.

The type of geography promoted via the three projects 'Geography 16–19', 'Geography 14–18' and GYSL is excellent for developing and spreading new ideas. The projects bring teachers together to produce their own materials and to discuss how best to teach. They all rely on a wide range of teaching styles and resources, using both small- and large-scale studies. In the examination set for GYSL, there is no longer a compulsory mapwork section, and there is in some cases a 50 per cent teacher-marked school-based assignment or project component. These assignments are frequently based on small-scale local studies relevant to the interests and experiences of teenage girls, and help the pupils to generalize about the known, and then use these generalizations in a global context. The drawback of these assignments may be that they require an assertive questioning of the environment. The girls' upbringing may not have prepared them for this, and they may need more encouragement and guidance, initially, than the boys, to learn to work independently and to draw their own conclusions.

On a practical level, fieldwork and local surveys should be started as early as possible with pupils, and not introduced for the first time in the fourth year when external exams require it, by which time the girls will be more self-conscious and 'ladylike'. If the PTA could provide fieldwork kits, this would help enlarge the girls' perspective, and provide them with future leisure activities. Do not make the fieldtrip an endurance test in speed and length. Lagging behind, out of breath, is guaranteed to make a teenager feel fat, inadequate and impossible.

Teachers should also try to build on the experiences, interests and expectations of teenage girls. The justifications for teaching geography are as relevant to girls as to boys:

– Map reading is a survival skill.
– Spatial competence acquired in map reading may be transferred to other subjects.
– A well-planned environment is formed by the contribution of many

different types of people.
- Everyone should understand that resources are limited.
- Empathy and understanding for people in other countries are the foundation for peace.
- Pupils learn through their geographical education to make decisions in their own lives.

We do not wish to reinforce the stereotyped images of 'macho' man and cocooned, home-based woman, but to make all pupils aware of the whole spectrum of environmental factors, without emphasizing or ignoring any of the pupils' initial preoccupations and interests. For too long we have underplayed the girls' contribution and have almost shown contempt for their smaller world. When women refer to real-world examples we tend to regard this as an anecdote; yet when men do the same we probably call it a case-study.

Resources

There are no non-sexist geography teaching packs yet available, but the Women and Geography Study Group (contact through the Geography Department, University of Reading), are collecting material for a basic feminist geography text, and would welcome contributions. The two main areas of work so far are development and settlement geography, and the following list provides some suggestions for further reading.

Women and Geography (1982), vol. 6, no. 3 'Progress in human geography' – a 40-page account by three authors reviewing the present work within the topic.
Journal of Geography (1978), vol. 77, no. 5 – a complete issue on feminism in geography and geography teaching.
Perspectives on Women and Geography (1982), Geography Dept., Special Paper, University of Reading, 'Sexism in geography education, by John Bale, in A. Kent (ed.) (1982) *Bias in Geography Education*. University of London, Institute of Education.

On a more specific level, the following are good 'eye-openers' and possible sources of lesson materials:

M.F. Loutfi (1980) *Rural Women, Unequal Partners in Development*. Geneva, ILO.
Barbara Rogers (1980) *The Domestication of Women*. London, Kogan Page.

L. Leghorn and K. Parker (1981) *Women's Worth*. London, Routledge and Kegan Paul.

S. Ardener (ed.) (1981) *Women and Space*. London, Croom Helm.

R. Peterson (1982) 'Women and environments', *Environments and Behaviour*, December 1928, pp. 511–534.

Stimpson C.R. et al., (1980) *Women and the American City*. University of Chicago Press.

Women in the 80's, CIS Report, spring 1981 – about women at work in Britain today.

R. Hudson (1980) 'Regional development policies and female employment', *Area* vol. 12, no 3. He does write, however, that women only work to pay household bills!

The New Internationalist, summer 1980 – two issues on women. They use women's position as one criterion for assessing the quality of life in a country.

Oxfam and Christian Aid produce materials with 'visible' women. Often sample studies dealing with women are to be found in social anthropology:

World Bank (1979) *Recognizing the Invisible Women in Development*.

Christian Aid (1975) *Man's World, Woman's Work*.

D. Elson and R. Pearson (1981) 'Nimble fingers make cheap workers', *Feminist Review* vol. 7, spring 1981, pp. 87–107.

CHAPTER 12

SOCIAL STUDIES

JANIE WHYLD

Nature and status

Social studies is not an obviously sexist subject. Girls like it, it is people orientated, it is frequently taught by women, and is usually assessed using essays and projects, at which girls do well, rather than the objective tests which they find more difficult (Murphy, 1982). Yet it is not a 'girls' subject', like domestic science. The reputation which sociology often has, for being left-wing and 'subversive', for example regarding its analysis of poverty and delinquency, may lead people to assume that all areas of oppression are confronted with equal critical awareness. In school, social studies is the slot in the curriculum where pupils are most likely to be encouraged to notice the power structures which affect their lives; and even in some cases to analyse and evaluate the school hierarchy. Almost all social studies courses pay some attention to the changing role of women (though not of men), to gender socialization and to the requirements of the Sex Discrimination Act. However, it would be facile to argue that because the issue of sexism is raised, social studies is no longer sexist. This chapter looks at the subtle ways in which the sociological approaches most often used at secondary school level include sexist assumptions about the characteristics and behaviour of women and men; and suggests ways of introducing pupils to a study of society without enforcing these assumptions.

According to Lukes' survey of social studies in Humberside schools (Lukes, 1979) there is an enormous variation in what counts as social studies, and topics taught range from health and sex education, through aspects of psychology and sociology, to economics, welfare problems and civil rights. In relatively few courses is the structure of social institutions, and therefore of the dominant ideology, critically examined. Dr Lukes suggests that in many courses there is an emphasis on personal and social problems (e.g. drugs, vandalism, unemployment, divorce, homelessness) because these are seen as 'relevant' to pupils, who are themselves regarded as potential social problems. This approach treats women who work, leaving children unattended, as a problem, rather than the society which fails to provide adequate childcare and thus denies women the right to work and to financial independence. It may label women 'irresponsible' if they do work.

The status of social studies varies considerably. The present government leaves us in no doubt of their views on the merits of sociology with massive cuts in their grants to the SSRC. In schools which have departments of sociology, and where sociology 'A' Level is offered as a sixth-form option, the status of the subject will be high. However, in many schools, social studies is made 'invisible' by its inclusion in other subjects, and only surfaces in its own right as a CSE option, as a timetable filler for non-examinees, or 'what's done by those pupils who are no good at foreign languages' (Lukes, 1979, p. 53). Certainly, at one school where I taught, community studies was reserved for fifth-form ROSLA girls, with the latent objective of getting them out of the staff's way for a while.

Tied in with the status of social studies is the question of how it is taken up by the sexes; the breakdown by sex of GCE entrants in 1979 is shown in *Table* 1.

Table 1   Breakdown by sex of GCE entrants for social studies examinations (1979)

	1 'O' Level (Summer 1979)	
	Total entry	Pass grades (%)
Boys	10 862	45.4
Girls	27 604	51.6

	2 'A' Level (Summer 1979)		Grades				
	Total entry	Passes (%)	A	B	C	D	E
Boys	5 038	45.9	3.4	5.0	9.0	14.7	13.9
Girls	10 758	51.2	3.3	6.5	9.9	16.6	15.2

Source: DES, *Statistics of Education* (1979). Reproduced by permission of the Controller of HMSO.

At 'O' Level, well over twice as many girls as boys take sociology, and there is a higher percentage pass rate. Relatively fewer girls go on to take 'A' Level, reflecting the fact that girls are less likely than boys to continue study of the subject after the age of 16, but there are still twice as many girls as boys taking social studies at 'A' Level. Figures are not available for non-examination courses, and the proliferation of CSE courses with their diversity of content makes analysis cumbersome, but in schools I surveyed, social studies was taught either to an equally mixed class or to more girls than boys. The affinity of social topics such as family, methods of childcare, education and housing to the 'feminine' role of caring, and the fact that social studies at 'O' Level and below is a non-technical, non-numerical subject where the assessment depends on verbal ability and ease of expression, is likely to make social studies a popular choice with girls. Not unrelated to this is the fact that it has low employment currency. In technical colleges, whereas sociology is taught at 'O' and 'A' Level to mixed groups, social studies is concentrated in female courses such as nursery nursing and pre-nursing. So, in many cases, social studies is a low-value option for girls.

Syllabus content

Since the contents of social studies courses are so variable, I shall deal with any topic which may be included in social education courses, and which shows particular sexist bias. It may seem that I am concentrating on the 'worst' aspects of social science teaching and theory. To a certain extent this is true, and I do not intend to imply that all social science is taught in such a sexist manner. The analyses of sexist bias in this chapter should be familiar to anyone who has undertaken a higher level social science course within the last few years, but not every teacher has qualified so recently; and given the nature both of the teaching profession, and of social studies, there will be many people teaching social studies who are not qualified sociologists. There is also the problem of assessing how much work from university level filters through to the school classroom. While recognizing that feminist perspectives in sociology are being extensively developed in higher education, I have taken as my guide to what is being taught in schools the material and exercises produced in the most popular school texts.[1]

Structural functionalism, the perspective still most commonly adopted for secondary school sociology,[2] is inherently sexist. 'Actors' in the system are male. Women are expected to be passive and supportive of male actors. Women who become 'actors' and compete with men, instead of sharing their man's success, are disruptive, dysfunctional. The differences between the sexes are functional, helping to maintain society which, based on such institutions as the family, naturally tends towards an equilibrium. Social stability is emphasized at the expense of social change – which bodes ill for those who are not satisfied with society as it is. Jane Thompson (1980) challenges this view nicely in her 'O' Level textbook: 'Sociologists (who predict the death of the family) . . . usually ask what the effects of the increasing emancipation of women from the role of housewife and mother will be on the domestic arrangements in the home and the care of children rather than why the woman should still be assumed to have the major responsibility for childminding and housecleaning' (p. 47).

The above quote also illustrates how it is possible to introduce simply the concept of perspectives. Although a knowledge of perspectives is not required for CSE or 'O' Level, and my colleagues shy away from dealing with them, I think it is worth while trying to give pupils at least the understanding that there are a variety of ways of interpreting any one piece of behaviour. This in itself leads them to start questioning the normality of conservative, consensus judgements, which form the basis of gender stereotyping. I limit the perspectives I describe to evolutionary, functionalist, conflict and an interactionist approach. I give a brief outline of each, usually choosing to describe Marx's theory of social development from feudalism to communistic anarchy, and pointing out what an interactionist would look for in a conversation between teenage boys and girls.[3]

This could be a suitable point to introduce some explanation of women's inferior position in society, comparing the structural analyses of women's oppression (Marx, Rich, Delphy) with theories which place greater emphasis on cultural factors such as language and knowledge (Spender, 1980c, 1981a, b) and mythology (Figes, 1970; Daly, 1978).

I would illustrate the difference between consensus and conflict interpretations by example: why does a wife get her husband's meal ready? (duty; her role; loves him; he earns money, she serves – or fear of husband withholding money, or violence). I check pupils' grasp of perspectives with an exercise where they are asked to identify people talking from the different perspectives.[4] A similar exercise would be to present pupils with a summary (very simple, of course) of different approaches to one topic, discuss these, and then ask them to classify excerpts from books or newspapers.[5]

A problem which many social studies teachers seem to share is the lack of intellectual inspiration needed to translate a perspective only encountered in academic jargon into terms which fourth-year pupils can understand. It is easy to slip into the functionalist approach because there is so much material already prepared in textbooks – most of us have had our basic grounding in sociology in functionalism – and it lends itself to lists of points and diagrams of structures, which are a standard teaching technique. A non-structuralist approach would allow pupils to draw more on their own experience, and see that as being important in defining what counts as knowledge (thus challenging our male-defined culture). A phenomenological approach would be to examine what is taken for granted; for example, how do individual families develop a sense of 'our family'? Pupils could be asked to notice differences in relationships in friends' homes.

The structural functionalist approach seriously hinders a sympathetic study of the family. 'Normal' families are either extended working-class kinship groups, or geographically mobile nuclear units, with a working dad, and a mum at home looking after the children or in part-time work. Dual-career families, single-parent families, people in larger groups not related by blood, like communes, childless couples and people who live alone are seen as exceptions;[6] their families have either not yet formed or have broken down. The concept of set roles leaves no room for the possibility that men and women may supplement each other, and change according to moods, the father sometimes disciplining the child, for example, and the mother at other times. Even in the relatively progressive study of dual-career families by Rapoport and Rapoport (1971), babies are referred to as belonging to the woman, not to both parents.

The movement of women into the labour force is frequently mentioned, but not that of men into women's work, e.g. nursing and full-time parenthood, despite the fact that one in ten single parents is a man. Gillespie-Woltemade (1978) suggests ways in which men would benefit by sharing conjugal roles. They would no longer need to bear sole responsibility for providing financially for the family. They would become more independent by learning how to cook and care for themselves (and others). Childcare would bring them more in touch with their emotions. However, where the man sharing in the housework is mentioned, it is usually noted as helping the woman by lightening her responsibilities, and not as benefiting the man.[7] Rapoport (1978) suggests that in studying the family, less attention be paid to patterns of activity – who does what and for how long – and more attention concentrated on what partners feel about what they do: do men like working, and looking after children? Do women like shopping, and having children?

When I teach 'the family', I try to get pupils to explore the concept. Sometimes I provide them with a variety of source material, e.g. Thompson (1980) or *People Talking: Family Life* (see 'Resources') and ask them to list as many different family groupings as they can, also drawing from their own experience. This should provide a wide range, from which we conclude that it is not possible to define family by membership alone. Alternatively, I may start by asking pupils to name who they count as their family. Some of them will immediately include relatives who do not live with them, others will not, so introducing the 'unit family'. One pupil spoke of how her family's relationship with the older brother gradually changed as first he went to work away from home, but still counted as being a half-member of the family, and later dropped from family membership when he married, and formed major allegiances elsewhere. Using 'living together' as a basis, we go on to look at how related you have to be – by blood, married, 'living in sin' (at what age, and for how long?), adopted, fostered, lodging – and whether there have to be children (young couple living together; old couple, child-less, or whose children have moved away; and the requirements for obtaining council housing when homeless). We compare people who have chosen to live together, from families to communes, to people living in institutions, and compile a list of common features and differences: eating together; sharing income, resources and skills, sexual relationships; providing material, physical and emotional support for all members; and rearing children. We find that 'traditional families' and other living groups equally show most of the characteristics, although few show all. Single parents and many married couples do not have a sexual relationship within the group, many couples do not have children, extended family groups do not usually eat together or share income. The information collected is sufficient to answer questions on the functions of the family, if they arise in an examination, without giving the impression that one type of family is more proper or desirable than another.

Following on from 'the family', socialization provides an excellent place for looking at the development of gender identity. There are now many excellent teaching materials available which are designed to stimulate pupils to challenge gender stereotypes and the inequalities of power between the sexes (see 'Resources'). A common way of starting 'gender' is to make pupils aware of their own dependence on stereotyping by looking at jokes or riddles, which are based on gender confusion, such as the one about the woman surgeon,[8] or by checking pupils' own stereotypes. Ask them to jot down their mental image of several, sex-typed occupations – doctor, secretary, canteen assistant – and compare results. Check for age, sex and race stereotyping.

The questionnaires developed by GIST (see 'Resources') to check on the home background, aspirations and attitudes of the pupils taking part in their intervention project (see Chapter 7) could be used at the start of a lower-school social studies course. They cover a wide range of gender-linked activities such as 'who usually does what in the home', to attitudes about whether certain school subjects, jobs and household tasks are suited to males and females. As well as provoking discussion, the completed questionnaires could provide valuable information and form the basis of an exercise in statistical analysis, possibly carried out by the same pupils later in their school career.

Project Baby X (see 'Resources'), the story of a child raised as neither boy nor girl, is an excellent discussion starter on how we develop concepts of gender for groups of all ages. It engenders plenty of follow-up activities, such as looking at the toys pupils were given, how they were dressed, adults' reactions to them, what games they played. This analysis of sex roles can be continued to take in school and adult life, but I also like to encourage pupils to see how their own expectations of others can affect others' reactions. Judge's idea[9] of getting pupils to list the qualities they would like in their ideal or fantasy partner, and analyse whether those qualities are important or realistic, can be used as a starting point for examining how we are socialized into the expectation of heterosexual monogamy. Point out how you, as the teacher, have just suggested that there should be one partner rather than several, or none, and that the public nature of the exercise would dissuade people from admitting to homosexual or celibate impulses, thus reinforcing the heterosexual norm.

Thorne (1978) argues for an interactionist approach in teaching gender, rather than an emphasis on sex differences or roles. Certainly most 'O' Level textbooks have a section on the 'changing role of women',[10] although no mention of how men's role must change simultaneously, nor anything on how a sense of gender is acquired. Recent questions at 'O' Level invite an interactionist approach:

> The woman, delicate and timid, requires protection . . . The man as a protector is directed by nature to govern; the woman, conscious of inferiority, is disposed to obey. (Source: *Encyclopedia Britannica*, 4th ed., 1800–1810.)
> a) . . .
> b) How does society continue to reinforce the kind of attitude shown above?
> (AEB, June 1980)

The question to ask is, who makes gender relevant in a given situation, and how? The classroom and the school provide an excellent environment for a study of interaction between the sexes, although this obviously requires sensitive handling and direction. A basic technique would be to chart patterns of relationships throughout the school day – who comes to school with whom, talks to whom, and sits next to whom? Look at seating plans in terms of pupils' own relationships, teacher–pupil interaction, the type of lesson (science may dictate benches) and the teaching style (authoritarian, democratic). For breaktime, compare the formal segregation of things like toilets (on grounds of sex) and areas reserved for staff and sixth-formers (class/status) with the informal segregation of the playground. Who controls the main space? Is it as boys or as football players? Can girls become football players? How? What, if anything, prevents girls joining in? Explore the power relationships, and what creates the power.

Tony Marks (1981) proposes that instead of teaching gender as a discrete topic, it be incorporated as a variable, alongside class and ethnicity, which will enter into analysis of all areas of study, such as deviance, socialization, distribution of wealth and income. Social studies for 11–16-year-olds is much more topic based than 'A' Level social studies with its current 'perspectives' approach, but as the basic concern of social studies is how people relate in groups, and what conditions those relationships, it should be considered necessary to draw pupils' attention to the effects of gender in all areas studied.

An area where gender can be a most useful aid to study is 'the media', since references to men and women occur more frequently than references to race, violence and politics, which are the other topics usually examined to show how media 'selectivity' creates an impression. Although many texts, e.g. Nobbs et al. (1979), do not mention gender stereotyping in relation to media, there is now a wealth of material suggesting approaches. A 'one lesson' idea is to take one or two issues of a popular newspaper like *The Sun* or, alternatively, one day's edition of as many papers as possible, and to look at all the pictures and/or words describing men and women. Longer individual projects could be based on advertising, or teenage or women's magazines. Pupils should be given a checklist for identifying sexism in written and visual material (this could be adapted from the one in Chapter 4) and then asked to discuss: what messages we get about men and women; how men's/women's bodies are used; what the effect is on people who do not fit the stereotype; what is revealed about the interest of men and women, their roles, age, race, illness, disability, beauty, intelligence. For high-ability pupils preparing for one of the less traditional examination boards, such as JMB, or not bound by an examination syllabus, a study of language could provide an interesting and unusual 'micro' exercise. The *New Society* 'Society today' on language (18 October 1980) is an excellent introduction, which could be expanded for analysis of sexism by reference to Miller and Swift (1976), Spender (1980c) and this book (see pp. 70–75).[11]

Despite the current interest among educational sociologists in the effects of gender on educational success, very little has percolated down to secondary level teaching material. A person's sex is arguably the most important factor affecting his or her life chances, and should be given as much attention as race or class. Discussions of career choices, subject options, timetabling, parents' and teachers' attitudes, and maybe even the sexist bias in teaching material, are both informative and usually popular, because they draw on pupils' actual experience. As written exercises, instead of presenting statistics on the relationship between class and academic achievement (numbers entering further or higher education), give the figures relating to pupils' sex and exam success, and ask them to interpret and explain these. I have modified a 'life chances' card game[12] to include the effect of gender. There are five rounds: pre-school, infants, junior, secondary and higher education. For each round, pupils will pick cards, some of which will be marked with events which may cause the player to lose or win points: you have less than six books in your home, lose 3 points; your mother is chairperson of the PTA, add 3 points; your teacher comments on you wearing a skirt from the dressing-up box – if a boy, lose 5 points; a careers film on the building industry only showed men – if a girl, lose 3 points, etc. If the players are able to explain fully why points would be deducted for the situations on their cards, they do not lose the points. All plus points are kept – privilege is not easily disposed of, but awareness can mitigate deprivation. The player must have scored points to get into higher education.

It is difficult to know what to do about the omission of women when teaching social class for 'O' Level, except to make pupils aware that this vital element is ignored. We must await theoretical work which devises a way of including sex as significant. To change the present analysis of class, it may be necessary to change the idea of the family as the basic unit of classification. Jackie West (1978) argues that women do not necessarily acquire their class positions through their families. The wife of a steelworker who works as a nurse and therefore has an independent income, has different life chances and status to the steelworker's wife who is a housewife. Women are more likely to be regarded by colleagues and neighbours in terms of what they do, paid or unpaid – teacher, dinner-lady, playgroup leader, councillor – than to be classified according to their husband's occupation.

A mother's education is often far more important in determining a child's attitude and early aptitude for education, than the father's job. In terms of life chances, quality of life and job satisfaction, there may be more similarity between the unwaged wives of an architect and a school caretaker, whose husbands may control them by keeping them short of money and by beating them, than there are differences because of their husband's income and social standing. A system of social classification which ignores the contribution and position of over half the members of society, is now widely recognized as invalid. In his review of two major new works on education, class and social change, Donald McRae remarked: 'The major fault here is that we are concerned exclusively with males only. Now in British society the proportion of women in gainful employment is and has been unusually high. Second, women are probably more mobile than men. Third, women are certainly less 'classbound', less involved in the business of stratification than men. Surely this matters?' (*Times Educational Supplement*, 18 January 1980).

Baroness Lockwood, chairperson of the EOC, commented with some anger on 'women's statistical invisibility' in the Nuffield Social Mobility Survey (*EOC News*, February 1980). Ann and Robin Oakley (1979) have identified five levels at which sexism enters into the production of official statistics: in the areas chosen for statistical analysis, the concepts employed to organize and present the statistics, the collection of data, the processing of the statistics, and the presentation, for example which sex category is consistently presented first.

Fertility tables analyse childbirth in relation to the married female population, men only featuring in order to give the husband's social class. The *New Earnings Survey* covers part-time employment among women, but not men, thus giving the impression that part-time work is a purely female phenomenon. Statistics on women are usually broken down into marital status, whereas those for men are not.

The concept of 'head of household' is so regulated that nearly four-fifths are men. Of the female heads of household, three in five live alone and are therefore head of household by virtue of being the only household member. Other female heads of households would be single mothers, or women in households where the males are either juvenile or retired. A woman who is the major or sole breadwinner will not be defined as head of household if there is an unemployed adult male in the household. The whole concept of 'head of household' brings into question why a household needs a head, which can only be resolved by recourse to the patriarchal concept of dominance. Official statistics are not collected for the benefit of social scientists, but to satisfy the needs of government departments, and these needs are linked to the preservation of a sexist social order. Statistics can be sexist simply by omission: unemployment figures are collected through those registering for unemployment benefit, and many women do not register as they are not entitled to benefits.

Textbook sections on work tend to ignore the 40 per cent of the workforce which is female. Research has concentrated on the problems of absenteeism and strikes which occur more in production industries, whereas women workers are mostly concentrated in the service sector, and have been relatively passive in conflict situations. Studies have been made of 'managers and their wives'. Myths abound that women only work till they marry, are not dependable, and are not breadwinners (Land, 1975). These ideas need to be actively challenged, with statistics and explanations of why women do not get promoted.

Where women are considered in relation to work, it is nearly always to examine the 'conflict' with their domestic roles. How do women fit in work with their family responsibilities? Do working mothers lead to maternal deprivation? How do couples reach the decision as to whether the wife should work? (It is even still suggested that working mothers may contribute to juvenile delinquency (Nobbs et al., 1979, p. 274).) These questions are almost never asked of men. Many men share in childcare and collect the children from school, but we do not study the effect on men's 'self-identity' from crossing 'sociocultural barriers' as we do for women entering the world of male work. Margaret Mead (1950) commented on the possible effects of paternal deprivation on Western society, but this link is never considered, nor is the effect of the father's state of employment (unemployed, away from home for long periods, working late at the office) often taken into account as a cause of juvenile delinquency.

In schools, it is necessary and relevant to discuss factors affecting equality of job opportunity, and ways in which these can be improved for women and men. Identifying ways in which work systems could be altered to fit in with the demands of family care can be linked with the study of the rise of trade union power, and the consequent improvement in working conditions. Pupils could compare the work done by men, women and children in other parts of the world with the type of waged and unwaged work performed in Britain. Introduce examples of polyandry and polygyny, societies where women build homes and where men look after children, and consider how technology and 'development' have changed the patterns of work.

'Work', in most people's eyes, is synonymous with waged work. The work which is traditionally performed by women – housework, childrearing and care of the elderly and the sick, both at home and in the community – is unwaged. Because the GNP does not take housework into account, and housework does not disrupt the social or economic system, it is often ignored or counted as 'not work' by sociologists who, following Parsons and Bales (1955), consider it as part of woman's 'expressive role' in the family. Ann Oakley has succeeded in bringing the study of housework into sociology, and there is now some material for pupil use (see 'Resources'). A difficulty when dealing with unwaged work is to get pupils, especially boys, to take it seriously. I would try to overcome this by looking at how women feel about their work, and stressing the two jobs that women in waged work are expected to do. Get pupils to make a list of the jobs done in their own home over a period of time. Who does what? Do people like doing these jobs? If not, why do they do them? What would they rather do? How would their lives need to change so that they could do as they liked? If possible, get some mothers to come into the class and talk about what their day entails, the problems they face fitting a job into looking after the home, the voluntary and caring work they do, and their interests; or get pupils to interview their mothers, or the person who takes most responsibility for running their home, and record them on a cassette, so the interview can be edited and shared in class.

Youth culture is another area where the normal and conformist – the Guides, the Scouts and the Methodist Youth Club – have been ignored by academics in contrast to the disruptive and the sensational. Most male researchers have been concerned with gang culture partly because of its relevance to the 'social problem' of delinquency, with its attendant destructiveness and high economic cost, and partly out of simple fascination with the hard, 'macho' image of, for example, the motorbike culture. McRobbie and Garber (1975) suggest that girls have been seen as peripheral to gangs, and as having no culture of their own, because girls associate in small groups, at home, hidden from public view – much less visible than a gang. Nava (1981), on the other hand, claims that girls are not studied because they are not seen as a problem, their labour and sexuality being carefully controlled in the home. The study of youth has suffered from considering young people as a homogeneous group (like the elderly), with similar aims, interests and problems. Starting from pupils' own experience of their lives could avoid the problem of presenting one group as more important or interesting than another.

Ask students to chart their leisure time (time not at school, or time between coming home from school and going to bed) for a week. What did they spend most time doing? Why? How much time did they spend with people outside their family? Where? What did they enjoy most? What would they like to do more of? What do they talk about with their friends? What do they read or watch on TV? Where do they get ideas from? What do they spend money on? How do they get money?

Certain themes, if they arise, could be developed in discussion, or as projects:

- Cultural differences and sexual morality: the double standard (it's alright for boys, but not for girls), and religious, ethnic and class attitudes to morality.
- Pop music: the history and development of various 'sects' (Brake, 1980; Widgery, 1981); analyse the words and messages of all the numbers in the top ten; look at the political associations of movements like punk and reggae, and the trend towards androgyny (Bowie, Adam Ant).
- Youth and adult control: do pupils feel controlled, oppressed? How are young people controlled by parents, teachers, the law? Discuss the conflict between adult responsibility for minors, and the development of autonomy. Outline the areas where the state controls children, but not adults (drinking, sexuality), but allows assault/corporal punishment.

Closely associated with the study of youth is the theme of delinquency. Neither Nobbs et al. (1979) nor Selfe (1981) pay any attention to girls in their sections on delinquency. Selfe, both in the chapter on delinquency and in the excerpts for study, talks mainly about 'youth', although one extract refers specifically to boys. The photographs in the section show the inside of a borstal, a little girl, and a teenage boy beating a woman over the head (yet violence against women is not mentioned). The functionalist perspective implies that males 'naturally' commit offences against property when they are frustrated in achieving their expected role of worker and economic provider, and females commit sexual offences, since their role in life hinges on their sexual relationships with men. In fact, as Wilson (1978) has found, young girls are frequently taken into care for 'sexual offences', like staying out late at night, which would go unnoticed in boys. Shacklady Smith (in Smart and Smart, 1978) has dispelled the common notion that 'the female mode of personality, more timid, more lacking in enterprise, may guard against her delinquency' (Cowie et al., 1968) but confirms that girls are most likely to be controlled because of their sexuality.

Formal control starts in school, where the pretext of school uniform is used to stop girls dressing provocatively. This can be compared to the way girls and women are controlled through their sexuality. Men use sexual harassment – wolf whistles, groping and verbal abuse – to humiliate and intimidate women (see Chapter 2).

Any non-sexist approach to deviancy and delinquency has to deal with the question of who makes and enforces the rules of society, and why. When I teach about crime, I usually begin by creating a problem-solving exercise (see Chapter 21, p. 312) so that pupils explore their own opinions about the seriousness of a crime. Then we compare their results with the punishments actually given, and see how these uphold the 'norms and values' of society. I also stress 'statistical' rather than 'psychological' explanations – shoplifting is a female crime, because more women than men go shopping.

Teachers used to working from established sources and written material will find it hard, and perhaps unacceptable, to build so much from pupils' experience. One of our defences against the charge that social studies is 'just common sense dressed up' is to make the subject academically respectable with prepared notes and lists of causes, and there is always the real danger that experience simply related but insufficiently examined, will remain at a superficial level, and only serve to reinforce prejudice. Yet, to rid social studies of sexist bias, we need to be prepared to change what we count as knowledge. Hanmer and Leonard (1980) argue: 'The problem is much greater than that of just "not leaving women out" . . . It is not enough to extend existing sociological concepts and methods to cover women as an addendum. Rather a different paradigm is required; one which pushes men to the side, giving them only half the stage . . . We want women's experience of being, of society, of social and personal process and women's problems, to be taken and given equal form and expression in the culture . . .'

The problem, however, is an immediate one. We cannot wait until sufficient new work has been produced to reflect adequately women's experience, and champion feminine values. We can start by explaining to our pupils not only that women have been excluded, but why; that a functionalist view of politics counts women's abstention as 'natural' and men's as political choice, and that women have been prevented from active participation by their responsibility for the home and childcare. We can explain that psychology commits 'the common error of equating "human" with "male" ' (Sharpe, 1976). We can explain that anthropology assumes that the sexual division of labour evolved naturally from the earliest times, despite challenge by Mead (1950); that maternal deprivation is a guilt-inducing myth to trap women into staying at home unwaged, to look after children, thus freeing jobs for men (Comer, undated); and that the lack of any equivalent theory of paternal deprivation takes from men and boys the concept that it is their right to share in childrearing. We need to look at ways of altering the bias of material to include a fairer, more positive analysis of women's contribution; for example, expanding a mention of the women's movement by outlining and discussing its aims.

Sexism in social studies is particularly insidious because sociology purports to examine all social relations; but in fact certain relationships go by way of default because they are felt to be so normal that it is not worth commenting on them. This practice maintains the dominant ideology, and therefore requires a high level of awareness to 'suss it out'. On the other hand, social studies offers a legitimate place to examine these relationships. The sociologist should be working to make people more aware of the forces acting upon them, thus leaving them greater opportunity to take control of their own lives. People may finally opt for the conventional roles, but that, then, is their *choice*.

Exams

Past examination papers probably have more influence on what is taught than the formal syllabus outline. I examined the AEB 'O' Level papers for the last five years (1977–1981) for evidence of sexist bias. I could find none. Every paper contained at least one question on either gender socialization or the position of women. Some of these included stimulus material which, in itself, was extremely instructive. There were no questions which used the words 'man' or 'men', instead of people, even in quotations, which is an improvement on the previous five years. The AEB has just issued a revised syllabus, which includes, under the heading 'Family', 'the changing position of men, women and children in the family and in society generally'. One of the specimen questions asks pupils to 'distinguish between biological sex differences and sex roles' as part of a question from a stimulus on the Tchambuli tribe where men are 'shy, coy, timid and embarrassed'.

According to the *New Society* review extra on examinations (4 October 1979), the Oxford Local Board adopts a more structural functionalist approach, and it will be difficult to avoid sexism in teaching for it. Those schools which write their own CSE mode 3 courses may be interested to know that the precedent for a CSE in women's studies has already been set. The Metropolitan Regional Examining Board (of South London) has accepted a syllabus, designed by Liz Waugh, which covers a core of socialization, division of labour, the media, women in other cultures, and life-styles, with options on the arts, history and biology.

Social studies textbooks

Marianne Kjellgren (1977) investigated ten social science textbooks for secondary schools published after 1972, looking particularly at sexism in the illustrations and the treatment of women. Only one book (Selfe, 1981) discusses women's liberation, as part of a whole section on the changing role of women, which shows a slight bias in favour of women's rights. O'Donnell (1975) is strongly in favour of equality and quotes a study confirming that children of career mothers show greater independence and resourcefulness. Harvey (1974) has a politically active young woman as a central character. Otherwise, the overall impression in these books was discouraging. Little attention was paid to discrimination against women in employment, but concern was expressed about the effect of women's employment on relationships within the marriage, and the disadvantage to children. Two books had no entry on women.

Out of the five illustrated books, four contained between two and three times as many male-dominated pictures as female-dominated pictures. Of illustrations of people in positions of authority, Kjellgren (1977, p. 18) remarks: 'Judges are very popular: they appear again and again and they are all men. There is the occasional woman magistrate, but lawyers are all male. Pictures of policewomen involve different activities from those of policemen: policewomen are talking to children and lifting a child up so that he can pat the horse on which the policeman sits, or they are giving evidence in court. Policemen drive motorbikes, investigate road accidents and hold back crowds.' In Selfe (1981) a picture of a young boy and girl together is entitled 'The skinhead and his girl' (even though this revised version contains an extra section on the Sex Discrimination Act).

The generic term 'man' is commonly used in social studies. The very influential 'Man, a course of study' (MACOS), developed at Cambridge, Massachusetts, on which the Manchester Oxfam project was based, has, in its second-year course, 'Prehistoric man', for which the source material includes 'Man, the artist', 'The first men', 'Clues to man's past', 'Man and the Ice Age' and 'Man's works' (tools, not baking and eating vessels). Hambling and Matthews (1979), throughout their first chapter on pre-industrial society, use 'man' and 'men' in both a generic and non-generic sense, so that there are statements like 'Men have control over the other people around them' (p. 4), where 'people' must be used to mean 'women'; and, in one paragraph: 'Man is creative . . . Men expressed their feelings by painting, dancing and making objects out of wood, clay and stone. Sometimes people used their art to try and make things happen.' This could be interpreted to mean that women's art is instrumental, men's merely decorative! This books also includes statements like 'Traditional jobs for women include looking after children, and fashion modelling', and has a picture of boys in Upper Volta learning about agriculture, with no mention of this being women's work (see Chapter 11, p. 172).

By far the best 'O' Level textbook I have found is Jane Thompson's *Examining Sociology* (1980). She avoids a functionalist perspective, favouring an ethnographical approach, which she realizes in the book by presenting pupils with the minimum of formal explanation (which means that the teacher who likes to explain a topic to a class first, is not merely repeating what is in the text) and a wealth of extracts from research and journals. Women have 'more than half the stage' for a change. Two-thirds of the section on work deals with the experience and problems of women as workers, and considerable attention is given to gender socialization and adolescent girls. At least half the extracts are by women, including Margaret Mead, Ann Oakley, Lee Comer and Polly Toynbee.[13] Thompson's book for pupils in the early years of secondary school, *It's a Matter of People* (1978a), manages equally well to bring women into the limelight more often, without ever appearing 'anti-men'. The very first section starts with a picture of a girl interviewing her father while he is doing the washing up, before the mother comes home from work.

Resources

For teacher and pupil reference

Sociology Without Sexism (British Sociological Association) – a sourcebook compiled by the BSA Women's Caucus, listing and commenting on hundreds of academic texts useful for teaching without sexism.

Women, Sexuality and Social Control by Carol and Barry Smart (Routledge and Kegal Paul, 1978) – a collection of papers on the position, status and treatment of women in the areas of crime, delinquency and sexual promiscuity.

The Sex Role System: Psychological and Sociological Perspectives, edited by J. Chetwynd and O. Hartnett (Routledge and Kegan Paul, 1978) – a collection of essays on socialization, education, marriage and the family, work, psychiatry, the social security and tax systems, and social science.

Housewife and *The Sociology of Housework* by Ann Oakley, are both invaluable sources of material on women's lives.

The Social Science Teacher is the journal of the Association for the Teaching of Social Sciences. Vol. 6, no. 4, April 1977, was on sex roles in society, and contained a board game for teaching sex role socialization. Vol. 10, no. 5 was a special edition on youth and music, and girls in youth culture. Vol. 11, no. 1 was on family, gender and community. The ATSS also run a Resources Unit, based at Didsbury Faculty of Community Studies, Manchester Polytechnic, Wilmslow Road, Manchester M20 8RR. This is an exchange scheme for teaching materials, some of which are mentioned in this chapter.

For use in the classroom

The Gender Trap: A Closer Look at Sex Roles by Carol Adams and Rae Laurietkis (Virago, 1976) – three volumes of quotes, stories, cartoons, sayings, poems, interviews, facts and figures. Book I: *Education and Work*; Book II: *Sex and Marriage*; Book III: *Messages and Images*.

Taking Liberties by Jean Coussins (Virago, 1979) – a set of workcards on equal rights in education, work, marriage, and social and political life, for use with pupils from 14 years upwards.

Project Baby X by Lois Gold, available from the ATSS Resources Unit (see above) – a story about a baby whose sex is kept hidden. It is a marvellous discussion starter for all ages from six to sixty.

Male and Female by A. Jones, J. Marsh and A.G. Wates (CRAC Lifestyle Series, 1974) – looks at sex roles and how they affect your choice of career. More useful for looking at gender stereotyping than careers.

Prejudice and Discrimination by Peter Moss (Harrap, 1976) has a large section covering mental and physical differences between men and women, work, attitudes and dress; also looks at class, race and homosexuality. For 14–16-year-olds.

Investigating Society: People Talking by Nance Lui Fyson and Sally Greenhill (Macmillan Education, 1979) – five booklets of source material based on interviews. The topics covered are Older People, Work, New Commonwealth Immigrants, Family Life and The Law. Anti-sexist and anti-racist. Usable with all ages. There is an accompanying pupil workbook, *Talking to People*.

Women with a Past by Annmarie Turnbull (WRRC, 1981) – a pamphlet on women's history with a large section on domestic life in the 19th and early 20th centuries.

Finding a Voice by Amrit Wilson (Virago, 1978) – Asian women and girls living in Britain talk about their experiences at home, school, work and in the community.

The Living City (BBC TV) – a series of half-hour programmes for 'O' and 'A' Level, which takes a non-sexist approach. The single parent, in the programme on the family, is a man; segregated and shared conjugal roles are compared; girls are shown doing metalwork at school; and a pensioner cleaning the bedroom while his wife is out at work, says it is only fair he should do half the housework now.

GIST Questionnaires – *Gender Stereotype Inventory*, *Occupational Stereotype Inventory*, *School Questionnaire* and *Background Questionnaire*, along with the booklet *Initial GIST Survey: Results and Implications* which details original findings from the questionnaires. Available from Girls into Science and Technology, 9a Didsbury Park, Manchester M20 0LH.

Notes

1   The *New Society* Review Extra 2: *Textbooks* (4 October, 1979) recommends Nobbs et al. (1975, 1979) and Selfe (1981) as among the most 'competent texts . . . for the average 'O' level candidate'. Kjellgren (1977) finds Selfe, if anything, slightly biased in favour of women's rights. These two books, from which I have taken most of my references, would seem to represent fairly the 'middle way' of school sociology, neither being particularly old-fashioned, nor particularly striving to avoid sexism, like Thompson (1980).

2   Nobbs (1979) describes only the historical and functionalist perspectives, and adopts a functionalist approach. Selfe (1981) does not describe any perspectives directly, although he does stress that society is based on 'constant human interaction' (p. 3). He outlines Marxist theory of class, and lists the functions of the family.

3   Spender's *Man-made Language* (1980c) will give ideas on this.

4   Available from ATSS Resources Unit (see p. 196).

5   Thanks for this idea to Roger Gomm (*Social Science Teacher*, vol. 11, no. 1, p. 17).

6   See statistics on the family (*Social Science Teacher*, vol. 11, no. 1, p. 18).

7   See A. Oakley (1974) *The Sociology of Housework* (Oxford, Martin Robertson); Thompson (1980, pp. 67–68) has a student exercise on Oakley's findings.

8   See Chapter 17, p. 252.

9   'Ideas for a sex roles course', by Lorraine Judge, in *Social Science Teacher*, vol. 6, no. 4, pp. 25–27. This article outlines many other teaching ideas and pupil activities, resources and statistics.

10   Kjellgren (1977) (see this chapter, p. 194) found that only O'Donnell (1975) suggested part-time work for men so that they could share in childcare.

11   Sydney Pereis comments on the ideological aspects of language: 'Performing roles often involves "ideological language" i.e. the use of language that has the function of structuring the meanings, perceptions and emotions of some in ways that are functional for the interests of the others. For example, in our society, "Mary is John's widow" is a common form of utterance, but not "John is Mary's widower". Such language uses tend to stabilize roles in favour of the more powerful and to limit the consciousness of the less powerful.' From 'On teaching the concept of role', in *The Social Science Teacher*, vol. 6, no. 2, November 1976.

12   I believe this game originated from the School of Oriental and African Studies, University of London, Malet Street, London WC1 7HP.

13 No book is perfect. Thompson lacks a glossary of terms and the language in some of the extracts is too difficult for many 'O' Level pupils, but this is true of the explanations in many 'O' Level texts.

CHAPTER 13

HOME ECONOMICS

BARBARA WYNN

Is home economics a subject which encourages girls to think only of marriage and motherhood or one which can help to educate and liberate both sexes? This chapter will look critically at both the past and present teaching of home economics and consider some of the contradictions involved.

Home economics can form a progressive and essential element of the curriculum, developing a wide range of intellectual, creative and practical skills needed by everyone. Historically, however, home economics has often reinforced traditional attitudes towards women and men.

Until fairly recently home economics and textile studies were taught almost exclusively to girls. This is not surprising when you consider the traditional male distaste for 'womanly work' and the hierarchy of knowledge which exists in our education system. For too long a high status has been awarded to abstract, rarified, 'male' knowledge and a lower status assumed for applied knowledge of relevance to everyday life or to people.

Since the passing of the Sex Discrimination Act in 1975 it has been illegal to offer a different curriculum to boys and girls in mixed schools. In fact it has been possible to teach cookery and other domestic subjects to boys for over a hundred years.[1] A Nottinghamshire school log book of 1878 pointed out that 'there is no law forbidding boys domestic economy as an extra subject'. Even today when this teaching is a legal necessity there are schools getting around, ignoring or undermining this law,[2] and it has hardly touched the lives of pupils in single-sex schools.

In mixed schools the facilities are theoretically available for both sexes to study all subjects and in a number of schools this has been happening for many years. Yet when pupils are able to choose options they frequently revert to their 'traditional' subjects as is shown by the differences in examination entries in *Table* 1.

Many parents may regard the choice of home economics or textile studies as a 'cissy' option for boys. Even where it is taught to both sexes the teachers themselves may make different assumptions about the purpose of

Table 1   Examination entries for boys and girls in domestic subjects[3]

Level	Home economics		Textile studies		Other	
	Girls	Boys	Girls	Boys	Girls	Boys
CSE	112 360	12 776	40 200	135		
'O'	51 719	1632	18 473	28	6877	496
'A'	All domestic subjects				5122	26

Source: DES, *Statistics of Education* (1978). Reproduced by permission of the Controller of HMSO.

the subjects. A number of books and surveys have suggested that girls need to know 'how to run a home' whilst boys need only be prepared for an emergency or for survival if they do not get married! (Schools Council, 1971; Wynn, 1974; Gilbert, 1975).

These attitudes provide a hidden curriculum which encourages pupils to conform to stereotyped roles.

Historical origins and development

It is difficult to understand the issues involved in changing home economics and other aspects of education without some knowledge of the past. The historical roots of domestic subjects teaching show that there were divisions along class as well as gender lines.

One of the outstanding features of domestic subjects teaching in the 19th and early 20th centuries was the highly differentiated approach to girls from different social backgrounds. Teachers received different courses of training and consulted different textbooks on 'plain' cookery for the working class, 'household cookery' for the middle class and 'superior cookery' for the upper class.[4] A student who completed only one course was qualified to teach only that particular class of pupil.

Officially schools were concerned to train girls for the 'household duties which devolve more or less on all women' (Major, 1899) and 'to be good wives and mothers',[5] but unofficially the inspectorate also encouraged many working-class girls to study domestic economy in order to prepare them for domestic service (Newsholme and Scott, 1902). As late as the 1930s correspondence from the Board of Education made this assumption 'for certain types of girls'.[6]

Upper-class girls studied domestic economy in order to train servants. It would help them to run a large household of servants, either in Britain or in the colonies. A well-informed mistress would be in a better position to exploit her servants to the full (Fedden, 1922; Mallock, 1935).

Thrift was certainly a dominant theme in the teaching of working-class children in the late 19th and early 20th centuries. Almost all the textbooks of the period stressed the 'self-help' virtues of saving and careful spending in order to maintain a bare living from the very low wages.

Some domestic subjects pioneers openly called for greater obedience and conformity from working-class girls (Gordon, 1889; Pillow, 1897; Bidder and Baddeley, 1911), but many other ways of persuading the girls to accept their inferior social position were employed. The solutions proposed were almost always individualized and centred around concepts of better management or increased thrift. Greater efficiency would certainly have brought improvements in the homes of the poor, but the overall effect of the proposed reforms was to convince women that the solutions to the problems that beset them were personal, home-based and within the power of isolated individuals.

An important change in the teaching of domestic subjects occurred as the heavy emphasis on thrift gradually gave way to the middle class 'ideal home' image, thus ensuring a market for mass-produced consumer goods.

By 1927 the Board of Education was no longer insisting that teachers should only use equipment that could be found in working-class homes.[7] Sillitoe (1933) urged teachers to make sure that 'the outlines of the ideal home stand out more clearly in the schoolgirl's mind'. She was confident that the ideal is latent in every normal girl, however much she may dislike and sometimes despise the troublesome mechanism of home-making'.

This ideal home presumably needs an ideal woman and the teachers of domestic subjects at this time were in no doubt that women should see their role as being within the home.

The traditional approach to home economics has tended to glorify the most tedious aspects of so-called 'women's work', sometimes elevating it to a religious (Gordon, 1889) or patriotic[8] duty. An 1878 handbook advised teachers to 'lead the scholars to set a high value on the housewife's position and to understand that the work of women in their homes may do much to make a nation strong and prosperous'.

Similarly women were expected to help men to get on with the 'real' work of taking decisions and running the country: 'The cleverest *men* in the world may make good, wise laws and strive with all their might to make the nation prosperous but unless *women's* work is well done they cannot succeed' (Hitching, 1910).

Although women were considered to offer only a supportive contribution to the nation's welfare, their 'willful ignorance' (Pillow, 1897) was held to blame for the poor state of health 'owing to unthrifty habits' (Head, 1904). The possibility that poor housing, overcrowding, poor wages, inadequate medical care and unclean milk may have been the real culprits was not fully realized for many decades.

Recent trends

There have been many changes in attitudes towards sexual divisions in society in recent years with the increasing involvement of married women in the labour market and the questioning climate that the women's liberation movement has started to create. Sexual inequalities are beginning to be noticed and some attempts have been made to reduce overt discrimination through the Sex Discrimination Act and the Equal Pay Act. It will be argued that the situation has changed a great deal on the surface in the teaching of home economics and textile studies, but that much remains to be changed.

Self-effacement and passivity have been assumed in many home economics texts and a confusion between gender and sex roles has been equally common.

> A woman's great strength lies in her truly feminine qualities and skills as a homemaker for her man and her children. This is a role which cannot be reversed.
>
> (Hunt, 1964)

The job of the domestic subjects teacher has often been regarded as essential in convincing women that household chores are not only a duty but also a pleasure. It is not unexpected that a book written in 1910 (Hitching) should have emphasized the need for 'proper tuition in the performance of a housewife's duties' and urged teachers to 'spare no pains to eradicate the widely prevalent view that housekeeping is menial and unskilled labour'. It is rather more disturbing to find that a book published in 1975 and widely used in schools emphasized that 'running a home is not just *one of the sacrifices a girl must make in order to gain a house and husband*', but 'on the contrary it can have a positive aspect, needing intelligence, creativity, imagination and organization' (my emphasis) (Good Housekeeping Institute, 1976).

Many household chores are tedious and until this is admitted by all concerned, pupils are unlikely to be convinced by such appeals. The consequences of a lack of application to household tasks have been clearly pointed out to girls. In the social conditions of 1887 it may not have been so surprising for a middle-class domestic subjects pioneer to claim that 'perhaps the best antidote to the public house' is 'a wholesome appetising meal at home', but this quotation from a book published in 1970 has the same implication:

> . . . husbands resent housework taking priority over their comfort, and nothing sends a man to the local night after night more quickly than washing, ironing and eternal cleaning.
>
> (Ruth, 1970)

A number of themes which were found in domestic subjects teaching in the early part of this century can be traced in more recent home economics books. An obsession with the creation of order is one such theme. To create order it is obviously necessary first for disorder to be perceived. One of the pernicious aspects of home economics has been the widening of boundaries of this concept of disorder so that women are encouraged to become obsessed with trivial household tasks, as 'the houseproud woman'. Compare the life-styles implicit in these two excerpts:

> Next comes tea, which should be one of the most enjoyable meals of the day. The tea table should be laid as neatly and daintily as possible. Everything should be bright and cheerful.
>
> (Colley)

and

> Afternoon tea should be a leisurely meal served at four o'clock. . . . It is a gracious meal. Use lace or fine linen cloths on a small table or tea trolley. Small tea napkins should be provided. This is the opportunity to use your best china and to show your silver to advantage.
>
> (Cullen)

The first excerpt was written in 1895, the second in 1973. Home economics teaching has frequently encouraged a ritualization of meal patterns, another form of maintaining order and ceremony in the home. Such a ritualization is also to be found in examination questions which require the candidate to prepare a traditional type of meal or range of dishes. When they do not make this requirement, they may assume that girls should cook, clean and launder for their male relations. From the Oxford 'O' Level examination in 1976 came the following questions:

> Two boys have spent an energetic morning on social services work. Plan, cook

and serve a dinner for them to include a steamed pudding and a sauce. Make some small cakes for tea.

and

Prepare, cook and serve a breakfast for a hungry young man on a cold morning . . .

Your brother is riding in a series of races at the local cycle track. Prepare, cook and pack a lunch for your brother and his friend to eat after the races.

(Joint Matriculation Board pilot exam for the 16+, 1979)

Even in 1982 the following question was found in a London 'O' Level examination paper:

The average weekly expenditure on food is a major item in the family budget. How can *the mother* ensure that in a time of inflation *she* can provide nutritious and interesting meals for her family of husband and two teenage children? (my emphasis)

An occasional sortie into the world of work has been integrated into home economics teaching with an acceptance of a 'dual role' for women. A dual role is seldom considered for men, even the idea of one and a half roles for both sexes has rarely merited serious treatment.

Many home economics textbooks approach life in a very narrow, individualized way. They concentrate almost exclusively on the nuclear family and rarely consider wider issues or alternative life-styles. There are many issues which need to be considered in more depth and in relation to wider economic and political factors. The home economics teacher may well discuss the problems of high-rise flats; it is doubtful whether the social pressures which reinforce isolation and loneliness are adequately considered.

Our society encourages the private accumulation of wealth and makes little provision for families which do not consist of mum, dad and two children. More emphasis is needed on the importance of sharing work in the home, of better childcare provision, of more communal facilities and similar issues.

One consistent feature of school home economics books has been the way that they are addressed to the 'housewife'. In the same breath these books talk to the housewife and the pupil as if they were the same person. Two school books published in the 1970s start 'If a housewife is to feed her family wisely' (Foster, 1976) and 'One of the most important tasks for the housewife' (Picton, 1975). Assignments given to pupils in class in preparation for examinations follow similar lines. From a book published in 1976 comes the following:

> As a newly married housewife an important occasion will be the first time you entertain your parents-in-law to a meal in your new home. . . . Your mother-in-law will be interested to see what sort of a housewife you are and whether you are going to feed her son properly.
>
> (Gawthorpe, 1976)

A book published in the same year and advertised in the publisher's catalogue as being suitable for use with boys and girls, suggests assignments which are obviously directed towards girls, and which are almost all illustrated with pictures of girls, until page 47, where at last we find:

> As a young teenage boy of fifteen you are going to your cousin's wedding. Press the trousers and jacket (or suit) you are going to wear, and clean your shoes.
>
> (Lamb and Lamb, 1976)

Home economics has changed superficially but not fundamentally in the way it ritualizes a home-based role for women. One area where there has been a change in recent years is the possibility of housework being shared between men and women. This varies from asking for a little assistance to a belief in some equality. Occasionally, the sexual division of labour in the home is rejected:

> Seriously, you must try to share all the household duties fairly and happily and this includes the kitchen . . .
>
> (Clarke, 1971, 1976)

As this author points out, sharing which involves men decorating and women doing the chores is not really sharing because 'decorating ends, chores don't'. Similarly, another cookery book explains:

> The purpose of this cookbook is to get couples, particularly younger couples whose ideas are more flexible, to stop thinking of themselves as cookers and eaters (like apples) and start operating as a team.
>
> (Selby, 1972)

In general the situation of women, where housework is basically their responsibility, even when men lend a hand, is typical of current approaches in home economics. There is more sharing in the home, but:

> On the whole this has not reached a stage where participation of men in

domestic activities is not only an act of good will towards the wife, who still retains responsibility, but an activity viewed as their own responsibility, at least in part. Most men who do things at home do so to 'help' their wives. They help with the washing up, they help with changing the nappies and so on, but there is still a tendency to regard it as *her* job they are helping with.

(Rapoport and Rapoport, 1971)

When we look at household routines suggested in textbooks, we can see this quite clearly. Even books which suggest that men should help in running the house, usually address these routines to women. These routines have changed little over the last hundred years, apart from the use of modern equipment. They frequently exaggerate the amount of work necessary, in suggesting daily, weekly and monthly tasks, and spring cleaning. Jobs are to be done not when the need arises, but according to arbitrary and prescriptive standards usually set out as 'routines' or timetables for the day's activities.

Home economics teachers who are concerned to reduce the drudgery of, and commitment to, outmoded household routines, might be better advised to recommend sections of *The Feminine Mystique* (Friedan, 1971) to their pupils, rather than giving them the usual home economics textbook. Compare for example:

The time required to do the housework for any given woman varies inversely with the challenge of other work to which she is committed. Without any outside interests, a woman is virtually forced to devote her every minute to the trivia of keeping house.

with an excerpt from a 1976 textbook ironically entitled *Running a Home is Fun*:

A Wife out at Work. The wife who does go out to work has to organize herself rather differently. But there are one or two things she really ought to do before she leaves in the morning – especially making the beds and washing the breakfast dishes. Unmade beds and dirty dishes are quite loathsome to come home to after a day's work.

7 am Make tea or talk your husband into doing it or have canned orange or grapefruit juice instead. Wash and dress.
7.15 am Make breakfast.
7.30 am Wash the dishes, and wipe over the kitchen working surfaces. Make the beds. Put away any clothes that are lying around. Dust the dressing-table. In the living-room, plump out the cushions, pick up stray newspapers and magazines, wipe over any surfaces like coffee tables which tend to collect ash and rings from the coffee-pot. In the bathroom, wipe round wash-basin with a damp cloth and detergent. (It sounds like an awful lot to do, but you can just squeeze it into 45 minutes!)

8.30 am Make up your face and do your hair, then run for the train.
6.15 pm Arrive home, prepare the evening meal and set the table.
7.15 pm Serve the meal.
8.00 pm Clear and wash up the dishes. (*Get your husband to help, right from the day you're married. Husbands have to be taught early if they're to be properly trained!*)
8 pm You don't have to slave at housework *every* evening as long as
to you've spent those vital 45 minutes at it each morning. You
10.30 pm might give two evenings a week to it – one of them doing the carpets and surrounds (*send your husband out for a game of darts or something*) and the other doing the rest of the thorough dusting and cleaning. If you live in a tiny flat you might manage to do the lot in just one evening.
10.30 pm Wash up if you haven't done it already. Lay the table for breakfast.
Weekends for the working wife are the time for doing the washing, major shopping (day-to-day food is usually bought at weekday lunchtimes) *and extra cooking*. (my emphasis)
(Good Housekeeping Institute, 1976)

One might be tempted to think that home economics teachers were running a conspiracy to keep women in their place, but this would be a distortion of the situation. The view of women as second-class citizens has many elements, including the idea that a woman's main role is in the home, and that the labour she provides there is one of 'love'. To become accepted by a large number of people, such a position must appear to be neutral, fair and normal, and this is exactly what happens in the traditional teaching of home economics. Values and stereotypes are taken for granted, accepted without question by many teachers and pupils.[9]

What changes are needed?

The image of women presented in these books and papers is an unrealistic one. Women today spend far less of their lives bearing and rearing children, and most work outside the home for much of their lives. These changes are in fact reflected in the teaching of home economics in most schools; after all, many home economics teachers are themselves working parents, but the available textbooks need to be drastically altered to remove the bias that still remains in many of them. The invisibility of men in these books is as striking as the invisibility of women in many science texts.

One other very important point is the limited range of life-styles assumed by many home economics texts. Far more consideration needs to be given to single people, those living in groups of friends, single parents and other life-styles. According to *Social Trends* (1981), 69 per cent of households are not married couples living with dependent children, and this situation should be recognized.

The emphasis of home economics teaching should be on basic living skills which everyone needs; on understanding the principles involved in all aspects of the subject; on creativity and decision-making. Other aspects may be included, but a great deal of the traditional rote-learning, much of it quickly outdated, and the unnecessarily time-consuming household routines, have to go. Consumer and health education, home science and technology, community and social aspects are all relevant.

The social control implied in many home economics books and examination papers should not be part of the school curriculum. It is not for home economics teachers to impose life-styles on people – giving them information and skills in order to take decisions for themselves is as far as this should go.

One step in the right direction might be the banning of the word 'housewife' from new home economics textbooks and examination papers. School books should address the interests of pupils at school in food and other topics, and not some predestined model of a future way of living.

A detailed study of home economics textbooks and educational documents (Turnbull, 1980) concludes that the image created in these texts is of a 'clean, dutiful, selfless, conforming, neat, gentle, home-centred pacifier with little suggestion of the experimental, independent individual'. It is important that teachers are aware of this hidden curriculum and that they teach pupils to become more aware.

First-year boys and girls in my own school are asked to write about the amount of housework they do and to consider the importance of sharing work in the home. Second-year pupils take the issues a little further by relating the questions we have raised to possible ways of running the home. They are given two descriptions of two families, one very traditional and one more egalitarian, then they are asked to work out which household job might be done by which member of the family. They are then given a description of a working couple where the wife does all the shopping, cooking and cleaning and are asked how a couple might organize their lives differently. Both male and female pupils create very positive images in their alternative models and all of them claim to prefer this way of living.

Pupils are also encouraged to examine sexism and bias in home economics textbooks and advertising materials. It is not necessary or desirable to throw out all the old textbooks if pupils have been taught to be critical and to notice sexism and racism in books. This approach could even be more useful than a more neutral curriculum which did not encourage them to think for themselves and develop powers of observation, analysis and criticism.

The recent emphasis by many home economics teachers on food education, and by textiles teachers on design education, would seem to give good possibilities of developing curricula which avoid many of the old traps and biases outlined in this chapter.

The modern emphasis on food education must, of course, be relevant to the quick preparation of basic foodstuffs. The old emphasis on time-consuming techniques and on over-elaborate garnishing of food, perpetuates the myth of the domesticated little woman with endless time on her hands. There is no place for the disapproval of convenience foods and quick methods still sometimes found in home economics teaching. It is also important to encourage the use of fresh ingredients such as vegetables as they are cheap and nutritious but quick methods of preparing and cooking them are far more likely to be of use to most people.

The practical side of home economics courses should include an emphasis on basic survival skills and should help people to look after themselves, but this should not be the sum total of the subject. Home economics can contribute to many aspects of education; there is a genuine purpose in acquiring skills of literacy and numeracy when they will help you to follow a recipe or pattern, weigh out ingredients or work out a time plan. Many skills of observation, criticism, analysis and communication can be encouraged through an experimental approach to the subject.

Pupils can also learn the importance of good design and planning by designing articles to make, and planning meals. Efficient organization of time is a most useful life-skill and one which the subject teaches probably better than any other. Leisure skills can also form part of the courses.

Examination syllabuses are vital in this respect, and in the development of the 16+ examinations replacing 'O' Levels and CSE it is essential that new syllabuses are of value to girls and boys living in the society of the 1990s and beyond, and that they help to promote sexual equality. Unless this is the case the courses will become increasingly irrelevant, and teachers could rightly be criticized for not learning from the mistakes of the past. Home economics should relate to pupils' interests and needs while at school, and should also help them to organize their lives after school in whatever sort of group they choose to live in, so that household tasks take up the minimum time possible to leave time for whatever else they decide to do.

Similarly, in the teaching of textile studies the emphasis should not be on elaborate and time-consuming methods of neatening seams but on designing and producing articles and clothing which will be used by pupils.

Teachers in boys' schools need to raise these issues and ensure that the teaching of home economics is extended to boys wherever possible. Without this aspect of school life the education of boys is incomplete; boys need to be encouraged to be self-sufficient, and need to know as much about food, nutrition, fabrics, decision-making, organization of time and all the other aspects of the subject as do girls.

The development of sexual equality is, however, a very long and complex process and the inclusion of short courses for boys is not on its own going to change the world. It is interesting to note that where boys have been involved in home economics courses, the aims of these courses have sometimes been adapted so that less challenge is made to the prevailing domestic ethic of the place of women. Home economics courses for girls may assume that they are preparing for domesticity whereas for boys at examination level the emphasis may well be on preparation for a career as a chef. Even in further education where girls have chosen to take catering as a vocational subject they may well be directed towards work in hospitals, schools and the public sector whilst boys go into the better paid and more prestigious jobs in hotels and restaurants.

Some encouraging trends

In criticizing textbooks and examination papers used in home economics it should be pointed out that they by no means represent all that is going on in the subject. They are inevitably out of date very quickly and very many teachers use their own teaching materials and strongly oppose the images of women and men presented in the textbooks.

Some of the worst and most sexist books are reprints of earlier books written at a time when challenges to the traditional role of women were less common. It is encouraging to see that some of these worst excesses are being removed in the new editions of books. For example, *Home Economics* by Beryl Ruth, which has already been quoted in this chapter, has been extensively changed 'to appeal to pupils of both sexes in line with the growing number of boys taking the subject' (Preface to the 4th ed., 1981).

No mention is made of separate household chores for boys and girls, of 'entertaining the menfolk' or of the dangers of driving men to drink by women doing housework in the evenings. Now 'the family can share the housework' and a number of the illustrations have been changed to include men. This is a considerable improvement. Unfortunately, the basic outline of the book was so directly addressed to girls that some bias still remains, such as an emphasis on an over-elaborate and unnecessary routine, and a section on make-up.

Books proclaiming that 'Perhaps the culmination of every girls' dream is to look beautiful on her wedding day' (H. Davy, 1970) are fortunately rare today, but 'good grooming' books for schools are still being produced and the message, although more subtle, still exists. Most of these books are still aimed at girls and even those which claim to have been 'extended to include advice for boys as well as girls' and to consider 'the needs of different ethnic groups' (Cullen, 1979) still include advice on how to apply face packs and similar trivia.

Although this approach to pupils is sometimes justified as an alternative to the housewife-oriented approach, it is in reality just the other side of the same coin of female subservience.

About the House (McGrath, 1980) assumes that household work will be shared: 'the important thing is to realise that both should have a fair share of work and leisure time' and women who do all the housework are warned that they will not be helping their children to grow up as independent people. Illustrations show both men and women caring for children and the needs of single people are considered to some extent. A book by this author published in 1982, entitled *All About Food*, takes a similarly non-sexist approach to teaching about food and nutrition, and the Nuffield Home Economics scheme assumes that the subject will include boys, many of whom are shown in the illustrations in the pupils' books.

There have been many other positive changes in home economics teaching. The emphasis in CSE courses on teacher-based examinations has enabled schools and teachers to develop courses more relevant to boys and to today's society. A little searching amongst the examination boards, as well as consultation with schools which have developed their own courses, can help teachers to find a more suitable examination course if they are not satisfied with the one they are using. Far more curriculum development work along these lines is needed.

There are numerous examples in different parts of the country of more enlightened approaches such as the design-based approach to food education and textiles developed in Leicestershire, and the 'Food and the community' course which has proved popular in London.[10]

It is important that teachers are vigilant and that they write to examination boards and to publishers when they see sexist or racist examples to ensure that future examination papers and textbooks look forward, not back. If we do not raise these objections then we cannot be surprised if few changes take place. Both examination boards and publishers are open to change, provided that they are sure that a different approach is demanded by a large number of teachers and schools.

For teachers designing lower-school courses it is not enough to assume that pupils will consider issues such as sexism unless they are raised with them. Developing criticisms of books, teaching and advertising materials is all part of the encouragement of a critical and thinking approach to society. Slides, books and other teaching materials which encourage the sharing or collectivization of household tasks can be contrasted with those adopting a more traditional approach.

A homework task for first-year pupils at a mixed London comprehensive school which asked pupils to wash up after a main meal at home and then asked parents to 'mark' their work, produced a very positive response from over 100 parents. Only one parent wrote a negative comment: 'R. thinks that washing up is women's work and I agree' – a response which elicited an excellent debate in class the following week.

Even using a very traditional curriculum in a very traditional school allows plenty of scope for teachers to try to include more progressive approaches and to create a positive atmosphere which assumes that house-hold tasks are not just 'women's work'.

It is important not to ignore the social and political aspects of teaching home economics, textile studies and child development. For example, any course about food should alert pupils to the nature of food additives and to big business exploitation of food technology. Courses in child development ought to take a cross-cultural approach. References to countries like Sweden, where attempts are being made to challenge traditional roles, may be particularly helpful. However, unless boys as well as girls take these courses, any changes will be of limited value.

An anti-racist approach to all these subject areas can be encouraged by developing an appreciation of the validity of the practices and experiences of ethnic minorities and other cultures.

Fourth-year option schemes where pupils choose which subjects they wish to study to examination level should be examined carefully. If home economics is blocked against craft, design and technology, this may encourage pupils to assume that they are expected to revert to traditional roles, however much they have enjoyed different lower-school courses.

One of the main problems of teaching home economics to boys is the false expectations they may have regarding the subject. It is essential for the teacher to make it clear to pupils what is involved in the course right from the start, and a brief written outline of the content of the course, explaining what is expected of the pupils and what they can expect to learn, is most helpful.

It is not difficult to devise courses which boys enjoy and find relevant, as the large increases in numbers of boys entering examination courses in home economics shows. The introduction of mixed classes can be an incentive to update the curriculum – if the courses are not relevant for boys then they are probably not relevant for girls either.

Conclusion

Some feminists' opposition to home economics is often based on the assumption that an outmoded syllabus is still being taught. Knowledge and consideration of the changes which have taken place, are limited. There is also a certain disdain among some teachers and parents towards practical subjects, without an understanding of the intellectual rigour involved in so-called practical tasks or an appreciation of the creativity required. These attitudes show a lack of understanding of much current teaching of home economics, and of its potential. Very many pupils find the subject relevant to their immediate interests, and it can help them in the long term to organize their lives after they leave school, however they choose to live.

A further problem is the assumption that the traditional male approach to curriculum content and to education as a whole is the correct one. This is dangerous, and will lead to an impoverished curriculum, lacking richness, which assumes that women need to compete with men on men's terms. Sexism will not be removed in this way – what we need is an updated curriculum of educational value to all pupils, and a fight for wider changes in society, so that male dominance and female subservience are eventually abolished.

Resources

Child development books

Any feminist bookshop will have a range of more progressive child development books, although there is no one anti-sexist textbook that will solve all problems. Some which may prove helpful are:
Brant Margaret (1980) *Having a Baby* (Macdonalds Guidelines).
Brooks-Gunn Jeanne (1979) *He and She* (Prentice Hall).

Badinter Elizabeth (1980) *The Myth of Motherhood* (Souvenir Press).

Carmichael C. (1977) *Non-Sexist Childraising* (Beacon Press).

Cohen Michelle and Reid Tina (1981) *Ourselves and Our Children* (Penguin).

Dowrick Stephanie and Grunberg Sibyl (1980) *Why Children?* (The Women's Press).

Greenberg Selma (1979) *Right from the Start, A Guide to Non-Sexist Child-rearing* (Houghton Mifflin).

Kitzinger Sheila (1981) *Women as Mothers* (Fontana).

McGrath Helen *About the House* (1980) and *All About Food* (1982) (Oxford University Press).

Phillips Angela and Rakusen Jill (1979) *Our Bodies Ourselves* (Penguin).

Other resources

Contact BSSRS, 9 Poland St., London, for publications on the politics of food.

Wardle Chris (1977) *Changing Food Habits in the UK* (Earth Resources Research Ltd – associated with Friends of the Earth).

Notes

1   Boys in seaport towns also had the opportunity to study cookery, as did boys who wished to enter the armed forces or catering. See T. Atkins (1921) *The Nautical Cookery Book*, 10th ed. (Glasgow, James Brown).

2   The Sex Discrimination Act 1975.
It is very hard to obtain information which is accurate on this issue. Local education authorities will obviously not admit to allowing their schools to break the law but everyone who has visited a large number of secondary schools knows that this happens; unfortunately no one has carried out any detailed research to discover the extent of the problem.
A court case brought by a parent at the Croydon County Court in December 1979 against a school and local authority for not allowing her daughter to study woodwork was dismissed by the judge as he felt that the home economics course was no less advantageous to her. In fact, the case was quite complex and the girl was offered a place on a fourth-year course on an individual basis, but it might be used by other schools to undermine the spirit of the Sex Discrimination Act.

3   This is an increase of 400 per cent for 'O' Level and over 1000 per cent for CSE entries by boys in home economics over a period of ten years.

4   The official handbooks in use at the National Training School for Cookery were:

Mrs C. Clarke   *Artisan Cookery Book* (1896 and 1910)
Plain Cookery Recipes (1896)
High Class Cookery Recipes (1890)
New High Class Cookery Recipes (1896, 1902)

(all Chapman & Hall)

See also:

Mrs Black   *Household Cookery* (William Collins, 1882)
Superior Cookery (William Collins, 1887)

Miss Briggs   *Cookery Book and General Axioms for Plain Cooks* (Chas. Straker, 1890)

M. Gordon   *Cookery for Working Men's Wives* (Alexander Gardner, 1889)
  To some extent this class bias is still found, for example *The Manchester Cookery Book* (Altrincham, John Sherratt, 1961) which I was expected to use as a student, has basic and advanced cookery sections, a division based more on the cost of ingredients than on the skill required.

5 Revised instructions to HM Inspectors, in H. Major, *Newmann's Housewifery* (Newmann, 1899, p. 170).
  Board of Education, *Suggestions for the Consideration of Teachers and Others Concerned in the Work of the Public Elementary Schools* (HMSO, 1905, p. 61).
  Mrs Pillow, *Domestic Economy Teaching in England*. (BPP, 1897, vol. XXV, p. 186).
  J. Hassell, *Lessons in Domestic Economy*, 3rd ed. (William Collins, 1893, p. 170). See also Newsholme and Scott (1902) and Sillitoe (1933).
  Mrs Lord 'Domestic economy', in T. Spalding, *The Work of the London School Board* (P.S. King, 1900, p. 228).
  C. Morley, *Studies in Board Schools* (Smith & Elder, 1897, pp. 135–141).

6 Public Records Office (PRO) *Elementary Education File*, Ed/11 278/E 472 (1937–1941).

7 *Suggestions for the Consideration of Teachers* (Board of Education, 1927).

8 See also the Hadow Report 1926: 'on efficient care and management of the home depend the health, happiness and prosperity of the nation'.
  Even in the 1950s books referred to 'That heroine, the housewife . . .'. 'Creating a good home is a form of patriotism as well as a purely personal and deeply satisfying joy' (Household Management, 1952).

9 An experienced Inspector of home economics found that many home economics teachers fundamentally believed in the sex role stereotyping that they were often promoting. They would make statements such as 'Yes, but *realistically* they will all be wives and mothers' when challenged about their approach, and did not always have the confidence or imagination to try a non-sexist approach (Personal correspondence).

10 For the Leicestershire courses contact County Hall, Leicester. For the London courses contact the London Regional Examination Board who will tell you who you should contact.

CHAPTER 14

CRAFT, DESIGN AND TECHNOLOGY

MARTIN GRANT

If differential enrolment patterns in any subject area of the curriculum could be judged as a measure of prejudice towards any single group of people, craft, design and technology (CDT) would emerge as one of the most strongly sex-stereotyped areas of the secondary school curriculum. At GCE 'O' Level girls accounted for only 3 per cent of entries in design and technology in 1980 and 1 per cent of entries in woodwork and metalwork (see Chapter 1). Equal opportunities legislation has done little to improve the participation of girls in CDT at examination level. Statistics show an insignificant rise in the proportion of girls entering CDT examinations in recent years (*Table* 1).

Table 1   Girls as a percentage of total entries in CDT examinations (1972–1980)

	1972	1973	1974	1975	1976	1977	1978	1979	1980
Design and technology GCE 'O' Level	0.3	0.9	1.8	2.0	2.0	2.4	3.0	3.2	3.0
Woodwork/metalwork GCE 'O' Level	0.3	0.4	0.8	0.5	0.5	0.6	0.8	0.9	1.0
Woodwork/metalwork CSE mode 1	0.4	0.4	0.6	0.7	1.0	1.0	1.5	1.6	1.6

Source: Compiled from DES, *Statistics of Education* (1980). Reproduced by permission of the Controller of HMSO.

While entry to examination courses is optional, it is generally accepted that the same legislation guarantees equal participation by both sexes in the pre-examination common curriculum. However, according to a recent HMI Survey of the curriculum prior to the fourth year (DES, 1979):

> . . . differentiation by sex in the craft subjects occurred in practice if not by design in something over 65 per cent of the 365 schools.

Clearly, the mere provision of equal access does not result in equal ease of entry to subjects traditionally followed by only one of the sexes. Before exploring possible reasons for the absence of girls from CDT and the possible strategies which might bring about change, it is necessary to examine the implications for girls and for the whole of society of the continuation of the present situation.

The importance of CDT for girls

The absence of girls from technological-type courses may well have profound social and political consequences for a society that is highly dependent on technology. Individuals lacking the necessary skills and knowledge to understand and cope with the technology that impinges on every aspect of their daily lives will increasingly have to rely on technical experts – be it for simple technical repairs or for more important decisions regarding the very nature of our society. At present most women have little influence on technological decision-making at any level. This non-participation of half the nation's population in directing technological change must surely strike at the very foundations of democracy. To disenfranchise women from the politics of technology by denying them an adequate technological education is to deny them a most basic freedom and can only lead to alienation from and ignorance, or worse still, fear, of technology. The Council of Europe forcibly states the problem in this way:

> An educational system which will not accept technology is an educational system which turns out cultural cripples.
>
> (Deforge, 1972)

There are other important reasons why we should be concerned to increase the technological skills and understanding of girls and women. Recent years have seen a marked change in the pattern of women's employment. The impact of new technology on traditionally female jobs – in banks, offices and the distributive trades – together with the contraction of industries such as textiles, clothing and footwear, and education, are likely to increase the level of female unemployment. Career possibilities are improved by facility with tools, ability to communicate graphically and general technological competency. The pursuit of workshop-based courses will help to provide girls with greater opportunity and greater freedom of choice in future careers.

Mathematics and physics are both subjects of critical importance in career choice. Craft, design and technology, by its interdisciplinary nature, has a major part to play in contributing to the everyday relevance of mathematics and science subjects, in which the performance and participation of girls are also a cause for concern. By encouraging technological competence amongst girls it is likely that their interest in the mathematical and physical sciences will be heightened and that their attitudes to these subjects will be made more positive.

Craft, design and technology is characterized by its problem-solving approach and by its emphasis on the manipulation of materials such as metal, plastics and wood. As well as being concerned with analytical approaches to knowledge, great importance is given to the concrete, pictorial and global ways of knowing the world. Unfortunately, the latter modes of thought are relatively neglected in our education system. All cognitive modes of thought are equally important in the individual's development from child to adult, and it is in CDT that pupils are likely to be given the opportunity to practise, through exploratory and investigative activities, those cognitive processes which help them to make sense of the world in concrete terms (Philips, 1981). By the time girls reach secondary school their experience of constructional and manipulative activities is likely to be less than that afforded to boys, through play with Lego, Meccano, model kits and chemistry sets. While daughters' domestic chores are more likely to be concerned with cooking, washing and ironing, sons are more likely to be called upon to help with car and appliance maintenance and DIY activities. To limit further the practical and constructional experiences of girls by excluding them from CDT may have important implications for the development of concrete modes of thought. In addition, because of the probable hierarchical nature of cognitive development, it may also have implications for the development of symbolic and abstract modes of thought.

Whatever shape one's career eventually takes – be it plumber, accountant, clerk or unwaged parent – one is required to react to the products and processes of modern technology and industry. Craft, design and technology not only contributes to active design skills but also to the passive design skills of assessing, criticizing, accepting or rejecting all those human-made products that make up our technological environment. CDT is also as much concerned with the communication of ideas as it is about creation. Since girls are relatively over-represented in the arts and languages, they are less likely to develop the graphical communication skills required to 'read' and understand all manner of design and operating plans, from simple assembly instructions to town planning and new motorway schemes. The individual who cannot cope adequately with graphical modes of communication is therefore at a disadvantage in interacting with consumer and industrial products and systems. Regardless of career aspirations, CDT is an important part of the general education of all girls and boys.

Nowhere in the school curriculum are pupils required to commit themselves to the responsibilities of their own actions as totally as in CDT. In attempting to solve problems through the use of materials, pupils are required to plan, implement and finally evaluate a solution or range of solutions. By its very nature, the design process demands self-evaluation, requiring pupils to measure the final outcome of their design work against initial specifications. External adult approval or disapproval becomes less important than personal satisfaction and the process can only lead to increased self-confidence.

It must be said that not all curricular activities carried out under the umbrella title of craft, design and technology are capable of sustaining the justifications made here for girls' design and technology education. Traditional woodwork and metalwork courses which emphasize the acquisition of motor skills undoubtedly go some way towards providing familiarity and confidence with tools and machinery, but their value in teaching for technological literacy may be limited.

The absence of girls from CDT

Where should we look to discover why so few girls appear to be attracted to CDT? The earliest and most profound cultural and socializing experiences undoubtedly pave the way for girls' later rejection of technological subjects. Our society determines that girls, from an early age, become more concerned to please, more dependent on adults, more interested in their appearance, more practised in verbal communication, more socially aware, less experienced with constructional, mechanical and electrical materials and less free to consider a wide range of possible future roles. The collective philosophy of our patriarchal society is strongly reflected in our educational institutions, which consciously or unconsciously promote sex stereotyping. Teachers carry on from parents the differential experiences and interactions offered to girls and boys. Girls are more often rewarded for neatness and organized presentation than boys, which results in the course of their personal satisfaction being dependent on adult approval rather than task completion.

Girls entering secondary school may already have strong predispositions to the different subject areas (see Chapter 4, 'Image'). These are likely to be confirmed by the organizational structure of the school, the predominance of males in positions of authority and in the technical and physical science areas, the careers advice girls receive, the multitude of messages they receive through the hidden curriculum regarding their femininity and the strong emphasis on male interests in the traditionally male subjects. These influences result in pressure on girls to use subject choice to express gender identity and to avoid competing with boys, who are likely to have maintained and consolidated their lead in things practical and mechanical.

Encouragement for girls' CDT

Although the barriers to girls entering and remaining in CDT in numbers comparable to boys may seem enormous, there is much that teachers can do to counter stereotyped assumptions and to encourage girls to participate in workshop-based courses. Because of our history of educating girls and boys differently and because of the many strong influences outside the direct control of the individual teacher, no single initiative is likely to produce dramatic change. By concentrating on biological deterministic explanations of sex differences, educational research offers only meagre support to the teacher concerned with equal opportunities. The only consistent result from this strand of research lies in the degree of similarity between males and females in all cognitive abilities (Frieze et al., 1978). However, enough is known from a social–psychological perspective on equality of educational opportunity to suggest possible initiatives that, taken together, might result in lasting change. The outcomes of current projects such as GIST (Girls Into Science and Technology)[1] and GATE (Girls and Technology Education)[2] will no doubt offer additional support for schools and teachers concerned to promote equality. Initiatives can be taken at workshop level, departmental level and school policy level.

The initial training and subsequent teaching experience of CDT teachers is likely to have been in a largely male environment. Attitudes that have been unwittingly absorbed which reinforce the male image of CDT are virtually impossible to conceal, if one is unaware of their existence. These attitudes may be visible in the teacher's own behaviour and language, in his/her failure to challenge sexist behaviour and language of pupils where they arise, and in the acceptance of institutional factors which emphasize the 'maleness' of the subject. A number of studies have shown that, despite the belief that they interact equally with girls and boys, teachers spend a disproportionate amount of time responding to and encouraging boys (see

Chapter 3). In CDT, where the nature of the work allows considerable freedom of pupil movement, the difference may be even more marked than in the conventional classroom. Boys' tendency to be more assertive may result in their monopolizing scarce equipment and machinery, as well as teacher guidance.

Catton (1982) has shown that boys resort to a variety of tactics in order to secure equipment being used by girls. He describes an incident where a boy who needed a hand drill that a girl was using, stood close beside her, arms folded, and stared at the drill until she handed it over. In this case the teacher was able to intervene and the girl was allowed to complete the drilling operation. As well as such direct intimidation, boys' attitudes can also emerge in the way they poke fun at the attempts of some girls who warily approach machinery for the first time, and in the chivalrous 'helping' with girls' practical work. It would be helpful in such cases if the teacher were to point out to boys that a cautious approach to machinery is in fact the most sensible and safe attitude to adopt. It is also not unknown for teachers themselves to fall into the 'chivalry towards girls' trap in school workshops, as shown by this transcript of a tape-recording of 12 third-year girls talking about school:

- In woodwork or metalwork, the teachers think the girls can't do the work, the hard work, like the boys. (Chorus of agreement)
- It's like we're not strong enough. They think the girls can't cope.
- I don't like the way they help us more. It makes out we can't do it.
- Like the time we were making a box. He said that mine was the best and he sounded really surprised that mine turned out to be the best. He sounded surprised and I thought there was something the matter.[3]

Not only do such incidents perpetuate girls' lack of practical experience, but the girls quickly come to regard themselves as less competent than boys. Teacher assumptions about male and female roles can also be seen to underlie the division of labour found in many workshops. At the end of a teaching session, girls are more likely to be found sweeping bench tops and cleaning the sink, while boys return equipment to racks and clear waste material from machines. Girls are likely to be encouraged to spend longer recording design ideas and using magazines, the school library, etc. for research, while boys are frequently allowed to 'get on with the job of making'. Girls are also often considered to be better at the more tedious tasks of glass papering, polishing and obtaining 'finishes' and are persuaded to spend longer on them.

Occasionally, some direct obstacles to the greater involvement of girls in

CDT can occur through minor details of classroom management. Most teachers arrange their class lists according to the sex of the pupils. Delamont (1982) demonstrates the possible consequences of this practice in the following incident:

> In the woodwork room the new pupils are being allocated places at the benches, in alphabetical order, with the boys first. When Mr Beech found that he had 23 pupils in the group, it was the girls who were left without bench places – about three girls were left to work at whatever place was available through the absence of another pupil. This meant . . . starting each lesson by trying to find a space.

Delamont concludes:

> It is hard to imagine anything more likely to make girls feel uneasy in lessons which are in any case 'non-traditional' for them, than not giving them a permanent place in the class.

While such an outcome was obviously unintended, it shows that it is often in the small but important details of class management and classroom interaction that girls and boys recognize that they are being treated differently.

Our language is also well known for its ability to convey much more than the intended message. The underlying assumptions that CDT is a male subject can unwittingly be emphasized in the language used in the workshop. References to 'strong boys' to carry equipment; girls to 'stop gossiping'; a boy to 'show the girls what to do'; a girl to 'arrange a display artistically'; a girl who 'isn't just a pretty face'; 'girls first' when dismissing a class; and 'ask your dad for help/information' are some examples of how we unconsciously inform girls and boys of supposed differences between the sexes.

The maleness of CDT is also emphasized by the lack of role models for girls. Women CDT teachers are still in a small minority and younger pupils have little opportunity to see older girls in the school workshop. Safety posters and career literature relevant to CDT invariably depict males. Arranging for women craftspeople and professional designers and engineers to talk to pupils about their work or about the industrial applications of certain workshop processes would go some way to redressing the balance.

By far the most important area for potential change must be in the presentation of CDT knowledge and activities. Because of its history, the subject area is essentially geared towards male interests and a redefinition of technology as neutral rather than masculine is necessary. CDT textbooks are invariably overloaded with design problems, examples or blueprints that are obviously of more interest to boys.[4] Some attempts to interest girls in CDT have resulted in them acquiring a different set of experiences in the school workshop than boys. There is a danger of further emphasizing sex-role stereotyping by encouraging girls to pursue work in jewellery, silversmithing, lapidary and light crafts, while boys continue with 'real' technology. Material should be presented in a more neutral manner so that girls can feel more comfortable with its image. This is no easy task, since it requires a total re-evaluation of the CDT curriculum, and even then teachers are hindered by a lack of knowledge of the extent and nature of the differing experiences that girls and boys bring to the school workshop, and of what might therefore constitute areas of neutral interest. One of the surprising findings of the GIST project is that girls are likely to be less interested in finding out about domestic appliances than boys (Smail et al., 1982).

Very often it is the method used to present a topic which determines whether pupils see it as having more or less interest for one sex. For example, with a class of 12–13-year-olds I recently presented the problem of designing and making a stand that would hold a book upright and open at a particular page, in the following way. At the beginning of the lesson the class was confronted with a table containing items associated with (1) 'Airfix' model making – glue, paints, brushes, plastic components and plans; (2) breadmaking – flour, yeast, water, salt, a mixing bowl and a recipe book; (3) home decorating – paste, wallpaper, paints, brushes, crack-filler, glasspaper and a DIY magazine. Pupils were asked to design something that would hold the plans/recipe book/DIY magazine upright and open, thus saving table space and protecting them from water/paint spills, etc. In this situation boys and girls were free to choose the particular area that interested them while at the same time ensuring that they were each tackling what was essentially the same problem.

The problem of male bias in curricular materials goes deeper than packaging and presentation. Technological concepts and processes are presented in objective and impersonal ways. CDT textbooks and syllabuses attest to this; not only are they devoid of reference to females, but they display an almost total absence of people. Designing and making must surely be as much concerned with the solution of human problems, as with machinery, materials, equipment, mechanisms or structures. Concern for the social aspects of science and technology has been shown to be an important factor in the subject choices made by girls (Ormerod, 1979).

In the area of science education, there are increasing calls for the subject to be taught in the context of the needs of society and individuals (see, for example, UNESCO, 1981; Head, 1982). Any move designed to make science more relevant to all pupils, as well as attempting to interest more girls, is equally applicable to design and technology subjects. To fully incorporate the social aspects of technology into the teaching of CDT, will require teachers to examine their present teaching approaches. In broad-based design courses the starting point for any individual or group activity is usually the presentation of a problem statement, which asks pupils to design and make a device or system which will perform a given function. Knowledge of equipment, tools, processes and scientific concepts is gained as the pupils progress through the design process. In more structured technology courses, pupils are given a grounding in a series of knowledge units (e.g. structures, mechanisms, electronics) and are then required to apply this knowledge in design projects. Both approaches can all too easily convey an image of the subject area as being mainly concerned with technological problems, scientific concepts, equipment, products and 'things'. An approach which highlights the social implications of design and technological activity could start with a technological issue currently in the news (and there is no lack of these). By debating the issue, using newspaper cuttings, film and official reports, pupils can arrive at a wider understanding of the interaction between technology and society; and from such a starting point a number of technological problems can be identified and defined. Some proposed solutions may be rejected in favour of social solutions, while others can be pursued to design–make–evaluate activities.

Instead of, say, designing and making a burglar alarm, or applying knowledge gained in an electronics module, in such a design project, 15–16-year-olds might begin by examining the role of technology in the protection of property. Part of the process would involve pupils in assessing the impact of alarm systems on patterns of crime. Some pupils might reject the technological solution in favour of social solutions, and identify a number of other possible applications, such as fire protection, distress alarm, gas alert alarm, and alarm aids for the elderly and handicapped.[5]

Younger pupils (11–12-year-olds), instead of designing and making a model playground rocking horse, or using their knowledge of mechanisms to build such a model, might begin with the issue of accidents in children's playgrounds. Only from such a starting point could they discover why equipment such as a rocking horse is considered a major safety hazard. Their examination of the issue would not, however, end there. They could go on to design a variety of static and moving pieces of model play equipment, and in the process learn much about their immediate environment and social, economic and technological decision-making.

The humanization of CDT by approaching the subject from technologically related issues, would not only win the approval of girls but would benefit all pupils. The prime concern of technological activity directed at the improvement of the human condition has received little attention in schools. CDT is the ideal vehicle to carry the debate on the relationship between personal values and modern technology – which brings us back to the earlier point about the need to ensure the participation of women in technological decision-making.

Good, non-sexist teaching in CDT workshops can be supported or hindered by departmental or school organizational structures. During the middle and late 1970s there was a proliferation of 'circus' or rotational-type arrangements in the early secondary years, designed to accommodate the influx of girls into CDT as a result of the equal opportunities legislation. Much dissatisfaction with these systems has been expressed by teachers of CDT, home economics, needlework and art, because of the discrete nature of educational experiences offered to pupils (Association of Advisors, 1977). Not surprisingly, alternatives to rotational planning based on option choice systems in the second and third years, result in girls and boys reverting to their 'traditional' subject areas. The Equal Opportunities Commission (1981b) makes its condemnation of much option planning quite clear in its evidence to the House of Commons Education, Science and Arts Committee:

> We firmly believe that CDT should be taught to all pupils, and that the option between CDT and Home Economics should be discontinued, because these subjects are in no sense alternative areas of study.

Whatever the disadvantages of rotational systems of organization in CDT, they are preferable to any option system which allows girls to opt away from CDT in the early secondary years. Once that decision is made, girls are unlikely to want to, or be encouraged to, take up the subject again in the fourth year. Some of the more severe disadvantages of circus-type arrangements can be avoided by offering integrated or multi-media design courses or options within CDT, rather than a series of 'taster' courses in woodwork, metalwork, technical drawing, etc.

CDT departments can also encourage girls by giving some consideration to ways and means of reducing their lack of practice in mechanical experiences. Lunch-time and after-school clubs for girls only might go some way towards closing the gap between girls and boys. Comparative studies on the performance of girls in mixed and single-sex schools suggest that in mixed schools the polarization of sex stereotyping is more marked (Dale, 1974). The likely benefits of teaching CDT to single-sex groups could be considered. The content of such teaching, though separate, would have to be equal, and the treatment would need to be carefully monitored. Involvement in local and national design competitions and in schemes such as 'Young Enterprise' form an important part of the work of many CDT departments. Encouraging girls, including those not following a formal CDT course, to participate in these schemes, would not only benefit the girls involved but would provide role models for younger pupils.

The way in which schools operate their third-year option choice system often reflects assumptions about what subjects girls and boys 'naturally' choose. Option choice systems frequently involve girls rejecting CDT subjects in favour of those they may particularly enjoy, such as music, shorthand and typing, and home economics. While CDT and home economics may share some common objectives, they cannot be regarded as equivalent areas of study. Unlike home economics, CDT has a major role to play in teaching technological competence, as well as widening the range of possible career orientations. Home economics, on the other hand, is important for all pupils, but it is especially important for boys for the survival skills it teaches, and for the way it can prepare future fathers and husbands to participate fully in domestic and family affairs. To offer these subjects as alternatives leads to an imbalanced curriculum for all pupils.

Pupils who may wish to pursue both areas of study are then unable to do so and the 'easier' choice for girls will close off a range of future career possibilities. The fact that much career guidance in schools is given in the fourth and fifth years, after option choices have been made, does little to help. Careers education should be a matter of concern for all teachers and CDT teachers can help by pointing out to pupils the implications of opting away from the technical and physical science areas. Work experience courses form part of the careers education of many schools, and workplaces are often matched to girls and boys on the assumption that they are likely to choose careers in different areas. This practice further reinforces the idea that certain types of knowledge and skills are more appropriate for one sex than the other, both in school and in work.

Resources

EOC publications:
  Guide to Equal Treatment of the Sexes in Careers Treatment.
  We can do it now.
  Sidetracked.
  CDT Working Party Report (forthcoming).
EITB, *Insight* – careers literature.
GIST reports.
GATE reports.
Design for the Disabled (Community Voluntary Service).
Studies in Design Education, Craft and Technology (University of Keele, Winter edition, 1982).

Notes

1 GIST (Girls into Science and Technology) – a research project based at Manchester Polytechnic (see Chapters 7 and 21, and Appendix B).
2 GATE (Girls and Technology Education) – a research project designed to encourage girls' involvement in CDT, based at Chelsea College, University of London.
3 Quoted in the pre-conference pamphlet for Pimlico School Anti-Sexism Conference, 26 April 1982.
4 A recently published CDT textbook bears the title *Jobs for the Boys*.
5 For a fuller account of this example, see Grant, 1982, 'Starting Points' in *Studies in Design Education, Craft and Technology*, vol. 15, no. 1, pp. 6–9.

CHAPTER 15

ART

JENNIFER HATTON

Educational policy

In a recent issue of the *Times Educational Supplement* (26 February 1982), Sir Roy Shaw (Secretary General of the Arts Council) stated that he knew of one college of further education where information concerning the arts was placed on a board labelled 'Women's subjects'. It is certainly a fact that art, in common with other arts subjects, is taken by more girls than boys up to 'A' Level and more successfully (*Table* 1).

Table 1 Numbers of pupils taking art at 'O' and 'A' Level

'O' Level		Entries	Passes	Grade C and above (%)
	Boys	52 765	30 357	57.53
	Girls	68 435	43 699	63.85
'A' level				Passes (%)
	Boys	9111	6354	69.74
	Girls	14 581	10 330	70.85

Source: DES, *Statistics of Education* (1980). Reproduced by permission of the Controller of HMSO.

Yet the majority of art teachers in schools and colleges are men (*Times Educational Supplement*, 26 March 1982). So why do relatively few boys choose the subject? I believe that the reason is not that art is considered 'cissy', but that it is rarely thought to present any job opportunities for the school leaver (apart from teaching) or to have any intellectual content. It is thought by some to be a mode of self-expression, by others a leisure pursuit, neither having any marketable value or real educational validity. Boys, to a greater extent than girls, seeing their lives ahead in terms of a career, give art little serious consideration in school.

This attitude has developed largely because of changes in approach to art education. In the 19th century art education was important only in so far as it related to manufacturing industries – better designers could work quicker and greater production meant cheaper products and more profit.

Art found its way into elementary schools in order to provide a foundation for the more advanced studies in the schools of art and design. Children's art education was nothing more than the mechanical copying of adult work which gave some vocational training and as such was seen as being particularly relevant to boys.

In 1926 the Hadow Report saw other benefits in art education apart from the utilitarian, and outlined four main areas of study: (1) object drawing; (2) memory drawing: illustrative and imaginative work; (3) geometrical and mechanical drawing; (4) design (Hadow Report, p. 228).

Although much of this involved the acquisition of particular skills, there was a place for imaginative work and over the next 40 years art became much more child-centred. In 1963 the Newsom Report, *Half our Future*, saw a special value in art:

> . . . for some pupils these experiences may have a therapeutic value, and for most a strong emotional satisfaction. (para. 377)

In primary schools too, children were less constrained by adult standards and by 1967 the Plowden Report was able to say that,

> The essence of the new approach was to let children use large sheets of paper and big brushes, requiring larger movements of the hand and arm, more suitable to their age than the fine, delicate movement of the old tradition . . . and the children were allowed to 'paint what they liked'. (para. 677)

It is the proliferation of this expressive approach to the exclusion of the teaching of skills, that has resulted in art becoming undervalued and therefore relevant only to an undervalued section of society, i.e. females. At a time when vocational skills are considered all important, art has lost much ground and teachers now need to articulate very forcefully the value of an art education which encompasses *not only* freedom of expression, *but also* manipulative and design skills which will be of use in many occupations.

Art in the comprehensive school

Eileen Byrne (1980b) strongly advocates a compulsory core curriculum and argues that all pupils should take some form of art for the development of creative faculties and as education for leisure. In most schools art is usually only compulsory in the first two years and in groups so large (at least 30 in some cases) and for so short a time (usually one hour per week), that the aims of the art teacher are rarely achieved. Higher up the school when option schemes are in operation, art is often set against subjects in the craft faculty so that pupils must choose between art, woodwork, metalwork, technical drawing, needlework and home economics. Boys, who see no alternative to full-time employment, will choose (or more often be guided towards) a subject which they think will secure them a job or apprenticeship – usually one of the traditionally male crafts. Girls, on the other hand, despite careers lessons, tend to view the prospect of employment with a 'stop-gap' mentality, a way of passing the time between school and babies, and choose subjects which they enjoy rather than those which they think will be useful in the job market.

With a small amount of effort these misconceptions could be dispelled by the art and careers staff. There is, in fact, as much if not more likelihood of obtaining employment connected with art as with the traditional boys' or girls' crafts, and even greater opportunities when they are taken together – design work in furniture, fabrics, carpets, shop-fittings, graphics, theatre, etc. Art teachers would be well advised to keep such careers information available in the art room, for example Ruth Miller's *Equal Opportunities Guide*. Girls who have little inclination towards a career need to be reminded that even if they spend many years at home rearing children, they will still be likely to spend between 20 and 30 years in paid employment – a long time to be doing non-skilled, low-paid work.

Women as artists

Despite the fact that candidates in art examinations are mainly girls, very few succeed as artists, designers or even teachers. How many people could name even five female painters? Why should women suddenly fail in a subject in which they have previously excelled? It would seem that as long as art is considered a pastime it is taken by girls in large numbers, but beyond the confines of the school situation, art takes on a very different function and becomes a valid means of communication from which women are excluded. The reason for the dearth of women artists has been first, lack of access to places of training, and secondly, prejudice.

Prior to the Renaissance, the function of art was a purely practical one: to narrate the gospels for those who could not read, and to provide pleasing decoration for churches and other public buildings. Artists were therefore more aligned to craftsmen than they are today and served apprenticeships or worked in their fathers' studios. Women were no more likely to become artists than they were to become merchants or carpenters. There were female painters and sculptors but they were all either the daughters or close relatives (but not wives) of already established artists and received more than the usual amount of encouragement and opportunity (for example, Artemesia Gentileschi, Angelica Kauffman). The nearest many aspiring female artists came to success was in the supporting role of wife of a male artist.

Towards the end of the 16th century, art education became more formal and moved away from craft workshops into the academies to which women had even less access. In France a young artist had to win set competitions in order to gain a scholarship to the French Academy in Rome, and it was not until the academies' influence was in decline at the end of the 19th century that women were allowed to compete (Nochlin, 1971).

An essential part of this training was the study of the nude to which women were denied access even after they had gained admittance to the academies. Initially this was because only male models were employed but the bar continued when female models were used because of Victorian attitudes to morality. (The view that women should not be allowed to see other women naked is still common today and manifests itself in 'men-only' magazines and strip-shows.) Nochlin (1971) sees this as a major stumbling block for the female artist.

> To be deprived of this ultimate state of training meant to be deprived of the possibility of creating major art – or simply, as with most of the few women aspiring to be painters, to be restricted to the 'minor' and less regarded fields of portraiture, genre, landscape or still-life.

Men defined art's terms of reference, and in so doing excluded traditional female arts such as embroidery and quilting; these being apparently closely related to the home (sewing, mending), rarely achieve the acclaim afforded to paintings or sculpture. This prejudice is evident in galleries and art colleges where such items may not be included in 'art' exhibitions.

The problem of access to art training has diminished to some extent (there is no official sex discrimination in admittance to art colleges), but prejudice remains. Very few women artists have achieved exhibition space, let alone solo shows, and even fewer appear as subjects for study in art history degree courses. Lucy Lippard (1976) gives nine ways in which women are discriminated against in the art world. These include:

2. Refusing to consider a married woman or a mother a serious artist no matter how hard she works or what she produces.
4. Treating women artists as sex objects and using this as an excuse not to

visit her studio or not to show their work. ('She's such a good-looking chick I wouldn't know if I liked the work or her . . .')
5. Using her fear of social or professional rejection to turn successful women against unsuccessful and vice-versa.
9. Galleries turning an artist away without seeing her slides ('Sorry, we already have a woman . . .')

Some successful women artists would deny all of this (see 5. above), believing women's failure to be due to their lack of ability or determination.

> Women's Liberation, when applied to artists seems to me to be a naive concept. It raises issues which in this context are quite absurd. At this point in time, artists who happen to be women need this particular form of hysteria like they need a hole in the head.

(Riley, 1971)

One of the winners of the National Portrait Gallery's annual awards echoes this view,

> Artists are people who should paint by themselves for themselves, not in groups or workshops. Women haven't worked hard enough or long enough, that is why they haven't developed into great painters. They've done bitty, fluffy, decorative stuff between babies.

(Sergeant, 1981)

It is ironic that this statement should have been made by a female portrait painter, portraiture being one of the minor arts to which women have historically been limited. In the same article Polly Toynbee notes that the judges of the competition all praised the 'feminine' qualities of the work; 'delicately and perceptively characterised', 'a subtle and musical arrangement', etc.

The idea that there is such a thing as 'female art' is not unusual. Women have a different view of the world from men because of their experiences and conditioning in a patriarchal society, and it follows that they would express this difference through their work. In an effort to be taken seriously as artists, many women have deliberately avoided the 'feminine' – the pastel tints, the delicate line, etc. In other words, they have fallen into the trap of accepting the male standard and attempted to make their work 'masculine'. Some women have resorted to using men's names in the hope of getting their work viewed objectively.

Female imagery in school

Because school-age girls are usually unaware of the workings of the art establishment and of women's place in society generally, they make no attempt at this 'double think' and the difference between boys' and girls' work right through the secondary school is observable, whether or not we as teachers choose to admit it. *Most* girls are neater than *most* boys; *most* girls will choose organic rather than mechanical subject matter; *most* girls use colours which are more subtle than the primaries. When working from a list of themes, the pupils' finished pieces can still usually be identified as 'male' or 'female', even when the themes were thought to be essentially non-sexist. Recently, when using the idea of 'contrasts' with a group of fourth years, the girls, without exception, showed contrasts between people or animals, whereas all but one boy showed contrasts between buildings, vehicles or other mechanical objects. Although the use of organic form is a valid one it does mean that, left to themselves, girls tend to avoid subjects needing even the smallest amount of technical knowledge, such as perspective or lettering. Boys on the other hand would miss out on, for example, figure and plant studies. Here the art teacher is in a dilemma – does she force all pupils to tackle the same subject and use specific methods, techniques and colours, or does she allow more freedom of expression?

Just how much influence a teacher exerts on the pupils' work depends to a very large extent on her view of the purpose of art in the school curriculum, whether its function is to provide a vehicle for personal development, or whether it is to teach specific manual skills. Most art teachers devise courses which include opportunities for both. I believe that art lessons should be used to make pupils more aware of their environment, to observe natural and artificial forms more closely and to be more appreciative of the aesthetic qualities of their surroundings, thus widening their definition of art. If this awareness results in 'works of art', so much the better, but the end-product is not of prime importance, particularly in the early years of the secondary school. The teaching of skills is also important, introducing pupils to various media, tools and techniques, such as printing, pottery, batik, as well as the more traditional drawing and painting. It is only after pupils have been made aware of the existence of these elements that they are in a position to make choices of their own, even if that choice is to reject all that they have been taught. That being the case, it is obvious that both boys and girls should be strongly encouraged to experiment in all areas and not to limit themselves to their initial, possibly stereotyped preferences. If art is considered a serious subject then there is no more reason why pupils should opt out of certain areas than they should opt out of, say, arithmetic or mapwork. Teachers' guidance should therefore be seen not as interference but as a widening of horizons.

Non-sexist approaches to art teaching

A well-structured course in the first three years of the secondary school may mean that the teaching of techniques becomes the basis of art teaching rather than the means to an end, an approach strongly opposed by some art teachers, but;

> Leaving pupils to play with art materials in the hope that they will learn to use them properly is akin to giving children a lute or a piano and saying that they will learn how to play it. It is important to give people the weaponry to go beyond those who teach them.
>
> (*Times Educational Supplement*, 26 February 1982)

The 'discovery' method of education has its place but some aspects of art need to be *taught* – colour theory, pattern, perspective, lettering, etc., and it is these aspects which have most career relevance. Graphics, sign writing and printing require technical skills, and to allow girls to spend all their secondary years drawing plants and cats would be to deny them access to many careers in art. Girls can gain confidence in the use of rulers and compasses by making posters, an area where neatness is essential and at which they can excel. Boys also enjoy this type of work *because* of the technical skills involved but do tend to need more encouragement to keep their work neat. This work can be extended to the making of boxes and packaging, board games, record sleeves, etc.

Pattern can be related to lettering in the use of measurement and the need for accuracy and it can be a means of making boys take more interest in their home; patterns found in the environment can be adapted for fabric, carpet or wallpaper designs which they could use in a project to redesign their own bedrooms. Extending this idea, it should be possible (resources permitting) to interest boys in the 'female' area of textiles by introducing weaving, quilting and embroidery. All pupils should be encouraged to explore both delicate, organic patterns and hard, artificial designs. Girls can be made aware of how mechanical objects work by making studies of the pattern qualities inherent in machinery and boys become more appreciative of organic forms after only a few analytical drawings of plants.

A knowledge of colour theory is essential to any art work, but equally important is the use of colour for the evocation of emotions. Formal lessons on colour theory give girls the opportunity to see the pleasing effects of splashes of bold colour, and make boys aware of the more subtle combinations they would be unlikely to achieve by themselves. Showing how colour can be used emotively and symbolically gives pupils a non-verbal means of expressing emotion, which can be particularly beneficial to boys who have been conditioned to suppress their feelings.

All pupils can learn more about themselves and their aspirations using their art work as a starting point. Ask a class of 11-year-olds to draw or paint pictures of themselves as they are now, of their families and of themselves as they will be in 20 years' time. The results can be used as discussion material or as a basis for written work. It is interesting to compare the pictures of first-year pupils with those of 14-year-olds where girls' aspirations can usually be seen to have fallen considerably (DASI Project, 1982, see p. 303).

A similar idea can be used to check pupils' gender stereotypes, this time asking the group to depict a 'leader'. Young people are often completely unaware of the narrowness of their ideas but once this has been pointed out to them, they will frequently use their new awareness to challenge others.

Classroom organization

Cooperation between the sexes can be encouraged by careful classroom organization. If tables are arranged in groups rather than individually, there is room for sets of friends of both sexes to sit around them. Large-scale work can then be produced by boys and girls working together on the same piece. Initially this may lead to arguments and frustration, with the girls thinking that the boys are messy and the boys accusing the girls of being fussy, but eventually they will learn from each other and discover that cooperation produces the best results. Clearing up at the end of the lesson can be done by each group taking turns week by week. Asking for volunteers invariably results in the work being done by girls as most boys still see cleaning as 'women's work'. By making it clear from the outset that all pupils share the work, boys will understand that girls are not there to clear up after them and girls will understand that their sex will not protect them from messy or heavy jobs.

Three-dimensional work and interdisciplinary studies

A balanced, non-sexist art education can be achieved with little difficulty in two-dimensional work, but few schools have adequate facilities within the art department for three-dimensional work, and it is girls who suffer most here. Despite the Equal Opportunities Act and the use of craft circuses, very few girls opt for woodwork or metalwork when given a choice in the third or fourth year, so their three-dimensional experience is severely limited. Pottery is often the only three-dimensional area available in the art department and although it involves both heavy and dirty work, more girls than boys take the subject to examination level. If sculpture in other materials were also available as an element of all art courses, girls' preference for art could be exploited in order to give them experience in the use of tools and machinery. Boys could gain experience usually only available in needle-work rooms to make soft sculptures, possibly using a male artist such as Claes Oldenburg as an example. Another solution would be to break down completely the traditional divisions within the craft faculty and offer design-based courses which would integrate art, and the 'male' and 'female' crafts (see Chapter 14).

Recommended reading

Art and Sexual Politics, edited by T. Hess and C. Baker (Collier, 1973).
The Obstacle Race by Germaine Greer (Secker and Warburg, 1979).
Old Mistresses by Roziska Parker and Griselda Pollock (Routledge and Kegan Paul, 1981).

Resources

Women Artists of the Renaissance – a slide kit on Sofonisba Anguisola and Artemesia Gentilleschi. Available from History and Social Science Teachers' Centre, 377 Clapham Road, London SW9 9BT.
Women Artists and the National Portrait Gallery – workcards by Eileen Hooper-Greenhill, included in *Schooling and Culture*, no. 7, 1980, from ILEA Cockpit Arts Workshop, Gateforth Street, London NW8.

CHAPTER 16

BUSINESS STUDIES

PHIL KEELEY AND KATE MYERS

What is business studies?

Business studies means different things in different schools and although
we have confined our comments to state secondary schools in England and
Wales, the teaching of this subject is a good example of the lack of centrali-
zation in our education system and of the consequent autonomy and power
of the teacher. Even within one LEA, business studies departments can
incorporate any of the following: commerce, economics, computer science,
principles of accounts, shorthand and other forms of speedwriting, audio-
typing and office skills.

Some generalizations can, however, still be made about this diverse
provision:
1. The status of business studies departments within the school
   depends on whether the subject is biased towards skills or economics.
2. The majority of economics teachers are male (this is certainly true in
   ILEA and Avon and, we suspect, is a national feature).
3. The majority of office skills teachers are female.
Wherever it is taught, business studies tends to have a lower status when
associated with the skills, usually taught by women and headed by female
heads of departments. High-status departments usually include economics,
more often taught by men and administrated by male heads of departments.

Who studies business studies?

Subjects included under this heading do not appear in the curriculum in
most state schools until the fourth year. As most of these schools operate an
options system, the subjects are taken only by those pupils who choose
them.

Option choice became fairly widespread in the early 1970s following the
raising of the school leaving age, when it was thought that if young people
were to be forced to stay on at school until 16, they should at least have some

say in how their time was spent there. At face value, this democratic approach seems reasonable and just. On closer examination, however, it is flawed (Myers, 1980).

Particularly relevant to this chapter are the problems associated with 13-year-olds, who have to make informed choices from subjects of which they have had no previous experience lower down the school (e.g. commerce), and the consequences which this 'free' choice has in respect of a balanced curriculum. Business studies or commerce departments commonly offer 'package-deal' courses including commerce and office skills in two or three options. Opting for these may well preclude pupils from choosing a science subject (particularly a physical science subject), or another humanities subject. They spend a large part of their final two years in school in the business studies department and their study of other important aspects of knowledge is curtailed, with implications for career choice and the quality of their lives.

Pupils following these package courses are overwhelmingly girls. Boys in commerce departments usually follow single-subject choices such as principles of accounts or economics (see *Figs*. 1–3) and this is often chosen to complement another subject such as geography or computer science which, although it is a new subject for schools and should therefore be devoid of traditional sex differentiation patterns, is showing signs of fast becoming an all-male domain. Of particular concern is the number of girls taking office studies courses (*Fig*. 1) (96 per cent of ILEA 1980 entries were female) as these courses equip pupils for a service role in industry, i.e. to enable someone else's decisions to be carried out. The advantage of initially highly paid, clean and plentiful work is an undeniable attraction to pupils. They are less likely to consider the lack of long-term prospects.

It has been argued (although not by us) that 13-year-old girls were making safe, realistic vocational choices by learning these skills, but the present economic climate and the new technological advances have negated even this contention. In our experience, pupils following CSE office skills courses do not have easy access to word processors or any office equipment associated with the new technology. They are spending valuable school time learning outdated and outmoded skills. This particular problem may be a recent phenomenon, but we believe it has always been a waste of time to spend three weeks learning how and when to use a spirit or ink duplicator when, if this skill were needed, it could be taught in one morning in an office. That these skills are outdated is not the only worrying thing about them. The way in which the office practice syllabus and secretarial magazines groom girls to become the patient, servile and sometimes decorative handmaiden to the (usually) male boss, is iniquitous. The subservient attitude encouraged will not help girls to cope with the problems of sexual harassment which they may well encounter in offices. Hazel Downing examines the myth and reality of being a secretary in 'They call me a life-size Meccano set' (Downing, 1981). It would presumably be as easy to inculcate pupils with an 'efficient and equal' attitude.

Not surprisingly, single-sex boys' schools rarely include office skills in their curriculum. In fact, there is tremendous disparity in the choices made by girls and boys at all levels and in all areas of the subject. This is demonstrated by the ILEA exam entries for 1980 shown in *Fig.* 1. It must be remembered that ILEA is one of the few LEAs concerned about the issues of sexual equality in schools, and is currently trying to develop ways of combating sexism. Their examination results, however, illustrate just how much work still has to be done in this area. The results suggest that business studies may be one of the most divisively sexist subjects in schools.

The general conclusions which can be drawn from *Figs.* 1–3 are:

CSE Level: Girls predominate in all areas of the subject except for economics and computer science.

'O' Level: It is only in commerce entries at this level that girls predominate (office skills are not examined at this level).

'A' Level: Girls are outnumbered in all areas at this level except for the relatively new subject of business studies, which they entered in equal numbers.

How is business studies learned?

Leaving aside the attitudes and expectations of teachers and parents, the most persuasive influence shaping pupils' perceptions of the business world will be the materials with which they are presented during the lessons.

Standard course textbooks

Financial constraints have forced schools to use textbooks which predate the recognition among some teachers of the desirability of avoiding material which promotes sex stereotyping. To form judgements based on the use of these textbooks would clearly be unfair. However, a recent contribution to the range of textbooks (Anderton, 1980), which is regarded favourably by many teachers because it promotes a wider socioeconomic awareness than

Fig. 1   ILEA CSE entries by sex in commercial subjects (1980). (Used with permission of the Research and Statistics Department, ILEA.)

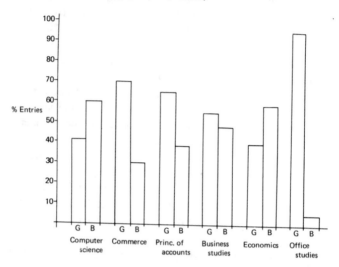

Fig. 2   ILEA 'O' Level entries by sex in commercial subjects (1980). (Used with permission of the Research and Statistics Department, ILEA.)

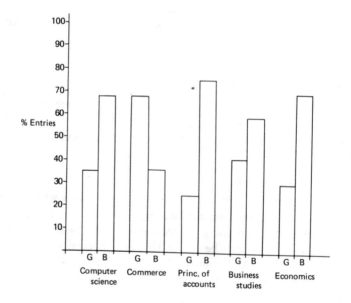

Fig. 3   ILEA 'A' Level entries by sex in commercial subjects (1980). (Used with permission of the Research and Statistics Department, ILEA.)

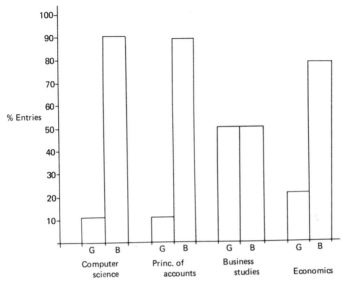

Fig. 4   Who are the people who can give you direct information about housing and furniture?
Source: *Pupil's Workbook in Money Education*, published by the Life Offices' Association and Associated Scottish Life Offices.

Fig. 5 Reprinted by kind permission of the Banking Information Service.

more traditional texts, fails completely to avoid a sex-stereotyped perception of the business/economic decision-making process. An example of its weakness is provided in this passage:

> In many cases he adds value to the goods or service. He might have after-sales service, promising to mend or replace goods which turn out to be faulty. He might prepare food – fishmongers will usually clean fish for the customer. He might install complicated goods such as electric cookers or dishwashing machines. He might give advice on which is best to buy, and once bought, how best to use it.

Would this be recognizable as a description of a shopkeeper?

This is not merely to take issue with the overuse of 'he' when 'they' would have been adequate and grammatically correct. It is, moreover, that an industry in which women do participate significantly is portrayed as male territory. Again, stressing that on other educational grounds this book would be regarded as excellent or 'progressive', it is not just sex stereotyping which emerges. Business decision-makers are portrayed to young people as white, middle class, middle aged and male. This constitutes not only a stereotyping process but also a factual inaccuracy. This is particularly so when, in reality, major contributions to the decision-making process in several areas of economic activity are made by ethnic minority groups and women. It is simply not true to say that all business people are 'WASP' men, so why imply that this is so?

A feature of books for use with the 14–16 age range is an attempt to personalize the business process, on the very good grounds that pupils can more readily identify with people than abstractions. This results, however, in the subliminal use of language – 'businessmen' with the subsequent reference to 'he' is the most common example. To avoid this unfortunate use of language would not be particularly difficult and we do not suggest an artificial avoidance of gender words; rather we suggest that examples in the business world could and should portray equal participation of the sexes. Men can be consumers and women decision-makers/entrepreneurs; a recent textbook for 'A' Level students in economics (Cairncross and Keeley, 1981) quite comfortably employs illustrative case-studies using women as professional, bread-winning, tax-paying and decision-making people.

An equally disturbing aspect of the sexist use of language, is the resultant distorted perception of the business world which boys receive. Exercises in a popular typing book always refer to the practices of a good secretary as 'her role'. Boys also receive an impression that male success in the world of commerce, industry and government is relatively commonplace and easily attained for them. It is possible that sex stereotyping in schools in business studies restricts female participation in industry and helps to explain why males do not regard management/business as a high status, challenging occupation.

Higher level courses tend to avoid the sexist deployment of language primarily through the use of abstraction. Thus economics textbooks typically obliterate people who are subsumed into collective concepts – the firm, the economy, the government, etc.

Sexist language is not just confined to textbooks. Secretarial students composing or copying letters are rarely encouraged to use the title Ms instead of Mrs or Miss. Married women are frequently addressed by their husband's forename, e.g. Mrs John Smith. Where the gender is unknown the pronoun 'he' is invariably used. We are aware that these practices are common elsewhere in the curriculum but an enlightened business studies department could very easily adapt a non-sexist 'house-style'. Presumably examination boards would be happy as long as the approach was consistent.

Visual aids

There are two uses of visual aids in classrooms; they brighten up the room with subject-related material, or they may form the focal point of a lesson. In the first category, sitting properly at a typewriter is exclusively illustrated with female models; it is evidently not the sort of thing which boys do. A set of posters from the Bank Education Service is typical of the second group. In a poster on 'Budgeting' complete with pupil handout, the woman is shown as a gum-chewing sex symbol, or as someone who collects state benefits, does the shopping and pushes prams of dummy-sucking babies around. In the same poster, the man is shown as someone who reads papers, speculates, invests, gets promotion and job satisfaction. (*Fig. 5*).

Resources and materials from commercial organizations

Teachers in this subject area frequently turn to commercial institutions for material to complement their textbooks. This material may have been specifically designed for classroom use or it may be intended for other purposes but have a classroom application. The Bank Education Service, the Building Societies' Association and the Life Offices Association are among the main suppliers of classroom-designed material, and the individual clearing banks and government departments provide, with varying degrees of enthusiasm, sundry public relations material. The significance of these materials is that they are prepared by participants in the business world and, therefore, present to young people the sex-stratified society which the participants themselves perceive. A publication from the Life Offices Association showed male decision-makers and female housewives: it has since been revised in response to criticism (*Fig.* 4).

These materials are distributed to schools as part of the City institutions' public relations budget. They are cheap, if not free, and are generally prepared with an awareness of the needs of teachers in the classroom. The sad condemnation of them must be that, despite being recently and professionally designed, often in consultation with teachers, they simply reinforce the male dominant/female subordinate roles which are a feature of the industries from which they emanate.

Similarly, a leaflet from a clearing bank on 'Starting your own business' makes it clear that all bank managers who can help are 'he's' and the Department of Trade and Industry's leaflet of the same title suggests that those likely to be in need of assistance are also male. Both publications are excellent in promoting ideas about business; they are useful teaching aids selected from hundreds with the same characteristics.

Economics/commerce/business studies are studies of people and how they operate in industrial society. It is undeniable that society's decision-makers are, at present, predominantly male and that this should be reflected in written material is not surprising. This pattern is changing, however, and it is disturbing that recently produced material does not reflect and encourage this change.

Teacher-designed materials

Counterbalancing the sexist bias in classroom material is likely to be the function of teacher-prepared resources. Subjects in this area are social and, therefore, material needs to be current. Developing material which teaches by means of current examples again reflects the low participation of women. Even the selection of material which positively discriminates in favour of those women who are, in the eyes of the media, 'decision-makers', is unlikely to succeed in portraying the business/economic environment in a way which encourages girls to contemplate the achievement of an equal participative role.

We are forced to conclude this section on how pupils are taught business studies, by stating that we know of no appropriate, educationally good (or even bad), teaching material which is non-sexist in its approach.

Recommendations

1. The place of business studies in the curriculum should be reconsidered. Instead of teaching some pupils to fulfil a handmaiden role in offices and others to take an active part in decision-making in the business world, it might be more appropriate now to ensure that all pupils are acquainted with technological developments in communications – many of which will not be confined to use in offices. It may, for example, be considered helpful to run keyboard familiarization courses for all, in order to facilitate use of computers (this is already being done in some schools, e.g. Clissold Park, ILEA and Billericay School, Essex). Business studies could be the focal point of a radical and integrated curriculum complementing mathematics, science and technology.

2. Non-sexist teaching materials must be developed. This will only occur on a significant scale if teachers use their market power, as consumers of textbooks, to put pressure on publishers. A coordinated curriculum project is needed, to develop and disseminate examples of good practice in this area. The Schools Council's successor and the Equal Opportunities Commission could well have roles to play here.

3. Schools need to monitor carefully the effects of their option choice systems. They could question whether in effect they produce two schools under one roof, divided on a sex basis. We would suggest that business studies/commercial subjects package courses are particularly divisive in this context, and recommend that they should be dropped from the curriculum of pupils in the 14–16 age range.

4. Teachers must be more discriminating in the recognition of the existence of the 'hidden curriculum' in business studies. Material must be selected with greater care and greater consideration given to the method of presentation in the classroom.

5. The outside agencies who use education for part of their public relations programme must be pressured to correct the sexist bias which exists in their attitudes to the business environment. If every teacher of business studies who invites outside speakers into the classroom insisted that every other year the insurance agent or bank representative was female, pupils' horizons would be considerably widened and, just as important, it might remind the commercial institutions that half their potential employees and clients are not invisible.

Acknowledgements

The authors are grateful to ILEA for obtaining the information shown in *Figs*. 1–3, and for allowing it to be published in this chapter. We would also like to thank Edith Jayne, Henry Reeves, Lucinda Anthony, Gaby Weiner and Betty Stewart for their help in the preparation of this chapter.

CHAPTER 17

CAREERS

GILLIAN PROUT

Until the mid-1970s vocational guidance, and careers education where it existed, not only reflected sex-stereotyped assumptions about male and female roles in society, but also overtly encouraged them. The Youth Employment Service (now the Careers Service) had separate sections for boys and girls, with separate staff, records and job vacancies. Literature referred to 'girls' jobs' and 'boys' jobs'. Pictures mainly showed men at work doing positive and demanding tasks, whereas women had the supportive roles of secretaries, the caring vocations of nurses, and the decorative feminine jobs such as florists and hairdressers. Mainstream philosophy of vocational guidance held the view 'that women's role as childbearer makes her the keystone of the home, and therefore gives homemaking a central role in her career' (Super, 1957).

Women have traditionally been discriminated against in provision of industrial training and further education. Only a very small percentage of school leavers entering apprenticeships are female (see Chapter 1), and hairdressing, the only 'female' occupation to offer apprenticeship, has the universal disadvantage of very low pay. The view that women were 'unreliable employees' and not suitable candidates for promotion was borne out by the fact that the percentage of young women released for industrial training during working hours hardly changed at all during the 1960s.

In the confines of stereotyped assumptions about 'men's work' and 'women's work', and with minimal opportunities for girls to go on to further education, careers guidance consisted of little more than occupational information on the eve of leaving school. Crucial option choices were made in the third year with pupils having little or no knowledge or discussion of the long-term implications of subject choice. Notions of male and female roles at work or in society went largely unchallenged, and pupils' choice of careers was severely limited.

Sexism in careers materials

At the end of 1975, the Sex Discrimination Act came into force. In terms of careers literature, this meant that information about or advertisements for jobs could no longer state or imply that the job was open to one sex only. The impact of this was slight in schools, despite the enclosure notices which appeared with the old familiar booklets, pointing out that the material was now meant to be applicable to both males and females. Large 'disclaimer' notices also arrived in schools and careers offices to be pinned up beside careers libraries, stating that although some literature referred to 'he' and 'she', sex discrimination was a thing of the past, and men and women now had equal opportunities in employment.

Literature and advertisements produced after the Act could not legally discriminate overtly between the sexes. Written reference to one sex in job descriptions and information was the most obvious sin to be avoided, although neutral job titles seemed to prove difficult. Pictures and illustrations began to appear with the token woman included in a booklet on traditionally male jobs, and vice versa.

More implicitly, sexism in careers materials has not disappeared. Many organizations wish to project an image or particular life-style by which to 'sell' their particular career, and such media techniques are often inherently sexist. For example, a leaflet on careers in a well-known building society depicts their successful (male) employee in front of his new car, complete with smiling wife and two children. Personal and physical qualities said to be required for a job can also be implicitly sexist. Stereotypes of temperament, e.g. the 'caring' profession of nursing showing female nurses, or the physical strength needed for some engineering jobs, are obvious traps. The Engineering Industry Training Board has a laudable scheme to encourage girls to join the industry as technicians. They produce special leaflets for girls which, while being excellent in showing girls succeeding in a traditionally male domain, still cling to sexist stereotypes of personal and physical characteristics. For example, a section entitled 'Is the work suitable for a girl?' begins, 'Much of the work of a technician requires mental rather than physical efforts in roles such as testing, maintenance, work study and sales . . .' Later the leaflet reassures girls '. . . whilst certain aspects of engineering are necessarily dirty, many other aspects are remarkably clean' (EITB, 1980).

Recent reports like the DES Report *Girls and Science* (1980) have pointed to girls' lack of experience in practical and technical areas which may put them at a disadvantage in particular skills like engineering. These are not innate inadequacies, however, and the HM Inspectors suggest positive action in schools to help girls 'catch up'.

So many problems still exist that five years after the Sex Discrimination Act, the Equal Opportunities Commission produced a booklet entitled *A Guide to Equal Treatment of the Sexes in Careers Materials* (1980). In its introduction it says:

> The need for a guide of this nature is clearly shown by the numerous requests for advice that the EOC continues to receive. These requests, from both individuals and organisations, highlight the fact that there is still a considerable amount of careers information which depicts males and females in traditional occupational roles. Such information maintains the false impression that there are 'men's and women's jobs'.

The guide suggests ways of rewording literature to ensure a neutral and balanced piece of information. For example, alternative job titles should be used to avoid reference to one sex, i.e. 'businessman' should become 'business executive' and 'cameraman' should become 'camera operator'. Job descriptions should not imply that jobs are suitable for one sex rather than the other, nor assume that the readers are of one sex only. Sentences like 'The secretary will need tact and diplomacy in dealing with *her* boss's clients' and 'We need *men* like you' should be avoided. Misleading generalizations about male and female characteristics and temperament often lead to discrimination. For example, in a film showing job interviews, the female said she wanted the job because she thought the pay was good, while the male asked about training and opportunities for going to the technical college. The guide points out that such stereotyping is to be avoided, and generally, where possible, both sexes should be shown when illustrating job opportunities and occupations.

Over recent years there has been a proliferation of resources for use in careers education. TV series for schools on careers vary from programmes such as the one which a girl in a Humberside comprehensive complained about last year, in which a lot of boys were shown saying they did not think girls should do certain jobs without giving the girls a chance to reply, to the *Wider Horizons* programme in a series for third-year pupils, which made an excellent attempt to encourage pupils to consider non-traditional occupations.

On the whole, it is obvious that attempts are now made to show opportunities for both sexes in specific occupations covered by schools television. However, traditional stereotypes of men and women, both at work and in relationships, portrayed in the more general careers programmes all too frequently go unchallenged. One aspect of this problem is the preoccupation to assure all concerned, and particularly the girls, that equal opportunity need not mean that they will lose their 'femininity'. There seems to exist here the same rationale as that which underlies the EITB *Girl Technicians* leaflet described earlier, and this in itself can be insidiously sexist. For example, a BBC careers programme about Sandra, one of five girl engineering apprentices in a factory with 250 apprentices, kept switching from Sandra at work to Sandra pursuing her hobby of ballroom dancing, complete with sequined taffeta outfit. A group of pupils with whom I watched the film found the idea of a girl engineer refreshing, and it gave us much to discuss. They were relieved, however, to see that being an engineer did not necessarily mean that Sandra, as one pupil put it, 'wasn't a real girl with girl's hobbies, even though she was doing a boy's job'. In seeking to break down sex stereotyping at the level of employment only, such material reinforces the overall traditional view of women's role.

A similar tendency often occurs in general careers books. For example, CRAC's *Your Choice at 15+* (1977) has a section entitled 'Equal opportunities' which is included to 'remind' girls that they 'will' be getting married and having children, but nevertheless must not see this as an alternative to achieving good qualifications and training for work to which they can return later on in life. Indeed, it is pointed out that it is more important for a girl to have good vocational qualifications for many reasons connected with the fact that she will have a gap of about ten years in her working life in which to raise a family. 'The better the qualifications, the greater the number of employment opportunities from which to select the one which best allows career responsibilities to be combined with family responsibilities.' And later, '. . . considering such problems at 16 requires a long term viewpoint. Girls must try to be particularly good at long range career forecasting.'

It is good that girls are being encouraged to think in terms of careers, but such approaches again do not question the overall role of women, nor of men. First, they assume that all girls are likely to get married and have children. Secondly, why should the particular 'problems' of marriage and family responsibilities impinge only on the woman's career? Without raising issues such as the need for men to share domestic responsibilities and parenting, the idea of equal opportunity at work is inevitably limited.

The image of 'industry' which is conveyed to pupils is still often blatantly sexist. In a booklet produced for schools to show how industry is organized, *Industry in Close-Up*, the pictures in particular show a very male-orientated company. The functions of the different departments of a typical firm are explained, and of the 60 individuals pictured, only 10 are women. They appear in typically unskilled or supportive settings: production line worker, secretary, clerk in 'support services', trainee in personnel – the other six are in a crowd scene with 14 men in a trade union training session. No women are shown in the management team, development team or marketing and sales, etc. Thus, although pains may be taken to point out equality of opportunity in theory in specific jobs, the overall message portrayed in careers education material remains that in firms and organizations where people actually work, men hold the positions of power and authority. This shows the ineffectiveness of the passive 'non-discrimination' approach whereby we simply alter the wording, 'open up' all careers to girls and let them take it or leave it.

An anti-sexist approach: proposals and problems

Careers education in schools has developed over the last two decades, from giving job information and vacancy advice to school leavers, to having a comprehensive set of aims and objectives in terms of pupils' overall growth and development. The DES *Educational Survey No. 18* (1973) stated that 'Careers Education is one facet of the total process of pastoral care, and it should thus be regarded as an integral part of the arrangements by which schools seek to promote the general well-being of their pupils'.

Fulfilling these aims includes promoting equal opportunity, and this means that careers education must be introduced well before subject options are chosen, if the long-term implications of the subjects opted for, and those excluded, are to be realized. The DES report *Girls and Science* (1980) claimed that a structured guidance programme at the time of choosing options was crucial, and HMIs felt that positive action was essential in schools, so that subjects were not seen as being for boys or girls. As John Mann, secretary of the Schools Council, put it: 'Careers educators have an uphill task to challenge and change such long-standing assumptions about the proper roles of men and women. Common justice and common sense require their success' (EOC, 1980).

Such assumptions can be challenged in a variety of ways (see Chapter 12, p. 184). A good way to introduce the topic is to tell the following riddle: 'A man was driving his son to school when they were involved in a serious accident. The father was killed instantly, and the boy was rushed to hospital. He required an emergency operation and was taken to the operating theatre. The surgeon came in, looked at the boy and exclaimed, "Oh God, it's my son".' The explanations offered by pupils are wide-ranging and imaginative, and the length of time taken for imagination to stretch to the idea that the surgeon may actually be his mother varies considerably!

The BBC TV programme *Wider Horizons*, referred to earlier, has an accompanying worksheet which encourages pupils to think about stereotyped characteristics, and to give reasons for their opinions. For example, 'Do you think men are more aggressive than women? Yes/No. Give your reasons.' This often gives rise to a lively and heated discussion.

Jane L. Thompson's book, *Studying Society* (1978b), has an interesting and well-presented section on 'Men's jobs and women's jobs' which can be used to question the roles of men and women in employment and current facts and figures. For broadening ideas on family responsibility and work, the chapter 'Who earns the bread?' in *Male and Female* (Jones et al., 1973) presents three couples with three different family set-ups. In one the husband goes to work, and the wife does not, in the second the roles are reversed, and in the third, both work part-time.

Simply to eliminate overt sex discrimination in careers materials and place equal opportunity 'cold' in front of pupils has so far tempted few to throw off years of conditioning, and to struggle for acceptance in an unconventional field. Pupils seem to have the message that they 'could if they wanted to', and 'somewhere some people do', but 'they don't want to'. Many regret this in later life. To widen pupils' aspirations before it is too late, a sustained positive campaign is needed.

Using materials

First, teachers should deliberately seek out and use what non-sexist and anti-sexist resources are available such as the EITB poster advertising for female engineers, which shows a girl apprentice. By displaying these around the school, we can begin to make others more aware of the possibilities of non-traditional job areas. A list of resources and agencies supplying non-sexist materials is given at the end of the chapter.

When teaching about the trades union movement as part of a careers course I like to use the video *Member of the Union* which, although a little outdated, has the advantage of featuring Hazel, a shop steward in an engineering company. Hazel is a very assertive character, and is shown negotiating with management, discussing problems with male and female workmates, attending meetings and at home with her husband. In general, pupils' initial reaction is one of surprise at seeing a woman shop steward. She is not always popular, particularly with the boys, and is usually referred to by someone as 'bossy' and 'always complaining'. This is partly due to the nature of the film which strings together a series of day-by-day situations to be dealt with on the factory floor. However, what this film does give rise to is a discussion not only about the role of the shop steward and trade unions, but also the role of women at work, and their level of commitment compared with that of men.

Unfortunately, non-sexist materials are scarce, but traditional (sexist) materials can be used to advantage. For example, in a fifth-year session on completing job application forms, a rather old form from a well-known bank was found to contain questions such as 'If female, state husband's occupation'. The completion of the form was halted, and we spent some time discussing the assumptions underlying these questions, and why they should be illegal in the light of the Sex Discrimination Act.

When newly produced sexist material is found, teachers should make a point of writing to or phoning whoever produced the item to complain. The outcome can then be publicized in the newsletter of the recently formed Association of Careers Officer and Teachers Opposed to Sexism (ACOTOS – see end of chapter). In addition, we should encourage pupils to watch out for sexist and other forms of bias in leaflets and advertisements. A follow-up exercise is to have pupils produce a non-sexist alternative to the offending leaflet.

Careers talks and guest speakers

A campaign of positive discrimination may mean that some well-established and well-intentioned practices in careers education have to be abandoned. The liberal view on careers talks is that it is more productive to allow pupils to choose which talks they wish to attend, since more will be gained by letting a few interested pupils have an intimate talk with a guest speaker, than embarrassing the speaker with a class of mostly uninterested pupils. The difficulty here is that pupils are unlikely to attend talks on non-traditional areas of work. Even if they are curious, the opposite sex may be reluctant to participate. A talk at my school advertised as being on 'Careers in the health services' produced a large number of budding (female) nurses and one boy, who was extremely embarrassed, and asked 'Is this a girls' talk, Miss?' He sat through the discussion trying to look as if he was nothing to do with what was taking place. I wondered how many boys did not even have his courage.

When inviting outside speakers into school, try to include in your programme people who work in non-traditional jobs, particularly women who have succeeded in traditionally male areas. (This is not being sexist, but since 'women's work' is much more limited than 'men's', and lower status and lower paid, it is more necessary to encourage girls to consider non-traditional areas of employment than it is boys who, theoretically, have a wider choice of careers. An equivalent anti-sexist approach for boys might be to invite as a speaker a man who had chosen to stay at home and look after his child.)

Finding people working in non-traditional areas of work is easier said than done. In urban areas it is usually possible to locate women working in 'neutral' areas of non-manual work, such as accountancy, or male nurses, but it is extremely difficult to find women working in 'male' manual work, who might provide role models for the less academic girl. The organization Women in Manual Trades may be able to provide contacts through their register and newsletter. They are a national federation of women who work in, are training for, or are interested in traditionally male manual trades, e.g. the building industry, motor vehicle repair, printing, engineering and gardening. The group's activities include research into training and job opportunities for girls and women in these trades, and support, information and careers advice. They have also produced a travelling exhibition and video film showing women and girls in various trades.

In the Manchester area, the VISTA programme (see Chapter 9, p. 140) is another possible source of contact of women in science-based occupations, although they have noted the difficulty of identifying women working at craft level.

There is now a substantial range of groups set up by women to promote women's opportunities in particular occupations and professions, e.g. Women in Publishing, Women in Computing, Women in Telecommunications (see 'Resources'). They provide information and support for women working in these fields, and could be a useful source of contacts for careers programmes and conventions.

Local trades councils may also be able to put you in touch with women who know of the problems of working in male industries locally. Some trades councils have women's subcommittees made up of active and sympathetic women trade unionists. Nationally, the TUC has a Women's Advisory Committee, and it is becoming more common for large trade unions to have national women's organizers and/or equal opportunity committees.

Parents can be an extremely useful and often neglected source of speakers. Contacts with women workers can be made by establishing a register of pupils' mothers, sisters and other female relatives who would be willing to take part in careers events. Although you are unlikely to find many women working in 'male' occupations, it is still important that women should be represented equally amongst outside speakers, so that women are seen to have the status of 'workers' as much as men.

Single-sex groups

One strategy to avoid the possible embarrassment and reluctance of pupils to show an interest in non-traditional areas of work would be to arrange sessions on a single-sex basis. Apart from the issues raised in the debate about single-sex education (see Chapter 21) and the ways that boys dominate the classroom (see Chapter 3), holding a series of 'girls only' careers sessions could go a long way to developing girls' self-confidence, and provide the opportunity for serious discussion on alternative careers for girls without the threat of ridicule from the boys. The National Advisory Centre on Careers for Women could provide useful experience and advice on how to encourage schoolgirls to use all the opportunities open to them.

Single-sex groups could also be useful when dealing with some of the practical problems of job seeking. Role playing an interview situation in the classroom can be useful in building up pupils' confidence and teaching basic interview techniques. Fellow pupils can be very critical as well as supportive, and it would probably make both boys and girls less nervous to be spared possible ridicule from the opposite sex.

However, a word of caution on single-sex groups seems appropriate here. Many teachers are quite opposed to single-sex teaching, especially if they see it as designed to give special attention to one group of pupils (girls). A talk on engineering for girls only could cause uproar in a mixed school if contrived out of the blue, instead of being part of a systematic course which had been explained previously to the staff. Establishing a tradition of single-sex teaching could also set a dangerous precedent if you move schools, and your place is taken by a sexist teacher who uses the opportunity to specialize in 'girls' and 'boys' activities (see Chapter 2, note 9). A survey of careers advice in Huddersfield (Benett and Carter, 1981) found that two out of the eleven mixed comprehensive schools surveyed separated boys and girls for careers lessons so that information on 'girls'' careers could be given to the girls, and vice versa.

Problems

Challenging sexism, particularly in relation to pupils' career aspirations, will arouse opposition. The YWCA research on girls in male jobs found that most of the girls were supported at home in their choice of career, although they had to work hard on persuading their parents that they were really serious: 'My mother was really upset and shocked at first' (YWCA, 1982, p. 2). Boys venturing into 'female' areas are more likely to encounter open hostility. For example, in 1978 a Devon mother wanted her son to do extra English instead of cookery or needlework, and a *Times Educational Supplement* report of the case (13 October 1978) showed a generally negative attitude to the idea of boys taking 'female' crafts.

Opposition may well come from local employers too, whose commitment to equal opportunity is merely skin-deep or blatantly non-existent. Some employers suggest that they could offer more jobs to young people (boys?), if it were not for all the married women who can now have their jobs held for them during maternity leave. Girls in the Huddersfield study certainly experienced prejudice from employers. One girl who went for an interview for an engineering apprenticeship, said of the firm's personnel officer: 'He made it clear that he didn't think I would get the job and that he didn't want me to get it. He said "We have never had a girl here yet" ' (Benett and Carter, 1981).

Work experience schemes for pupils during their final year at school are used widely now. Unfortunately, they tend to reinforce traditional sex roles, as girls go to shops and offices, and boys go into garages. Changing this pattern is particularly difficult because teachers rely on the goodwill of employers for these schemes to exist. However, it is worth asking employers if they will take someone of the non-traditional sex. They will probably not have considered it, and may be willing to experiment since the placement is only for a limited period.

Another possible source of opposition comes from within the school itself. It is unlikely that all the other teachers in your school will acknowledge the need for a policy of positive discrimination, and many are likely to maintain the sexist connotations of their own subject through the 'hidden curriculum'. Careers education cannot be isolated from other subjects and activities in the school, since in its widest sense it takes place in all subjects to some extent. In order to advise pupils on option and career choice, the careers teacher needs to be familiar with aspects of the curriculum, not only in terms of the formal structure of the courses offered and the subject combinations possible, but also in terms of the 'ethos' surrounding the subjects, which may vary from school to school. It is important to know, for example, if the science department actively discourages or encourages girls with ability, or is indifferent to them, and how individual members of staff in sex-typed subjects are likely to respond to pupils of the 'wrong' sex.

Active discouragement was experienced by some girls in the Huddersfield study who decided to try a non-traditional area of work: 'When she mentioned her interest in engineering, "the teachers just laughed at me" ' (Benett and Carter, 1981). The first responsibility of a careers teacher should be to offer support and encouragement to such pupils. A dilemma may arise for teachers here, however. To what extent should they try to balance their enthusiasm for the pupil to succeed in a non-traditional area with the need to prepare the pupil for the difficulties which may, and probably will, be met?

Careers advisers often find themselves caught between their own principles and the demands of sexist employers, and feel reluctant to build up the hopes of young people by encouraging them in an area where they are more likely to experience failure. One careers officer, experiencing this situation only too often, confesses '. . . so I find myself discriminating on sexist lines . . . while feeling very depressed and guilty about what I am doing'.

In the face of these doubts, we must not lose sight of the fact that a carefully conceived careers programme which results in such dilemmas will be likely to have benefited pupils in other ways: by developing confidence in decisions taken, awareness of difficulties ahead, and determination to succeed. We assume without any qualms that pupils are mature enough to choose their career at the appropriate time in all other respects – why not in this one? As Harriet Harman (1978) points out: 'Careers Officers find no difficulty in encouraging geographical mobility for the sake of wider opportunities; their fear of mobility across the sexual divisions of society should be looked at in that light.'

What counts as success?

One of the problems of trying to implement an anti-sexist approach to education is defining criteria for evaluation. There is no simple way of assessing the value of careers education courses. We can no more evaluate the anti-sexist aspects of a course by the number of pupils who enter non-traditional areas of work, than we can judge a careers course by the number of pupils who get the jobs they want at the end of it. The aims of careers education should not be simply instrumental. Job-seeking skills are an important component of careers courses, but careers education should also imply teaching about the world of work and the broader issues connected with it, such as sex discrimination, and the relationship of work to leisure and home life.

The current situation of high youth unemployment underlies this problem. Teachers do not control the labour market, but we cannot teach careers courses which ignore unemployment, or refer to it merely in the context of greater competition for jobs, and hence more refined 'employability skills'. We must set the issue of unemployment in context and deal with it as a social as well as a personal problem. This has particular implications for girls. Women are becoming unemployed at three times the rate of men. There are many reasons why women are more vulnerable in times of redundancy than men, not least of which is the historical view of women as a reserve force of labour. The deepening recession has led to women being forced back into the home when they would prefer to, and need to, have paid employment. This problem, combined with youth unemployment, is creating a new and worrying phenomenon of girls going directly into marriage and motherhood as a 'way out' of the dole queue and the scramble for jobs. Girls are resorting to marriage to confer upon themselves the status which is denied them in the labour market.

Another important example of how traditionally female areas of employment are being reduced at present is the introduction of the new technology. The biggest reductions in jobs as a result of this will be in the clerical field, where two-fifths of women are currently employed. Discussion of clerical work with pupils should include the long-term implications of the new technology and alternatives to redundancy such as job-sharing schemes, etc.

Considering the weight of traditional sex stereotyping already on pupils from within the school system, and the family, and the similar problems which the school leaver will encounter in employment, it is tempting to underrate the contribution which an anti-sexist careers education can make to equal opportunity. On the other hand, while recognizing limitations we should also remember that girls should be active participants in the learning process; what is achieved in terms of their personal development, self-confidence and general outlook on life, may not necessarily be measurable in crude statistical terms.

Resources

Books

Adams Carol and Laurikietis Rae (1976) *The Gender Trap. Book 1, Education and Work*. London, Virago.

Benett Yves and Carter Dawn (1981) *Sidetracked? A Look at the Advice Given to 5th Form Girls*. Manchester, EOC.

Coote Anna (1979) *Equal at Work? Women in Men's Jobs*. London, Collins.

CRAC (1982) *Women in Industry*.

EOC (1980) *A Guide to the Equal Treatment of the Sexes in Careers Materials*.

EOC (1981) *Breakthrough*.

Mackie Lindsay and Pattullo Polly (1977) *Women at Work*. London, Tavistock Publications.

McRobbie Angela and McCabe Trisha (eds) (1981) *Feminism for Girls — An Adventure Story*. London, Routledge and Kegan Paul.

Miller Ruth (1978) *Equal Opportunities: A Careers Guide for Women and Men*. London, Penguin Books.

New Opportunities Press *Advice* (periodical).

Thompson Jane L. (1978) *Studying Society*. London, Hutchinson.

Jones A., Marsh J. and Watts A.G. (1973) *Male and Female*. CRAC.

Films and videotapes

BBC, *It's Your Choice* series – 'Wider Horizons'. *Going to Work* series – 'Working Mothers', 'The Apprentices'. *Scene* series – 'Member of the Union', 'Changing Roles for Women'.

Engineering Careers Information Service, *What's a Girl Like You . . .?*

EOC/Thames TV, *What Are You Really Made of?*

Sheffield Film Co-op, *Jobs for the Girls*.

Women in Manual Trades, *Building your Future*.

Organizations

ACOTOS (Association of Careers Officers and Teachers Opposed to Sexism), c/o Liz Summerson, Careers Information Unit, 60a Fore Street, Trowbridge, Wiltshire BA14 8ET.

NACCW (National Advisory Centre on Careers for Women), 251 Brompton Road, London SW3 2HB.

NACGT (National Association of Careers and Guidance Teachers), c/o 9 Lawrence Leys, Bloxham, Banbury, Oxon. OX15 4NU.

Women in Manual Trades, 40 Noel Street, London W1.

British Women's Pilots Association, British Airways Terminal, P.O. Box 13, London SW1.

Women in Telecom, IN3.2.31, Room 116, Lintas House, 15–19 New Fetter Lane, London EC4.

Women's Farm and Garden Association, Courtland House, Byng Place, London WC1.

Women's Advisory Committee, TUC, Congress House, Great Russell Street, London WC1B 3LS.

Rights for Women Unit, NCCL, 21 Tabard Street, London SE1 4LA.

CHAPTER 18

SEX EDUCATION

YVETTE ROCHERON and JANIE WHYLD

This chapter does not set out a non-sexist programme of sex education, but outlines some of the issues which future programmes must deal with, and suggests some ways in which this can be achieved. We believe that issues such as 'compulsory heterosexuality', the double standard of morality, and the gender typing of young women into motherhood within marriage, can and should be raised alongside the traditional preventive concerns of sex education with unwanted pregnancies and sexually transmitted diseases. If we want young women to have real control over their fertility, images of masculinity and femininity must be explored with pupils.

Few schools have a planned programme for sex education; many do not teach it at all. It is one of the most contentious areas in the curriculum. In the late 1970s, a book on display at a parents' evening in a London girls' comprehensive was withdrawn after a parent complained to the governors. The book contained a picture of a couple lying together, and mentioned homosexuality. In 1979, the Education Minister, Lady Young, instructed the AEB to drop a question on contraception from the 'O' Level human biology paper, after a complaint from a Conservative MP, on moral grounds. This extremely conservative position aims to consolidate traditional gender relations within the family.

Teachers of sex education must give sufficient information to young people to stop them 'getting into trouble', while not giving so much as to encourage sexual activity. Consequently, there is an emphasis in sex education on the horrors of VD, a biological analysis of 'where babies come from' and a fleeting glance at 'how they got there'; and a survey of contraceptive techniques as 'a preparation for married life' – but rarely the address of the local Family Planning Association. When sex education is taught as part of religious education or social studies, there is a tendency to deal with the moral and social aspects; when it is taught in biology, sexual intercourse is presented as part of a sequence of biological events, emphasizing the internal functions of reproduction at the expense of the individual's experience. 'The most typical imagery is that of the noble sperm heroically swimming upstream to fulfil its destiny by meeting and fertilising the egg'

(Gagnon and Simon, 1974). The egg can never be heroic – it just waits around for the sperm, thus reinforcing the myth of female passivity.

The emphasis on reproduction as opposed to sexuality produces its own selective and sexist images of sexuality. A woman's body is regarded as a receptacle, first for the man's penis, and secondly for the growth of the baby. The male orgasm is dealt with because it is necessary for reproduction, but the female orgasm is not. The penis, being the organ for the elimination of liquid waste, for reproduction and for sexual sensitivity, has at least the first two functions described, but the clitoris is often omitted from diagrams of the female sexual organs. The 'liberal' line on masturbation is that it should be discussed with boys to avoid guilt feelings but, being far less common among girls, need not be discussed with them. Sex (for reproduction) is heterosexual intercourse, anything else is regarded as foreplay. Homosexuality is abnormal (because it is not for reproduction) and is regarded as something which needs to be cured. Boys cannot control their own sexual urges (which nature has made strong, for reproduction) but girls, being passive receptacles, can (or perhaps they have no sexual urges!), and it is therefore up to them to control the sexual scene by saying 'no'! The focus on reproduction reinforces the double standard of morality and paves the way for the 'she led me on' excuse for rape.

However, things are changing. The following dialogue occurred in a sex education lesson with a mixed group of 15-year-olds (1979):

Teacher: Girls at times don't take contraceptives because they don't like touching themselves. They may be afraid of touching their own bodies.

Boy: Why, miss?

Teacher: Listen, you. Ever since you were a little boy you had to touch your penis just to pee and not wet your pants. Right? (Great laughter from both sexes.) Well, girls don't have to touch themselves in the same way. Really! They touch their clothes, and they are told to be careful about their dress. They don't need to touch themselves the way boys do. (Laughter again.) That's why some women feel it's wrong to use the cap – 'Touching their bodies! Messing with themselves – no!' . . . Some women used to faint during intercourse. Even now, some women remain passive, don't move, let the man do the job.

Girl: Why?

Teacher: Because some women are afraid of showing their sexual

> feelings, afraid of letting go. They have been told never to. Perhaps they feel insecure towards the man. They'd rather pretend to give him something than to demand something – afraid of being rejected.

Same girl: Is that true, Miss?

This exchange took place within an authoritarian school run by male staff. Yet there was room in the class for the individual teacher to give an open acknowledgement of sexual pleasure and put forward female interests, despite lack of resources. A feminist approach to sex education will obviously avoid the prohibitive stance of telling girls 'Don't do it'.

Pupils should be clear that nobody really knows what sexuality is all about, although we have all experienced it. There are many conflicting theories about the ways people are affected by their sexual drive, and learning about sex goes on from birth to death. Sexual identity develops at various ages, and can change with our growing ability to communicate sexual feelings, as sexuality is about oneself in relation to others, and is often constrained by power relations.

Material for challenging stereotypes of sexuality can be found in descriptions of other cultures, and in historical accounts. Questions would fly from a class, on hearing Malinowski's comment about Trobriander women:

> On the whole, I think that in the rough usage of passion the woman is the more active. I have seen far larger scratches and marks on men than on women; and only women may actively lacerate their lovers.
>
> (Quoted in Oakley, 1972b, p. 111)

Parenthood can be examined from a cross-cultural point of view. The teacher could tell pupils how, in ancient Rome, the 'biological father' took the decision to become a father a week after the birth, by lifting the child in front of the ancestors' altar. The mother had little to do with the decision. In our society, when do men become fathers? They have to be 'told', and assured that no other man has had access to the mother nine months before the birth! How much do the biological differences in male and female reproductive roles affect men's attitudes towards women, birth and children? Among the Arapesh, childrearing was seen as a man's as well as a woman's job.[1] Examples like this may help to counter most pupils' assumptions that 'a woman's biology is her destiny'. The concept of being a mother can be challenged. When does a woman become a mother? At the moment of birth? During pregnancy? When leaving hospital? When the baby is a few months old, and the biological mother is thought to be strong enough to cope with the child without the help of female neighbours and relatives? And when does motherhood cease?

The work of Masters and Johnson can be used to introduce and challenge conventional notions of biological response. Their descriptions of the sexual responses of males and females give the teacher an unthreatening way of talking about female multiple orgasms and masturbation, but care is needed to avoid being too clinical and technical. Material from studies of sexual activity can also be used to introduce the fact that a large number of people have homosexual desires and relationships. Teachers could stress the variety of patterns and life-styles among homosexuals as well as hetero-sexuals. With older groups you might discuss the legal discrimination against gays, and why some decide to 'come out'. Ask which changes in the laws on homosexuality pupils would support. Another approach to homo-sexuality is to place it in an historical context. With the help of a history teacher, find material showing how 'respectable' homosexuality was in ancient Greece. You can use photos of Greek art, showing the male body, and point out that we see very few pictures of the naked male today, compared with the female. From this starting point you might explore social and cultural changes regarding 'gays' and why present masculine stereotyping makes most men fear homosexuality.

Attitudes towards observed sexual behaviour can best be explored around questions from pupils. The 'problem page' technique is a simple one which will elicit ideas from pupils who might otherwise hesitate because of embarrassment. Get them to select letters from published problem pages, or to write their own 'problem' letters. A variation on this is to get everyone to write down a question on a card. It is important to stress that the problems need not be personal, and you may also need to preserve anonym-ity. The object is for pupils to discuss questions about which they are unsure.

There are several direct techniques which can be used for starting discus-sion. Explain how large sectors of the population differ from statistical averages of height and weight; and that this also applies to aspects of sexual development such as the onset of puberty, the time of the first menstrua-tion, as well as to personal values and sexual interest. Some people may want many sexual partners, and others be celibate by choice. You might stress that there is a spectrum of sexual choice, and if the class has become confident with each other and with the teacher, you might suggest that they place themselves on a homo-/heterosexual scale, or a promiscuous/celibate one.

A way of breaking down myths attached to sex is to write down as many myths as possible on separate cards, or to list them on the board, e.g. 'A woman cannot become pregnant if she has sex standing up' or, 'Men have a greater sex drive than women'. Getting the class to continue the list once you have started it will show the level of knowledge of the group, which will be useful in planning further lessons.

Specific situations, such as a young girl telling her mother/friend she is pregnant can be role-played, and the issues thrown up will form a basis for discussion: abortion (shall she, shan't she?); contraception (whose responsibility?); the way pregnancy affects her life, but not her boyfriend's (she may not feel well); marriage; finding somewhere to live; childbirth; adoption; postnatal depression. A similar approach, either through role play or case-study, could be adopted towards the situation of a girl being persuaded by her boyfriend to have sex: what are the pressures, both social and physical, on the boy and the girl? What did they feel afterwards, emotionally and physically? Did the girl 'give in'? Was there any sexual harassment, physical violence or emotional blackmail? How do people who do not want to have sex cope with relationships? What type of relationships do they form? Because you have had sex with a person once, is it assumed that you will continue to have sex with them?

Gender typing related to sexual situations can also be explored through role play, or writing notes. Take this situation: 'John fancies Penny, whom he does not know very well. How does he tell her he finds her attractive? And how can she respond?' The pupils will quickly realize that there is a variety of language and gestures by which males usually express their sexual desires, and females respond. The situation can then be reversed: 'Cathy fancies Richard. How does she convey to him that she finds him attractive?' The class will compile a very different, and probably shorter list. If you have established a group where all the members feel confident and safe with each other, this situation could be developed into an assertiveness training exercise, where girls could practice inviting a boy out, and both sexes could practice saying and being told 'no'.

To get away from the idea that sex is just a physical response, you might present a selection, taped or written out, of different authors' descriptions of sex and love (e.g. Barbara Cartland, D.H. Lawrence, Marge Piercy). By using many different views, an impression of the uniqueness and individuality of feeling can be transmitted. If you discuss the way romance shapes girls' expectations of love and marriage, take care not to make the girls feel ashamed of their reading. Also examine the ways in which war games and war films shape boys' ideas of masculinity, and how it is difficult for them to escape the 'macho' stereotype. Sex education in too many schools looks at 'women's problems' such as depression or menstruation, and totally ignores the problems of being male. This in turn tends to reinforce negative impressions of women, and present them as chronic patients – the 'weaker sex'.

With any group where you are uncertain of how they have been taught before, or what they know, it is important to ensure that they have a basic knowledge of anatomy, contraception and conception, without embarrassing them by exposing their lack of knowledge. Puberty is a useful topic to start with, since it raises little controversy with colleagues and parents, and the development of the body can be explained. With an older group, general discussion can be introduced by asking pupils to select from cards presented face down, with parts of the anatomy such as 'clitoris' written on them, as well as terms such as 'orgasm'. In Jackson's study (1978) only two out of the 24 girls interviewed knew where their clitoris was, and that it was the source of sexual pleasure. You can talk about male and female masturbation, suggesting that to touch oneself is a good way of discovering one's sexual feelings.

It is also important to give practical advice on where to obtain contraception, early abortion (which should never be presented as a form of contraception) and welfare. We find it inadvisable to invite open discussion on controversial issues such as abortion and homosexuality, until a lot of information has been given, for instance on legal rights, and pupils have been encouraged to think about these issues in a sensitive way. Uninformed discussion only tends to reinforce established prejudice.

There is very little non-sexist material widely available. Cuttings can be taken from feminist magazines; and women's pressure groups, such as the National Abortion Campaign, have up-to-date leaflets and posters. But be careful not to suggest that the women's movement has answers to all the questions it raises! You can use sexist resources in a non-sexist way by asking pupils to spot stereotypes. If you think a film conveys gender-typed roles, but is otherwise useful, ask the pupils for an alternative script. Be careful not to set up norms of visual attraction. If your pictures show only glamorous people, insist that pimples, wrinkles or a flat or fat chest are no obstacle to sexual potential. If images of women are not explored elsewhere in the curriculum, spend a little time on this, and on images of men, and for comparison introduce pictures of men and women thought to be glamorous in other cultures, and in earlier times.

Ideally, sex education should be taught in small groups with time allocated for single-sex group discussion. It should be developed from an interdisciplinary approach with teachers from most subjects contributing, either within their own subject time, or within the context of a health and social education programme designed to run over several years. Setting this up will require confidence and determination. Few teachers are fortunate enough to find enough colleagues in their own school to establish a working party, but you may be able to find support from other teachers within the same authority, and from local health education officers. Try to involve parents, but be clear what you expect from them. If you suspect opposition, wait until you have some consensus within the school. Start with a modest programme for a trial period. Some schools have developed long-term programmes from initial informal discussions with girls at lunchtime over a six-week period.

When you decide on a programme, be clear why you wish to introduce a particular topic. Make sure that the classroom materials underline your objectives. This is nothing but sound teaching practice, but all the more important because sex education can create controversy. Make sure that you appeal to pupils' experience without embarrassing them. Make it clear that you do not want to probe into their sexual lives, nor allow them to investigate yours. Move slowly from familiar experiences to more controversial issues. Give local addresses of where to get help and information. Bring in some fun and humour. Above all, develop the feeling that relationships are not static. Reject the depressing thought that 'Men will be men, you know!' It is not so. Men have changed their attitudes to their work and families. So have women!

Resources

Many of the best materials have been cheaply produced and will not last, or are of an experimental nature. Less ephemeral non-sexist materials are in preparation, so it is important to contact some of the addresses below.

Who Tells the Children? (Community Education Project, Manchester Road, London E14) – a teaching pack designed for fourth-year pupils. It includes a pupil booklet, material for photocopying, cartoons, fact sheets, games, quizzes, and deals with sexual identity, caring, rape, contraception, VD, making love, and images of sex in society.
Somebody's Daughter (ILEA Resources Unit) – a five-episode drama on

video, which tells the story of a white girl, trainee hairdresser, 17, and her boyfriend, 18, black, full-time college student, and the dilemmas they face when she becomes pregnant. Many of the ILEA resources dealing with gender and race relations are useful for sex education.

Schools Council Projects: *Health Education 13–18*, Humanities Project *Family* and *Relations Between the Sexes*, and Moral Education Project *Lifeline* – parts of these are useful.

Birmingham Brook Advisory Centre, Education Service, 9 York Road, Edgbaston, Birmingham B16 9HX has produced tapes of interviews with girls and boys; excellent for starting group discussions on adolescents' sexual feelings, falling in love, and contraception.

Institute of Sex Education and Research Ltd, 38 School Road, Moseley, Birmingham B13 9SN has produced tape and slide kits showing the variety of body forms and developments – use selectively.

Taught to be Girls – an excellent film on femininity and gender roles. (Available from the Cinema of Women, 27 Clerkenwell Close, London EC1.)

Whose Responsibility – a film by the National Abortion Campaign which discusses how to get an early abortion. The story of the girl is movingly portrayed. Use extracts as it is rather long.

The Causes of Lesbianism – a series of cartoons on possible explanations for lesbianism in *Sourcream*. (Available from 136 Florence Street, London N1, or feminist bookshops.)

Spare Rib no. 109 on romance and rape, and no. 75 on sex education. Many of the best pieces written by young women for *Spare Rib* have been published in *Girls Are Powerful*, edited by Susan Hemmings (Sheba Feminist Publishers).

Make It Happy by Jane Cousins (Penguin or Virago, 1978) – a sex education book written for teenagers (15+), which deals positively with sexual identity and sexual techniques.

Growing Up Homosexual – a short pamphlet on the oppression of gays. (Available from Birmingham Gay Education Group, c/o Peace Centre, 18 Moose Street, Birmingham.)

Recommended reading

'How to make babies: sexism in sex education' by Stevi Jackson, in *Women's Studies International Quarterly*, vol. 1, no. 4 (Pergamon).

My Mother Said . . . The Way Young People Learned about Sex and Birth

Control by Christine Farrell (Routledge and Kegan Paul, 1978) – a survey of parental and young people's attitudes to sex education.

Feminism for Girls: an Adventure Story, by Angela McRobbie and Trisha McCabe (eds) (Routledge and Kegan Paul, 1981) – especially part 11.

Human Sexual Response by W. Masters and V. Johnson (Little Brown and Co., 1966).

Pregnant at School – a report on schoolgirl pregnancies (The National Council for One-parent Families, 255 Kentish Town Road, London NW5 2LX).

Working with Girls – newsletter from the National Association of Youth Clubs Girls Work. Issue no. 11, Sept/Oct 1982, is all about sex education in youth clubs.

Note

1   For comparative anthropological and historical materials see: Mead M. *Sex and Temperament in Three Primitive Societies* (William Morrow, 1935); Beah F. (ed.) *Sex and Behaviour* (John Wiley, 1965); and Ardener S. (ed.) *Perceiving Females* (Malaby Press, 1975).

Acknowledgement

The authors want to thank Jane Lethbridge of *New Grapevine*, many of whose teaching ideas we have borrowed.

CHAPTER 19

PHYSICAL EDUCATION

PAT BROWNE, LENE MATZEN and JANIE WHYLD

Physical education is not like other school subjects. Pupils spend a lot of their free time playing sport or practising gymnastics like handstands, but not much time talking French, writing poetry or even making stink bombs. Sexism in PE is not a matter of reading material which ignores women, although press coverage of sport is more likely to include pictures of women and written descriptions of men's achievements, implying that when men taken part it is the sport which is of interest, while in women's sport, women themselves are of interest.[1] In school PE, many sexist attitudes stem from ideas about the need for sexual modesty in women, which dictate that they should not come into physical contact with men; and assumptions about gender-linked physical differences – the muscle power and speed which men are supposed to have always being valued more highly than the control and suppleness attributed to women.

Although many girls and boys do PE together in primary schools, they are almost always separated in secondary school. Reasons given for this vary from the 'physiological' – 'They develop at different rates', to the practical – 'They (we) want (them) to learn different games'. If all PE was taught in mixed groups some of the 'boys'' activities might have to give way to 'girls'' activities. Sport is still the focal point of PE in many schools, especially where the teachers or perhaps just the head of department, are first and foremost sportspeople. What schools need are first-rate teachers, not first-rate sportsplayers. Barnard (1982) argues that the reason for this situation lies with teacher training institutions which select entrants to PE courses on the basis of their excellence in sport.

The amalgamation of PE and sport increases the gap between boys' and girls' attitudes to physical activity. Many girls reject PE because they confuse it with sport (male sport has high status, women's sport much lower status, and the 'jolly hockey sticks' image conflicts with developing femininity). Men and boys reject the idea of mixed PE because they say girls would not be able to compete with them (debatable, but competition occurs in sport rather than in PE). In some schools, a lot of emphasis in PE is put on getting into the house, school or area team. It should not be the aim of PE to select the best gymnasts, or to coach budding football players, but to develop the whole person. A well-implemented sports programme can have educational value, but its relationship to PE should be reassessed before the status and true nature of PE is trampled beneath the football boots or drowned in the swimming pool. Few would question the contrasting viewpoints underlying sport and PE, and it is difficult for one teacher to cope with the conflicting demands of both: egalitarianism, cooperation and improvement in PE; elitism, competition and performance for sport.

In Denmark, where state law gives guidance on the aims of teaching, the Education Act 1975 states that PE must 'improve the physical, psychological and social development of the students'. In Britain, the situation is less clear. A central strand of the philosophical debate is that PE is not education *of* the physical, but *through* the physical. So although PE deals mainly with physical activities, it implies intellectual and emotional appreciation of our own physical nature, and of the way we relate physically to others. PE should be about extending the physical potential of the individual. There should be a sound build-up of basic movement skills before the teaching of games. The teacher must consider the individual pupil's abilities, and should be able to give pupils the opportunity to experience movement as a means of communication and expression. If these ideals were achieved for all pupils, regardless of sex or individual ability, there would be no sexism in PE.

Evidence from pupils shows that often they are told to copy some activity without ever understanding why; and although PE is always taught in mixed-ability groups, exercises are frequently the same for all so that many are incapable of making any real attempt at the work, and may experience fear. Many pupils are unable to relate what they are learning to their own participation in sports, so they do not appreciate sport as spectators. This is one reason why girls, when they leave school, often drop any participation in physical activity.

School and teachers

If PE is well taught, it may and should be accepted as part of the complete process of education. We can learn as much through physical activity as through numeracy or literacy. But it is a non-exam, non-academic element of the curriculum. Although it is becoming more accepted as a worthwhile activity within the education system (with the introduction of an 'O' Level and CSE in dance, and a planned 'O' Level and existing CSE in PE), most people still regard PE as a fringe, low-status activity. Poor performance in academic or vocational subjects will provoke comment on a school report, but even non-attendance in PE may go unremarked.

The history of PE may go some way to explaining its low status, and the different attitudes to boys' and girls' PE. Three distinct styles can be identified in the development of physical training since the middle of the 19th century. Boys of the upper and middle classes in public schools played team games, particularly cricket and rugby. Organized games were thought to provide not only physical benefit, but also to instil qualities of self-reliance, initiative and a selfless team spirit, necessary for the development of leadership.

Physical training for girls was closely linked with the struggle for female emancipation. Medical experts in Britain and America held that academic study would be injurious to women's health, and that the resultant weakness should not be further aggravated by exposing them to physical strain. Despite this, Frances Buss included callisthenics, or physical training, as part of the curriculum in her North London Collegiate School. The therapeutic nature of these exercises was stressed as a remedial element to counteract the charge that mental exertion would lead to physical breakdown. These 'Swedish exercises', developed by Per Ling at the end of the 18th century, were based on a romantic ideal of free movement, but by the time they came to be taught in Madame Bergman-Osterberg's teacher-training gymnasium (which a century later provided women PE teachers to all the 'best' girls' schools), the emphasis was as much on coordination as on free expression. Based on flow, timing and graces these rhythmical exercises were performed with precision of movement at the command of the instructor, who had to keep strict control over her class. Many women PE teachers were committed to challenging the idea that women were naturally weak and sickly, and to show that, with self-discipline, women could be strong and healthy. Thus disciplinarianism and feminism became linked in the tradition of girls' PE.

Despite the fear that competitive games would make girls too 'masculine', by the end of the 19th century most girls' schools had introduced some team games which did not have masculine connotations, such as lacrosse and hockey. There was still debate between those who held that team games developed powers of organization, speed of thought and action, and self-lessness; and those like Sara Burstall, who thought they were 'a mere imitation of the ways of boys' schools'. In girls' PE more emphasis was laid on gymnastics and athletics.

In state elementary schools, physical training was mostly of the military drill type. It was believed that this would promote obedience and social order, and also improve the health of the lower classes (thus producing greater efficiency in industrial workers). Drill exercises for boys were carried out by instructors, often retired sergeant majors, who visited the school on a part-time basis. Their status was such that they were not allowed in the staff room. In many cases, girls had no physical training.

Gradually PE was absorbed into the curriculum, but until the late 1960s, many PE teachers had still only undergone a two-year training. Although today all PE teachers take degrees, and women PE teachers are educationalists, male PE teachers still tend to be coaches and instructors. In mixed schools, this has frequently led to two single-sex departments with different educational philosophies, traditions and experiences, coexisting under a single head of department (usually male). It is well known that in some primary schools, deputy headships 'happen' to be tied to football and/or boys' games; and as with headships, women are less likely to get head of department posts where this involves responsibility for boys' as well as girls' education. As the number of single-sex schools declines, so does the number of women heads of PE. In Rotherham there are now only two women heads of PE whereas a few years ago there were several, and in the boroughs of Redbridge, Newham and Havering, for example, there are no women heads of PE in mixed schools.

Pupils see the status of sport in society reflected in the school department. The head of department is male, since men's sport is more important than women's sport. Because the head of department allocates resources, boys' classes (which he may teach) have first claim on the space in the gyms, sports halls and fields. Announcing football results in assembly also gives competitive sports, mostly male, undue importance.[2] So girls learn that PE is more important for boys than it is for them. As Byrne says, 'The artificial split for PE at secondary level first endorses in girls' eyes the exclusive masculinity of prestige sports which is a generally harmful and unnecessary sex message' (Byrne, 1978, p. 127).

When children go to secondary school, they have, probably for the first time, a specialist PE teacher. It is very important to break the stereotype of the male PE teacher, as portrayed in the film *Kes* – aggressive, authoritarian, using his superior strength to terrify and punish. Children often idolize particular teachers whom they emulate, and PE teachers seem to run fairly high in the popularity charts because of their often superior physique, and because their subject can be a lot more fun than most, especially for the less academic pupils who are used to failure and frustration elsewhere in school. It is a great shame if the characteristics which are perpetuated in PE are rough behaviour, hardness and the 'stiff upper lip'. The effects of 'male' PE – going out in bad weather and over-zealous cross-country running – can themselves be brutalizing. It was pleasing to see the subject treated differently in the film *Gregory's Girl*, where boys were shown resenting their enforced PE, while a girl enjoyed her (voluntary) physical training. A film like that can do a lot to change attitudes.

The PE teacher has a moral obligation to help channel and diffuse the violence in society, particularly that surrounding male sport. PE teachers are in a unique situation to view the physiological development of their pupils, and to funnel growing energy and exuberance in a constructive way. Women PE teachers should try to make girls aware that they have been conditioned into passivity, and try to get them, by gentle persuasion and encouragement, to develop confidence and pleasure in their physical ability. Men PE teachers have more chance than most to show that it is possible to 'be a man', and still be caring and show emotion.

Mixed PE?

In planning a non-sexist PE curriculum, an issue of fundamental importance is whether groups should be mixed or not. Segregating the sexes for PE teaches children that the differences between the male and female bodies are more important than the similarities. The establishment message is clearly that with the onset of puberty, boys and girls should not be allowed to view each others' bodies, not be put in a situation where they are required to have physical contact. On a practical level, one of the main arguments for mixed PE is that girls would get an equal share of the resources, space, time and status that are at present allocated unequally in favour of boys. However, experience has shown that coeducation rarely leads to such equitable sharing (see Sections 1 and 3 of this book), and feminists are alarmed that if PE were taught in mixed groups, without a radical revaluation of aims and teaching methods, then girls would end up doing boys' PE, on the fringe and being pushed around. We favour mixed PE because we feel it is harmful to teach boys and girls that there are areas of their lives which should and must be separate, and we hope that the presence of girls, acting positively, could lessen the aggressive tendencies in male sport.

Until children reach puberty, there are no major physical differences between boys and girls, so there is no physical justification for having certain exercises for girls and others for boys. During and after puberty, changes occur in the body which put boys at a physical advantage. They become able to absorb more oxygen than girls, the amount of muscle in boys represents a higher percentage of their total weight, and they grow bigger than girls. This provides the physiological reasons for the segregation of the sexes, but social expectations of what is appropriate for boys and girls carry far more weight. It should be remembered that statistics relating to the physical development of the sexes refer to the *average* boy and girl, and there will be many individuals who do not fit this general pattern.

There is often the objection that if PE were mixed, boys, being stronger, would become bored if they were not able to use all their strength, and had to pay attention to the less able (girls) all the time. This is a question of grading exercises, which has to be faced by any teacher of mixed-ability classes. It must be shown, particularly to boys who have undergone 'traditional' sports training, that PE is not only concerned with muscular strength, but also with control and discipline of the body. Taking part in mixed physical activities might well encourage girls to assert themselves more, if the teacher is able to create an atmosphere where girls feel free to develop their physical potential at the same rate as boys. If girls are good at football, there should be no barriers to their joining a team, or forming one of their own. Probably they would gain experience faster by playing in the boys' team in league matches, as has already happened in a London junior school.

Some people enjoy mixed physical activities, and some do not. If the school curriculum allows a choice, so much the better. Schools which already operate mixed games sessions often find they end up with some mixed and some single-sex activities, simply through pupil choice. A Lincolnshire 11–18 comprehensive has mixed games for fifth- and sixth-formers (compulsory for the fifth, and optional for the sixth, although only half a dozen pupils choose private study instead). Games are chosen each term from soccer, rugby, hockey, netball, badminton, volleyball and basketball. All, in theory, are mixed, but girls are not encouraged by anybody to do soccer or rugby. If a girl wanted to do these, she would be allowed to, but none so far have wanted to. Some arguments are put forward, like 'It would spoil the boys' game', and 'The boys would be afraid to tackle properly'. The Rugby Football Union is unhappy about the insurance against injury for girls. The school would like to run an all-girls soccer option, but at present is restricted by staff shortage. Netball remains all-girls by choice; boys tend to choose basketball. The other games are fairly evenly mixed.

The pupils' reaction to mixed games is 'O.K. It appears to them a natural thing to do'. When they first start in the fifth form, there are questions like 'Can boys do hockey?' to which the answer is 'Yes'. 'It's as simple as that.' The girls like mixed hockey. 'Occasionally they complain that a boy is playing like a bull in a china shop. They usually deal with the boy themselves, maybe go over to him and say something like "Watch your stick".' The hockey team is coached by a male teacher. Play has always been aggressive, but now it is more skilful.

At this school, there is also one period of PE each week in single-sex groups. The reason given for this is 'tradition'. Boys and girls are timetabled for PE at the same time, so there would be no practical difficulties in having mixed sessions. There was once a mixed group of first years for PE because of a 'fluke' of timetabling. It was 'alright'. The pupils liked it. The girls were a bit shy at first, but it only took a couple of weeks to get over that. There were no complaints from parents. Boys and girls competed equally. On the whole, boys learnt skills more quickly and reached a 'plateau' of ability, and then, three or four weeks later, the girls would catch up. There was no adverse reaction from the other staff because they were 'only first years'. After discussing the issue of mixed PE the head of PE, a woman, said 'Your questions are making me think that maybe it is time to get such things discussed at our Curriculum Planning Board'.

Mixed PE is now being tried in several schools, including DeBrus School, Skelton, Cleveland (except for third-years) and in ILEA, at Battersea County School (for first-year games) and Abbey Wood School, who reported that their successful classes over the last two years had given rise to 'some unexpected problems such as girl footballers in our team who have had to fight disqualification from their all-girl outside football teams, because they were playing in mixed teams' (*Schools Council Newsletter*, November 1982, ILEA supplement).

Competition or cooperation?

One of the most widely accepted opinions about human nature is that people perform best when motivated, and in our culture motivation is usually provided through competition, which is held to be a natural instinct, and desirable – necessary for survival. We would argue that this is mistaken and that cooperation is more important than competition. People are taught to be competitive; 'Don't cheat' means 'Don't help or ask for help from others'. Competition engenders all sorts of unpleasant feelings, such as being pushy to win, and resentment inevitably accompanies failure.

To accept that people can be motivated without competition, it is necessary to understand the distinction between competition and challenge. Most of the positive effects of competition are, in fact, those of challenge – the thrill of success, managing to achieve something against difficult odds, like climbing a mountain or reaching a personal best time. All of these help to build self-confidence. Whenever there is competition, there is always a loser – and this involves loss of confidence which will only turn into a desire 'to do better next time' if there is a realistic chance of success; the problem is that many people learn early on that they are never likely to win, so give up making any effort whatsoever. Even worse are the unhealthy attitudes engendered in the winners – 'We're the greatest', 'Holier than thou', 'You're not worth bothering with now'. Most school games lessons are geared towards competitive sports, perhaps because hardly any non-competitive games exist in Britain now, although some are being developed or rediscovered (see 'Resources').

The present enthusiasm for marathon running is a good example of how a sport can be enjoyable for both participants and spectators, although little emphasis is laid on winning. In the 1981 London Marathon, the two leading runners Beardsley and Simonsen, made a point of finishing together, holding hands. Spectators regularly show as much interest in and support for those runners who finish against difficult personal odds – the old, the obese, those in weird garb, and those who collapse under the strain but crawl to the finishing post – as in those who finish first. This has encouraged the participation of many who would normally be excluded from competitive sport, where only the best are selected for teams.

All sports which are not team games can be practised in a non-competitive way by laying the emphasis on beating the clock, or improving on a personal or team best. For running over a short distance, each group (or the whole class, if space allows them to run at once) could have their times added together, with the aim of achieving a class record at the end of every lesson. Where pupils are performing the same type of activity, and there is bound to be comparison between personal performances, set different aims for each person, like a handicap race, and make it quite clear that they should be aiming at improving their own performance, and not at beating the person next to them. Group exercises can be designed to require a number of skills which might be provided by different group members: the teacher asks a group to jump a total length of exactly x metres; the last person to jump might not have to jump very far, but very accurately. The teacher's attitude is very important. If the same exercise is set for several groups, and the one which finishes first, or most accurately, is praised, then the exercise becomes competitive.

Where team games are played, attention should be given to how the teams are picked. Never let pupils pick their own teams so that the less skilled or unpopular ones are made to feel unwanted, or that they will be more of a burden than a help. A quick, unbiased way is to get the class to line up and count them off, one, two, three, etc. to the required number of teams (for more examples, see Chapter 2). When teaching team sports, take plenty of time to teach basic skills and rules, especially if the game is new to some pupils in a group, such as boys playing netball. If the game is dominated by a small group of good players, try using them as referees or coaches, so that the rest of the group is of a more even standard.

Another technique to lessen the effect of competition is to teach PE in an exploratory manner. The teacher's starting point is the difference between the pupils. The learning process does not depend on the acquisition of skills which are well defined from the outset, but on the individual experience and appreciation of movements (Luke, 1970). So the teacher puts forward certain conditions, and the pupils experiment and show each other various possibilities. For example, instead of saying 'athletics', the teacher might ask the group to create an exercise 'where you are doing something which involves running, jumping and throwing', or 'Move in different ways, e.g. fast, powerful, easy, coordinated, rhythmically, etc.'. Working in pairs will teach pupils to know what to expect from other people in situations where they have to adjust to the other person's energy and strength, will create confidence and sensitivity towards others, and help them to plan work with others. Activities which can be done in pairs are: one person making a statue of the other, lifting each other up in certain ways, and dance and gymnastic routines.

Building confidence – elements of a non-sexist curriculum

The relationship of PE to the emergent self-image is a very important one. If girls are constantly doing 'girls' activities' in lessons when boys play football, then the girls are going to have an image of themselves as dainty, non-ball players. It is important that all pupils try a large number of different activities in PE so that everybody has a chance of finding the activity for which they are best suited and which gives them the most pleasure. It is important to allow boys into dance classes without putting them down, to have female teachers teaching football, and to do anything which turns the traditional male/female images upside down. The self-image problem is equally serious for boys and girls. For a boy to take part in a feminine activity like dance, means a loss of prestige. This can be very damaging if not handled correctly by the teacher. It also means that many boys will miss out on what could be a positive and rewarding experience. For girls the problem is a bit different. When they play football, they get lots of encouragement from boys (as long as they don't have to play with them). They are learning to play the right sort of game, they are aspiring to something higher, but in the eyes of most boys they are still 'only girls'. An alternative could be to train the girls very thoroughly in the tactical and technical skills. Most boys could learn a lot from this too, as most of them just kick the ball round the field, not really playing at all.

All through the teaching of PE it is important to help the girls to build up confidence about their own capabilities and strength. We think that this is best done together with boys. It is impossible to build up confidence about some mysterious force, whose strength you don't know. If girls and boys are being taught together it is easier to show the girls that they have no need to feel physically inferior, and that the myth about what boys can do and what girls should do is quite false. The teacher can show pupils that in some areas there are differences in strength between girls and boys but that this isn't the be-all and end-all, because how does the weakest boy compare to the strongest girl? All these things are difficult to handle if you are only teaching the girls – yet another argument for mixed teaching. It is also very difficult to check the aggression in boys and the 'hero' image of the male PE teacher, if the teaching is segregated.

Eradicating sexism in PE is not simply a case of giving girls confidence to participate in 'male' activities, but also of attaching greater importance to stereotyped feminine pursuits, like dancing. Where dance is taught by specialist teachers, it is usually well received, but unfortunately the image among pupils and parents is still that dance is 'cissy' for boys.[3] It is difficult for dance teachers to break this image, particularly if dance remains an optional subject chosen by girls, but it is probably easier now than it has ever been, due to the popularity of disco dancing, and the possibility of using video material to motivate pupils. Modern dancing is an excellent form of physical exercise, requiring and developing suppleness, balance, control and cooperation, and needing sustained physical energy. If any boys are too uncontrollable or boisterous at the beginning of a dance session, they could always be invited to demonstrate their virility with a little Cossack or

Morris dancing. A good way to end a lesson is with a quick dance, so that everyone leaves feeling all warm and puffed out.

It is not usually the responsibility of the PE department to teach health education, but questions about sex arise naturally in PE sessions or the changing room, and should not be ignored. Girls often ask to be excused PE during menstruation, and this may give rise to discussion on reproduction. It is to be hoped that schools have an overall policy on sex education, and that back-up work will be available from other departments (see Chapter 18). An alternative to excusing girls from PE or forcing them to do it, if they are suffering from period pains, would be to show them some relaxation exercises and massage to relieve suffering. This would also demonstrate that PE is about more than toughening up the body, and can also be used to care for it.

One important social aspect of PE could include mixed changing. This suggestion usually arouses great hostility, based on envisaged embarrassment and shock at the threat to sexual modesty. But mixed changing would provide a wonderful opportunity to foster early healthy and natural attitudes to the body. It would be unrealistic to expect PE teachers to eliminate the guilt and shame about the body which children acquire at a very early age in our society, but it could be advocated as one of the aims of a good PE programme. Unfortunately, current practice is to provide separate changing facilities even in primary schools.

As part of her teaching practice in Denmark, one of the authors (LM) had the opportunity to teach a group of primary children and introduce mixed changing. (This is as unusual in Denmark as it is here, but as showers are compulsory, it involves total nudity.) She found that it was the parents who were shy rather than the children, but of course the parents' inhibitions rubbed off on them. During the first couple of weeks the children showed a lot of curiosity in each others' bodies, and asked lots of questions about bodies and sex, and after that it was accepted as normal. A colleague had the opportunity to teach a mixed class during puberty. According to her, the pupils rarely caused problems, and seemed to have a more relaxed attitude to things like menstruation. They asked questions about it, accepted it as a physical condition peculiar to girls, and no longer saw it as 'something dirty and rude'. Of course, this demanded a very open attitude from both teacher and pupils, and a willingness on the part of the teacher to deal with all questions and not to refer them back to parents or the biology teacher.

Self-defence

It must be made very clear that self-defence is a true defence, not attack. It must be used in a non-violent way, working with blocking and evasion, not one brute force against another. The negative energy in the attack can be turned against the aggressor. Self-defence should not be presented as a form of martial art.

Boys are constantly encouraged to test their strength against each other, whereas girls, after puberty, quickly lose confidence. Girls' fighting is discouraged at school as 'unladylike', whereas boys' is often tolerated (see Chapter 2), and there is no institutionalized test of strength or development of aggression in girls' sport which compares with the male rugby scrum. Lack of practice means that women do not acquire skills of combat. Also, being constantly told they are weak, they tend to forget their actual strength, unless it is tested. Heather Brigstocke, head of St Paul's Girls School and president of the Girls' School Association, maintains that all girls should learn self-defence at school (*Times Educational Supplement*, 13 November 1981), and has made self-defence lessons compulsory at her school. There is no doubt that violence occurs against women and girls, and it is arguable that all pupils should learn to defend themselves, at least against minor attacks.

Given that self-defence is more necessary for girls than it is for boys, and that the consideration of girls should be a priority in this area, opinions differ about whether girls would learn best in single-sex groups. Many people feel it is sexist and contradictory to argue for mixed PE (and general equality for women), and then demand special lessons for girls (but see Chapter 21). The need probably depends on what age group is being considered. Younger girls will be more used to rough-and-tumble in the playground, and may be nearer to boys of the same age in their ability to defend themselves. Fifth-form girls are more likely to have suffered the dreadful loss of confidence in physical ability which is part of women's socialization, and with them it may be necessary to have some practice in an all-girls group, where they have a safe place to experiment, and talk about their reluctance to use force, and fears of violence. Building up psychological confidence is as important as physical training. The girls must feel that they are worth defending, as well as being capable. Our experience is that boys very quickly get over their gentlemanly qualms about hurting a girl once they have been floored by one. The main problem for girls in a mixed group will be overcoming their socially induced tendency to passivity. It must also be remembered that the 'naturally aggressive male' is a stereotype, and there are less confident boys who will benefit from compensatory training in a safe, supportive situation.

'Women aren't physically capable'

Much of the discrimination against women in sport, and hence girls in PE, has been justified by arguing that women are physically weaker and more vulnerable than men. Evidence shows that the difference in strength between the trained male and female athlete is far less than between the average, or untrained man and woman (Crittenden, 1974). Evidence also exists to disprove the belief that women are physically weak. Endowed with a different kind of strength from men, the problem is that women are not encouraged to develop their physical potential. Women are very strong when carrying babies, young children and heavy shopping. You seldom see men do this. Janice Kaplan, the American sports writer, says 'I generally accept the studies of Dr Jack Wilmore, that suggests that under optimal conditions there would be a 5% difference between men and women in terms of strength . . . But what upsets me is that among most of us, this small gap gets enlarged to an abyss . . . a 50% differential' (Kaplan, 1979).

Two sports in which women seem to have proved themselves are swimming and running. Dr Ken Dyer (1977) admits, 'Differences in the past seem to have been more social than biological'. At the 1976 Montreal Olympics, the difference between the men's and women's world record for the 800 metres was 11.4 seconds. In the past 30 years, the women's record has improved by 13.5 seconds, the men's by 1.4 seconds. Just after the war, women were running world records at speeds which averaged 80 per cent of men's. Now they are running at 90 per cent the speed of men. In swimming, the gap is so small it is hardly worth mentioning, the female record for the 800 metres being 96 per cent of the speed of the male record. Katherine Switzer made history as the first woman to run the Boston marathon. During the 1970s, while the men's marathon record did not improve at all, women cut their best time from 3 hrs 7 min 26 sec to 2 hrs 25 min 41 sec. Women hold the speed record for swimming the channel in both directions; in 1978 Penny Dean beat the previous male record by more than 1 hour.

Despite this evidence of women's physical endurance, women are still not allowed to swim 1500 metres in international competition nor to compete in ski jumping or pole vaulting; and the IOC has only recently allowed a women's marathon to be added to the 1984 Olympic Games. It was not until 1960 that women were allowed to enter the 800 metres; the Committee found that the race was too exhausting for women, and also that a sweaty, panting woman was an unpleasant sight. That, for us, is where the real issue lies. It seems an odd sort of reasoning to exclude people from competitive sport because they are not good enough. If they keep losing, they will drop out anyway, or be knocked out in the heats. One can understand the weaker group demanding separate competitions so that they do not always get beaten, but not the stronger group – unless, of course, they are secretly afraid they might lose!

Dr Elizabeth Ferris, a bronze medal winner for diving in the 1960 Olympics, has applied herself to demonstrating that physiology is not the main obstacle to women's progress in sport. 'It became very interesting to juxtapose what people thought women were capable of and what women were clearly showing themselves to be capable of' (Walker, 1980). With regard to the discriminatory sex tests that women have to undergo, she points out that no one ever asked a man to produce a sperm sample before he could compete. Some would argue that men are less well equipped than women to compete in sport: 'Female genitals are compact and internal, protected by her body. Male genitals are so exposed that he must be protected from outside attack to ensure the perpetuation of the race. His vulnerability obviously requires sheltering . . . (A boy) remembers his sister jeering at his primitive genitals that "flap around foolishly". She can run, climb and ride horseback unencumbered' (Twin, 1979).

All in all, arguing that women are not physically capable of participating in top sport, whether this be true or not, is strange justification for excluding them at school level. The qualities which are often valued in connection with PE are the so-called 'masculine' qualities such as strength and aggression. Why not concentrate instead on the style and experience of a well-synchronized movement? Contrary to the popular opinion that it is the academically less capable who compensate through sport, Engström and Ahlgren (1974) have shown that pupils who spend six hours a week doing physical training get the highest marks in academic subjects, while those who do not spend any time in training, do not do as well. Certainly physical weakness contributes to lack of confidence in other areas, and magnifies both men and women's fear of violence. As Kaplan (1979) says: 'Men recognise in women's sports a final challenge to sexual domination.'

Resources

Winners All (Pax Christi, Blackfriars Hall, Southampton Road, London NW5) – a booklet of cooperative games for all ages. Suitable for use with lower school pupils.

Sports Manual of Co-operative Recreation (Family Pastimes, R.R.4 Perth, Ontario, Canada K7H 3C6) – designed for teachers of PE. Contains descriptions for cooperative athletics, gymnastics, target, court, team and stick-and-ball sports.

New Games U.K., 11 Plato Road, London SW2 5UP is an organization which trains people to use cooperative sports and games with all types of groups, including the handicapped, both indoors and outdoors. It also supplies information on new games, and organizes events.

Out of the Bleachers by Stephanie L. Twin (New York, Feminist Press) – two volumes of writings, one on women and sport, and the other a teaching guide with ideas for non-sexist sports projects.

Oliver Leaman (1982) 'Sport and the Feminist Novel' *Physical Education Review*, vol. 5, no. 2.

Girls and PE, Schools Council Research Project. Contact Dr. O. Leaman, Department of Education, Liverpool Polytechnic.

Notes

1　On Danish television a Swiss skier in the 1976 Olympics was described as having 'brown squirrel eyes and turned up breasts'.

2　The whole question of sport, competition and the status of boys' football has been the subject of much debate at Kidbrooke School, which has recently had its first intake of boys (see *Schools Council Newsletter* no. 3, ILEA supplement).

3　The report of the introduction of ballet for first-year boys at New Park Comprehensive School, Leicestershire, grandiosely described in *The Teacher* as 'a new step in curriculum development', found its way into the 'ridiculous British' column of the *New Statesman*.

Acknowledgement

The authors would like to thank Jenny Brundle for all the help she has given in the preparation of this chapter.

CHAPTER 20

REMEDIAL EDUCATION

MARGARET WINTER

The pupils considered in this chapter are those taught by remedial departments. Schools differ in their assessment and definition of remedial pupils, some regarding them as having specific difficulties, others considering them to be of general low ability with a poor level of school attainment. Differing approaches will dictate how remedial education is organized in schools. Space does not allow consideration of these different perspectives so these comments are general and relate to my own work experience. The organization of remedial education differed in the four schools where I have worked, but covered the most usual options:

1. Individual tuition on a withdrawal basis concentrating on the pupils' specific area(s) of difficulty.
2. Withdrawal groups or classes aimed at enabling the pupil to cope in the mainstream of the school by improving literacy skills and sometimes maths.
3. Remedial classes or bands in which pupils are taught most lessons with the exception, perhaps, of PE, RE and practical subjects.

When I refer to non-exam pupils I mean those in their fourth or fifth year who may have had remedial teaching earlier on. Many of the aspects covered by other contributors in this book will also affect pupils in remedial departments. However, there are some aspects which are particular to remedial education.

Most remedial teachers are women, which may be one reason why the remedial department in some schools is not accorded the same status as other subjects or pastoral care. The similarities that exist between the remedial classroom (with its emphasis on reading) and the primary school account perhaps for the fact that remedial work has a feminine image, which is furthered by the 'caring' aspect of the work.

Boys are in the majority in remedial classes, which tend to concentrate on literacy and communication skills, areas in which boys rather than girls have problems. Two points need to be made here. First, it is increasingly recognized that in the classroom, even when the ratio of girls and boys is equal, boys are generally allowed to dominate (see Chapter 3). When, as is usually the case in remedial classes, girls are outnumbered, their position becomes even more marginal. Additionally, in attempting to capture the interest of the slow or reluctant learner, teachers are even more likely to select stories, reading schemes, discussion topics, themes/projects and pictures they think are particularly relevant to the class. On closer inspection it is the boys' interests that are specifically catered for. This situation, though fairly common in my experience, is not perceived as a problem.

More attention should be given to areas where girls tend to do less well than boys, namely those of spatial and mechanical ability. Boys' under-achievement in literacy affects them across the whole range of subjects in the school curriculum, but it is not so widely accepted that girls' poor attainment in some areas could be improved by specific support or remedial programme. The work of Harris (1971) and Stanworth (1981) shows that adolescent girls tend to have a poor image of their academic achievement. The success of counselling as a means of boosting the self-image and subsequently the reading skills of remedial pupils (Lawrence, 1973) suggests that strategies like collective self-help or counselling might be appropriate means of working with girls. Remedial provision ought to deal more positively with those aspects of learning where girls do comparatively less well. Spatial and mechanical skills would make good starting points.

Materials

Reading material available in the remedial classroom needs some examination. In the mainstream English lessons pupils are likely to study books mainly written by men. They read, discuss and write about the lives of boys and men, their characters, hopes and successes; they may learn that the experiences of women are of less significance (see Chapter 5). Teachers may be able to present mixed classes with books solely about boys (*Joby*, *Run for Your Life*, *Kes*, *Lord of the Flies*) far more easily than they could books predominantly about girls or women. Despite this, the English teacher usually has available a range of good stories. This is not so likely in the remedial class.

To stimulate the interest of pupils with reading problems, a variety of schemes are available which cater for their assumed interests. In effect they present stereotypes of male/female characteristics, activities, aptitudes and interests. The now well-documented criticisms levelled at some primary readers (Lobban, 1976) also apply to those specifically written for pupils with reading problems in the secondary school. Such readers suggest that boys' horizons are more interesting, challenging and varied, while girls' concerns appear to focus around personal relationships and a fairly limited range of occupations. Most noticeably, however, girls and women are grossly under-represented. Stories are predominately based on football, motorbikes/mopeds, pop groups, adventures in space, animals, space police, westerns, discovery adventures, trouble at school or with the law, vandalism. Ten SRA cards picked at random by a pupil featured: (1) Admiral at the South Pole, (2) King Arthur, (3) Do animals talk?, (4) King and the spider, (5) Skip goes to school, (6) Around the world in 3 years, (7) Stubborn Captain Cook, (8) Lawrence of Arabia, (9) Animals with house, (10) Geronimo; namely seven extracts about men and their adventures and three stories of general interest.

Admittedly there are more boys with reading problems, so arguably there need to be more books that appeal to them, but for girls they present a world of very limited opportunity. They also serve as extremely limiting pictures of girls and women for the large number of boys who read them. The stories where girls do feature are often worse than ones where they are absent altogether. The following are just a few examples, chosen by Sharon (14 years) as some of her favourites.

1. *Inner Ring*, second series, by M. Hardcastle (Benn, 1969) – about Tony and his girlfriend Jan, a nurse, who says 'I get my money helping people in pain. I'd do it for nothing if I had to.' (p. 8)

2. Checkers *Fair Game* by J. Brown (Evans Brothers, 1974) – Julie didn't want to steal 'but Stu had dared her, she couldn't let him down'.

3. Heinemann Guided Readers, *Anne and the Fighter* by E. Laird (Heinemann, 1977) – on her first journey Anne is kidnapped by Sam. 'Anne could not run away, she was weak and slow, Sam was big and strong.' (p. 8)

4. Anchor Books, *When the Song Was Over* by A. Higgins (Cassell, 1976) – Susan 'wanted so much to be pretty' (p. 3) and go out with Tony. She ends up modelling clothes and marrying Samson, her agent.

5. Cassell's Encounter Series, *Debbie's Guy* by R. Vaughan Carr (Cassell, 1976) – Debbie is lonely. She has no dad and no boyfriend.

These schemes portray girls and women who have status in the story by virtue of their relationship to males, as girlfriends, sisters, wives or mothers. The occupations pursued by female characters are mainly in service industries or caring roles – cafés, shops, hospitals, offices, schools, hairdressers, and the home – jobs which the fourth- or fifth-form girl will find relate specifically to her school timetable. Asking colleagues for recommendations for a resource list has drawn a blank although there is some good work for discussion published by Action Research Project.[1]

Curriculum

The subjects studied by boys and girls start to differ more obviously from the age of 14 onwards and these differences are most marked in the timetables of non-exam students (Woods, 1976). Early on in their secondary schooling pupils categorize subjects as male or female (see Chapter 4). By the fourth year the vocational type of courses available to non-exam pupils are usually seen as either girls' or boys' lessons, e.g. office skills, engineering, woodwork/metalwork, childcare, mechanical/technical studies, design work, home economics, needlework, general/rural sciences. Unless the school actively gives encouragement, non-exam pupils are even less likely than others to make untypical subject choices.

First, they would find themselves in groups without most of their friends of the same sex at an age when peer support is very important. Secondly, pupils with little confidence in their school ability are less likely than able girls to make unusual subject choices (Slee, 1968). Courses most usually taken up by boys relate to a wider range of occupations. Girls of similar background and ability follow courses more related to domestic life, confirming them in traditional caring and servicing roles in the home and in employment.

The association of girls' education with domestic life has been an historically explicit aim (see Chapter 13), but while this is being challenged for more able girls today, it is still thought that childcare and home economics, with their emphasis on caring and servicing the needs of others, are relevant for all non-exam girls. I do not suggest that being able to respond to the needs of others is not important, but one needs to ask why it appears so much less important for boys. With the present shortage of permanent employment, particularly for the unskilled, many more boys/men are likely to be involved in domestic life and childcare.

Teachers' perceptions of remedial pupils

From talking to other teachers I find they generally perceive low ability girls fairly negatively. The most frequent comments seemed to be 'They're only interested in boys', 'They're sulky', 'The girls will only act as a group, never as individuals'. They are seen as preferring repetitive tasks, being too dependent on friends, moody, with a tendency to petty quarrelling and a reluctance to join in discussions. Boys of similar ability are seen more favourably. They are regarded as being more lively, their work is more slapdash but a common comment is 'You can always have a laugh with the lads'. Even when such boys are rebellious, teachers seem more tolerant of their behaviour. Girls' rebellion was seen to manifest itself in 'filthy looks', sullen silence or 'unladylike' behaviour. Some girls are seen to use their sexuality as a way of rebelling and teachers are quick to make comments about girls' sexual behaviour, whereas the sexual behaviour of boys is largely ignored (see 'Sexual harassment', Chapter 2).

Teachers observe that girls sit in groups, frequently on the periphery of the classroom, are generally more keen to have work marked and to 'get on' with written work. Boys demand more time and attention and ask more questions. Some teachers would apply some of these comments to pupils in the mainstream of the school, but they are more frequently made about non-exam pupils. While the school's explicit aim is career choice and personal fulfilment for more able girls, there is a tendency to assume low ability girls are 'only going to get married in a couple of years anyway' and use this to justify a limiting curriculum and low expectations.

Positive action

However, there are ways of challenging stereotypes in the classroom:

Reading material

Basing work on the stories and workshop materials, I have used several approaches to increase awareness. With, for example, a story like *When the Song Was Over* (Anchor Books), I would ask several pupils, both boys and girls, to consider questions such as:

1. Is the girl typical – in what ways is she like you or girls you know?
2. Why is looking attractive so important to her? Why is it important to you?
3. Do boys have to be attractive? Do they care about how they look?
4. What things do boys and girls do to improve their appearance? Who is it for?
5. Why does Susan marry Samson – who is he named after and why?

Sometimes a group might suggest alternative endings. As the characters in these stories are usually like cardboard cutouts it's quite easy to meddle with the plot! Simply conveying to the pupils that all girls in these stories are stupid is likely to further the assumption that girls in general are 'like that', i.e. silly, unassertive, etc. There needs to be discussion about why the characters are portrayed as they are. It is not my experience that pupils in remedial classes are unable to consider such questions. Following the example of the role reversal version of the Cinderella story, some girls have taped stories which have then been typed for others to read, or taped as short plays.

Talk

Any pupil is more confident talking about what they know and have experienced, particularly those in the remedial classroom. This involves listening to their experiences, hearing about babysitting, family life, music, football, clothes, going to the club and valuing these activities. Many girls get the message from their teachers and other pupils, that their concerns and activities are not as interesting as those of the boys. Boys' talk is given more time and attention in the classroom (see Chapter 3). When there are more boys in the class, in my experience there always needs to be positive discrimination in favour of girls. Usually the boys will dominate the talk and then in an attempt to include them, the teacher will turn to a cluster of girls and ask 'and what do the girls think?'. Seating arrangements should preclude girls being on the edge of the activity. A non-competitive and supportive environment will encourage greater participation, especially among pupils with little confidence in their school performance.

Writing

Improving the standard of written work is usually one of the concerns of the remedial department. Girls' work is usually better presented and organized than boys', for which they are praised, sometimes to the extent that girls are more concerned with appearance than content. It should be no less permissible for boys to present untidy work than it is for girls. Girls often need encouragement to write from their own experiences and not try to produce 'nice' stories. Short plays (about 20 lines) are a good medium for girls, and encourage them to use their own language and experience, be more direct, and cut out incidental details. Some very good plays have been written called *It's not Fair*. The themes most common in the girls' writing are: having to look after younger children, not being able to wear what they wanted at home and in school, not being allowed out at night, having to do housework when brothers don't – all issues relating to their feminine role.

When pupils work in small groups it is easier to be supportive, challenge assumptions which pupils have of one another, and question stereotypes.

Pupils in remedial classes also suffer from teachers' assumptions about their thinking ability. In terms of output and school knowledge these pupils may well be poor performers, but when thinking about matters within their own experience they often show a surprising grasp of issues thought too abstract for them to grapple with. Consequently, while some teachers may raise questions about sexism or equal opportunity with more able and verbally competent pupils, teachers in remedial classrooms over-simplify and resort to using stereotypes. Using their own words, experiences and views of the world, I have found remedial pupils able to explore areas such as wages for housework, men sharing childcare, girls/women portrayed in pop songs, the 'Big boys don't cry' image, advertising, violence, etc. The issues raised reveal a level of thinking seldom credited to these pupils.

It is not simply that girls need more options so that they all run off and do woodwork, for example, but that the masculine and feminine behaviour roles need to be re-evaluated and seen as complementary areas of positive behaviour. I have sometimes taught groups consisting only of boys and it has emerged over the months that the masculine role constrains their behaviour – it took time for them to be supportive, share experiences or talk about feelings. One talked about being 'packed in' by his girlfriend, another about his parents splitting up. When I asked if we could carry on after break: 'No fear!' they said, 'The girls will be here and skit us.'

The constraints on girls are more limiting as they encourage them to adopt passive behaviour and restrict their choices. While academic girls may aspire to an increasing range of jobs, the reduced availability of semi- and unskilled work means the choices of less able girls are decreasing. These girls are further encouraged to undervalue traditional women's work, and yet is is towards these areas that the school guides them. With changing work patterns, it is my hope that home, family and community will be regarded as more important, and women's and men's place within them and the work environment more flexible.

Note

1.   Information about the Action Research Project and its publications is available from Carola Adams, 27 Hodge Bower, Ironbridge, Telford.

SECTION 3

STRATEGIES

CHAPTER 21

MORE THAN ONE WAY FORWARD

JANIE WHYLD

So far this book has looked at the various ways in which sexism operates within the school as a whole, and within each subject, and has tried to suggest how teachers, as specialists, can counteract such sexism. In this chapter, I shall try to indicate how all concerned people, teachers, parents and pupils, can work against sexism, not as specialists, but as people committed to achieving a non-sexist education.

Aims

In order to work out detailed long-term strategies for providing an equal education, it will be necessary to clarify our aims. The criterion for sex equality is frequently taken to be the number of women in top positions. The strategy for achieving this would be to encourage the bright girl to take 'A' Level physics, and to widen her horizons through career lessons. Certainly everyone should have a grounding in science, in order to gain the confidence to handle and maintain the technological equipment which is becoming an ever greater part of our lives at home and at work; and unless more women become well qualified in science, the type and applications of technology, which will be a controlling element in our lives in the future, will be determined entirely by men. However, ensuring women get their fair share of top jobs in industry and commerce will benefit mainly the bright and generally middle-class girl who might be expected to fill these posts – and only for as long as she remains childless. There may be some benefits to women as a group, such as increased promotion prospects, and more attention to areas of specific concern to women, but up until now, the increased academic achievements of middle-class women have done little to improve the position of working-class women.

With the increase in automation of industrial and commercial processes, and the need to conserve dwindling natural resources, which implies a reduction in manufacturing industry, it is inadequate to measure sex equality in terms of women's increased 'saleability' on the labour market.

(As Anna Coote, 1981, has pointed out, most women are already 'over-employed', although unwaged.) We need to think in wider terms, of changing the way we reward work, the attitudes about who is responsible for the home and childcare, and the relationship between home and work, before most people will see how women could benefit from an independent career as well as marriage.

Eileen Byrne (1980a) has identified two models for achieving sex equality. The socialist countries have a planned policy of high formal economic involvement for women, but still presuppose that it will be the mother who should bear final responsibility for the home and childcare. Substantial support services are available to mothers: a high child allowance, nursery and creche facilities, job security for a considerable period around childbirth, and provision for time off work to deal with domestic crises such as a sick child. Women are expected to work, but men are not expected to assume responsibility for the home and children. The Swedish system, on the other hand, expects both sexes to have equal and interchangeable roles at home and at work. Extensive childcare facilities are backed by legislation providing parental leave for family emergencies, and for nine months following a birth. A government poster campaign encourages fathers to take advantage of this leave. Guidelines for education, issued in 1969 and 1970, required that pupils be made 'aware that a pre-requisite for equality between the spouses, on the labour market, and in society as a whole, is the equal division of childcare and home chores between men and women in the family'. Domestic science, including childcare, was made a compulsory school subject for both sexes.

In 1975 the government Green Paper *A Freer Choice*, suggested that 'the curriculum should be altered so that every girl and every boy will have to try fields where their sex is at present in the minority', thus recognizing that unless a positive attempt is made to present alternatives, no individual's choice is 'free'. Particular recommendations in the report were that technology and economics were to be made compulsory, PE to be taught in mixed groups, more vocational guidance to be given, science and technology teaching to be made less male-orientated, and the school hierarchy divided more equally between men and women. In 1978, the Sex Role Project report formed the basis for an equality programme in schools, with a common core curriculum and a state-led campaign to eradicate sexism from school books. But since then, the decentralization of the control of education has hindered progress, and concern with unemployment has taken over. In her assessment of Sweden's *Right to be Human*, Hilda Scott (1982) observed: 'As things stand today, there has been no appreciable change since the beginning of the seventies in study changes made by boys and girls at secondary school level'. Employers have been reluctant to hire local women, and have preferred to import male labour, but more women are entering higher education in cross-sex areas, particularly girls who come from families where the parents have undergone higher education.

Such a comprehensive attack on sex role divisions seems unlikely to happen in Britain, and many feminists feel that no progress can be made until the economic position of women is improved. Marxist-feminists attribute women's inferior position to capitalism (Deem, 1978, 1980), which benefits from the sexual division of labour in that it is getting the labour of two people for the price of one. The argument is that since a function of any educational system is to pass on the culture of the society, as long as society is controlled by capitalists, they will demand schooling which will ensure that men go out to work, pay for their own children, and have wives at home to look after them. Figes (1970) and Spender (1982a) place much more emphasis on the necessity to change the patriarchal attitudes and control of knowledge which, some will argue, gave rise to capitalism, and in any case maintain it, by keeping men and women in their separate and unequal positions. I see this as a chicken-and-egg situation. Sexism in education and the sexual division of labour in the economy and at home are indisputably linked, but it is only of theoretical and ideological importance to establish which came first. I can see no reason why, apart from the pressure of political mud-slinging, people cannot work in education both as radicals and reformists. While recognizing that there will never be equality between the sexes without a massive shift of economic power to women, which will not occur under our present form of capitalism, there is much that we can and must do to produce an awareness of socially induced injustice, and to restore women's confidence, so that future generations will be better equipped to face the struggle. Working within the system does not mean giving up the fight to change it. Practically, there is a place for working at national and regional level to change the structures which encourage the sexual division of labour, and at the same time countering the worst effects of patriarchy in the classroom. It is up to each individual to decide where her or his energies and time may be used to best effect.

Means

Just as ideas about what we should be aiming for differ in detail, but share many similar characteristics, so do ways of achieving these aims. Suzanne Schafer (1976) suggests a group of reforms, based on her study of West German schools: (1) coeducation, (2) coeducational sex education, (3) additional maths and science for girls, (4) non-sexist textbooks in all subjects, (5) promotion of women teachers to senior posts, (6) basic domestic survival skills for all boys, and (7) counselling for girls, to encourage achievement. All these, except the promotion of women teachers, could be achieved with very little money, but would require nationwide coordination.

Eileen Byrne (1980b) argues that the persistent refusal of the government to develop a national plan of education has been the biggest obstacle to the achievement of sex equality in the United Kingdom. She opts for a common core curriculum, including housecraft, parenthood, technology and manual skills, mathematics and some science, and at least one creative art, which would be compulsory for all boys and girls. Opponents of a compulsory common core curriculum have drawn attention to the dangers of central control of education. However, during the 1970s, educational policy emanating from the DES has been far more progressive than that practised by the majority of LEAs, although there is no guarantee that the same trend will continue during the 1980s. Both Byrne and Schafer advocate preparing children, regardless of sex, for domestic responsibility and working life, and for some form of compensatory programme in those areas where either sex may have fallen behind.

At a more immediate level, suggestions from researchers and teachers working in this area have centred on developing and publicizing a school policy on equal opportunities, and the creation of a special post of responsibility within the school; and measures such as careers advice and counselling for girls and parents to encourage girls to opt for maths, science and CDT, and making it compulsory to take one science in the upper school (Mortimore and Mortimore, 1981). Some teachers (e.g. Myers, 1981) stress the importance of changing boys' attitudes, not just directing energy at girls; others emphasize the importance of giving girls the confidence to succeed in a male world. Annie Cornbleet and Sue Sanders, coordinators of the DASI project (see p. 303), point out: 'An equal opportunities programme is a superficial attempt to answer a complex problem. Such a programme does not intrinsically contain a challenge either to the culture which produces stereotypes or to the language in which the curriculum is taught. An anti-sexist programme, however, has implicit in it not only these challenges, but it also incorporates positive action in an attempt to equalise the historical privileges which boys have always received at the expense of girls' (*Where*, January 1982).

I see three main areas of reform. Economic relations must be changed so that all work is recognized and rewarded, and women are no longer confined to unskilled, low paid work in the labour market, and unpaid work at home as childminder, housekeeper, cook, nurse and cleaner. Teachers can challenge this directly in their unions, and indirectly in the concepts and attitudes they bring to the classroom. In social relationships, the problem for women is to regain our confidence. There must be an end to male violence, and domination in social discourse. We must find ways to counter-act the attractiveness of the feminine stereotype, which requires girls to be shy, coy and submissive in order to get a boyfriend. Women must feel they are as good as men, value their own opinions and feelings, and expect to be listened to. Teachers can encourage this in the classroom, not only by giving attention to girls, but also by giving 'women's topics' serious attention. In this third area of cultural transmission we must ensure that women's actions and experience are no longer written out of history, but become half of all our knowledge.

Coeducation

Most secondary education was single sex for the first half of this century. Considerably fewer resources were allocated to girls' education (Byrne, 1978), since it was considered that women's primary role should be that of homemaker, with a working husband for financial support. Consequently even in the most advanced girls' grammar schools there were fewer science facilities than in equivalent boys' schools, and more emphasis was placed on cultural refinements. The move to coeducation was welcomed by those who thought that a common education would lessen the differences between boys and girls, and help them to get on better together in later life. Educational facilities, previously available only to boys, would be opened to girls, there would be wider access to subjects, girls would add a slightly civilizing element to boys, and boys would act as a spur and an incentive to girls. Such optimism has proved to be unfounded. There may be formal equality of opportunity, though often even this does not exist where schools contravene the requirements of the Sex Discrimination Act by reserving places on the basis of sex. The forces of socialization push adolescents, particularly girls who mature at an earlier age than boys, into developing their gender identity at the expense of their education. Girls who want to be feminine avoid competition with boys in masculine pursuits such as science, and there are fewer women in the hierarchy to present positive role models which might help to counteract the idea that success and 'femininity' do not mix. Far from bringing a 'civilizing' influence, the presence of girls makes boys more aggressive in demanding more than their fair share of teacher attention (Spender, 1982a, Chapter 3). Many feminists (Sarah et al., 1980) now view coeducation with suspicion, seeing it as girls going into boys' schools.

Research has shown that although pupils are more likely to be offered cross-sex subjects in a mixed school, they are more likely to take them in a single-sex school (DES, *Statistics of Education*, 1977). Where science is offered in a girls' school, it is clearly there for girls to do. A reversion to single-sex schooling would take a massive upheaval in the educational system (which is quite outside the influence of single feminist activists, or small groups). Apart from the problem of differential allocation of resources which would undoubtedly recur, it is debatable whether separating the sexes would go any way to helping girls cope with and challenge male domination later on. It merely removes the problem from the sphere of schooling. Certainly, attention must be paid to 'preventing girls from switching off when they are too heavily overwhelmed' (Margaret Maden, ex-head of Islington Green, North London, quoted in *The Guardian*, 11 March 1982) so that they do not fall behind in vital areas of the curriculum. Some of the advantages of single-sex schooling can be achieved within the coeducational framework, as has been demonstrated at Stamford School, Ashton-under-Lyme (*Times Educational Supplement*, 19 July 1980; *Schools Council Newsletter* no. 1; and Chapter 7). Some of the girls were taught maths in single-sex groups for two years, and made consistently better progress than their counterparts in mixed groups. Discussions with the girls revealed that although they almost unanimously approved of all-girl maths sets, they all liked mixed schools, too.

Positive action

Intervention strategies are designed to remedy situations where a group has already shown a disadvantage. This is nothing new in British education. Remedial teaching is commonly available to those who have fallen behind at primary school, particularly in reading. (The fact that no equivalent concern is traditionally shown for those who fall behind in science, mostly girls, is a facet of our culture which places more importance on men than on women; where boys fail, special efforts are made to compensate, but in the case of girls, their failure is blamed on their 'biological deficiencies'.) The EOC, in its guidance on how to apply for designation under section 47 of the Sex Discrimination Act, says that 'positive action, in the form of training and encouragement, is necessary to help overcome the effects of past discrimination', and the Act allows for positive discrimination in entry to training schemes for areas of non-traditional work. However, if a feminist teacher in a staff meeting suggests any form of positive discrimination in favour of girls, she may well face howls of derision and protest, particularly from supporters of 'equality' for women – 'very different from the special treatment they now seem to be demanding' – and will need to be well armed with arguments to support her case.

Although many teachers and parents will admit that after girls leave school, they may face discriminatory attitudes which will hinder their career chances, there is a common belief that the British educational system offers equality of opportunity, and that failure is a sign of individual inadequacy. If a whole social group fails (or succeeds), that is tantamount to saying that that group is naturally inferior (or superior); in the case of the performance of girls and boys, this view acknowledges supposed 'natural' differences between the sexes, and is the basis of the sexist stance. It is therefore necessary to show how schooling discriminates in favour of certain groups and against others. Most teachers are firmly committed to the principle of equality, but will be unwilling to accept that their treatment of pupils is in any way unfair, or discriminatory (Smail et al., 1982). Dale Spender (1982a, p. 56) notes that even where teachers try to spend more time interacting with the girls in a mixed class, to the extent that both the teacher and the boys thought that the teachers had spent far more time talking with the girls, not one managed to spend more than 42 per cent of the time interacting with girls. Similarly the GIST team (Smail et al., 1982) found that teachers voiced highly stereotyped opinions about the behaviour and abilities of girls and boys, but believed that they were being fair. This is hardly surprising, as we are all members of the same society in which we are taught that there are scientifically proved basic and incontrovertible differences between males and females, and that the characteristics which are deemed to be male are of value, while those that are female are of lesser worth.

It is my experience that it takes months, or even years, to 'internalize' the validity of these arguments, since they require both rejecting established culture and ways of thinking, and challenging one's own behaviour and

-image. Therefore, at least initially, any campaign in the staffroom to establish why girls, through no fault of their own, have fallen behind in ability and expectation, needs to centre on arguments which are not too threatening to other members of staff: how girls, by the age of 12, will have formed a picture of themselves as potential homemakers and childrearers, supported financially by husbands; how boys, through helping their fathers with repairs, will have gained some technical skills (tinkering ability), but will have already learned to crush their tender emotions; how educational materials and school staffing provide models of society divided along sex lines, with men holding the positions of economic power and prestige. The question of how boys control teachers will have to be dealt with at some time, but it is advisable to wait until there is a core of teachers who can give support to each other, in what will almost inevitably be a hostile situation.

Positive action does not necessarily entail reverse discrimination – although this may need to be accepted for a while, in areas such as appointing more women as heads, in order to overcome the effects of past discrimination (see the case of Anne Gameau, Chapter 1, and Helen Gates, *EOC News*, March 1982). Positive action in favour of girls need not have an adverse effect on boys. The Stamford School experiment gave girls the opportunity to learn in a cooperative and harmonious group so that their performance improved considerably, without any detriment to the boys. Since sexism also limits men, by crippling them emotionally, positive action to eradicate sexism can also benefit boys. The development of single-sex assertiveness training groups for third-year pupils at Clissold Park School, taken by a teacher of the same sex, led to some boys having the confidence to take their needlework home.

The first intervention project receiving publicity outside the USA was at Falcon Street Alternative High School, in New South Wales, Australia, in 1977–1978. With funding from the Australian Schools Commission to pay for extra staff, an options programme 'to deliver role-breaking skills to both sexes' was run. For girls there was a course in basic technology, including carpentry, electrics, and electronics and motor maintenance. The female teachers joined in, and the most competent boys were kept away. Women bicycle mechanics, motor mechanics and motor cyclists were brought in. For boys, courses in interpersonal skill areas were given in an attempt to foster self-awareness and a caring attitude to others, although the boys reacted with ridicule and trivialization if one of their group showed signs of 'softening'. The third part of the options programme was assertiveness training in age- and sex-split groups. These personal areas are not usually dealt with in British schools, but the experience of this Australian alternative school shows that countering the boys' dominance of girls is fundamental to girls gaining confidence. This project is detailed more fully in *Women and Education*, nos. 14 and 15.

Not unlike the Falcon Street project is DASI (Developing Anti-Sexist Initiatives). Funded jointly by the ILEA and the EOC, two women teachers, both of whom happen to have worked in New South Wales where the state policy declares that 'combating discrimination based on a student's sex should be the teacher's priority', worked for a year to 'combat the inherent sexism that is implicit within the school's overt and hidden curriculum'. The aim was to give girls a positive self-image, and make them aware of the way society controls them rather than to direct them into 'male' areas of study and work. As well as building up resources of anti-sexist teaching materials, the team worked with women teachers at Clissold Park and Woodberry Down Schools in London to develop anti-sexist teaching programmes. The main emphasis was on teaching in single-sex groups, half the usual size, so that girls could have the space to develop their abilities. The coordinators withdrew the girls from selected years for support work in english, maths and drama, while male teachers worked with the boys to challenge their attitudes. The first-year pupils at Clissold Park all took a foundation unit on sex-role stereotyping, which started by looking at interaction in the classroom, and how girls are 'put down' by boys. Third-year pupils took a single-sex assertiveness training programme. A measure of its success was that persistent truanters would turn up early for this class, which was held during registration time and generally seen to be peripheral to the curriculum. This area of work is still experimental, and does not lend itself easily to written description, but it is becoming increasingly obvious that some training in social skills will be necessary if girls are ever to challenge the verbal and physical domination of boys in the classroom, and sexual harassment through the school. For help and advice on setting up an assertiveness training course, contact the DASI Project coordinators, and the National Association of Youth Clubs.

Two intervention projects with more vocational aims of encouraging girls to participate more fully in 'male' areas of science and CDT are GATE (Girls and Technology Education) and GIST (Girls into Science and Technology). GATE, funded by BP, has broad objectives of identifying problems which girls have when they take CDT, and of developing teaching programmes based on successful practice (see Chapter 14). A large element of the work is involved with teacher groups in mixed and girls' schools.

GIST, funded by the SSRC, EOC, Department of Industry and Schools Council, is an action research project working in eight schools in Greater Manchester. In the first year, the researchers organized sessions, in school time, with the science and technology staff of the schools involved, to raise teachers' awareness of why girls were under-represented in physical science and technical subjects. Science and technical staff tended to value research based on factual knowledge more highly than psychological and sociological theories about behaviour. Discussions on de-stereotyping were more enthusiastic when humanities staff were present, and the researchers felt that meetings with all the staff of the school were most important, partly because they indicated that the idea of positive intervention had received the official seal of approval from senior management. Teachers' willingness to commit themselves to the scheme depended to some extent on how much time the researchers could spend with them. The level of interest and participation of the teacher also affected how pupils responded to women scientists and technicians coming into the school to talk about their work (Smail et al., 1982; see also Chapter 9). The intervention strategies centre on an anti-sexist careers programme, and ensuring that girls have frequent practical experience of work which seems relevant to them.

A measure of how concern with equal educational opportunities for girls and boys has penetrated mainstream educational thinking is the Schools Council funded curriculum development project *Reducing Sex Differences in School*. Details of the project, and up-to-date information on other projects, including those described above, are given in free newsletters sent out by the Council to all schools liaison officers, teachers' centres and other interested parties. Apart from providing advice, contacts and facilitating the spread of information by printing and distributing papers and reports, an asset of this project which should not be undervalued is its respectability. New or established feminist education groups are able to attract the attention of the LEA and local school management by organizing a meeting to which they invite one of the Schools Council project workers to speak.

Over the past few years, from 1980 onwards, there has been an increasing number of initiatives on equal opportunities coming from within schools: Billericay School, Essex; Clissold Park, Haverstock, Kidbrooke, Islington Green, Pimlico and Hackney Downs, all in London. I was interested to find out whether there was any pattern of development, or common factors in these schools, for example an active PTA, union pressure, feminist teachers. From very brief enquiries, several factors emerged. In 1979, when the EOC published *Do You Provide Equal Opportunities?*, ILEA circulated their schools to find out how they matched up to the EOC guidelines (the deputy leader of the ILEA, Frances Morrell, is also actively promoting equal opportunity for boys and girls). This initiative from the top acted as a catalyst in some schools where there was already a nucleus of feminist teachers, provoking discussion in staff meetings and sometimes leading to the setting up of a working party on equal opportunities and a whole-school conference. An initiative from the authority is not sufficient – there are many ILEA schools which have done nothing – nor is it necessary, since some activity has occurred in schools in authorities which have not shown particular concern. The initial commitment seems most likely to come from classroom teachers lower down in the hierarchy who group together to combat sexism informally and put pressure on school management to institute formal procedures. Where there is authority back-up, it is difficult for the head to be seen as not supportive, although a head who is determined to be obstructive will usually find a way to quash even well-established groups, perhaps resorting to charges of 'feminist propaganda'.

Initiatives are most likely to flourish where there is an organized group of anti-sexist teachers and a woman head, or a progressive male head and some women high up in the school hierarchy. At Islington Green, for example, a mixed ILEA comprehensive which has had a positive policy on eradicating sex discrimination for over two years, the head and the chairperson of the governors are both women, so are the majority of heads of departments. Governors' support can also be useful in 'persuading' school management. In some schools, the initiative has come from within a department, which can make statements about its policy, and which books it is going to use. Obviously it is easier to gain consensus (or control) within a smaller group, and where the department teaches across the school, for example English or PE, the initiative may spread, but the chances seem equally likely that it will not. Two schools so far have created posts of special responsibility for equal opportunities which, according to Kate Myers, who first held this post at Haverstock, gave status rather than power. The holder of this post has the authority to go to heads of departments and ask about their policy on equal opportunities, and to raise the subject at staff meetings. 'But', said Kate, 'with all the advantages here which most schools haven't got (educationally concerned governors and parents, a woman head who is interested in developing girls' potential, and having had a whole-school conference) it is still not easy. The problem is making other people realise it is a priority. There is little antagonism from the staff, only inertia from those who have other concerns.'

Working with others

It is becoming more apparent from the experience of the GIST team and the initiatives described above, that successful action must necessarily involve the cooperation and interest of a majority of the staff, and at least the compliance of the head, governors and parents. There is a natural human tendency, when faced with success stories, to think 'we could never do that, not starting from our situation'. But some successful action has sprung from the most unlikely ground. Anne Whitbread (1980) has described how a women's group was set up in a boys' school, because of sexual harassment of the women staff, and this has now initiated an anti-sexist 'Skills for living' course; and Bethell and Keith (1980) describe how they raised the question of sexism in a staff meeting, in the face of opposition from the head who was actively discriminating against women. A small group of committed feminists, especially with the support of some non-sexist men, may be able to give each other the support and expertise necessary to counteract the hostility and derision which pushing for action against sexism is likely to provoke (Bruley, 1977). If you are fortunate enough to work in a school where the staff are willing to look further into sexism, then Valerie Hannon's sourcebook for school-based workshops *Ending Sex Stereotyping in Schools*, available free from the EOC, gives some excellent ideas for running a session yourself. The Schools Council Sex Differentiation Programme newsletters, and particularly the supplement to issue no. 3 on initiatives in ILEA, describe in detail the way action groups have been set up in schools, the areas they have tackled and the difficulties they have encountered.

Another way of effecting changes within a particular school could be through the Parent–Teacher Association, or the governors. On the whole, governing bodies are notoriously 'establishment' and unwilling to involve themselves in educational policy, but this need not be the case. It is usually within the remit of the governing body to oversee policy, and to ensure that the school is carrying out its legal obligations – you can obtain the constitution of the governing body, and the names and addresses of governors, from the LEA. One difficulty common to all members of committees made up of lay people, who may be addressed by officers in attendance, is that the agenda seems to be predetermined. One way to circumvent this, and to give a sympathetic governor ally a break, is to send a letter to the secretary or chairperson of the governors, perhaps asking what steps the school is taking to fulfil its obligations under the Sex Discrimination Act, so that the matter will be raised under correspondence.

Although most PTAs are more concerned with fund raising than with controversial political standpoints, they can be quite powerful (contact ACE and CASE for advice). Three or four enthusiastic parents and teachers might persuade the PTA to have an evening discussion or a day school on sex discrimination. The EOC keeps a list of speakers willing to address such bodies.

Using the SDA and the EOC

When the Sex Discrimination Act was first passed, feminist educationalists breathed a sigh of relief that education was included. Their joy was premature. The Act has had so little impact in education, that schools which initially conformed to its requirements by providing all crafts equally for girls and boys, are now reverting to cookery for girls and woodwork for boys. The number of education cases brought under the Act has been minimal, and the court's judgement in the only case which has reached court (Whitfield vs the London Borough of Croydon) contravenes the spirit of the Act.[1] Discrimination has to be proved against an individual on the ground of his/her sex, so a group of parents cannot claim that all their children are suffering because of the sexist nature of school materials. The court process is long and expensive (there is no separate tribunal) so even if the case is won it may be too late to be of benefit to the child concerned.

Legal difficulties aside, most people assume that because a law has been passed, it has to be obeyed, and for this reason alone the Sex Discrimination Act is still of some use. In the classroom, teachers can outline the conditions of the Act, along with other legislation which affects the position of women, or raise questions about it in general knowledge quizzes, thus making sure that pupils know their rights. If there is a sympathetic headteacher, the authority of the Act can be used to justify any changes which prove unpopular. If proposals which contravene the Act are suggested at staff meetings, you can say, 'You can't do that, it's illegal' and the EOC can still use the threat of prosecution, even if it is unlikely that it will be carried out.

Criticism of the EOC from the women's movement has focused on its inadequacy in taking up cases of discrimination, and thus ensuring that the Sex Discrimination Act is enforced. However, for cases which do not need financial support, it can be very useful. In Lincolnshire, a case of boys and girls being separated for craft at primary level was resolved by the EOC writing a formal letter to the LEA. The LEA decided not to oppose this and instructed the headteacher concerned, and surrounding local schools, to change the situation. This action was successful, where previous requests from a parent to the headteacher had failed.

Although under the Act individuals can only complain of particular cases of discrimination, the EOC can take up complaints of a more general nature. This has two distinct advantages. First, the name of the person who lodged the complaint does not have to be made public, which may help to alleviate the fear that individual children concerned may be victimized. Secondly, it is possible to complain about situations in which you yourself are not directly involved. 'All that is required is for someone to send us the details and we will take it from there.'[2] The EOC will also supply speakers, produces reports, some of which are excellent, and operates a library and resource centre for material on sex equality.

On the international scene, the EEC Directive 76/207/EEC on equal treatment for men and women includes provisions with regard to vocational guidance and access to vocational training. It has not yet been decided if it applies to education or not. The UK government maintains that it does not, but only the EEC's Court of Justice can determine this. For the adventurous, confident and rich there may be potential for challenging any educational practice which could be legally construed as giving access to vocational training (i.e. leading to qualifications that must be acquired to join vocational training courses) if they discriminate against women or girls.

Using your union

The major teaching union, the NUT, is developing a reasonable policy on the position of women teachers (see *Promotion and the Woman Teacher* (NUT, 1980), and the 1982 conference resolution on equal opportunities); and NATFHE, the union for further and higher education, has produced an excellent, progressive policy statement, *The Education, Training and Employment of Women and Girls* (1980). This does not mean, of course, that these unions are non-sexist. The arguments on how unions discriminate against women are well documented (Coote, 1980; Women in the NUT; Ellis, 1981). However, the existence of a national policy does mean that you can use it to deter sexist fellow unionists from taking discriminatory actions, by referring them to the agreed policy of their union.

Many women teachers find their union no use at all in combating sexism at school. Most women do not get involved in their unions, because of the added burden of domestic responsibilities and childcare. Those who do go along to meetings and who have the courage to speak, find that there are few matters which relate to women, and surmise, quite rightly, that any attempt to raise the question of sexism in schools would most likely be howled down as trivial in comparison to the important, and ever-present, issues of salaries, redundancies and conditions of service. However, NATFHE has regional women's panels, to which branches can send a delegate, and several divisions of the NUT now have equal opportunities groups. Although these are not as affective as branches, they can be a good and supportive place in which to plan action. They can also provide a 'direct line' to the divisional executive (or in NATFHE, to the national executive) so that initiatives do not get blocked at branch level.[3]

The problems which many women face at branch level are one aspect of women's difficulties in unions. Activists, on the other hand, frequently complain of the ineffectiveness of established policy. For all that, I do believe that the teaching unions can provide a very useful channel to combat sexism. Both the NUT and NATFHE are well represented at local and national level on policy making bodies such as education committees, examination boards and subject advisory panels, so that teachers who succeed in being selected for such a position are in an ideal position to check the content and wording of policy documents, subject syllabuses and examinations.

Influencing teacher education

Most people, including the NUT, NATFHE and the EOC, agree that the single most effective way to counteract sexism in education would be through teacher education. Even the TUC policy document, *Priorities in Continuing Education*, says that to further 'the educational and vocational opportunities for women . . . a start should be made through a change in the emphasis given in teacher-training to male and female roles'. All teachers are state registered, so it would seem a relatively simple matter for the state to ensure that its teachers were given the training it required before they qualified. But the autonomous organization of higher education in this country makes this impracticable. A survey carried out by NATFHE in 1979–1980 showed that only one institution included a compulsory element on sex typing in its education course, and although several offered advanced options, the majority gave no formal attention to gender differences. Under the present system of academic organization, the onus lies with staff and students to press their college to offer modules on sexism. This may not be such a difficult procedure. At the moment, education staff are receptive to student-initiated learning, and if you are a student in a college where no member of staff is willing to give a course (maybe they do not know what to teach), then try to get your tutor to allow you to prepare and present material yourself, as an individual assignment. If you have student representation on the academic board, then this is the place to push for a course. Academic board approval also means that the course is less likely to disappear if the member of staff teaching it is no longer available. Many lecturers in education have succeeded in setting up their own courses – a list is available from the EOC or WRRC. Pressure must also be put on validating bodies, particularly the CNAA, to demand that the issue be dealt with in every course.

Working alone

Within the classroom, teachers are faced with two major areas where sexism operates: interpersonal relationships, and the syllabus and materials. If you do have a chance to buy new materials, finding non-sexist books is not easy (but see Chapter 4 for identifying sexism in materials, and the specialist chapters in Section 2 for recommendations). Relatively little non-sexist material is available, although several projects are currently developing material which may be available for general use (see the section on 'Positive action' earlier in this chapter). Often, hard-pressed teachers cannot afford to reject a textbook which is ideal in every other way except for its sexism. In this case, or if you have to make do with existing sexist material, you can redress the balance, to some extent, with your own material, wall-charts, pictures of women at work and men with children, and oral examples. Very sexist material lends itself to analysis in class, or to the odd remark: 'One can mutter subtle hints about princesses who say "Yes" to the first man to reach them, just for the sake of something to do, and princes who have only marriage at the end of a great adventure' (Tabraham, 1980).

Publishers are becoming more sensitive to teachers' demands. The Educational Publishers' Council, a subgroup of the Publishers' Association, and the EOC, set up a working party to look into sex stereotyping in educational books, and published a report (EPC, 1981) which was circulated to members; some publishers have produced their own in-house guidelines on avoiding sexism. It is worth writing to publishers whose books you reject; Longmans revamped their Nuffield maths project only one year after its publication because of the number of complaints about sexism.

Your own behaviour, appearance and speech can have a considerable influence in the classroom. I prefer not to try to start discussions on gender and sexism by introducing these as 'the subjects we are going to deal with today' but to provoke pupils into asking me questions because of casual remarks I make, or badges I wear. So a sexist remark like 'Next time your mother does the cooking, watch her . . .' can become a role-breaker by being changed to 'Next time your mother or father does the cooking, . . .'. Obviously, you should try to avoid all sexism in your own language, although this is easier said than done, as language reflects knowledge which has been given to us by a male-controlled education (Spender, 1982b). I have found that once the question of sexism in language has been discussed with pupils for even a very short time, they will pick up on sexist remarks made by other teachers (but will not necessarily challenge them, or modify their own speech).

Galton (1981) has identified three styles of asking questions in science teaching: in the form of problems, simple recall questions and the 'Nuffield' pupil-centred approach. Girls seem to be wary and diffident of the first approach, and consequently the boys get yet another chance to become the focus of attention. However, many teachers are reluctant to relinquish what would seem to be an educationally valuable way of teaching (in favour of straight recall, at which girls seem to do well). Judy Samuel, in Chapter 9 of this book, offers sensitive advice on how to phrase questions to encourage girls – relevant to all subjects, not just science.

Class discussion is another commonly adopted learning method which seems to worsen sexual divisions. Apart from the problem of the most vocal and confident, usually some boys, monopolizing the discussion, while the rest doze or chatter in cliques, there is the danger that without a considerable input of background material first, class discussion merely reinforces prejudices. If the teacher intervenes to 'redress the balance' (and I can rarely resist doing this, when I hear dangerous idiocies), then the whole lesson may dissolve into a class versus teacher contest. I find this particularly true of groups of older boys, who seem much more reluctant than girls to step outside the codes of behaviour which their peers have defined for them. I have known teenage boys be pulled into line with a sneer by their 'gang leader', if they show too much interest in a topic which has not been approved by the dominant clique, or is seen to threaten the ideological basis of the group.

If I want pupils to explore their own ideas on a subject, a technique I often use is to split the class into small groups and set the topic in the form of a problem for the group to solve. For example, on crime, I give a list of offences and ask the group to rank them in order of importance or severity, and then to suggest punishments for each. In environmental studies, the group could be asked to suggest reasons why a town has grown up on a particular site. Results are then pooled and compared, thus involving the majority of the class. Sometimes I precede this with exercises specifically designed to make pupils aware of the way they function in groups.[4] Observers take note of individual group members' behaviour and participation rate. This is discussed afterwards, and sometimes groups are reorganized so that all the pupils who talk a lot are put together. This has been quite successful, especially with older boys in all-boy groups.

Instead of checking pupils' understanding of work by asking questions to the whole class, or even to named individuals, which allows the boys to dominate, or puts individuals into a position of feeling uncomfortable, I prefer to ask pupils to jot down the answers to questions on a scrap of paper, and then to check the answers when they have had time to think. I find this works well with those who do not usually offer questions in class, and gives no space to the aggressive. (Further ideas for group work are given in Chapter 5.)

Surviving

I have tried to suggest many ways for people in various situations to work towards a non-sexist education. But, on reading these suggestions, there will be some people whose reaction will be 'But I couldn't do that in my school, town, union'. For a lone feminist, life can be difficult enough without inviting extra snubs and ridicule in the staffroom, and hostility from parents.[5] To these women I say, do what you feel you can, and no more.

Waugh and Foster (1978), the two women involved in the Australian intervention project, stress the dangers to pupils: 'The teacher cannot afford to be a lone feminist in a misogynist environment. It may be counter-productive. She may break under the strain, and leave an example of failure behind her – enough to put a younger, less experienced student off the idea of feminism forever'. The best support comes from meeting other like-minded people. Women's groups are springing up all over the country. *Spare Rib* carries a list of new groups forming, and WIRES keeps a list of all groups (see Appendix C).

It has taken me many years to grow in confidence. I live in rural Lincoln-shire, and work in a college in Grimsby, a typical provincial town – not a centre of progressive ideas. I have now identified a number of sympathetic and supportive women and men locally, but for years my only contact with the women's movement was through *Spare Rib*. I did not feel strong enough to initiate any action on my own at college, and often felt pangs of guilt at meetings of women in the union, when women from other colleges talked about their action to set up a creche, or organize a demonstration on abortion. My only contribution to feminism was collecting a lot of informa-tion, which has subsequently proved useful, and providing a role model to my students which challenged their assumptions about the capabilities of women. Do not expect to change your pupils' ideas; most of the other influ-ences socializing them are working against you. Count two or three in a class who 'see the light' as a major breakthrough. Value positively everything you do.

Notes

1 In the Whitfield case, December 1979, the judge considered that it was not discriminatory that the girl pupil had to apply to do metalwork and woodwork, which were normal curricular activities for boys, as boys had to apply to do home economics, and that cooking and needlework were more advantageous to girls than woodwork, metalwork and design technology. The EOC originally assisted the plaintiff, but withdrew its assistance before the case was heard, as it no longer had any reasonable prospect of success (EOC Annual Report, 1979). Advice on how to use the Sex Discrimination Act to fight on education is best given in the NCCL publication, *Sex Discrimination in School: How to Fight It*, by Harriet Harman (1978).

2 Quote from a letter to me from the then Principal Education Officer of the EOC, Wilf Knowles, dated 14 August 1979.

3 In areas where there is no likelihood of an equal opportunities group being established, or for women who do not feel their group is sufficiently effective, Women in the NUT, an unofficial body, campaigns on issues which affect women teachers and girl pupils. Contact Vida Bond, 83 Banbury House, London E9.

4 The best book I know, which gives lots of practical lesson ideas, is *Joining Together* by D.W. Johnson and F.P. Johnson (Prentice Hall, 1975). Unfortunately, the book is designed for adult groups, so a lot of the material needs to be simplified. I have prepared a

'group observation sheet' for use with teenagers, and will send a copy free on receipt of a s.a.e. See also Waugh and Foster (1978) for further justification of group dynamics, and cooperation rather than competition, and Monika Henderson (*New Society*, 8 April 1982) who recommends this as treatment for violent criminals.

5. In *Spare Rib* no. 75, Sally Shave, deputy head of a primary school, wrote an article on how to counter sexism in a junior school. *Spare Rib* no. 76 documents the reaction this raised in the community, including hostile parents, a special meeting of the governors, a petition for her dismissal, and mudslinging from the national press!

APPENDIX A

GENERAL RECOMMENDED READING

This is a small selection of books I have found interesting and usable. It is not an exhaustive resource list; there are many of these available from organizations such as the EOC, Schools Council, the WRRC, CASSOE, the Women and Education Newsletter Group, and in books like *Learning to Lose*.

Just Like a Girl, Sue Sharpe, (Penguin, 1976).
Some Processes in Sexist Education, Ann-Marie Wolpe (WRRC, 1977).
Women and Education, Eileen Byrne (Tavistock, 1978).
Learning to Lose, edited by Dale Spender and Elizabeth Sarah (The Women's Press, 1980).
'Dinosaurs in the classroom', Kathy Clarricoates, *Women's Studies International Quarterly*, vol. 1, no. 4 (1978).
Gender and Schooling, Michelle Stanworth (WRRC, 1981).
The Missing Half: Girls and Science Education, edited by Alison Kelly (Manchester University Press, 1981).
Invisible Women, Dale Spender (Writers and Readers Publishing Co-operative, 1982).

The following are available free from the EOC:
Ending Sex Stereotyping in Schools, Valerie Hannon (revised 1981).
Sidetracked, Dawn Carter (1981).
Research Bulletin no. 6 (1982).

APPENDIX B

POSITIVE ACTION SCHEMES

DASI (Developing Anti Sexist Innovations). Co-ordinators: Annie Cornbleet and Sue Sanders. Project reports from D. Hicks, Room 283E, County Hall, London SE1 7PB.

GIST (Girls into Science and Technology). Co-ordinators: Alison Kelly, Barbara Smail and Judith Whyte, 9a Didsbury Park, Manchester M20 8RR.

APPENDIX C

CONTACTS AND ADVICE

Spare Rib – a women's liberation magazine, published monthly, available from alternative bookshops, and some newsagents, or from 27 Clerkenwell Close, London EC1R 0AT, for news, general articles, events, and the addresses of organizations listed below.

WIRES (Women's Information, Referral and Enquiry Service), whose address changes periodically; keeps a list of all women's groups, and information on events and campaigns (women only).

WRRC (Women's Research and Resources Centre), 190 Upper Street, Islington, above Sisterwrite bookshop – feminist library, including rare and unpublished papers; keeps list of ongoing research on feminist issues.

CASSOE (Campaign Against Sexism and Sexual Oppression in Education), 17 Lymington Road, London N16 – has produced excellent, comprehensive resource list on sexism in education, and publishes regular newsletter giving details of initiatives.

Equal Opportunities Commission, Overseas House, Quay Street, Manchester M3 3HN – government body to promote sex equality (see Chapter 21). Free advice and publications on all aspects of sex discrimination.

ACE (Advisory Centre for Education), 11 Victoria Park Square, London E2 9PB – publishes *Where* magazine; will give advice on campaigning on all aspects of education, as will CASE (see below).

CASE (Campaign for the Advancement of State Education), 186 Headington Road, Oxford OX3 0BS – publishes *Parents and Schools*, useful for parents and governors, rather than teachers.

BIBLIOGRAPHY

Adams Carol (1981) 'Who did the sewing?', in *Clio* (History and Social Science Teachers' Centre Review, ILEA), vol. 2, no. 1.

Adams Carol (1982) *Ordinary Lives 100 Years Ago*. London, Virago.

Anderton A.G. (1980) *An Introduction to Social Economics*. London, Heinemann.

Arnot Madeleine (1980) 'Socio-cultural reproduction and women's education', in Deem R. (ed.) *Schooling for Women's Work*. London, Routledge and Kegan Paul.

Association of Advisors in Design and Technical Studies (1977) 'Design and technical studies in the middle years', presented to conference in April 1977.

Bain G.S. and Price R. (1972) 'Union growth and employment trends in the United Kingdom 1964–1970', *British Journal of Industrial Relations*, no. 10, November 1972.

Barnard Peter A. (1982) 'Boys and girls come out to play', *British Journal of Physical Education*, 2 March 1982.

Bartlett V.L. (1979) 'A measure of pupil interest in learning activities in School Geography', *Geography Education*, vol. 3, pp. 377–386.

Beach F.A. (1948) *Hormones and Behaviour*. New York, Hoeber.

Bell et al. (1971) *New-born and the Pre-Schooler: organization of behaviours between periods*. Monograph of the Society for Research in Child Development no. 36, referred to in Birns B. 'The emergence of sex differences in the earlier years', *Merrill-Palmer Quarterly of Behaviour and Development* (1976), no. 24(3).

Belotti Elena Gianni (1975) *Little Girls*. London, Writers and Readers Publishing Co-operative.

Benett Yves and Carter Dawn (1981) *Sidetracked*. Manchester, EOC.

Bethell Andrew and Lois Keith (1980) 'Staffroom strategy', *Teaching London Kids*, no. 15.

Bidder M. and Baddeley (1911) *Domestic Economy*, 2nd ed. Cambridge University Press.

Blackstone Tessa and Weinreich-Haste Helen (1980) 'Why are there so few women scientists and engineers?', *New Society*, 21 February 1980.

Brake Mike (1980) *The Sociology of Youth Culture and Youth Subcultures*. London, Routledge and Kegan Paul.

Broadman D. and Towner E. (1979) *Reading Ordnance Survey Maps: Some Problems of Graphicacy*. Birmingham University Dept. of Education.

Brophy J.E. and Goode T.L. (1970) 'Teachers' communication of differential expectations for children's classroom performance: some behavioural data', *Journal of Educational Psychology*, vol. 61, no. 5, pp. 365–374.

Broverman D.M., Klaiber E.L., Kobayashi Y. and Vogel W. (1968) 'Roles of activation and inhibition in sex differences in cognitive abilities', *Psychology Review*, vol. 75, pp. 25–50.

Broverman I.K. et al. (1970) 'Sex role stereotypes and clinical judgements of natural health', *Journal of Consultancy and Clinical Psychology*, vol. 34.

Brown G.W. and Harris T. (1978) *Social Origins of Depression: a study of psychiatric disorder in women*. London, Tavistock.

Bruley Sue (1977) 'Fighting sexism in F.E.', *Women and Education Newsletter*, no. 12.

Burkhardt H. (1981) *The Real World and Mathematics*. London, Blackie and Son Ltd.

Burstall S.A. and Douglas M.A. (eds) (1911) *Public School for Girls*. Longmans, Green and Co.

Burt Cyril (1917) *The Distribution and Relations of Educational Abilities*.

Byrne Eileen (1975) 'Inequality in education allocation in schools', *Educational Review*, vol. 28, no. 3.

Byrne Eileen (1976) *The Rationale of Resource Allocation*, unit 16, course E321. Open University.

Byrne Eileen (1978) *Women and Education*. London, Tavistock.

Byrne Eileen (1980a) *Women, the Work Ethic and the Dual Home/Work Role*. Annex to the UNESCO report to the Education 80 conference.

Byrne Eileen (1980b) *Women, Education and Development in the Eighties*. Helen Wodehouse Memorial Lecture, 8 May 1980.

Cairncross Frances and Keeley Phil (1981) *The Guardian Guide to the Economy*. London, Methuen.

Campbell Bea (1981) 'Schoolgirls, are equal opportunities enough?', *City Limits*, 11 December 1981.

Carey G.L. (1958) 'Sex differences in problem-solving performance', *Journal of Abnormal and Social Psychology*, vol. 56.

Catton J. (1982) 'Girls in CDT – Some teacher strategies for mixed groups' in *Studies in Design Education, Craft and Technology*. vol. 15, no. 1.

Chandler E.M. (1980) *Educating Adolescent Girls*. London, George Allen and Unwin.

Chester J., Harper E. and Price G. (1980–1981) *Maths Matters (Books 1 –6)*. London, Addison-Wesley.

CILT (1980) *Modern Languages Examination at 16+, a Critical Analysis*. London, CILT.

Clarke Margaret (1971, 1976) *Homecraft*. London, Routledge and Kegan Paul.

Clarricoates Katherine (1978) 'Dinosaurs in the classroom', *Women's Studies International Quarterly*, vol. 1, no. 4.

Clarricoates Katherine (1981) 'The experience of patriarchal schooling', *Interchange*, vol. 12, no. 2/3, pp. 185–205.

Cockcroft W.H. (1982) *Mathematics Counts*. Report of the Committee of Enquiry into the Teaching of Mathematics in Schools. London, HMSO.

Colley A. (1895) *Domestic Economy for Students and Teachers*. London, Simpkin and Marshall.

Comer Lee (undated), *The Myth of Motherhood*, Spokesman Pamphlet no. 21. Bertrand Russell Peace Foundation.

Condry J. and Condry S. (1976) *The Development of Sex Differences: a Study of the Eye of the Beholder*. Ithaca, NY, Cornell University Press.

Coote Anna (1980) 'Powerlessness and how to fight it', *New Statesman*, 7 November, 1980.

Coote Anna (1981) 'The A.E.S.: a new starting point', *New Socialist*, no. 2.

Coussins Jean (1976) *The Equality Report*. London, NCCL.

Cowie J., Cowie V. and Slater E. (1968) *Delinquency in Girls*. London, Heinemann.

Crittenden Ann (1974) 'Closing the muscle gap', in Twin. S. (1979) *Out of the Bleachers*. New York, Feminist Press.

Crowther (1959) *15–18*. Report of the Central Advisory Council for Education. London, HMSO.

Cullen M. (1971, 1973) *Feeding the Family*. London, Heinemann.

Cullen M. (1979) *Good Grooming and Clothes Care*. London, Heinemann.

Dale R.R. (1974) *Mixed or Single Sex School*, Vol. 3. London, Routledge and Kegan Paul.

Dale R.R. (1975) Education and sex roles, *Educational Review*, vol. 27, no. 3.

Daly Mary (1978) *Gyn/Ecology*. London, Women's Press.

Davie R., Butler N. and Goldstein H. (1972) *From Birth to Seven*. Report of the National Child Development Study. Harlow, Longman.

Davies Lynn (1973) *The Contribution of the Secondary School to the Sex Typing of Girls*. Unpublished MEd dissertation, University of Birmingham.

Davies Lynn and Meighan Roland (1975) 'A review of schooling and sex roles, with particular reference to the experience of girls in secondary schools', *Educational Review*, vol. 27, no. 3, pp. 165–178.

Davies L. (1977) 'Butter wouldn't melt in her mouth?', *The Social Science Teacher*, vol. 6, no. 4.

Davies Lynn (1979) 'Deadlier than the male? Girls' conformity and deviance in school', in Barton L. and Meighan R. (eds) *Schools, Pupils and Deviance*. Driffield, Nafferton Books.

Deem Rosemary (1978) *Women and Schooling*. London, Routledge and Kegan Paul.

Deem Rosemary (ed.) (1980) *Schooling for Women's Work*. London, Routledge and Kegan Paul.

Deforge M. (1972) *The Teaching of Technology*. Council of Europe (72, 14).

Delamont Sara (1976) *Interaction in the Classroom*. London, Methuen.

Delamont Sara (1978) 'The double conformity trap', in Delamont S. and Duffin L. (eds) *The Nineteenth Century Woman: Her Cultural and Physical World*. London, Croom Helm.

Delamont Sara (1980) *Sex Roles and the School*. London, Methuen,

Delamont Sara (1982) 'Sex differences in classroom interaction', *EOC Research Bulletin*, no. 6.

DES (1975) *Curricular Differences for Boys and Girls*. Education Survey no. 21. London, HMSO.

DES (1979) *Aspects of Secondary Education*. London, HMSO.

DES (1980) *Girls and Science*. HMI Series: *Matters for Discussion*, no. 13. London, HMSO.

Douglas J.W.B. (1964) *Home and The School*. London, McGibbon & Kee.

Douglas J.W.B., Ross J.M. and Simpson H.R. (1968) *All Our Futures*. London, Peter Davies.

Downing Hazel (1981) 'They call me a life-size meccano set', in McRobbie A. and McCabe T. (eds) *Feminism for Girls*. London, Routledge and Kegan Paul.

Duncan Tom (1969, 1970) *Exploring Physics, Books 1–5*. London, John Murray.

Dyer Ken (1977) In *New Scientist*, 22 September, 1977.

Educational Publishers Council (EPC) and Equal Opportunities Commission (EOC) (1981) *Sex Stereotyping in Children's and Educational Books*. London, EPC.

Education, Science and Arts Committee (1981) *Second Report on the Secondary School Curriculum and Examinations* (with Special Reference to the 14–16 Year Old Age Group). London, HMSO.

EITB (Engineering Industry Training Board) (1979) Report on the Training Scheme for Girl Technicians. Stockport, EITB.

EITB (1980) *Girl Technicians*. Stockport, EITB.

Ellis V. (1981) *The Role of Trade Unions in the Formation of Equal Opportunity*. Manchester, EOC.

Engström Lars M. and Ahlgren Rose Marie (1974) *Behavioural Sports Studies in Sweden*. Stockholm, Lärerhögskolan.

EOC (1979) *Education in Schools – a consultative document: the Response of the EOC*. Manchester, EOC.

EOC (1980) *A Guide to Equal Treatment of the Sexes in Careers Materials*. Manchester, EOC.

EOC (1981a) *A Response to the MSC Document, 'A New Training Initiative'*. Manchester, EOC.

EOC (1981b) Supplementary material submitted to House of Commons Education, Science and Arts Select Committee.

EOC (1982a) *Getting It Right Matters – A Parents' Guide to Subject Options*. Manchester, EOC.

EOC (1982b) *Women and Teaching* – conference report. Manchester, EOC.

Evans Terry D. (1978) 'Creativity, sex-role socialization and pupil–teacher interaction in early schooling', *Sociological Review*, vol. 27, pp. 139–155.

Fagot B.I. (1973) 'Sex related stereotyping of toddler's behaviour', in *Developmental Psychology*, vol. 9.

Fedden M. (1922) *Simple Housecraft*. London, Pearson.

Ferry Georgina (1982) 'How women figure in science', *New Scientist*, 1 April 1982.

Feschbach N.D. (1969) 'Student teacher preferences for elementary school pupils varying in personality characteristics', *Journal of Educational Psychology*, vol. 60, no. 2, pp. 126–132.

Figes Eva (1970) *Patriarchal Attitudes*. London, Virago.

Foster M. (1976) *Learning to Cook*. London, Heinemann.

Fox L.H., Brody L. and Tobin D. (1980) *Women and the Mathematical Mystique*. London, John Hopkins.

Foxman D. et al. (1980 and 1981) *Assessment of Performance Unit Mathematical Development*. Primary and Secondary Survey Reports nos. 1 & 2. London, HMSO.

Frazier Nancy and Sadker Myra (1973) *Sexism in School and Society*. New York, Harper and Row.

Friedan Betty (1971) *The Feminine Mystique*. London, Victor Gollancz.

Frieze I.H. et al. (1978) *Women and Sex Roles*. New York, Norton and Co.

Fuller, M. (1978) *Dimensions of Gender in a School*, unpublished PhD thesis, University of Bristol.

Fuller, M. (1980) 'Black Girls in a London Comprehensive School' in Deem (ed) (1980).

Gagnon J. and Simon W. (1974) *Sexual Conduct*. London, Hutchinson.

Galton M. (1981) 'Differential treatment of boys and girls during science lessons', in Kelly A. (1981).

Galton M. and Simon B. (eds) (1980) *Progress and Performance in the Primary School*. London, Routledge and Kegan Paul.

Gavron H. (1966) *The Captive Wife*. London, Routledge and Kegan Paul.

Gawthorpe L. (1976) *Family Meals*. Amersham, Hulton.

Gilbert E. (1975) *Your Style*. Edinburgh, Oliver and Boyd.

Gillespie-Woltemade N. (1978) *Sex Equality: Some Implications for Men*. Unpublished paper, Dept. of Sociology, Ohio State University.

Good Housekeeping Institute (1976) *Running a Home is Fun*, 2nd ed. London, Ebury Press.

Gordon M. (1889) *Cookery for Working Men's Wives*. Gardner.

Gray J.A. (1981) 'A biological basis for the sex differences in achievement in science', in Kelly A. (1981).

Groves John and Mansfield David (1981) *Making Sense of Science: Chemistry*. London, Addison-Wesley.

Hambling L. and Matthews P. (1979) *Human Society*, 2nd ed. London, Macmillan.

Hamburg D.A. (1967) *Effects of Progesterone on Behaviour: Endocrines and the nervous system*. Baltimore, Wilkins and Williams.

Hanmer J. and Leonard D. (1980) *Men and Culture: The Sociological Intelligentsia and the Maintenance of Male Domination, or Superman meets The Invisible Woman*. Paper given at BSA conference, 1980.

Hannon V. (1981) *Ending Sex-Stereotyping in Schools*. Manchester, EOC.

Harding J. (1981) 'Sex differences in science examinations', in Kelly A. (ed.) (1981).

Hargreaves D.H. (1967) *Social Relations in a Secondary School*. London, Routledge and Kegan Paul.

Harman H. (1978) *Sexism in Schools and How to Fight It*. London, NCCL.

Harris (1971) 'Scholastic self-concepts in early and middle adolescence', *Adolescence*, no. 6.

Harrison L. (1975) 'Cro-Magnon woman in eclipse', *The Science Teacher* (USA), April 1975.

Harrison M. (1982) Letter to the *Sunday Times*, 17 October 1982.

Hartley D. (1977) *Some Consequences of Teachers' Definitions of Boys and Girls in Two Infant Schools*. Unpublished PhD thesis, University of Exeter.

Harvey J. and Harvey M. (1974) *Government and People*. London, Macmillan.

Head H. (1904) *Manual of Housewifery for Elementary Schools, Secondary Schools and Technical Classes*. Lee and Nightingale.

Head J. 'Personality and Attitudes to Science', in Head J. (ed) *Science Education and the Citizen*. Chelsea College/British Council, 1982.

Hey V. (1982) *Managing Femininity*. Unpublished MA dissertation in Women's Studies, University of Kent.

Hitching W. (1910) *Home Management; a Three Year Course for Schools*. Edinburgh, Chambers.

Horner M. (1974) 'Towards an understanding of achievement related to conflicts in women', in Stacey J., Beraud S. and Daniels J. (eds) *And Jill Came Tumbling After*. New York, Dell.

Hunt J. (1964) in Bone G., *Setting Up Your Own Home*. London, Mills and Boon.

Hutt C. (1979) 'Why girls underachieve', *Trends in Education*, vol. 4, pp. 24–28.

Jackson S. (1978) 'How to make babies – sexism in sex education', *International Women's Studies Quarterly*, vol. 1, no. 4.

Jones A., Marsh J. and Watts A.G. (1973) *Male and Female*. CRAC.

Jones C. (1982) 'Sexual harassment of women in schools', in *DASI Resource Booklet*.

Kaplan J. (1979) *Women and Sport*. New York, Avon Books.

Keeves J. (1973) 'Differences between the sexes in mathematics and science courses', *International Review of Education*, no. 19, pp. 47–62.

Kelly A. (1976) 'Women in Science: a bibliographic review', *Durham Research Review*, no. 7, spring 1976.

Kelly Alison (1980) *Bridging the Gap in Science Education*. Paper presented at the Sex Differentiation and Schooling Conference, Cambridge.

Kelly Alison (ed.) (1981) *The Missing Half, Girls and Science Education*. Manchester University Press.

Kelly A. (1981a) *Research on Sex Differences in Schools in the UK*. Paper given for UK National Report for the Council of Europe Educational Research Workshop in Sex Stereotyping in Schools, Hønefoss near Oslo, 5–8 May.

Kelly Alison, Smail Barbara and Whyte Judith (1981) *Initial GIST Survey: Results and Implications*. Manchester, Girls Into Science and Technology.

Kelly Elinor (1981) 'Socialisation in a patriarchal society', in Kelly A. (ed.) (1981).

Kessler Suzanne J. and McKenna Wendy (1978) *Gender: an Ethnomethodological Approach*. New York, John Wiley and Sons.

Kjellgren A.M. (1977) 'Sex roles and schooling: an investigation of social science textbooks', *The Social Science Teacher*, vol. 6, no. 4.

Lai Po Kan (1980) *The Ancient Chinese*. London, Macdonald.

Lamb B. and Lamb D. (1976) *Care and Clean*. London, Edward Arnold.

Land Hilary (1975) 'The myth of the male breadwinner', *New Society*, October 1975.

Lawrence D. (1973) *Improved Reading through Counselling*. London, Ward Lock.

Lee Anne (1980) 'Together we learn to read and write: sexism and literacy', in Spender D. and Sarah E. (eds) (1980).

Leghorn L. and Parker K. (1981) *Women's Worth*. London, Routledge and Kegan Paul.

Leinhardt S., Seewald A.M. and Engel M. (1979) 'Learning what I taught: sex differences in instruction', *Journal of Educational Psychology*, vol. 11, no. 4.

Levitin T.E. and Chananie J.D. (1972) 'Responses of female primary school teachers to sex-typed behaviours in male and female children', *Child Development*, vol. 43, pp. 1309–1316.

Lewis Jane (1981) 'Women lost and found: the impact of feminism on history', in Spender D. (ed.) *Men's Studies Modified*. Oxford, Pergamon.

Lippard Lucy (1976) *From the Centre*. New York, Dutton.

Llewellyn Mandy (1980) 'Studying girls at school: the implications of confusion', in Deem R. (ed.) (1980).

Lloyd Barbara (1980) 'Young children's understanding of gender', *Women Speaking*, October 1980.

Lobban Glenys (1975) 'Sexism in British primary schools', *Women Speaking*, no. 4.

Lobban Glenys (1976) 'Sex roles in reading schemes', in *Sexism in Children's Books*. London, Writers and Readers Publishing Co-operative.

Lobban Glenys (1978) 'The influence of the school on sex-role stereotyping', in Chetwynd J. and A. Hartnett O. (eds) *The Sex Role System: Sociological and Psychological Perspectives*. London, Routledge and Kegan Paul.

Long M. (1953) 'Reaction to geographical pictures', *Geography*, vol. 38, pp. 100–107.

Long M. (1970) 'The interests of children in school', *Geography*, vol. 56, pp. 177–190.

Love C. (1980) *Sexist ideology of girls' education*, South Bank Sociology Occasional Paper no. 2, London, Polytechnic of the South Bank.

Luke H. (1970) *Gymnastik som Opgaveløsning*. Copenhagen, Christian Elders.

Lukes J. (1979) 'School sociology and social studies in Humberside', *The Social Science Teacher*, vol. 19, no. 2.

Maccia E. et al. (eds) (1975) *Women and Education*. Springfield, Ill., Charles C. Thomas.

Maccoby E.E. (1972) 'Sex differences in intellectual functioning', in Anderson S. (ed.) *Sex Differences and Discrimination in Education*. California, Wadsworth.

Major H. (1889) *Newmann's Housewifery*. Newmann.

Mallock M. (1935) *Economics of Modern Cookery*, 2nd ed. London, Macmillan.

Marks P. (1976) 'Femininity in the classroom', in Mitchell J. and Oakley A. (eds) *The Rights and Wrongs of Women*. Harmondsworth, Penguin Books.

Marks T. (1981) 'Teaching the sociology of gender at 'A' level', *The Social Science Teacher*, vol. 11, no. 1.

Martin R. (1972) 'Student sex behaviour as determinants of the type and frequency of teacher–student contacts', *School Psychology*, vol. 10, no. 4, pp. 339–347.

McGrath H. (1980) *About the House*. Oxford University Press.

McGrath H. (1982) *All About Food*. Oxford University Press.

McRobbie A. (1978) 'Working class girls and the culture of femininity', in Women's Studies Group, *Women Take Issue*. London, Hutchinson.

McRobbie A. (1980) 'Settling accounts with subcultures', *Screen Education*, no. 34.

McRobbie A. and Garber J. (1975) 'Girls and subcultures', in Hall S. and Jefferson A. (eds) *Resistance through Rituals*. London, Hutchinson.

McRobbie A. and McCabe T. (eds) (1981) *Feminism for Girls*. London, Routledge and Kegan Paul.

Mead M. (1950) *Male and Female*. Harmondsworth, Penguin Books.

Meyer William J. and Thompson George C. (1963) 'Teacher interaction with boys as contrasted with girls', in Kuhkens R.C. and Thompson G.C. (eds) *Psychological Studies of Human Development*. New York, Appleton-Century-Crofts.

Miller Casey and Swift Kate (1976) *Words and Women*. Harmondsworth, Penguin.

Ministry of Education (1952) *Teaching History*, 51.

Mortimore Peter and Mortimore Jo (1981) *Sex Differences in Achievement in Schools*. ILEA Research and Statistics.

Murphy R.J.L. (1982) 'Sex differences in objective test performance', *British Journal of Educational Psychology*, June 1982.

Myers Kate (1980) *Sex Stereotyping at Option Choice: an Attempt at Intervention*. Unpublished MA dissertation, London Institute of Education.

Myers Kate (1981) 'Boys on the defensive', *Times Educational Supplement*, 25 September 1981.

Nava Mica (1981) 'Girls aren't really a problem', in *Schooling and Culture*, no. 9. Cultural Studies Dept., ILEA Cockpit Arts Workshop.

Newsholme A. and Scott M. (1902) *Domestic Economy*. Swan Sonnenschein.

Newsom John (1948) *The Education of Girls*. London, Faber.

Newsom John (1963) *Half Our Future*. London, HMSO.

Nightingale Camilla (1977) 'Sex roles in children's literature', in Allen S., Sander L. and Wallis J. (eds) *Conditions of Illusion*. Leeds, Feminist Press.

Nilsen Aleen Pace (1975) 'Women in children's literature', in Maccia E. et al. (eds).

Nobbs Jack, Hine Bob and Fleming Margaret (1975, 1st ed.; 1979, 2nd ed.) *Sociology*. London, Macmillan.

Nochlin Linda (1971) 'Why have there been no great women artists?', in Hess T. and Baker C. (eds) *Art and Sexual Politics*. New York, Collier.

Nuffield (1982) *Home Economics*. London, Hutchinson.

NUT (1980) *Promotion and the Woman Teacher*. NUT/EOC.

Oakley Ann (1972a) 'Nature, culture and women's liberation', *Women Speaking*, July 1972.

Oakley Ann (1972b) *Sex, Gender and Society*. London, Temple Smith.

Oakley Ann and Oakley Robin (1979) 'Sexism in official statistics', in Irvine J., Miles I. and Evans J. (eds) *Demystifying Social Statistics*. London, Pluto Press.

O'Donnell G. (1975) *The Human Web*. London, John Murray.

Ormerod M.B. (1975) 'Subject preference and choice in co-educational and single sex secondary schools', *British Journal of Educational Psychology*, no. 45, pp. 257–267.

Ormerod M.B. (1979) 'The "social implications factor" in attitudes to science', *British Journal of Educational Psychology*, no. 41.

Ormerod M.B. (1981) 'Factors differentially affecting the science subject preferences, choices and attitudes of girls and boys', in Kelly A. (ed.) (1981).

Parker Angela (1973) *Sex Differences in Classroom Intellectual Argumentation*. Unpublished MSc thesis, Pennsylvania State University.

Parsons T. and Bales R.F. (1955) *Family, Socialization and the Integration Process*. New York, Free Press.

Perl T. (1978) *Maths Equals: Biographies of Women Mathematicians and Related Activities*. Reading, Mass., Addison-Wesley.

Peterson R., Werkele G. and Morley R. (1978) 'Women and environments', *Environment and Behaviour*, December 1978, pp. 511–534.

Peterson S. (1971) Swedish survey of mapreading ability, *Vad vet grundskoleeleven om karten?* Unpublished dissertation, Gothenburg University.

Philips E. (1981) *Developing by Design*. Research note from the Open University Design Education Research Programme.

Picton M. (1975 and 1980) *Understanding Cookery*. Glasgow, Blackie.

Pillow Mrs. (1897) 'Domestic economy teaching in Britain', in *British Parliamentary Papers*, vol. 25, p. 157.

Pimlico School (1982) Pamphlet prepared for the Anti-Sexism Conference, at Pimlico School, ILEA, 26 April 1982.

Pitcher R. and Harris A. (1978) *Man Makes His Way*. Harlow, Longman.

Rapoport R. (1978) 'Sex role stereotyping in studies of marriage and the family', in Chetwynd J. and Hartnett O. (eds) (1978) *The Sex Role System: Psychological and Sociological Perspectives*. London, Routledge and Kegan Paul.

Rapoport R. and Rapoport R. (1971) *Dual Career Families*. Harmondsworth, Penguin Books.

Reynolds D. (1976) 'The delinquent school', in Hammersley M. and Woods P. (eds) *The Process of Schooling*. London, Routledge and Kegan Paul.

Ricks F.A. and Pyke S.W. (1973) 'Teacher perceptions and attitudes that foster or maintain sex-role differences', *Interchange*, vol. 4, pp. 26–33.

Riley Bridget (1971) 'The hermaphrodite', in Hess T. and Baker C. (eds) *Art and Sexual Politics*. New York, Collier.

Robins David and Cohen Philip (1978) *Knuckle Sandwich: Growing up in the Working Class City*. Harmondsworth, Penguin.

Ruth Beryl (1970, 1975, 1981) *Home Economics*. London, Heinemann.

Saegert S. and Hart R. (1978) *The Development of Environmental Competence in Children*. Unpublished, from the Environmental Psychology Programme, City University of New York.

Samuel J. (1981) 'Feminism and science teaching: some observations', in Kelly A. (ed.) (1981).

Saraga E. and Griffiths C. (1981) 'Biological inevitabilities or political choices? The future for girls in science', in Kelly A. (ed.) (1981).

Sarah E. (1980) 'Teachers and students in the classroom: an examination of classroom interaction', in Spender D. and Sarah E. (eds) (1980).

Sarah E., Scott M. and Spender D. (1980) 'The education of feminists: the case for single sex schools', in Spender D. and Sarah E. (eds) (1980).

Schafer S. (1976) 'The socialization of girls in the secondary schools of England and the two Germanies', *International Review of Education*, no. 22.

Schools Council (1968) *Young School Leavers*. London, Schools Council.

Schools Council (1971) *Home Economics Teaching*, Curriculum Bulletin 4. London, Methuen.

Scott H. (1982) *Sweden's Right to be Human*. London, Allison and Busby.

Scott M. (1980) 'Teach her a lesson: sexist curriculum in patriarchal education', in Spender D. and Sarah E. (eds) (1980).

Selby L. (1972) *The Together Cookbook*. London, New English Library.

Selfe P. (1981) *Sociology*. Sunbury on Thames, Nelson.

Serbin L.A., O'Leary D.K., Kent R.N. and Jonick I.J. (1973) 'A comparison of teacher response to the pre-academic and problem behaviour of boys and girls, *Child Development*, nos. 39 and 44.

Sergeant Emma (1981) Letter to *The Guardian*, 11 December 1981.

Sharma S. and Meighan R. (1980) 'Schooling and sex roles: the case of GCE 'O' level mathematics', *British Journal of Sociology of Education*, vol. 1, no. 2, pp. 193–205.

Sharp Rachel and Green Anthony (1975) *Education and Social Control*. London, Routledge and Kegan Paul.

Sharpe Sue (1976) *Just Like A Girl*. Harmondsworth, Penguin.

Shaw Jennifer (1980) 'Education and the individual: schooling for girls or mixed schooling – a mixed blessing', in Deem R. (ed.) (1980).

Sheffield City Polytechnic (unpublished) Report of the Research Project *Mathematics Education and Girls*. Dept. of Mathematics, Statistics and Operational Research.

Sheffield NUT Equal Opportunities Group (1982) Report on the Secondary School Questionnaire. Available from 52 Conduit Road, Sheffield S10 1EW.

Sherman J.A. (1978) *Sex-related Cognitive Differences*. Springfield, Ill., Charles C. Thomas.

Sillitoe H. (1933) *A History of the Teaching of Domestic Subjects*. London, Methuen.

Slee F.W. (1968) 'The feminine image factor of girls' attitudes to school subjects', *British Journal of Educational Psychology*, vol. 38.

Smail Barbara, Whyte Judith and Kelly Alison (1982) 'Girls into science and technology: the first two years', *EOC Research Bulletin*, no. 6.

Smart C. and Smart B. (eds) (1978) *Women, Sexuality and Social Control*. London, Routledge and Kegan Paul.

Smithers Alan and Collings John (1981) 'Girls studying science in the sixth form', in Kelly Alison (ed.) (1981).

Solomon Joan (1980) 'Science and society studies in the school curriculum', *School Science Review*, vol. 62, December 1980.

Southern Examining Group (1982) Draft Reports on 16+ National Criteria: Chemistry.

Spaulding Robert L. (1963) *Achievement, Creativity and Self-Concept Correlates of Teacher–Pupil Interaction in Primary Schools*. Co-operative Research Project no. 1352. Washington, DC, US Dept. of Health, Education and Welfare.

Spender D. (1980a) 'Talking in class' in Spender D. and Sarah E. (eds) (1980).

Spender D. (1980b) 'Disappearing tricks' in Spender D. and Sarah E. (eds) (1980).

Spender D. (1980c) *Man-Made Language*. London, Routledge and Kegan Paul.

Spender D. (1981) *Gender – a Question of Equality*. BBC TV, December 1981 and report in *The Listener*, 31st December 1981, p. 816, 'What will we do about the girls?'

Spender D. (1982a) *Invisible Women*. London, Writers and Readers Publishing Co-operative.

Spender D. (1982b) *Women of Ideas*. London, Routledge and Kegan Paul.

Spender D. and Sarah E. (1980) *Learning to Lose: Sexism in Education*. London, The Women's Press.

St John-Brooks C. (1981) 'Are girls really no good at maths?' *New Society*, 5 March 1981.

Stanworth Michelle (1981) *Gender and Schooling. A Study of Sexual Divisions in the Classroom*. London, WRRC.

Stevens Gareth (1978) *Famous Names in Medicine*. Hove, Wayland.

Stones Rosemary (1980) 'Sex roles and the primary school', *NUT Primary Education Review*, no. 8.

Super D. (1957) *The Psychology of Careers*. New York, Harper Bros.

Sutherland Margaret B. (1982) *Sex Bias in Education*. Oxford, Basil Blackwell.

Tabraham H. (1980) Letter in *Spare Rib*, no. 93.

Thompson Jane L. (1978a) *It's A Matter of People*. London, Hutchinson.

Thompson Jane L. (1978b) *Studying Society*. London, Hutchinson.

Thompson Jane L. (1980) *Examining Sociology*. London, Hutchinson.

Thorne Barrie (1978) *Gender – How Is it Best Conceptualised?* Michigan State University, Sociology Dept.

Turnbull Ann-Marie (1980) *Women in the Making*. South Bank Sociology Occasional Paper no. 2.

Twin Stephanie (1979) *Out of the Bleachers*. New York, Feminist Press.

UNESCO (1981) International Congress on Science and Technology Education and National Development. Final Report, Paris.

Vaering M.M. (1946) *Feminine Character*. Oxford University Press.

Walden R. and Walkerdine V. (1982) *Girls and Mathematics: The Early Years*. Bedford Way Papers no. 8, University of London, Institute of Education.

Walford Geoffrey (1980) 'Sex bias in physics textbooks', *School Science Review*, vol. 62, December 1980.

Walker Ian (1980) 'Girls and boys go out to play', *New Society*, 18–25 December 1980.

Waugh Pam and Foster V. (1978 and 1979) 'Down girl', reprinted in *Women and Education Newsletter*, nos. 14 and 15.

Weiner G. (1980) 'Sex differences in mathematical performance: a review of research and possible action' in Deem R. (ed.) (1980).

Weinreich-Haste H. (1981) 'The image of science' in Kelly A. (eds) (1981).

Weitzman Lenore J. et al. (1976) 'Sex role socialisation in picture books for pre-school children', in *Sexism in Children's Books*. London, Writers and Readers Publishing Co-operative.

West Jackie (1978) 'Women, sex and class', in Kuhn Annette and Wolpe Ann-Marie (eds) *Feminism and Materialism*. London, Routledge and Kegan Paul.

Whitbread Anne (1980) 'Female teachers are women first', in Spender D. and Sarah E. (1980).

Whyte Judith (1981) 'Sex-typing in schools', in Kelly A. (1981).

Widgery David (1981) 'The rise of radical rock', *New Socialist*, no. 2.

Willis Paul (1977) *Learning to Labour*. London, Saxon House.

Wilson Deidre (1978) 'Sexual codes and conduct', in Smart C. and S. (eds)

Wolpe Ann-Marie (1977) *Some Processes in Sexist Education*. London, WRRC.

Wood R. (1977) 'Cable's comparison factor: is this where girls' troubles start?', *Mathematics in Schools*, vol. 6, no. 4, pp. 18–21.

Woods P. (1976) 'The myth of subject choice', *British Journal of Sociology*, no. 2.

Wynn Barbara (1974) *Aspects of the Teaching of Domestic Subjects*. MA thesis, University of London Institute of Education.

Wynn Barbara (1977) In *School Knowledge and Social Control*, Open University Course E202, *Schooling and Society*, block 111, 'Knowledge, ideology and the curriculum'.

YWCA (1982) *Girls in Male Jobs*. Research findings from Girls Apprentice Course no. 3, 11–15 January, from Brookfield House, 24 Eccleston Square, London SW1.

INDEX